JUSTIFYING JEFFERSON

The Political Writings of John James Beckley

JUSTIFYING JEFFERSON

The Political Writings of John James Beckley

Edited by

Gerard W. Gawalt

MANUSCRIPT DIVISION

LIBRARY OF CONGRESS · WASHINGTON · 1995

LIBRARY OF CONGRESS CATALOGING-IN-PUBLICATION DATA
Beckley, John James, 1757–1807
        Justifying Jefferson : the political writings of John James
    Beckley / edited by Gerard W. Gawalt.
            p.   cm.
        Includes bibliographical references.
        ISBN 0–8444–0875–1
        ——— ——— Copy 3 Z663 .J87 1995
        1. United States—Politics and government—1789–1809—Sources.
    2. United States. Congress—Rules and practice. I. Gawalt, Gerard
    W.   II. Title.
    E302.B43 1995
    081 s—DC20
    [973.4'092]   95–8875
                                                          CIP

Cover: Bill of Rights with John Beckley's signature.

∞ *The paper used in this publication meets the requirements for permanence established by*
the American National Standard for Information Sciences "Permanence of Paper for Printed
Library Materials" (ANSI Z39.48–1984).

For sale by the U.S. Government Printing Office
Superintendent of Documents, Mail Stop: SSOP, Washington, DC 20402–9328
ISBN 0–16–048431–6

Contents

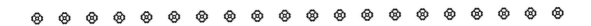

Foreword
BY JOHN Y. COLE
7

Introduction
BY GERARD W. GAWALT
9

Editorial Method
15

THE POLITICAL WRITINGS OF JOHN JAMES BECKLEY
17

CONGRESS of the United States

begun and held at the City of New York, on

Wednesday the fourth of March, one thousand seven hundred and eighty nine.

The Conventions of a number of the States, having at the time of their adopting the Constitution, expressed a desire, in order to prevent misconstruction or abuse of its powers, that further declaratory and restrictive clauses should be added: And as extending the ground of public confidence in the government, will best ensure the beneficent ends of its institution;

Resolved by the Senate and House of Representatives of the United States of America, in Congress assembled, two thirds of both Houses concurring, that the following Articles be proposed to the Legislatures of the several States, as amendments to the Constitution of the United States, all, or any of which Articles, when ratified by three fourths of the said Legislatures, to be valid to all intents and purposes, as part of the said Constitution; Viz.

Articles in addition to, and amendment of the Constitution of the United States of America, proposed by Congress, and ratified by the Legislatures of the several States, pursuant to the fifth Article of the original Constitution.

Article the first. After the first enumeration required by the first Article of the Constitution, there shall be one Representative for every thirty thousand, until the number shall amount to one hundred, after which the proportion shall be so regulated by Congress, that there shall be not less than one hundred Representatives, nor less than one Representative for every forty thousand persons, until the number of Representatives shall amount to two hundred, after which the proportion shall be so regulated by Congress, that there shall not be less than two hundred Representatives, nor more than one Representative for every fifty thousand persons.

Article the second. No law varying the compensation for the services of the Senators and Representatives, shall take effect, until an election of Representatives shall have intervened.

Article the third. Congress shall make no law respecting an establishment of religion, or prohibiting the free exercise thereof; or abridging the freedom of speech, or of the press; or the right of the people peaceably to assemble, and to petition the government for a redress of grievances.

Article the fourth. A well regulated militia, being necessary to the security of a free State, the right of the people to keep and bear Arms, shall not be infringed.

Article the fifth. No soldier shall in time of peace be quartered in any House, without the consent of the owner, nor in time of war, but in a manner to be prescribed by law.

Article the sixth. The right of the people to be secure in their persons, houses, papers, and effects, against unreasonable searches and seizures, shall not be violated, and no warrant shall issue, but upon probable cause, supported by oath or affirmation, and particularly describing the place to be searched, and the persons or things to be seized.

Article the seventh. No person shall be held to answer for a capital, or otherwise infamous crime, unless on a presentment or indictment of a Grand Jury, except in cases arising in the land or naval forces, or in the Militia, when in actual service in time of war or public danger; nor shall any person be subject for the same offence to be twice put in jeopardy of life or limb; nor shall be compelled in any criminal case to be a witness against himself, nor be deprived of life, liberty, or property, without due process of law; nor shall private property be taken for public use, without just compensation.

Article the eighth. In all criminal prosecutions, the accused shall enjoy the right to a speedy and public trial, by an impartial jury of the State and district wherein the crime shall have been committed, which district shall have been previously ascertained by law, and to be informed of the nature and cause of the accusation; to be confronted with the witnesses against him; to have compulsory process for obtaining witnesses in his favor, and to have the assistance of counsel for his defence.

Article the ninth. In suits at common law, where the value in controversy shall exceed twenty dollars, the right of trial by jury shall be preserved, and no fact tried by a jury, shall be otherwise re-examined in any court of the United States, than according to the rules of the common law.

Article the tenth. Excessive bail shall not be required, nor excessive fines imposed, nor cruel and unusual punishments inflicted.

Article the eleventh. The enumeration in the Constitution, of certain rights, shall not be construed to deny or disparage others retained by the people.

Article the twelfth. The powers not delegated to the United States by the Constitution, nor prohibited by it to the States, are reserved to the States respectively, or to the people.

Frederick Augustus Muhlenberg, Speaker of the House of Representatives.

John Adams, Vice President of the United States, and President of the Senate.

John Beckley, Clerk of the House of Representatives.

Sam. A. Otis Secretary of the Senate.

Foreword

The foundation of the federal government rests securely on the accomplishments of eighteenth-century American patriots. Washington, Jefferson, Madison, Adams, Lee, Monroe, Jay, Hamilton, and Franklin are names celebrated in American history as responsible for creating our national government and the institutions for operating that government in a free, republican society. The founders wisely created three branches of government—the executive, congressional, and judicial—to share the responsiblity of maintaining our democratic society and to administer the myriad functions of our federal government.

The House of Representatives has performed a key role in preparing the legislation essential to the creation of our federal government since its first quorum was achieved on April 1, 1789. On that day the House elected its first Speaker, Frederick Augustus Conrad Muhlenberg of Pennsylvania, and its first Clerk, John James Beckley of Virginia.

John James Beckley served concurrently as the first Librarian of Congress. His mentor, President Thomas Jefferson, appointed him to the post in 1802, two years after the Library of Congress was established. (The job of Librarian of Congress was not separated from the job of Clerk of the House of Representatives until 1815.) As the first Librarian of Congress and the first Clerk of the House, John James Beckley, whose writings are published in this volume, established administrative and parliamentary procedures that supported these great institutions in their fledgling years. As director of the Center for the Book and as a scholar keenly interested in the history of the Library of Congress, I have had the opportunity to appreciate Beckley's important role in helping to shape these federal institutions. I am pleased that the Library of Congress through this volume of political writings and personal letters is making it possible for others to share in this knowledge.

Facsimile of an original copy of the Bill of Rights, presented to the Library of Congress on February 21, 1945.

Readers of this book can explore rules that Beckley established for the Clerk of the House and for the operation of the legislative process in one of the world's greatest deliberative bodies—the Congress of the United States. As a political confidant of Jefferson, Madison, and Monroe, Beckley was a founder of the American political party system. He collaborated with Jefferson to formulate the parliamentary rules and procedures that have been a manual for the smooth operation of the legislative process. After January 29, 1802, when Jefferson appointed Beckley to the concurrent post of the first Librarian of Congress, he began the program of broad-based acquisitions and laid the foundation for the future growth of the Library of Congress.

Congress will celebrate the bicentennial of its library in the year 2000, and the Congress is marking the decade by supporting publications and other projects that share this remarkable institution's resources with the nation and the world. *Justifying Jefferson: The Political Writings of John James Beckley* gives all Americans the opportunity to read documents important to understanding the formation of our basic political and legislative institutions.

John Y. Cole
Director, Center for the Book
Library of Congress

Introduction

Beckley is a man of perfect truth as to what he affirms of his own knolege, but too credulous as to what he hears from others."

Thomas Jefferson, June 7, 1793, MSS Note, Library of Congress

On March 4, 1801, two American politicians reached the pinnacle of their political careers. In Washington, D.C., at a small, quiet ceremony, Thomas Jefferson was inaugurated as the third president of the United States of America. In Philadelphia at a large boisterous celebration, John James Beckley delivered an oration marking that event—the political revolution of 1800.

Jefferson has rightfully remained one of the most well-known and respected American founders and presidents. His able lieutenant and one of the people most responsible for his presidential election victory has become a mysterious, almost unknown person appreciated chiefly by specialists in American history and political culture. Although their backgrounds and opportunities were widely diverse, their careers became intertwined during their common experiences in the maelstrom of military and political warfare of the American Revolution and molded together in the crucible of the early years of American national government.

John James Beckley (1757–1807), son of obscure English parents, was sent by his uncle James Withers, an employee of the mercantile trading firm John Norton & Son to Virginia in 1769 as an indentured servant. This "clever, lively boy"[1] proved to be remarkably skilled as a scribe and particularly suited to the personal interaction of a general clerical assistant to his master John Clayton, amateur botanist and clerk of Gloucester County, Virginia. While Beckley was laboring as an indentured courthouse clerical assistant, Jefferson was embarked on his career as lord of the manor, lawyer, and politician. And even though Jefferson was legal counsel in 1769 for two cases of Gloucester County men,[2] it would have been highly unlikely that Jefferson and Beckley experienced any meaningful encounter at that time.

After Clayton died in 1773, Beckley's indenture terminated, but he remained in Virginia, perhaps because he could not afford the cost of returning to England or he perceived greater opportunities in America. By late 1774 Beckley was clerking for Thomas Adams, clerk of Henrico County, where Clayton's son John resided. Beckley was the beneficiary of the many opportunities created by the revolutionary movement, and in February 1775 he was elected clerk of the Henrico Committee of Safety. Beckley's clerical skills, his friendship with revolutionaries, such as Edmund Randolph and John Pendleton, and probably his political acumen, earned him the post of assistant clerk of the state Committee of Safety on February 7, 1776.

When the new state government began operations on July 5, 1776, Beckley began closing out operations for the Committee of Safety. For more than a year he served as a committee clerk and accountant for the House of Delegates and in November 1777 he replaced John Pendleton as clerk of the Senate. While his clerical duties sustained him, Beckley began reading law with Virginia attorney general Edmund Randolph, in Williamsburg. In 1779 he began practicing law in Gloucester court and joined the Phi Beta Kappa chapter in Williamsburg as a nonstudent member. As secretary of the chapter he became well acquainted with other young members, such as John Marshall, John Brown, William Short, William Cabell, and Bushrod Washington, who would play prominent roles in his life and the political life of the country. When Randolph was elected to the Continental Congress in June 1779, Beckley replaced him as clerk of the House of Delegates and handled his legal clients in his absence.

In these critical years of the revolution, Beckley's relationship with Jefferson emerged. As Beckley moved up the administrative ladder from committee clerk to assistant clerk to clerk of the Senate, clerk of the Court of Chancery, and clerk of the House of Delegates, Jefferson moved up the political ladder from state delegate to member of the Continental Congress to governor of Virginia in 1779. Their relationship was never personally close, but Beckley provided key political and administrative support for Jefferson's public leadership.

When the state government moved to Richmond in 1780, Beckley took his household with him. Two British invasions of Virginia in 1781 threw the state government into turmoil and put additional pressure on elected officials, such as Jefferson, and the few permanent state employees, such as Beckley. In what proved to be a litmus test of Jefferson's leadership abilities, the chief executive and chief clerk were hard pressed to get the military supplies and government records out of Richmond ahead of forces commanded by British generals, Arnold in January and Cornwallis in May 1781.

After the war Beckley's life settled into a comfortable routine in Richmond. Work was divided between his state clerkships and his legal practice. In his spare time he began investing in city lots and western lands and participating in city government as a councilman and mayor. His household prospered in Richmond, and by 1783 it included his sister Mary Jane and a staff of six male slaves and two female slaves. But Beckley was still restless, and when his friend and mentor Edmund Randolph went to Philadelphia as a Virginia delegate to the Federal Constitutional Convention, Beckley "accompanied the Governor up, in expectation of being appointed clerk."[3] William Jackson caught the prize of clerk to the Convention, but Beckley became infected with nationalism and caught the earliest form of "Potomac fever."

After unsuccessfully running for a seat in the Virginia constitutional ratifying convention, Beckley served as its secretary and prepared to move onto
the national platform. In the early months of 1789 Beckley laid the political
groundwork for his selection as Clerk of the House of Representatives by
soliciting support and letters of recommendation. In a display of his political
connections, Beckley armed himself with the recommendations of Randolph
and James Madison and the support of the large Virginia delegation in Congress, and with the help of well-planned advance work, for which he later
became well-known, Beckley narrowly defeated William S. Stockton of New
Jersey to become the first Clerk of the federal House of Representatives.
When Samuel Otis became Secretary of the Senate, Massachusetts and Virginia had divided the chief administrative offices of the legislature, just as
they had the presidency and vice-presidency.

As the first Clerk of the House, Beckley was confronted with assisting in
the creation of new administrative and procedural systems for the smooth
and effective operation of the House. To this end Beckley helped prepare
the operational and parliamentary rules for the House, prepared housing
plans, preserved the records, acquired books and newspapers, controlled the
contingency fund, and maintained a personal file of constitutional precedents and procedures established by the House. From his office in the newly
rebuilt Federal Hall in New York, Beckley had instant access to the Bar of
the adjacent House Chamber and the House committee rooms. When Congress moved to Philadelphia, Beckley's office in the nearby west wing of the
State House and a desk on the House Chamber floor put him in the center
of action. Beckley's access to the House paperwork and his control of its
flow were the nexus of his legislative role and critical to his political power.[4]

When the national government became divided by partisan politics,
Beckley quite naturally sided with his Virginia friends and political allies
and eagerly jumped into the private and public campaigns on behalf of the
Jefferson-Madison coalition and its programs. As early as 1790 Beckley
became deeply involved in the political quagmire involving funding and
assumption of revolutionary war debts and the location of the national capital. His rapid rise to insider influence as well as his vulnerabilty to disin-
genuousness was recognized by William Maclay, U.S. senator from
Pennsylvania, who noted in his diary: "We can move from here only by
Means of the Virginians. The Fact is indubitable. I could write a little Volume to illustrate it. Buckley [i.e. *Beckley*] is very intimate with the speaker
on the one hand and Madison on the other. I can thro this Channel communicate What I please to Madison, and I think I know him. But if he is
lead it must be without letting him know that he is so. In other Words he
must not see the String." Later Maclay complained to his diary that Beckley
was playing on both teams and that President Washington's private secretary William Jackson had learned some privy information about his negotiations for the removal of the national capital from Beckley: "I cannot

account for Jackson having medled in this business, or his knowing any thing of it, by any other Means than thro' Buckley."[5]

Writing letters, pamphlets and newspaper essays, leaking official documents to the public, public speeches, planning local, state, and national campaigns, and soliciting funds for the activities of the Jeffersonian-Republican Party were just a few of many actions undertaken by Beckley. Beckley wrote over a number of pseudonyms, such as Calm Observer, Mercator, Senex, Subscriber, and Andrew Marvel, and corresponded with geographically scattered political partisans, such as John Brown (Kentucky), DeWitt Clinton (New York), Ephraim Kirby (Connecticut), James Monroe (Virginia), James Madison (Virginia), William Irvine (Pennsylvania), Tench Coxe (Pennsylvania), Albert Gallatin (Pennsylvania), William Eustis (Massachusetts) and John Milledge (Georgia). Documents and letters published in this volume attest to his political insights and energy.

Supporters of Beckley have credited him with being the first party manager (in Pennsylvania) and with writing the first campaign biography (of Jefferson in 1800). Critics have accused him of writing the first direct public political attack on George Washington (as Calm Observer in 1795) and of leaking confidential Congressional documents that destroyed the political hopes of Alexander Hamilton before the election of 1800. He worked hard on the state and national levels for Jefferson's presidential candidacy in 1796 and 1800, and for local and state Republican candidates in New York, Pennsylvania, and Virginia. Beckley was a master of political polemics and an early proponent of techniques now known as attack advertising and wedge issues. His writings reveal that no detail was too large or too small for his careful attention and pointed instructions to fellow Republicans.

His considerable efforts brought him only modest public rewards. Federalist revenge turned him out of office as clerk of the House in 1797, but Pennsylvania republicans found several minor positions to sustain him and his family. The Jeffersonians' victory in the 1800 election elevated Jefferson to the presidency and gave Beckley the opportunity to recover his clerkship in the House. After nearly a year of anxious and frustrating office seeking under the new administration, Beckley was restored to the House clerkship by a majority vote on December 7, 1801.

On January 29, 1802, just three days after President Jefferson approved legislation creating "the Library for the use of both Houses of Congress" headed by a librarian appointed by the president, Jefferson named his political ally and protegé Beckley to be the first Librarian of Congress. Beckley held these dual appointments until his sudden death on April 8, 1807, in his house in Washington, D.C.

This precedent of one person serving as Clerk of the House and Librarian of Congress begun by Jefferson and Beckley was continued by the joint tenure of Patrick Magruder until 1815. In that same year Congress agreed to accept Jefferson's generous offer to sell his private library to Congress as a replacement for the books destroyed by British troops when they captured

Washington and burned the capitol on August 24, 1814. Jefferson's personal book collection forms the core of the world's preeminent library, thus helping to meet Jefferson's expectation that there was "no subject to which a Member of Congress might not have occasion to refer."[6]

Beckley, like many other members of the national government, such as James Monroe, Elbridge Gerry, James Madison, and Rufus King, found personal as well as political success in the national capitol. Beckley met his wife, Maria Prince, daughter of James Prince, a retired West Indies merchant, during a session of Congress in New York City, where they were married in 1790. Although this marriage linked Beckley to Alexander Hamilton through Maria's uncles, Hercules and Hugh Mulligan, the connection did little to lessen Beckley's animosity toward Hamilton and his government programs. The Beckleys had one daughter, Mary (1798–1800), and one son, Alfred (1802–1888), who graduated from West Point (1823) and served in the U.S. Army till 1837.

Beckley's contacts in Congress also served as a base for his private investments and business deals. From official if not privileged sources on foreign news, Congressional actions, and government policies, Beckley gleaned valuable information, which he provided to family members in the mercantile field, such as James and Isaac Prince, to partners in land speculation, such as former Congressmen John Milledge and Andrew Moore, to foreign investors, such as William Anderson and Peter Galline, and to fellow speculators, such as Isaac Polock, Tench Coxe, and Ephraim Kirby. Often politics and speculation were mixed as his letters in this volume to Ephraim Kirby, John Brown, William Irvine, John Milledge, and Tench Coxe amply demonstrate.

Despite the attention Beckley lavished on his real estate investments in Philadelphia, Virginia, Georgia, Kentucky, and the District of Columbia, he was unable to obtain financial security for his family before his death. The absence of family wealth or public pensions forced his wife and family to try to operate a boarding house before becoming dependent on his friends, John Brown, James Monroe and William Henry Harrison. Only after more than thirty years of litigation did the Beckley family obtain clear title in 1835 to 85,000 acres of land in what was formerly Montgomery County, Virginia, where Beckley is now the county seat of Raleigh County, West Virginia.

Alfred Beckley resigned from the army and moved to his property in 1837 with his wife Amelia, daughter of Neville Craig of Pittsburgh, Pennsylvania. They were joined there by several members of the Prince family. The legal triumph came long after John's death and too late to benefit Maria Beckley, who had died in 1833. Alfred, however, was able to develop his property and prosper in the West Virginia countryside. The preservation of the Beckley homestead, Wildwood, for public use, and this publication of Beckley's political writings provide the well-deserved legacy that John James Beckley worked so hard to achieve for his family and his adopted nation.

Gerard W. Gawalt
Manuscript Historian, Early American History

1. John Clayton to John Norton, August 3, 1769, quoted in Edmund and Dorothy Smith Berkeley, *John Beckley: Zealous Partisan in a Nation Divided* (Philadelphia: American Philosophical Society, 1973), p. 3. The biographical facts of John Beckley used in this introduction are taken chiefly from the Berkeleys' biography of Beckley and the following two articles: Noble E. Cunningham, Jr., "John Beckley: An Early American Party Manager," *William and Mary Quarterly*, 3rd ser. 16 (1956): 40–52; and Philip M. Marsh, "John Beckley: Mystery Man of the Early Jeffersonians," *Pennsylvania Magazine of History and Biography* 72 (1948): 54–69. Many other important sources for understanding Beckley are cited in footnotes to the documents printed in this volume.

2. Case Book, photostat of original at Huntington Library, Jefferson Papers, Library of Congress.

3. James Monroe to Thomas Jefferson, July 27, 1787, Jefferson Papers, Library of Congress.

4. For the location of Beckley's offices, see Kenneth R. Bowling and Helen E. Veit, eds., *The Diary of William Maclay and Other Notes on Senate Debates*, vol. 9 of *Documentary History of the First Federal Congress of the United States of America* (Baltimore: The John Hopkins Press, 1988), pp. 3n. 1, 127, and 337n. 9.

5. January 17 and May 20, 1790, entries, William Maclay Diary, Library of Congress. See also the January 31 and May 19, 1790, entries in Maclay's diary.

6. Jefferson to Samuel H. Smith, September 21, 1814, Jefferson Papers, Library of Congress.

Editorial Method

This edition of the writings of John James Beckley strives to achieve a middle ground between modernization and facsimile reproduction. The original spelling, grammar, punctuation, and capitalization have been allowed to stand except that all sentences begin with a capital and end with a period, and personal and geographical names are capitalized. Abbreviations, contractions, and monetary signs have been retained, except abbreviations have been expanded when marked by the writer.

Marginalia, manuscript footnotes, and postscripts are marked in the text. Documents are arranged chronologically, and documents dated by month or year are placed at the end of the respective month or year. Conjectured dates appear in brackets. Newspaper essays are arranged by the date assigned by the writer, or in its absence by the date of the newspaper. Place-and-date lines always appear on the same line with the salutation regardless of their position in the manuscript. Footnotes are numbered for each document and appear at the end of the document. Gaps in the text are indicated by ellipses in brackets for missing words. Conjectured readings are supplied in roman type in brackets, and editorial assertions in italic type in brackets. Material canceled in the manuscript but restored in the printed text appears in angle brackets in italic type.

A descriptive note at the end of each entry provides abbreviations indicating the nature of the document, and its collection and location appear in parentheses. RC=recipient copy; Tr=transcript (used to designate not only contemporary and later handwritten copies, but also printed copies); MS=manuscript; FC=file copy; LB=letterbook.

The Political Writings of

John James Beckley

❁ ❁ ❁ ❁ ❁ ❁ ❁ ❁ ❁ ❁ ❁ ❁ ❁ ❁ ❁ ❁ ❁ ❁

JOHN BECKLEY TO JAMES MADISON

Sir,   New York 13th March 1789.

In appealing to your Candor I feel a confidence that no apology will be necessary for the present <u>mode</u> of address. Before I left Virginia I communicated to my good friend Mr. Randolph, the reasons that induced me to become a Candidate for the appointment of Clerk to the House of Representatives of the United States, and for that purpose to relinquish the public situation in which I stood there; he was pleased to approve those reasons, and to favor me with Letters of introduction here, (one of which I enclose for your perusal)[1] couched in terms which his friendship, rather than any merit of mine, prompted. At the same time I took the liberty to write to you on the subject, submitting the hope I entertained of your friendship and countenance therein, to your own knowledge of my public and private Character, but the casualty of the conveyance did not permit me to state the more particular and private reasons by which I was influenced; these I now beg leave, briefly to explain, referring to your Candor and goodness, how far the hope I have expressed, may be indulged: the adoption of the new Government by Virginia I have always regarded as a certain and considerable reduction, in point of emolument, of the Clerkship of the House of Delegates, added to this, the new arrangement of our Judiciary, created the necessity of a new field of practice in my professional line; thus circumstanced, and having parted with nearly all the savings of ten Years service, in the marriage and settlement of an unfortunate Sister,[2] I found myself unable to make the necessary remittance for the support of aged parents, reduced by misfortune to a dependance on me, and oppressed with the care of an unhappy son deprived of his reason, Considerations, Sir, which, altho' they may excite your sympathy, I hope you will regard as merely intended to explain the seeming incongruity of applying for Office here, in the certain relinquishment of Business, apparently better at home; for altho' I do not expect the Office I seek will be one of great emolument, yet as affording the means of longer and more constant employment, it will of consequence become more productive.[3] These reasons and my public pretensions I submit to that general sense of propriety with which I am sure you will regard this and every other application for your friendship and favor, being with true regard and esteem, Sir, Your most obedient, and very humble Servant,

John Beckley.

*George Washington.
Portrait by Gilbert
Stuart.*
LC–USZ62–96385.

RC (MADISON PAPERS, LIBRARY OF CONGRESS).

1. Beckley's enclosure is not in the Madison Papers, but it was undoubtedly a letter of recommendation written by Edmund Randolph (1753–1813), former governor of Virginia (1786–88) and member of the Confederation Congress (1779–82). Randolph wrote a similar letter on February 10, 1789, recommending Beckley to Caleb Strong, a U.S. senator

from Massachusetts, which is in the Virginia Historical Society. Randolph also joined the new government, serving as the first attorney general of the United States (1789–94) and then secretary of state to 1795.

2. That is, Mary Anne Beckley, who married Nathaniel Gregory, a Virginia farmer.

3. After Beckley was elected the first clerk of the House of Representatives on April 1, Madison wrote to president-elect George Washington on April 6: "The papers will have made known that Mr. Mulenburg was the choice of the Representatives for their Speaker, & Mr. Beckley for their Clerk. The competitor of the former was Mr. Trumbul who had a respectable vote: of the latter Mr. S. Stockton of new Jersey, who on the first ballot had the same number with Mr. Beckley." (Washington Papers, Library of Congress).

JOHN BECKLEY TO WILLIAM ANDERSON

Dear Sir,[1]   Philadelphia. 1st January 1791.

The River Delaware being closed with Ice, no Ship from hence will probably be able to Sail for some time, I therefore now write via New York to enclose yo. the presidents Speech to Congress at the opening of the present Session, and also a report which has been made by the Secretary of the Treasury for instituting a National bank and in Conformity to which a Committee of the Senate is now preparing a Bill, the sketch of which I have seen and is completely in pursuance of the Secretary's plan. In my opinion his plan will be adopted without any material alteration, however the Moment the Bill passes both houses I will send yo. two or three Copies by different Conveyances. Congress are also busily employed in organizing the militia of the United States and in providing further funds for paying the Interest of their whole debt, including the debt of the particular States, and there is every reason to beleive that this will be done during the present Session, without imposing either an Excise or one Shilling of Land tax; the annual Sum wanting is about 2,700,000 Dollars, of which the Annual impost alone yeilds 2,300,000 Dollars, and the deficiency can be supplied from Stamp duties, the post office, and small additional duties on Wines & spirituous liquors. This circumstance yo. will not be surprised at the rising Credit & encreasing Value of American Stock, the present rates of which are, six per Cent Stock 15/ on the pound; three per Cent ditto 7/6 to 7/9d; deferred six per Cent Stock 6/ to 6/3d. Altho' indeed a few Sales have been made for more. However, it is impossible that a debt of 40 Million, can rise to par and so remain until full evidence be given by Congress of the sufficiency, punctuality and immutability of their funds; an evidence which Congress is fully impressed with the necessity of giving in every instance, and which produced a few days ago the rejection of a petition from a body of public creditors, who are dissatisfied with the present provision and prayed an alteration of the funding system in their favor, and on which rejection the Senate of the U.S., to whom the application was made, were unanimous Save one member.

Congress have also ordered in a Bill Concerning the Navigation of the U.S. precisely on the principles of that of last Session, copy of which I enclosed yo. I believe it will pass without any material change and as soon as it does, I will forward yo. Copies thereof.[2]

The establishment of a Bank here upon the principles of the Secretarys report; the present State of American funds, the stability & energy of our Government; our increasing wealth, population, & resources; the peace your government has concluded with Spain; and the probability of some Commercial Connection between the U.S. & Great Britain in the course of the present Year; all combine to open an extensive & certain prospect for speculation to such monied men of your nation as are in Condition to adventure here, and for which purpose I again repeat my offer of Services as an Agent to yourself, or to any individual or association of individuals who may incline to form a Company & to whom your goodness & friendship may recommend me, assuring yo. that upon any plan of business which such a Company may device, I will assiduously, & faithfully execute all their views & instructions to the utmost of my ability, upon a Commission corresponding with Commissions for similar agencies with yo., or such as is Customary here, or referring it to the Company to interest me in such a Share of the profits only, as they shall deem reasonable & generous, naming it in the instrument of Agency. At the same time I would suggest that I will negotiate also & upon like principles subscription to the Bank, and by power of Atto. execute all business respecting it. Permit me also to remind yo. of what I stated on this Subject in my former letter, and to observe that there now is and must be for a Considerable time, sources open for investing Money here to a profit of from 20 to 25 per Cent at least. If therefore, as I am now married & settled at Philadelphia, and have totally disengaged myself from all law business, yo. will use your friendship to serve me generally, on the Subject of this Letter, I shall ever deem it an Act of the highest friendship & confidence and such as every principle of honor & gratitude will induce me to justify in all my conduct; being with true regard and esteem, Dear Sir, Your mo. obedt. & very humble Servt.

John Beckley.

FC (BECKLEY FAMILY PAPERS, LIBRARY OF CONGRESS).

1. William Anderson, London merchant and factor of Virginia tobacco.
2. For the official records and supporting papers of the first U.S. Congress, March 4, 1789–March 3, 1991, see the multivolume edition, Linda G. DePauw and Charlene B. Bickford, eds., *Documentary History of the First Federal Congress of the United States* (Baltimore: The Johns Hopkins Press, 1972–) and *Journal of the House of Representatives of the United States, First Congress* (Washington: Gales and Seaton, 1826).

JOHN BECKLEY'S BOOK OF MINUTES ON PARLIAMENTARY PROCEEDINGS

October 26, 1791–March 27, 1792

Papers ordered to be printed. See the other end of this Book.[1]
Call on the printer for all Original papers.
States that have ratified 1st Article of Amendment to the Constitution of the United States[2]—

    1. New Hampshire.
    2. New York.
    3. Maryland.
    4. So. Carolina.
    5. No. Carolina.
    6. Rhode island.
    7. New Jersey.
    8. Pennsylvania.
    9. Virginia. (also all others)
    10. Vermont. (whole)

Appendix to Journal matter for—[3]

    1st. Treasurers accounts.
    2d. Ratification of Amendments to Const. U.S.
    3. Statement in purchases of public debt.
    4. Census of Enumeration.
    5. resolution of 30th Decr.—annual statement of Expenditures.
    6. proceedings on Secret Journal.

Book for Standing rules & orders—joint rules &c.[4]

Purchases of public debt—[5]
        dollars cents
    1,131,364.76 purchased
      699,163.38 paid for it
      432,201.38 profit to the U.S.

26 October— Standing Committee of Elections—[6] Mr. Livermore, Mr. Boudinot, Mr. Gerry, Mr. Giles, Mr. Bourne (R.I.), Mr. Hillhouse & Mr. Steele.
Schedule of Enumeration—Have it executed by Mr. Lambert and framed to be hung up.[7]

22d November. Case of resignation William Pinkney, Member for Maryland & a return of John Francis Mercer in his room—see report of Committee of Elections thereon.[8]

Same day—In Committee of whole on a Bill to apportion representation acco[rding] to first Enumeration—see original Bill.—also amendts. agreed to in Committee. (Note Arguments.)[9]

10th Novemr.   Report Secretary State on Unappropriated Lands—21 millions of acres in NW. territory, at disposal of UStates.[10]

25 Novr.   Report on Gen. Jackson petn. of a mode of investigation[11] clause "that facts found by the Committee should preclude the House from all further Enquiry as to evidence." struck out—contended to be unconstitutional because no more power to delegate power over fact than over law—equally incommunicative case of Jury inapplicable that being integral part of a Comt wch. possesses power to judge.

December 1st.   Bill for the releif of Widows, Orphans &c. passed, and delivered therewith, to Mr. Otis, all original reports of Secy. at War on the cases therein provided for, together with the petitions & Vouchers of the respective Claimants.[12]

5th. Treasurers Accot. presented for receipts & expenditures between 1st July & 30th September 1791.
     679,579 dollars & 99 Cents in Treasury on 1st October.

Same day, a report of 147 manuscript pages, from the Secretary of the Treasury, on the subject of Manufactures.[13]

7th.   In Committee of Whole on Post Office Bill. Motion to strike out 1st. Section containing a demarkation of the post roads, and to insert a clause in lieu thereof vesting a power in the president of the U.S. to declare & establish the same—-Obj. that the grant of such a power is unconstitutional, & so decided by vote of the Committee—[14]
          Ayes 12.} Mo: by Sedgwick, Bourne, Laurance, Smith (SC)
                    Barnwell, Bourne (R.I.) &c.
          Noes 45.} Oppos: Gerry, Vining, White, Livermore, &c.

13th & 14th. first day, Amendments of Senate to Enumeration Bill,[15] committed to a Committee of who[le]: (Note-two am[endmen]ts. only, first, change of ratio 30 to 33,000 & also leaving it to remained until altered by law) Second amendt. a mere verbal correction.)
          The Committee reported a disagreemt. to first amt. and agreemt. to second—(obs. ought not to have refrd. agreemt.

28th Decr.[16]	A Meml. of the Legislature of New Hampshire, complaining of the inequality and injustice of Assumption—referred to Secretary of Treasury for information. Qu.
29th Decr.[17]	First instance of Sections or parts of a Bill Recommd. to a Select Committee, after a Commitment to whole House, the Bill itself being before the House. (Post Office 18th & 19th sections)

1792

January.	5th. Post Office Bill. Mo. to add a clause "to grant Mail carriers privilege of carrying passengers."
	Obj. as unconstitutional—because post roads are not highways and carrying passengers wholly irrelative to necessary means of conveying Mail.—because the principle involves an unlimited & exclusive power over highways, and yet by Constitution no power to punish felonies on the highway that power being expressly confined to cases on high Seas—it goes also to ferries, turnpikes &c. &c. toll bridges. Negatived.[18]
	11th. Communications from President—War dept. Statement of pacific measures—Instructions for Campaign &c.[19]
	12th. Resumed & finished reading of the foregoing.
	13th. Commd. to whole House on Monday.
	16. In Committee of the who. Muhlenberg repd.[20]
	17th. first instance. Mr. Laurance from a Committee to whom was refd. generally a Letter from Atto. General repd. a Bill without leave or instruction.—Objected to, and House ord. Committee to take it back.[21]
	Note—power to bring in a Bill must always be expressly given & cannot be taken by implication, and no variance in principle, is admissable between a Bill and the leave or Order on which it is founded—Speakers duty "ex officio" as the custom of order to remand a Bill with a variance in principle even without a question, altho' if it be attempted to justify the House must decide.

23 d. January. Mo. to refer the report of the Secretary of the Treasury to a select Comtee (by Fitzs.) negd. 21/24—(On Subject of Manufactures.)

Note. this motion was properly refd. to a Committee of the whole House, as all National subjects ought to be—particularly those treating finance, aids of Money, bountys &c.— standing rule of House of Commons that all such propositions shall be so disposed of:[22] See Hatsell Volo. 3d. pages 120–122.[23]

Also ruled in House of Commons that in all votes of Supply, aid, or tax, the sum voted in Committee of the whole cannot be augmented but may be lessened—and the Qus is to agree or disagree, or if it be desiredto augment, the Qu: is to recommit for that purpose.

31st January— In discussing Frontier Bill=Memo: After commitment, & tho mendments reported and agreed to, the House proceeded to consider the Bill at Clerks table—Observe, this mode of proceeding is dangerous & should be used with great caution, because it admits amendmts. new & important in principle without due consideration—practice & rule in House of Commons that every amendt. to a Bill in the House, not merely verbal or corrective, shall be committed & go thro' all the previous stages of discussion wch. the Bill itself has undergone, before it shall be brought up to the Speakers table for admission into the Bill.

NB. on 3d reading of the Excise Bill, some of the most important clauses in it were added with little or no discussion.[24]

24th February—On frontier Bill—a mistake discovered in transcribing Senates amts. by omitting in an amt. to the Second Section for raising three additional regiments, these words "each of which exclusively of the commissioned Officers, shall consist of 960 noncommissd. officers, privates & musicians; and that one of these regiments be organized in the following manner, that is to say two battalions of Infantry."

(Note) the effect of this mistake was to change the organization of the regiments from 960 each to 320 infantry & a squadron of dragoons of 320—making each regiment to consist of 320 infantry & 320 Cavalry. Debate ensued and a difficulty how to proceed, pending this, a message was received from the Senate avowing the mistake & desiring a return of the Bill. Qu:—shall the message be complied with?

Agreed by a large Majority, and Clerk ord. to carry the Bill & amts. to the Senate for thepurpose of having their proceedings on the Bill verified—wch was done.

Note—contrary to parliamentary usage. Memo. 12th July 1790—a mistake of Senate in amts. to a Bill to regulate trade & intercourse wth. the Indian tribes—by omitting an amt. to strike out 4th section from appropriating 10,000 dollars therefore—rectified—see Journal p. 171.[25]

25th Feby.   In considering amts. to frontier Bill=Mo. to allow six cadets to each regiment with pay & clothing of Serjeants=by General Wayne—opposed as price of a standing Army (by Sumpter)—withdrawn![26]

27th February—Assigned for the trial of the contested Election on the petn. of James Jackson against Anthony Wayne, one of the Members from Georgia,—Speaker reminded the House thereof, but before any proceeding could be had, the sitting Member in his place moved (in writing, see A) a postponement of trial until [ ] Monday in March, on which a debate arising, Speaker declared it out of order, whereupon the House voted to take up business for consideration and to admit the petitioner to the Bar, when, application was renewed on the part of the sittingmember, the petition being fully <u>heard</u> in objection thereto, and the House resolved further to postpone the trial one fortnight.

Note. two things occurred in this case worthy remark—first, a doubt as to the point of order,—and secondly, a question on the sufficiency of the reasons offered for a postponemt.

In regard to the first, whether the sitting Member had not equal rights with other members until a decision against him? it may be observed that he certainly has equal rights with any members in all cases other than that in which it becomes a Question whether he is a Member or not, but in such case altho' the curtesy of the House permits him a seat from which he may debate & defend himself, yet he cannnot make any motion or give a vote, the latter he is prohibited from by express rule and the former would involve the difficulty, not to say absurdity, of his moving to adjourn, or to postpone as in the present case, when the petitioner was not admitted & could not object or debate.

In regard to the second question, the House waved much enquiry respecting them, because the petitioner did not strongly urge opposition to a postponement, saying that he should submit but not <u>consent</u> thereto. If however the objection had been insisted on, it should seem that the reasons for postponement were insufficient, because the first essential proof was wanting to wit "that the testimony expected was Material."[27]

Note, Annex to the Laws of the present Session a Copy of the treaty at fort Harmer.[28]

7th March:[29]—Mo: to refer to Secretary Treasury—Ways & Means—(see Mo: on Journal) debate ensued—and the proportion was contested on principle, as unconstitutional, dangerous, and tending to relinquish Legisl. powers of Government, creative also of Ministerial influence & corruption—supported on principle as sanctioned by Law establishing the department, as expedient for sake of best & most accurate information, and the support of System in fiscal measures—other arguments as to fitness &c. Adj[ournmen]t called & prevailed.

8th March.   Motion renewed & debate resumed—opposition say Law does not justify it, because that speaks of "plans to improve revenue" which must refer to existing revenues and cannot extend to the creation of revenue; moreover if it could be justified by Law, and a law ought to be repealed, since all Bills to raise revenue must by the Constitution Originate here, and even the other branch of Legislature are precluded, much more than any individual or Officer of the Executive department, that to originate & begin or commence a thing, are Synonimous; that such a direlection of the Legisl. power destroys the meaning & design of Const. in the exclusion of the Senate, and is a total transmutation of the Governmt., itself from that of the people to the will or projects of an individual & that the addition of "Be it enacted" to a Ministerial plan is a mockery of Legislature & will never justify an abandonment of trust & duty—In respect to responsibility it was said that the Legislature ought not to transfer that which they themnselves owe to their constituents to any individual or officer whatever.

   E Contra—Law & practice justify us, dangerous now to innovate, destructive of system & impeachment of minister—Const. not opposed, because Originate must refer to the Sanction or vote of adoption, and to ask Secy to report is no more to originate than a comparison of ideas or convivial conversation out of doors which gives rise to suggestions or motions made in the House, can be so termed—Improper to expect responsibility & refuse power to propose revenues. Question taken Ayes 31/ Noes 27.

10th March—   Motion for a Committee to prepare expressions, as to French Kings Letter (by Tucker) debated & mo. to amend by inserting a joint Committee—agd. 26/24 after which on the main question proposition negatived 29/17. Another motion then made by Tucker for reconsideration by this House (see Journal)—debated & on Question divided, first part agd. 50/2 Second part 35/16.[30]
Note, Arguments on this occsasion very singular, last part being vehemently opposed on the ground of being an explicit approbation of french Constitution whereas the first sentence says "that this House receive wth. highest satisfaction, the notification of the <u>important event</u> of the acceptance of the Constitution by the King" &c. &c. &c." (see Note of Argumts. pro and con. & names of Yeays & Nays.)

12th March.   Contested Georgia Election.[31]—parties appeared at the Bar. & petn. being read—Counsel for sitting Member moved a further postponement Wednesday sennight—opposed & negatived 19/26. Proceed to hearing & petition opened proofs & exhibits, and was heard Argument so far as first charge. (see & state proofs).

13th March.[32]

23d March.   On representation Bill—Qu. of order taken—precedent to main qu.—does a Question to recede conclude any other question & amount to an agreemt. Yeays 44/ Nays 18
same occasion—Main qu. to recede detd. Yeas 31/ Nays 29
After which subsequent qu. taken that the vote to recede as to 1st amt. included all others to number of 11. (note what disorder prevailed.)[33]

24th March.   In Committee of who. on Mint Bill[34]—Mo. to strike out provision for impressing head of the president on Coins & to substitute an emblamatique figure of Liberty;
opposed by Smith (S.C.) Livermore, Sedgwick, Hillhouse, Thatcher. supported by Page, Key, Giles, Madison, Williamson agd. 25/20
Ridiculed on one hand, and declared little, departing from dignity, affrontive of president, unmeaning, uncertain, ambiguous—what is emblem of liberty, a bear breaking from his chain, Indian or savage freedom, a device, symbol,

hieroglyphic, sculptured image or what? Head of president proper, certain, & dignified, impress reverence, represent Governmentl. authority &c.

Those in support of Motion, say, it is improper, unprecedented, creature of Kingly power, glancing at Monarchy, designed to do so, & incompatible with republican principles. In Monarchys it is treason to counterfeit, because offence agst King whose money it is whose impression it bears & who by prerogative creates it, whereas in republics offence against Law & Governmt. & punishable as other felonies. Other argumts. also as to inconvenience, a King nevers dies, president may die, resign, be removed, or left out & a recoinage wd involve loss & confusion.

26th March— Same amendmt.[35] Sent back by Senate disagreed to. Animated debate ensured on Qu. to recede, and same ground of Argument gone over on both sides. Qu. to recede Negative Ayes 24/Noes 32—Motion to Adhere carried.

27th March— Motion for president to institute an Enquiry as to defeat &c.[36] division of motion called—21/35 motion negd.
Another Motion for a Committee—agd 44/10 Fitzsim., Giles, Steele, Mercer, Vining, Clarke, Sedgwick.

2d April.[37]

MS (BECKLEY FAMILY PAPERS, LIBRARY OF CONGRESS).

1. "This Book" was labeled as a "Rough memorandum Book" by Beckley when he made these first entries in October 1791, but he later refered to it as a "Book of Minutes on parliamentary proceedings." Beginning at one end of the bound volume Beckley entered his notes on important procedural and constitutional occurrences in the House for the first session of the Second Congress, October 24, 1791, to May 7, 1792. Beckley used the "other end of this Book" as a letterbook, 1797–99.

When Beckley was helping Thomas Jefferson prepare his *Manual of Parliamentary Practice*, he sent Jefferson extracts from what he called his "Book of Minutes on Parliamentary Proceedings." The extracts from this document for December 29, 1791, and January 31, 1792, which Beckley probably enclosed in a March 15, 1798, note to Jefferson are in the Jefferson Papers, Library of Congress.

Beckley also wrote an essay on parliamentary and Congressional practices, of which a surviving fragment is printed in this volume under a March 1798 date. Beckley certainly kept additional memorandum books of parliamentary procedures and constitutional interpretrations essential to the operations of the House during his terms as clerk, but they have not been found.

2. The proposed first amendment to the Constitution regulated the apportionment of repre-entation in the House of Representatives. During this session of Congress, notice was received of Virginia and Vermont's ratification of some of the proposed amendments to the constitution. Virginia's action on December 15 ratifying articles 2–12, ensured the

acceptance of ten amendments to the Constitution, which have come to be called the Bill of Rights. *Journal of the House of Representatives, Second Congress* (Washington: Gales and Seaton, 1826), pp. 483 and 493; and *The Debates and Proceedings in the Congress of the United States. . . Second Congress* (Washington: Gales and Seaton, 1849), pp. 54 and 75.

3. It is not clear to which documents Beckley was referring because no documents were apparently appended to either the manuscript or printed journal of the first session of the Second Congress, although they had been added to those of the First Congress and were added to those for later sessions of Congress.

4. The clerk of the House had been responsible for maintaining a collection of standing rules and orders since April 7, 1789. *Journal of the House, First Congress*, pp. 8–11.

5. For further information on the reports on public debt, see Harold C. Syrett, ed., *The Papers of Alexander Hamilton*, 27 vols. (New York: Columbia University Press, 1961–87), 10:538, 548–51.

6. For further information on the debates leading to the appointment of a standing Committee of Elections, see *Journal of the House, Second Congress*, p. 439; and *Debates and Proceedings, Second Congress*, pp. 144–45.

7. The "Schedule of Enumeration" based on the 1790 census was essential to the debate on apportionment, which began on October 31. *Journal of the House, Second Congress*, p. 444; and *Debates and Proceedings, Second Congress*, pp. 148–50.

8. For debate on the replacement of Representative Pinckney by Mercer, see *Journal of the House, Second Congress*, p. 459; and *Debates and Proceedings, Second Congress*, pp. 205–7.

9. See *Journal of the House, Second Congress*, p. 459; and *Debates and Proceedings, Second Congress*, p. 207.

10. Jefferson's Report on Public Lands of November 8, 1791, was presented to the House on November 10. *Journal of the House, Second Congress*, p. 459; *Debates and Proceedings, Second Congress*, pp. 1034–42; and Julian Boyd, Charles W. Cullen, and John Catanzarini, eds., *The Papers of Thomas Jefferson* (Princeton: Princeton University Press, 1950—), 22:274–88.

11. For the report on the petition of Gen. James Jackson protesting his contested election against Anthony Wayne in Georgia, see *Journal of the House, Second Congress*, p. 463; *Debates and Proceedings, Second Congress*, pp. 211–12; and note 27 below.

12. For debates on the widows and orphans pension bill, see *Journal of the House, Second Congress*, p. 466; and *Debates and Proceedings, Second Congress*, pp. 212–13. Beckley's interest in this bill no doubt increased when the Supreme Court in the Hayburn Case (1792) refused to review the pension claims as required by the act, declaring that it was unconstitutional for Congress to require the Supreme Court justices to perform nonjudicial actions that were subject to congressional and executive department review.

13. For Hamilton's Report on Manufactures, see *Journal of the House, Second Congress*, p. 468; *Debates and Proceedings, Second Congress*, p. 227; and Syrett, ed., *Hamilton Papers*, 10:340.

14. For the debate on the constitutionality of the establishment of postroads by Congress or the executive branch, see *Journal of the House, Second Congress*, p. 469; and *Debates and Proceedings, Second Congress*, pp. 229–41.

15. The House debate on the Senate amendment of the apportionment bill stretched over many days before the House voted to notify the Senate that "the House do adhere to their disagreement to the said amendment." *Journal of the House, Second Congress*, pp. 474–77; and *Debates and Proceedings, Second Congress*, pp. 243–74.

16. On December 28 the petition of the New Hampshire legislature protesting the "inequality" of the act of assumption of state debts was read in Congress. *Debates and Proceedings, Second Congress*, p. 289.

17. On December 29 the House recommitted sections 17 and 18 of the post office bill to a select committee, and on January 3, 1792, it approved the report of the committee. *Journal of the House, Second Congress*, pp. 483, 486; and *Debates and Proceedings, Second Congress*, pp. 299, 304–6.

18. See the *Journal of the House, Second Congress*, pp. 487–88; and *Debates and Proceedings, Second Congress*, pp. 307–11.

19. For Washington's confidential message enclosing recommendations to strengthen the frontier defense and improve relations with the Indians, following the November 4, 1791, defeat of Gen. Arthur St. Clair by the Indians in the Northwest Territory, see *Debates and Proceedings, Second Congress*, p. 327; and John C. Fitzpatrick, ed., *The Writings of George Washington*, 39 vols. (Washington, D.C.: U.S. G. P. O., 1931–44), 31:456.

20. The House continued debate on Washington's message concerning frontier defense and St. Clair's defeat. *Journal of the House, Second Congress*, p. 492; and *Debates and Proceedings, Second Congress*, p. 328.

21. Perhaps January 18 when the Journal reported that "Mr. Laurance, from the committee to whom was referred the written message from the President of the United States, of the twenty-eighth ultimo, covering the copy of a letter to him from the Attorney General, made a report; which was read, and ordered to lie on the table." *Journal of the House, Second Congress*, p. 493; and *Debates and Proceedings, Second Congress*, pp. 289 and 328.

22. The Journal reported simply that "the Report of the Secretary of the Treasury, on the subject of manufactures, be committed to a Committee of the Whole House on Monday next." *Journal of the House, Second Congress*, p. 495; and *Debates and Proceedings, Second Congress*, p. 329.

23. That is, John Hatsell's four-volume *Precedents of Proceedings in the House of Commons* (London, 1785–96).

24. The Journal reported that "the House resumed the consideration of the bill for making farther and more effectual provision for the protection of the frontiers of the United States; and the same being further amended at the Clerk's table, was, together with the amendments, ordered to be engrossed, and read the third time to-morrow," when the bill was passed and sent to the Senate. *Journal of the House, Second Congress*, pp. 500–501.

25. For further information on how the House handled "mistakes" in bills sent from the Senate, see *Journal of the House, Second Congress*, p. 520; *Debates and Proceedings, Second Congress*, p. 427; and Bickford, ed., *Documentary History of the First Federal Congress. House of Representatives Journal*, 3: 506, 508–9.

26. *Journal of the House, Second Congress*, p. 521; and *Debates and Proceedings, Second Congress*, p. 428.

27. House action on the contested election of Wayne and Jackson was postponed until March 12, when the election of Wayne was upheld by one vote. *Journal of the House, Second Congress*, pp. 534–43; and *Debates and Proceedings, Second Congress*, pp. 428–29, 458–79.

28. Beckley did not annex to the journal a copy of the treaties signed at Fort Harmar on January 9, 1789, by Gen. Arthur St. Clair for the United States and the Indians of the Six Nations, Wyandots, Delaware, Ottawa, Chippewa, and other tribes of the Northwest Territory. The treaties, which were ratified on September 29, 1789, are in *American State Papers: Indian Affairs* (Washington, D.C., Gales & Seaton, 1832), 1:5–8.

29. After considering the issue on March 7, the House voted on March 8 to direct the Secretary of the Treasury "to report to this House his opinion of the best mode for raising the additional supplies requisite for the ensuing year." *Journal of the House, Second Congress*, pp. 530–31; and *Debates and Proceedings, Second Congress*, pp. 437–52.

30. On March 10 after debates expressing fear that their resolution would be considered an approval of the new French constitution, the House resolved "that this House has received, with sentiments of high satisfaction, the notification of the King of the French, of his acceptance of the constitution presented to him in the name of the Nation." *Journal of the House, Second Congress*, p. 533; and *Debates and Proceedings, Second Congress*, pp. 456–57.

31. See the *Journal of the House, Second Congress*, p. 534; and *Debates and Proceedings, Second Congress*, p. 458.

32. On March 13 the "House resumed the hearing on the contested" election in the case of Jackson vs. Wayne. *Journal of the House, Second Congress*, p. 535; and *Debates and Proceedings, Second Congress*, pp. 458–70.

33. The "disorder" is not mentioned in the *Journal of the House, Second Congress*, pp. 546–46 or the *Debates and Proceedings, Second Congress*, pp. 480–83.

34. For further information on this debate with its monarchical overtones, see *Journal of the House, Second Congress*, pp. 547–49; and *Debates and Proceedings, Second Congress*, pp. 483–86.

35. That is, the Senate amendment for the "Act establishing a mint" discussed on March 24. *Journal of the House, Second Congress*, pp. 549–51; and *Debates and Proceedings, Second Congress*, pp. 486–90.

36. For further information on the motion and debate on a proposed investigation into the defeat of Gen. St. Clair's army by the Indians of the Ohio region, see *Journal of the House, Second Congress*, pp. 551–53; and *Debates and Proceedings, Second Congress*, pp. 489–94.

37. The manuscript entries end here.
The House spent most of the day debating Treasury Secretary Hamilton's reports on duties and the public debt. *Journal of the House, Second Congress*, pp. 556–58; and *Debates and Proceedings, Second Congress*, pp. 533–34.

Frederick A. C. Muhlenberg (1750–1801). Painting by Samuel B. Waugh after Joseph Wright, in U.S. capitol. LC–USA7–34331.

JOHN BECKLEY TO JAMES MADISON

Dear Sir,   Philadelphia, 1st August 1792.

I took the liberty by favor of Mr. Jefferson, to forward to you sundry papers,[1] which I thought would be useful, for your information respecting the progress of the Virginia accounts; and it has been my constant purpose, hitherto, to follow them by a communication of such other circumstances on the subject as I might be able to collect, but, until yesterday, I have not been successful in obtaining satisfactory information.

Colo. Davies, has, at length, undertaken to exhibit to the Board, within one Month, a general Statement of the Claims of Virginia particularising the several items of demand, specifically, & periodically, and to arrange and present his proofs and Vouchers in support of each respective item. I find however, that he does not yeild to this idea, without reserving to himself a right to make such exceptions & demands, previous to any submission of the accounts, as may eventually, and both General Irvine[2] & myself, greatly fear, will prevent a <u>timely</u> settlement of them, or perhaps any settlement at all; and altho' our fears proceed more from a knowledge of his litigious disposition, than from any actual difficulty that he has <u>yet</u> presented, we are still of opinion that it will be extremely seasonable, if not indispensable, that the Executive should peremptorily instruct him to present and submit his accounts to the Board, within the time specified in his letter to them, referred to in their report to the last Session, making any protest, or reservation, in respect to particular charges, which he may think proper and necessary, as a future or subsequent Security to the State; against inequality or injustice in the final settlement. Should you approve of this idea, and an instruction to that effect could come to him from the Executive, as suggested by & originating from themselves, without any communication of it to the Board of Commrs. it would doubtless be decisive.

We have no recent intelligence from abroad; the June packet is arrived, but brings nothing new. Our domestic proceedings are rapidly progressing in favor of republican views: from N Hampshire I learn by Mr. Langdon[3] the Commissr. that their representative ticket is predicated, & will certainly be carried, to the exclusion of all the present Members, on that express principle as avowed & published by the Western Counties; and he says that Livermore, received nine tenths of the votes of the Legislature, as Senator, altho' personally disliked, solely because he voted against the funding System & Assumption. The same spirit, he also says, is spreading in Massachusetts, and both Ames & Sedgwick, he thinks, will be dropped.[4] In New York, Benson has declined, and as the Jayite party all admit, that Clinton has a decided Majority in the Assembly, it is supposed that the Electors, who are appointed by them, will not be Antirepublican Men. In New Jersey, great exertion is making to leave out Dayton & Boudinot, but I doubt it will not be successful.[5] In this State, violent means have been attempted to produce a Conference,[6] at Lancaster, for the purpose of fixing a fœderal ticket, and yesterday, being the fourth trial of the Conference party, (Morris, Wilson, Bingham, Powell &c.) after a tumultuous proceeding in which nothing was done, a disgraceful riot & severe contest vi et armis was shamefully brought on by the Antirepublicans, who were, as they meritted, totally defeated and driven from the State house & its Yard, after a severe drubbing to several of them. It appeared too, that so great & decided a Majority of the Citizens were opposed to a Conference, that nothing but the most unbounded & palpable desire to influence the general ticket, could have directed the proposers of it, in pursuing the attempt. Their discomfiture, it is thought, will ensure success to the republican ticket, which stands thus, Findley, Woods, Smilie, Gregg, Montgomery, Heister, Irvine, P. Muhlenberg, A. Muhlenberg, Hartley, Kittera, & Fitzsimons & Bingham, or Tilghman & Fisher. I perceive too, that the defeated party are artfully endeavoring to stimulate Mifflin to become a Candidate for the Vicepresidency, from a real apprehension of Clintons succeeding. A like apprehension prevails too, with certain persons, that Mr. Lee[7] will be superceded as a Senator for Virginia, and that the general complection of our phalanx, both of representativs & Electors, will be equally republican & hostile to their views. General Irvine & myself take an excursion tomorrow as far as Carlisle, I shall be absent a fortnight, and on my return, should be happy to be favored with any communication from you, respecting the politics of our own State. I am, with great regard, Dear Sir, Your most obedt. Servant,

John Beckley

RC (MADISON PAPERS, LIBRARY OF CONGRESS).

1. Beckley enclosed copies of the letters of William Davies to William Irvine, 26 June 1792, and Irvine to Davies, 18 July 1792, and an Abstract of the Claims of Virginia against the United States, all of which are in the Madison Papers, Library of Congress.
2. That is, William Irvine (1741–1804), an Irish-born physician in Carlisle, Pennsylvania, former Revolutionary War general and member of the Confederation Congress. Irvine commanded the Pennsylvania troops during the Whiskey Rebellion of 1794 and served in the House of Representatives, 1793–95. He was a political ally of Beckley and a frequent correspondent.
3. That is, Woodbury Langdon, brother of Senator John Langdon. Contrary to Langdon's report, all of the New Hampshire congressional delegation was returned to office, although Paine Wingate moved from the Senate to the House and Samuel Livermore moved from the House to the Senate.
4. Fisher Ames and Theodore Sedgwick, Federalist spokesmen, were returned to the House from Massachusetts.
5. Elias Boudinot and Jonathan Dayton were returned to the House from New Jersey.
6. "Conferees" and "Correspondents," representing Federal and Republican interests, were wrangling over the proper way to nominate candidates for the selection of federal representatives and presidential electors as provided for in the Pennsylvania election law of 1792. Beckley soon became embroiled in Pennsylvania's partisan poltics. In the October 9 election for thirteen House seats, seven men were sponsored by both parties and were elected to Congress, but only three men solely listed on the Federalist ticket—James Armstrong, Thomas Fitsimons, and Thomas Scott—and three from the Republican ticket were elected—Andrew Gregg, William Montgomery, and John Smilie. Harry M. Tinkcom, *The Republicans and Federalists in Pennsylvania, 1790–1801* (Harrisburg, Pa.: Historical and Museum Commission, 1950), pp. 51–68; and Noble E. Cunningham, Jr., *The Jeffersonian Republicans. The Formation of Party Organization, 1789–1801* (Chapel Hill: University of North Carolina Press, 1957), pp. 38–45.
7. That is, Richard Henry Lee, who resigned and was replaced by John Taylor.

JOHN BECKLEY AS MERCATOR[1]

Aug. 30, 1792.

FOR THE *NATIONAL GAZETTE*[2]

REMARKS ON A LATE AUTHENTIC DOCUMENT, PUBLISHED BY THE TREASURY DEPARTMENT, UNDER THE SIGNATURE OF JOSEPH NOURSE, REGISTER[*3]

The object of this publication seems to be, to impress the public mind with a belief, that under the present administration of its fiscal concerns, the public debt has been actually reduced to the amount of 1,845,217 dols. and 42 cents; and that the sum of 397,024 dols. and 15 cents remains to be applied to the same object. That this is not the case, but that the public debt, instead of being diminished one farthing, has been really augmented to the amount of upwards of *one million and a half dollars*, since the present administration commenced, will I think manifestly appear by a reference to a few plain facts and documents not less authentic than the one signed by Mr. Nourse.

The Secretary of the Treasury in a report to Congress, dated 23d January, 1792, states that the whole expenditures or demands against the government from the beginning of the year 1791, to the end of the year 1792, amount to dols. 7,082,197.74.

That amount of the nett product of the public revenues during the years 1791 & 1792 is 7,029,755.26.

Leaving as a deficiency against the government dols. 52,442.48

It appears by Mr. Nourse's document, that the whole amount of the revenues of the United States from the time the first impost law took effect, which was the 1st of August 1789, until the 31st Dec. 1790, was dols. 3,026,070.65.

That the total demands upon that, agreeable to the appropriations made by Congress exclusive of any interest on the public debt, was 1,687,194.81.

Leaving a surplus in favour of the revenue, of dols. 1,338,875.84.

It appears too, from Mr. Nourse's document, that the treasury department claims credit for having disposed of the said surplus of 1,338,875.84, so as to purchase and redeem to the amount of 1,845,217.42 of the public debt, and to have left 397,024 dollars and 15 cents to be applied to the same object. Be it so; I admit the fact in its fullest force—but what follows? That if the treasury claims credit for the use and whole amount of the revenue of the United States, from its commencement on the 1st of Aug. 1789 to the 31st of Dec. 1790 towards lessening the public credit; so it ought to be debited with the whole amount of the interest, that accrued on the public debt, during the same period, which by the treasury returns amounts to 4,036,359 dols. and 19 cents. I am aware that in objection to this it will be said, that agreeable to the act of Congress, no interest was payable on the public debt until January 1791. Granted; but what became of this interest? Has it been paid? No—Does it remain to be paid? Yes.—Was it added to and made a part of the principal of the public debt, thereby encreasing that debt to the amount of 4,036,359 dols. and 19 cents, in addition to its former principal? Yes. Did not, the Secretary of the Treasury himself propose that it should be so added? Yes.—Is it not therefore an efficient act of his administration, and can he now claim credit with the public, upon the fallacious idea of having *bona fide* reduced the public debt upwards of two millions, when, as I have shewn above, he has produced an actual addition to the public debt of more than one million and a half of dollars?

A simple state of the case with the Treasury department stands thus—

	DEBIT.	dols.	cts.
For the amount of interest which accrued on the public debt between the 1st of Aug. 1789, and 31st Dec. 1790.		4,036,359.19	
For the deficiency of revenue to answer the demands of government in 1791 and 1792		52,412.48	
	Dollars	4,088,801.67	

CREDIT.

By the amount of public debt redeemed and
discharged out of the surplus of the revenue arising
between 1st Aug. 1789 and 31st Dec. 1790   1,843,217.42
By balance of surplus remaining on hand of dollars
397,024.15 and which may probably redeem   500,000.
By a deficiency against the treasury department, since
its establishment, which forms an actual addition to
the public debt.   1,743,584.25

                                                  Dollars   4,088,801.67

That the facts and conclusions above mentioned are just, and that it is a
sad and serious truth that the public debt has encreased in the hands of its
present administrators, is also manifest to two important classes of men in
the community. I mean the MERCHANTS and FARMERS, by the present
amount and encreasing weight of the duties of Impost and Excise.

MERCATOR

TR (*NATIONAL GAZETTE* (PHILADELPHIA), SEPTEMBER 1, 1792).

1. Authorship of the two essays (August 30 and September 5, 1792) signed "Mercator" has
   been attributed to Beckley by Berkeley, *Beckley*, pp. 66–67. Beckley displayed pride in the
   Mercator essays in his letters of September 2 and 10 to Madison, but made no direct
   claims to authorship.
2. Mercator was responding to documents prepared by Joseph Nourse, register of the treasury, for Alexander Hamilton, which are printed in Syrett, ed., *Hamilton Papers*,
   12:267–70.
   The Mercator essays prompted two responses by Hamilton over the pseudonym
   "Civis,"which are reprinted in ibid., 12:320–27, 357–61.
3. At the end of the essay the newspaper editor had inserted at the asterisk, "*See the last
   page*," where Joseph Nourse's August 24, 1792, letter to Hamilton and his enclosed reports
   on "the abstract statement of the debt incurred by the late government" were printed.

JOHN BECKLEY TO JAMES MADISON

Dear Sir,   Philadelphia, 2d September 1792.

A severe indisposition, the consequence of a violent cold which I caught
on my return from Carlisle, has prevented an earlier acknowledgment of
your favor of the 12th. ultimo. Its effects, however, are now subsiding, and I
hope soon to be perfectly restored.

I have not been able to discover any material change in the situation of
the Virga. accounts, the Commissioner[1] pursues his former course, says he
shall have them ready in time, and withholds of late any communication
with the Board. Mr. Randolph has been urging him lately, and I think to
good effect. A hint, from the Executive, might now be serviceable.

The state of our foreign intelligence has differed but little since I wrote yo. last. The success of Cornwallis in India, and a report of the death of the King of Hungary are the only material circumstances. Should the latter prove true, it will certainly produce important consequences in relation to the affairs of France—perhaps the former may prop Mr. Pitts administration a little longer, and enable him for a year, or two, to stem the current of popular opinion in favor of reform, which is rapidly advancing thro' the influence of the Constitutional clubs, and the spirit and energy of Paines continued and reiterated publications.

Our domestic affairs, seem to me, to be fast verging to the issue of a contest between the Treasury department and the people, whose interest shall preponderate in the next Congress; the anxiety and fears of the former, are strongly manifested by the means they are pursuing, both publicly and privately, to acomplish their object. The late insidious attack on Mr. Jefferson, which is generally imputed to Mr. Hamilton, marks the lengths they will go and the Arts they will practice.[2] The former, being regarded, as the head of the republican party, this premidated attack has been pointed as to time and manner, and is now industriously circulated thro' all the Eastern papers. It would have met, here, with its merited contempt, but for the artful misrepresentation of Mr. Jeffersons letter respecting the French debt, of which, the public at large being uninformed, many, are disposed to think, that the writer speaking from official information, would not have dared so to state it, if untrue. For myself, I know it to be unfounded, but am not now at liberty to disclose my information, and, if I were, should deem it injudicious to do so, until, the accuser, being challenged to his proofs, should either recede from the charge, or, by producing the proof, convict himself of falsehood. Accident has led me to the knowledge of a circumstance which confirms the suspicion that Mr. H. is the author. Arthur Lee is now here, as also Corbin, and Heth; the former and the latter have been a good deal closetted with the Secretary, and I find, from hints drop't by the latter, that the reference to the scruples of family connection &c. mentioned in the last publication, is privately said by Mr. H——to allude to the two brothers Arthur & R.H. and their kinsman H. Lee, whose conversations with Freneau, at New York, you and myself well remember. Corbin too, thro' his intimacy with A. Lee, and the Shippen family, communicates another curious fact, that when R.H. Lee, was nominated to the chair of the Senate pro. tem. Mr. H. & his friends, at a private meeting, objected that he was their declared opponent, and the author of the publications signed Caius[3] which, dictated by him & written or copied by his nephew, young Shippen, found their way to the press thro' that source—from which suspicion, the other, meanly, condescended to exonerate himself.

Heth,[4] also informs me that Mr. H. unequivocally declares, that yo. are his personal & political enemy. Another means of public deception & electioneering trick, is, a publication from the Treasury, signed by Nourse, affecting to shew a reduction of the public debt of nearly two Millions, which has been instantly attacked by a publication signed Mercator, proving an actual increase of it, by Mr. H's administration, of more than a Million & a half.

Private endeavors to influence are not less industriously urged, and I am told that to obviate the chagrin and prevent the effects of their late defeat here in the attempt to produce a Conference, Mr. H——has advised a private correspondence and exertion of the friends of Government thro' the Union, particularly in Maryland, Virginia, & No. Carolina—himself too, is endeavoring to amuse the Western people with an idea, that he will relinquish the Excise, and by a deeper stroke yet, which he communicated to General Irvine in seeming confidence, to wit, that the negotiation with Spain for the free navigation of the Mississippi drags too slowly, and that his opinion is, without delay, to seize it with a strong hand. Any comment to you, on this last suggestion, would be superfluous.

How far, these, and the various other means to influence, which are now pursuing may be effectual I know not, but I cannnot help indulging a sanguine expectation that a decided weight of Interest will appear in support of republican measures, in the next Congress. The N Hampshire choice will be decided, Massachusetts, Connect. & R. Island nearly of the same complection with their last. N. York, will greatly depend on the issue of the impending contest in their Assembly, respecting Governor, about which Clintons party are very sanguine. In Jersey, no material change. In this state the republican ticket will prevail. In So. Carolina too, Smith will be reelected, if he pleases, but all the others will be republican—Barnwell declines—Huger will be left out.[5] In the other States, my information fails.

Mr. Brown, was to start from Kentucky, yesterday: he says, that Clinton will have all the votes there, as Vice President. His Colleague Edwards, he does not altogether approve. Their representatives were not chosen when he wrote.[6]

The papers will shew yo. the proceedings at Pittsburg respecting the Excise,[7] of the result of which Mr. H——has manifested great anxiety. They are no less united & firm in that quarter against many other of his measures, and their union, decision, and influence thro' the State, will I believe, occasion him much further disquietude.

I am sorry at the lethargy which, I am told, prevails in Virginia, as to public men and measures in the general government. A general disposition, seeming to succeed, for relinguishing it altogether. To shake of the former, would be wise, effectual, and worthy of the Viriginia character; to indulge in the latter, is desperate folly, little short of madness. It is in critical times, that exertion is most honorable, and, our country has been used to give wise example, rather than to receive it.

I shall be happy to hear that the people are beginning to stir, respecting concerns in which they are so deeply interested. Your future communications on this subject, will be highly gratifying, and will receive the best return I am able to make. At present, my little stock is exhausted, and I conclude, with my best regards, Dear Sir, Yr. obedt. hble Servt.

John Beckley

P.S. An Account is, this morning, come to town, by the way of Boston, that the French & Austrians have had a general engagement, and that, after a bloody contest, the Austrians were defeated leaving 10,000 killed & wounded. The french lost 5000 or upwards—they have since taken Menen and several other places. Mons was besieged & expected to fall in a few days.

The Poles have had several severe rencounters with the Russians, and in two or three considerable skirmishes cut up some of their bravest Corps, particularly one of about 2000, which was esteemed the best in the Russian Army. Mindful of their former military glory, and eager to avenge their Countrys wrongs, the poles now fight with the most desperate valour. That success may crown their efforts, and in the total defeat of all their enemies, procure them that peace & liberty they so just merit, is my most fervent wish.

J.B.

RC (MADISON PAPERS, NEW YORK PUBLIC LIBRARY).

1. That is, William Davies.
2. Beckley is referring to the three essays written over the pseudonym, "An American," which were published August 4, 11, and 18, 1792, in the *Gazette of the United States*. They have been reprinted in Syrett, ed., *Hamilton Papers*, 12:157–64, 188–93, and 224.
3. Beckley is probably referring to the series of essays attacking Hamilton which appeared over the pseudonym "Caius" in *Dunlap's American Daily Advertiser*, January 11 and 21, February 1 and 4, 1792.
4. William Heth was the collector of customs at Bermuda Hundred, Virginia.
5. William L. Smith was reelected to the House and Robert Barnwell and Daniel Huger, as well as Thomas Sumter and Thomas Tudor Tucker were not returned to the House from South Carolina.
6. John Brown and John Edwards were the U.S. senators from Kentucky. Kentucky electors cast four votes for Washington and four for Jefferson. *Debates and Proceedings, Second Congress*, p. 875.
7. Beckley is referring to the convention of "sundry Inhabitants of the Western Counties" of Pennsylvania who met at Pittsburgh on August 21–22, and denounced the federal excise tax on whiskey, promising peaceful resistance. See Syrett, ed., *Hamilton Papers*, 12:307n.5–309; and Thomas P. Slaughter, *The Whiskey Rebellion. Frontier Epilogue to the American Revolution* (New York: Oxford University Press, 1986), pp. 109–24.

JOHN BECKLEY AS MERCATOR[1]

September 5. [1792]

FOR THE *NATIONAL GAZETTE*

MERCATOR TO CIVIS:

Containing further Remarks on a late authentic document, published by the Treasury Department, under the signature of Joseph Nourse Register.

When you, CIVIS, avow and declare the object of the Treasury Department in making the publication alluded to, I presume you speak from that intimate, accurate, and precise knowledge of *the intention* which the Secretary himself can alone possess. Would it not have been candid then, to have come forward in *propra persona*, and, under the official sanction of office, declared what the *real intention* was? To attempt a public deception through indirect means, may avoid personal impeachment, but can seldom escape detection. You say, that Mercator "*has endeavored to shew that the contrary of what was intended, is true.*" Now Mercator, has simply supposed that it was intended to impress the public mind with a belief that under the present administration of its fiscal concerns, the public debt has been *actually* reduced: This supposition then, as you declare, *was contrary to the real intention,* and, and as Mercator, is not disposed to *doubt your knowledge of what the real intention was* he rests satisfied in the admission that the public debt, has not been diminished. But Mercator has *unluckily* suggested that the public debt, instead of being diminished one farthing, has, under *your* administration, been augmented to a considerable amount. This you regard as a deliberate act of hostility, a malicious endeavor to lessen the public confidence in you, to drive you from office, and, in the true spirit of a certain junto, to grasp all the powers of the government into their own hands. Indeed, my good Civis, you discover too much anxiety, fear, and passion—your zeal betrays you, and in the apprehensions for the *reputation and continuance in office* of the Secretary of the Treasury, manifestly shews the inseparable connection between you and him. Do not, however, elevate Mercator beyond his views; give him an importance that he does not seek, or rank him with men that he does not know. Humble and moderate in his wishes, with no avidity or desire for the loaves and fishes of office, unconnected with any junto, if any there be, and disdaining the use of any power but that of truth and reason, Mercator came forward to examine a plain fact, and to assist the public investigation of it, by a reference to *other authentic documents* of the treasury department itself. Wherefore then do you impeach the purity of his motives, and accuse him of want of accuracy and candor? You have surely forgotten the scriptural admonition "to cast the beam from your own eye before you pluck the mote from a brother's." Remember that an accuser should never be guilty of the thing he condemns. You accuse Mercator of charging you with the arrears of interest from the day the public revenue commenced, that is, on the 1st of August,

1789, until your department was organized on the 13th of September following, and complain that this arrearage of interest accrued prior to the existence of your department; and yet you have no scruple to avail yourself of the use of the whole public revenue from the said first day of August. I leave it to a more plausible sophistry than you exhibit, to reconcile this absurdity. Your next complaint is, that Mercator's standard of calculation is erroneous, because he charges you with the arrears of interest made principal, and the amount of the affirmed debt. Now, as to the arrears of interest made principal, was there not allowed an interest upon it equal to that of the original principal? Did not this operate as compound interest, or interest upon interest? And have you not the *unballanced* claim of merit with the public for the proposition which such an operation demands? In respect to the assumed debt, I ask to know at what period, prior to the assumption, the interest upon that ceased? If then, Mercator has kindly taken a lower standard of calculation than he might have done, or if instead of eliminating upon the *present* rate of interest on the public debt, equal to about four and a half per cent, he had charged a full rate of six per centum upon the principal of the foreign and domestic debt, the arrears of interest and the assumed debt, thereby adding to the statement he made two or three millions more,—what becomes of this charge of inaccuracy and want of candor? Mercator's design was, to expose a plain and obvious principle to the public view, without regard to nice calculation or fractional certainty: that he has been under, and not over the mark, is pretty certain, and may be easily demonstrated by figures. You can best ascertain the *precise* amount of the addition that has been made to the public debt.

Whether the language and conceptions of Mercator justify the idea, that "to *provide* for a debt; and to *reduce* it, amount to the same thing," will be left to the public to determine: to whom also it is referred, how far in the principles and practice of Civis and of the Secretary, to *reduce* the public debt and to *add* to it, are synonymous?

The review of certain leading facts respecting the establishment of the funding system, is too tedious and unimportant for the pursuit of Mercator: he has little time, and less inclination to remark upon them; like *another* elaborate report of the Secretary of the Treasury, time and truth will discover their fallacy. The boast that is made of benefit to the public first, in the saving by purchases in the public debt at the market price; secondly, by the advanced price given by foreigners in their purchases of the public debt; thirdly, by the reduced rate of the new loans for paying off the foreign debt; and lastly, by the institution of the national bank, may be regarded as so many circumstances of little and temporary expedient, producing partial or insignificant advantage or convenience to the government, and which like all temporising expedients predicated on the sacrifice of justice and of principle, leave behind them the bitter sting of future, extensive and permanent evil. The beneifts, if any, are nearly passed away; the evil but begins to be felt and understood. What may be the issue of the public mind upon them, is left for Civis to verify.

MERCATOR

TR (*NATIONAL GAZETTE* (PHILADELPHIA), SEPTEMBER 8, 1792).

1. Mercator's second essay was written in response to Hamilton's Civis essay of September 5. See Syrett, ed., *Hamilton Papers*, 12:320–27.

JOHN BECKLEY TO JAMES MADISON

Dear Sir,   Philadelphia. 10th September 1792.

Since I wrote you last, a considerable change has taken place in the state of our foreign & domestic intelligence. Advices from France as late as the 14th July, exhibit a crisis in the internal affairs of that Country, which 'ere this must be determined and would probably decide the issue of the revolution; the Marquis Fayette appeared at the bar of the National Assembly & denounced the Jacobin club, as the cause of all the evils under which the Nation labours; it appears that he had a favorable hearing, and that notwithstanding violent attempts to impeach him &c., he had been permitted to leave Paris & rejoin the Army, but without effecting his object. On his return to the Army, Luckner immediately left it, and on the 14th July appeared in Paris on the same errand, but there our account ceases. It should seem that the contest is now fairly at issue, between the violent democrats who would overturn the Monarchy, and the friends of the present System. In respect to their external affairs, Prussia is come decidedly forward in support of Austria, and utterly renouncing all Guarantee of Poland, lends its utmost exertions against France. Poland is thus left to an unequal struggle with Russia, and France has one more formidable Enemy without, to contend with. The Poles act with unexampled unanimity and bravery, and have defeated one of the Russian Armies, killing upwards of 4000 and taking 14 pieces of Cannon; but I find that the account in my last of a victory by the French, is not confirmed. The occurrences of the present Year seem, alike, awfully important to both nations, and deeply interesting to the cause of liberty throughout the Globe.

Our domestic concerns are progressing in the struggle between the Treasury department and the republican Interest, which shall preponderate in the impending Elections; the former has been, lately, greatly checked & mortified by the Pointed attack on its authentic document, and the no less pointed answers by different writers, both here and at Boston, to the attack on Mr. Jefferson, the two attempts being equally regarded as the weak, insidious & contemptible efforts of Mr. Hamilton himself. It is difficult to say, which endeavor he will most regret the failure of, the one to traduce Mr. J—— and thro' him to wound the republican Interest throughout the Union, or, the other, to Arm his friends at the ensuing Elections with a deceptive statement, under sanction of Office, to induce the public beleif that a considerable reduction has been effected of the public debt. The latter I know he is extremely solicitous about, and in a phrenzy of passion made a weak intemperate and futile attempt to justify, in a publication signed Civis, by way of Answer to Mercators remarks—which publication I happened to see brought to the Office by a servant of his, and appears (I am told) in the handwriting of one of his Clerks—to this Mercator, has again replied in a manner well calculated to excite farther anmiadversion to draw him forth into detail; But I rather think he will retire from this species of warfare; which accumulates upon him in a disagreeable manner, and cannot fail to injure him in the public mind both as a man and a Minister. Indeed I am told that it is a certain fact that the whole weight of supporting his own measures thro' the public papers, has, since the adjournment of Congress, fallen upon Coxe[1] & himself, not a single publication on that side having been sent to the press, from any pen but theirs. A better way of proceeding, perhaps, is by urging the private & united influence of his freinds thro' the States. In Maryland, I hear that a speculator Candidate is brought forward for every district. In Virginia, the same will be attempted wherever they dare appear. In this State an attempt is again making to revive a Conference, and as a further means to seduce the dutch & German Interest, a City ticket is circulated with six dutch names and seven approved Treasury men. However, as the election is on the 10th October, they come too late to promise much success.

I shall go to New York on tuesday, for a week, and hope on my return to be able to give you some certain assurance of the disposition of that State.[2] Mr. Burr, has been here and says, that he thinks the republican interest will prevail. Mr. Randolph also informs me that he has furnished his written opinion at large in favor of Clintons Election.[3]

I have a letter from Mr. Brown, of the 10th August—he gives a very gloomy accot. of Indian Affairs—confirms the murder of all our flags, & says that the voice & union for War is very general & formidable—an extract will appear in freneau's next paper.[4] He also reports that Clinton, will receive the votes of that State as V. President. Several Virginians are in town, your kinsman the Bishop, Mr. Andrews, General Wood &c.—but they give us little information.

General Irwin tells me that Davis will exhibit his accounts before the first day of October. I have nothing farther to add, than to repeat the assurances of esteem and regard with which I am, Dear Sir, Your obedt. hble Servt.

John Beckley

RC (MADISON PAPERS, NEW YORK PUBLIC LIBRARY).

1. Tench Coxe (1755–1824), wealthy Pennsylvania merchant and land speculator was assistant secretary of the treasury, but later became a Republican and political associate o[f] Beckley. See Jacob Cooke, *Tench Coxe and the Early Republic* (Chapel Hill: University o[f] North Carolina Press, 1978).

2. When Beckley went to New York he carried with him a strong letter of endorsement from Benjamin Rush to Burr: "This letter will be handed to you by Mr. Beckly. He possesses a fund of information about men & things, & what is more in favor of his principles, he possesses the Confidence of our two illustrious patriots Mr. Jefferson & Mr. Madison." See Mary-Jo Kline, ed., *Political Correspondence and Public Papers of Aaron Burr*, 2 vols. (Princeton: Princeton University Press, 1983), 1:137–39.

3. Although the Republicans did not oppose the re-election of President Washington, they unsuccessfully worked to elect either Aaron Burr or George Clinton of New York to replace Vice President Adams. Beckley was undoubtedly in New York to discuss this effort which was led by John Nicholson of Pennsylvania and Aaron Burr of New York. Cunningham, *Jeffersonian Republicans*, pp. 46–48. See also Beckley to Madison, October 17, 1792.

4. Beckley published this letter of John Brown, as an "Extract of a letter from a gentleman at Danville (Kent.) to his friend in this city, dated Aug. 10," in the *National Gazette*, September 12, 1792.

JOHN BECKLEY TO JAMES MADISON

Dear Sir,   Philadelphia, 17th October 1792.

Your favor of the 3d instant, and a preceeding one of 25th Septr. came duly to hand. I should have written yo. immediately on my return from N. York, had not several circumstances occurred to prevent it, particularly the delay of a Meeting which was had last evening between Melancton Smith,[1] on the part of the republican interest of NY. (specially deputed) and the principal movers of the same interest here, to conclude finally & definitively as to the choice of a V.P.—the result of which was, unanimously, to exert every endeavor for Mr. Clinton, & to drop all thoughts of Mr. Burr. Mr. S——pledged himself for those he represented, & has desired me to communicate to Colo. Monroe & yourself, this determination, with an assurance that not only the freinds of Clinton, including Mr. Burr, will instantly pursue every proper means to accomplish the object, as far as depends on the vote of N York, but moreover that he is positively certain of their obtaining the entire votes of Vermont & Rh. Island, for the later of which States, Massachusetts, & Connecticut, he will immediately set out himself, and doubts not of making a considerable division in Connect. & also, of two or three votes in Massa. He wishes extremely that the most influential & proper characters in the Virga. Assembly could be timely apprised of the thing, and invited to act in concert, and he earnestly desires that Col. Monroe would write to Mr. Henry & endeavor to influence him to interest his friends in No. Carolina.[2] Mr. Butler will write to So. Carolina by a vessel that sails to day, and letters are also sent by her to Georgia. A conjectural estimate of the

Thomas Jefferson as vice-president. Engraving by C. Tiebout. Presidential File.
LC–USZ62–3795.

votes, was made as follows N. Hamp: 4 for Adams—2 for Clinton—Massa. 16 Adams—Connect: 7 A. 2 C.—Vermont 4 C.—R. Island 4 C. Jersey 4 A. 2 C. Pennsylva. divided—N. York 8 A. 4 C. Kentuckey 4 for C. Delaware 2 A. 1 C. Maryland 6 A. 4 C. Virginia 2 A. 19 C. No. Carolina 3 A. 9 C. So. Carolina 3 A. 5 C. Georgia 1 A. 3 C.—total (allowing Pennsa. to be divided, say 5 to A. 5 to C & 5 scattered) for Adams 56. for Clinton 63. In addition to this prospect Mr. S. says that they are very sanguine in the hope of getting every vote from N.Y. for Clinton, as the Legislature appoint Electors, & the Jayite party from a fear of a Majority against them, have publicly declared their waver of all farther dispute as to Governor—this circumstance would allow for a much greater defection Southward than was calculated upon, and, upon the whole, serves to shew that there is at least great probability of Success. A nomination of Electors by the republican party here, accompanied with circular letters will be dispatched this day, by Expresses, to every part of the State. The gloomy prospect of success to the republican ticket for represents. of this State, operates as an additional stimulus to exertion in the present instance, and I am sure that Colo. Monroe & yourself will pardon a Wish, resulting from a pure desire to the success of the measure, without regard to the Man, that if, on receipt of this letter your arrangements to leave Fredericksg. are not definitively taken, yo. would devote one day to the object of urging our principal republicans, into a general concert throughout the State—present appearances are that Bingham only, will be excluded from the Conferee ticket—& Serjeant, Montgomery, or Gregg elected in his stead.[3] Maryland elections too are not very favorable, & I fear nothing will be done eastwardly, altho' there is some expectation that Boudinot will fail in Jersey. Connect. has reelected W[4]—N Hamp. has done better.

Mr. H——is still busy, to divert public attention, prevent a particular impeachment of his own measures, and further his Electioneering views; another insidious publication of Catulus appears to day.[5] His efforts direct & indirect are unceasing & extraordinary—perhaps his inflexible pursuit of the object,[6] has betrayed him into means, which may eventually betray him and sufficiently expose the positive & corrupt interference of the T——y departmt. I think I have a clue to something far beyond mere suspicion on this ground, which prudence forbids a present disclosure of. The republican party here have, however, obtained one important victory, in the exclusion of Lewis, from the State legislature, and the election of Swanwick—the object of electing Lewis, was to procure them a proper Senator to supply the existing vacancy in Senate from this State; so extremely attentive is Mr. H— to this important point, & so cruelly mortified at the disppointment of his hopes, as to have explicitly declared "that the interests of the General Government, received a greater shock, than it would do by the total failure of the Conferee ticket."[7] A jealous eye is cast toward Virginia in her impending choice of a Senator and the most marked anxiety for the reelection of R.H.L.[8]—perhaps an attentive observer on the spot, might mark the secret workings of Mr. H. even in the Virga. Legislature, thro' the agency of one or more of those closetted friends of his, of whom I wrote yo. during the summer—it would be wise to be watchful; there is no inferior degree of sagacity in the combinations of this extraordinary Man, with a comprehensive Eye, a subtle and contriving mind, and a Soul devoted to his object, all his measures are promptly and aptly designed, and like the links of a chain, dependent on each other, acquire additional strength by their union & concert. In a conversation at the Levee yesterday, I discovered that another & not a small source of uneasiness is, the apprehension of a Virginia Convention to revise their Government; whether this results from the guilty fear of an inquisition by that body on certain fœderal measures, or the idea of its reform being generally hostile to their opinions of what are the interests of the General Government, I know not, but the questions to me & the persons they came from, manifestly betrayed great anxiety on the subject.

Are your districts marked? Is the time of Election decided? Will Electors be by choice of the people or the Legislature? ; the latter would now be desirable. Will a Convention be called, or is the progress of public opinion yet too tardy for the measure? These, or any other topic, on which, before yo. leave Fredericksburg, you could drop me a line, would be acceptable. With my respects to Colo. Monroe & his lady, I remain, Dr Sir, Yr. obedt. hble Servt.

John Beckley

[*P.S.*] Nothing particular occurred at N. York, worth mentioning, except Colo. Burrs assurances to me that he would cheerfully support the measure of removing Mr. A—& lend every aid in his power to Cs. election—but perhaps he has written yo. to this point?

RC (MADISON PAPERS, NEW YORK PUBLIC LIBRARY).

1. Melancton Smith (1744–98), a New York merchant and former member of the Continental Congress, was a firm supporter of the vice-presidential candidacy of Aaron Burr.
2. For the activities of Madison and Monroe related to the effort to replace George Clinton with Burr as the Republican vice-presidential candidate, see William T. Hutchinson, Robert Rutland, John Stagg, eds., *The Papers of James Madison* (Chicago: University of Chicago Press, 1962–), 14:376–87; and Kline, ed., *Burr Papers*, 1:135–42; and Cunningham, *Jeffersonian Republicans*, pp. 46–48.
3. William Montgomery and Andrew Gregg were elected to the House of Representatives from Pennsylvania. William Bingham and Jonathan D. Sergeant were omitted from Congress in the 1792 election.

   For the results of the 1792 election in which John Adams received 77 votes for vice-president and George Clinton received 50, including 21 from Virginia and only one from Pennsylvania, see *Debates and Proceedings, Second Congress*, pp. 874–75.
4. That is, Jeremiah Wadsworth.
5. This was the fourth in a series of six anti-Jeffersonian essays by "Catullus," a pseudonym of Hamilton, see Syrett, ed., *Hamilton Papers*, 12:379n. 1–2, 578–87.
6. That is Hamilton's clandestine support for George Clinton as the republican alternative to John Adams.
7. John Swanwick defeated William Lewis in the Philadelphia election to the state House of Representatives and was instrumental in the successful efforts to replace William Maclay with Albert Gallatin as U.S. senator.

   Roland M. Baumann, "John Swanwick: Spokesman for 'Merchant-Republicanism' in Philadelphia, 1790–1798," *Pennsylvania Magazine of History and Biography*, 97 (1973): 148–50.
8. Richard Henry Lee resigned as U.S. senator on October 7, 1792, and was replaced by John Taylor.

JOHN BECKLEY AND JAMES MONROE

An Examination of the Late Proceedings in Congress,
respecting the Official Conduct of the Secretary of the Treasury.
PRINTED WITHIN THE UNITED STATES.[1]

UNITED STATES,   8th March, 1793.

'Tis the right and the duty of a free people, to watch attentively the movements of every department of public trust. Whether those whom they
employ, fill executive, judicial, or legislative stations, still they are equally
the servants of the people, and amenable to them, for their conduct. This
great political truth, is now rapidly spreading itself throughout the other
regions of the earth, and liberating mankind from the tyranny which has
long oppressed them. In America, it was never doubted.

'Tis particularly their duty to watch attentively the conduct of the legislature. Whilst that branch preserves its independence and integrity, they are
safe. They have nothing to apprehend either from the noxious qualityof the
laws, or their invasion by the other departments of the government. It
forms a bulwark of sufficient strength, to baffle every danger, that may
assail them from without. But whenever it loses these indispensible qualifications, their security is gone, unless they can immediately repair the
breaches that are made.

Unhappily, this branch from which alone real danger may be apprehended, is best fortified against the suspicion of it. 'Tis the nature of an executive
trust, where the operations are directed by a single hand, especially if they
are extensive and important, to inspire jealousy and distrust; to warn every
citizen to stand on his guard, and observe its course. But with the representative, the case is different: Many considerations arising from the mode of
his appointment, and his duty, tend to connect him, in more intimate confidence, with his constituents. This propensity should therefore be resisted
with decisive force, for otherwise it will open a door, through which the
public rights may be invaded with success.

These observations apply in a greater or less degree to every free government; but they apply with peculiar force to the government of these States.
Many circumstances exist in our system which tend in a certain degree, to
weaken the checks of the several departments upon each other, and to
lessen the responsibility of the representative to his proceeding from causes
beyond the reach of human remedy. Others of the adventitious kind have
been added. That we may however perfectly comprehend our true situation,
and the ruling policy of our councils, from the adoption of the government
to the present time, it may be proper to notice a few of these in both
respects. They will enable us to decide with greater propriety, on the transactions which I mean more particularly to lay bare, to the public inspection.

'Tis inseparably incident to a federal government, for reasons too well understood to require illustration, that the representation should be comparatively thin. Hence it follows, that as each member must represent a great extent of territory, and considerable number of inhabitants, he can in general be but little known to his constituents in the commencement. They must of course take his merits, and vote for him, in a great measure, in the first instance, upon trust. And the extent of the territory over which our government in particular is organized, will prevent their ever being well acquainted with him afterwards. 'Tis scarcely possible to communicate that regular and thorough information, of all transactions, from the seat of government to the extremities, so indispensibly necessary to enable the constituent to judge with propriety of the conduct of his representative. This, in equal degree lessens the responsibility; for a representative acting on a distant theatre, never seen, and seldom heard of, by his constituent, except through the medium of his own correspondence, has little to fear from his censure.

In a single well organized government, the wisdom and purity of its administration, are essentially promoted by the jealousy which takes place between the several branches of each other, and especially between the legislative and the executive. This justifies the policy of the distribution, and preserves in full force the check intended by it. But the obvious tendency of the federal principle is to dissipate this jealousy, and enfeeble the check between the several departments of the national government. A coalition with the State sovereignties, naturally unites them together, to resist a foreign pressure. And this proportionably contributes to destroy the independence of the legislature, and diminish the responsiblity of its members.

These infirmities, and especially the latter, are in a great measure without cure; it were however rational to expect, that the most wholesome remedies would have been applied, so as to fortify the system against any malign effects which could possibly be avoided. But the contrary has been the course of our administration. Active and successful efforts have been made to increase the evil where it was a natural one, and to accumulate others of the artificial kind. The best expedient which policy could dictate, to remedy those inconveniences resulting from the extent of territory, was by opening their doors, to subject their legislative discussion to the free and common audience of every citizen, and to promote the free and rapid circulation of the newspapers. But has this been done? On the contrary, have we not seen with amazement, one branch of the legislature, withdraw itself into a sequestered chamber, and shut its doors upon its constitutents, still guarding them with obstinate perseverance, although more than one half the union have required that they be opened?[2] Have we not likewise seen the free circulation of the news-papers, clogged with taxes which amount almost to a prohibition? Are these things the mere effect of accident, or are they the result of cool deliberation? contemplating objects dreadful to this country.

These considerations demonstrate, that it is difficult to preserve in the members of the national legislature, that degree of responsibility to their constituents, which the principle under other circumstances admits of; and that those who have been called to that station, since the organization of the government, have shewn an earnest desire to rid themselves of that portion of which it is capable. They likewise demonstrate that from causes which are natural, the several branches, instead of forming a perfect check upon each other, and thereby securing to the people a purity in the administration of each, are to a certain degree impelled in a contrary direction, and forced together, into a constrained and politic harmony, for common defence.

But this propensity, however strong it may be, has been powerfully aided by some institutions of great force and efficacy. A charm has been formed of sufficient strength to draw them together, if the repulsive power had been naturally ten times greater than the attractive one really is. An immense debt has been accumulated, from every region of the union, and of every possible description, constituted into funds of almost perpetual duration, and subject from its nature upon the slightest incidents, to constant fluctuation, with a power in the Secretary of the Treasury, through the medium of the sinking fund, to raise it at pleasure*. [It has depended on the Secretary to say when the money could or could not be furnished for the sinking fund, out of the funds appropriated for the purpose, and even out of monies borrowed for and legally applicable to no other purpose. And under his direction has ultimately fallen the execution of the purchases.][3] And upon the basis of this debt, a bank of discount has been formed, allied by its charter to the government itself, and in a great measure subjected to the direction of the same officer.

The experience of other countries has shewn that the dealers in the public funds, and especially those whose fortunes consist principally in that line, have no interest and of course feel but little concern, in all those questions of fiscal policy which particularly affect the land-holder, the merchant, and the artist. Although these classes should groan, under the burdens of the government, yet the public creditor will be no otherwise affected by the pressure, than as he receives what has been gleaned from their industry. The tax never reaches him, till the money is counted out quarterly from the public coffers, in discharge of his claim. They are the tenants of the farm, he the landlord and the man of revenue. The disparity of their interests, and the difference of their sensations, respecting the objects to which they point, in a great measure separate them in society. Knowing that they live upon the labour of the other classes, the public creditors behold them with jealousy, suspect a thousand visionary schemes against their welfare, and are always alarmed and agitated with every the most trifling incident which happens. And having one common interest which consists simply in the imposition of high taxes and their rigid collection, they form a compact body and move always in concert. Whilst the administration finds the means to satisfy their claims, they are always devoted to it, and support all its measures. They therefore may be considered in every country, where substantial funds are established, and their demands punctually paid, as a ministerial corps, leagued together upon principles to a certain degree hostile to the rest of the community.

But this dread of the other classes, and subservience to fiscal policy, have been increased here beyond what was ever experienced before, and by causes extremely natural. The trifling consideration given for the debt, by the present holders, with the comparative merit of their characters, with that of the officers and soldiery of the late army, and the well known sense which the community entertain on that subject, must inspire a distrust that will disquiet their peace for a time. The claims of justice although from motives of policy, they may be suppressed, yet the cries which they raise, are terrible to those who live on the usurpation. Nor can the gay festivity, nor the pomp and splendour it supports, shield them from the admonition. This throws them blindly into the hands of those who patronize their interests. In addition to which, the policy and operation of the sinking fund, by which the rise of stocks is in a great measure regulated, must contribute greatly to subject the party interested to the controul of those who direct its application.

If then the certificate-holders or dealers in the funds in general, are subservient to the views of a department faithful to their interests, is it reasonable to expect that such as have, or may hereafter become members of Congress, will prove less so? Being on the great theatre of speculation and gain, and possessed of more correct information, with the means of turning it to better account, will they abandon their occupation and slight the opportunity offered, of becoming thrifty? In what condition would the land-holder, the merchant, and the artist, find themselves, if they should be represented in the national legislature by persons of this description only? might they not count at least upon high taxes and their rigid collection? 'Tis the first principle of a free government, that those who impose the tax should feel the effect, but here it would be not only violated, but reversed. What security would the people have in any of the departments of government, whose checks were destroyed by an interest which supervened every consideration of public good?

But the proprietors of bank stock, are still more subservient to this policy, than any other class of public creditors. The institution itself being founded on the same paper system, must communicate the same interests to those within its sphere. And in other respects, it possesses a strength and energy, to which the common members of the fiscal corps, are strangers. The superiority of its gains invigorates the principle common to all; but the constitutional subordination to the head of that department, sanctifies under the cloak of authority, that degree of subservience which a sense of shame, among independent men, might occasionally forbid.

The bank however should not be considered simply in the light of an institution, uniting together with greater force, the members of the fiscal corps. As an engine of influence, capable under the management authorized by its principles, of polluting every operation of the government, it is entitled to particular attention. In this view a concise illustration, may not be deemed improper. The stocks are low, and the command of money for a short term only, would enable the holder to clear with certainty such a sum. A question of moment is depending, and a member of Congress may obtain a discount with the bank for that sum. He makes the purchase. The party aiding this operation with the bank, has likewise the direction of the sinking fund: its monies are *seasonably* and *publicly* exhibited at the market, and the stocks rise. The gain has been made, and the demands of the bank may likewise be answered. Or perhaps he is indigent, pressed by difficulties, and seeks to be thus relieved: or his note has been already deposited in the bank, and to some amount, and the day for repayment approaches, has he the means? and if he has not, how shall he be relieved from this painful dilemma? Shall the indulgence be extended again and again, and by the intercession of this person? Have the members of the legislature sufficient independence, virtue, and firmness, to withstand these temptations? And are those not occasions in the operations of every government, when those possessed of such means of influence, will find it their interest to avail themselves of it, to quiet the opponents to their measures? Have not such arisen in the course of our government, which commenced, as it were but yesterday?

The contamination would however have been partial, and the practicable means of influence abridged, if the alliance of the bank had been confined to an executive department only. With a minister in that branch, a negociation with the members of the legislature, would have been difficult, as certain forms subsisting between the departments of government, put them at a distance from each other. Seduction does not operate by means direct or overt. If not abandoned and at auction, the integrity of a member must be assailed more gently, and without the appearance of a bribe. It must be forced on him, under the mask of friendship. It became therefore necessary, to bring the legislature into more intimate contact with this monied machine, and for this purpose to appoint several of its members bank directors. In England, the minister of finance is a member of parliament; by him negociations may be carried on in person; but here the constitution forbade it; this then was the next best alternative. Thus organized, the game becomes more easy. In all operations upon the legislature, whether for the particular emolument of the bank, the fiscal corps in general, or any other purpose, in which the views of the party are interested, the prospect of success is greatly improved. And in all inquiries relative to the conduct of the officer, in the mangement of the public monies, these members of Congress, *bank directors*, and the bank itself, give him their firm and uniform support. In *their eyes* his conduct will appear *immaculate, angelic*, and partaking perhaps of something still more devine*.[See the speech of William Smith, of South Carolina, on the late proceedings, where he says,"That the

Secretary would in the issue rise above every calumny, as fair as the purest angel in heaven"—Mr. S——, it is well known, holds between three and four hundred shares in the bank of the United States, and has obtained discounts, *ad libitum.*]

If we take an impartial review of the measures of the government, from its adoption to the present time, we shall find its practice has corresponded, in every respect, with this theory. The demonstration strikes us in every page of the law, that a faction of monarchic speculators, seized upon its legislative functions in the commencement, and have directed all its operations since. We shall find that to the views of this faction, an apt instrument has been obtained in the Secretary of the Treasury, and to whose emolument and advancement, all his measures have been made subservient.

If the public debt has been accumulated by every possible contrivance, buoyed up by means of the sinking fund, made in a great measure perpetual, and formed into a powerful monied machine, dependent on the fiscal administration, to this combination it is due. If by means of this sudden elevation of fortune, a dangerous inequality of rank has been created among the citizens of these States, thereby laying the foundation for the subversion of the government itself, by undermining its true principles, to this combination it is due. If those found and genuine principles of responsiblity, which belong to representative government, and constitute its bulwark, and preserve its harmony, have been annulled or weakened; if a practicable means of influence, whereby the members of the legislature may be debauched from the duty they owe their constituents, has been formed; if, by implication and construction, the obvious sense of the constitution has been perverted, and its powers enlarged, so as to pave the way for the conversion of the government from a limited into an unlimited one, to this combination they are due. The catalogue of enormities is a lengthy one, but its truth is well known to those who have marked the course of public proceedings, or examined the acts.

A more thorough developement of these measures with their pernicious tendency, may perhaps be presented in a future essay; the object of the present one is more particularly to demonstrate, that by virtue of this combination, all regard for their constituents has been abandoned by the parties to it, and that the public can neither count upon the independence or integrity of the legislature, or the responsibility of the other departments, whilst it lasts.

That the Secretary of the Treasury has been faithful to this corps, and performed his part of the covenant, is well known. Every report from his department furnishes the proof. Through him propositions for assumption, after assumption, with all the properties of the debt, for the establishment of the bank, and for loans from the bank, for the latitude of construction contended for in the powers of the government, &c. have been ushered into Congress. By them firm support has been given to these propositions. But it remained for an experiment still more interesting to the parties, and alarming to the community, to try the strength of this combination, and evince its turpitude; the particulars of which I will now detail.

In the course of these transactions and for the term of four years, the real state of the public finances was never searched into by the legislature. It was however manifest to the more observant, that the affairs of that department had gradually assumed a complexity and obscurity, which rendered them almost impenetrable. To every succeeding session reports had been made that there was a surplus of revenue, and yet reasons were urged for an increase of the public burdens, and with which the legislature had complied. Foreign loans were likewise announced, but no intimation given, how far the foreign debt had been discharged, or in fact how these loans had been applied. In this situation, early in the late session, a well known partizan and member of the fiscal corps*, [Mr. S——K, of Massachusetts][4] introduced a bill into the house of representatives, for applying a sum said to be on hand, to the amount of two millions of dollars, in discharge of the debt due the bank, on account of the shares taken by the United States. It seemed strange how there could be lying idle such a sum, and in the course of discussion only it appeared, that it consisted of the foreign loans, which had been drawn into this country by the Secretary of the Treasury.

It became immediately an object worthy enquiry, why this money had been drawn here. If it was idle, the demonstration must be deemed satisfactory, there had been no occasion for it: Of course that the domestic resources had been amply adequate to their objects, and in particular those of the sinking fund, to which alone any foreign money was applicable.

The subject assumed a still more extraordinary aspect from the consideration that a proposition was then depending, and forming a part of the appropriation bill for the current year, for a loan from the bank of 800,000 dollars. The motive to measures in themselves so opposite and contradictory, the one founded on the idea of a large surplus lying idle, and the other of a poverty in the treasury, was inexplicable. Nor could it be accounted for upon any rational principle, why the bank should allow a payment to extinguish a loan at 6 per cent, one tenth of which only it was bound to receive, and make one immediately after at five. It could not be presumed that the individual adventurers in the institution, would sacrifice their interests to the public; it is well known that such sacrifices are seldom made, nor ought they indeed to be expected. It was natural to infer that inducements of a different kind led to this arrangement between the bank directors and the Secretary of the Treasury, and which no public documents exhibited.

The draft however of the money from Holland, especially if not called for by indispensable and legal obligations, was an interesting fact, and which required explanation. Had our engagements been fully and punctually fulfilled to France? and if they had, would they not have accepted and thanked us for the service, of a reimbursement of all we owed them? The parallel in their present situation, with our own when the money was advanced, called upon us for the offer; and America must feel mortified and humbled if it was not made, at least so far as we had it in our power to comply with it. In every view an explanation became necessary, and as so much had been already confessed, in the course of discussion, a proposition for it could not now be resisted, with even the appearance of decency. An order accordingly issued to that effect from the house of representatives upon the motion of Mr. Giles some time in December last*. [In the House of Representatives of the United States. Thursday the 27th of December, 1792. Resolved, That the President of the United States be requested to cause this House to be furnished with a particular account of the several sums borrowed under his authority by the United States; the terms on which each loan has been obtained; the applications to which any of the said monies have been made agreeable to appropriations; and the balances, if any, which remain unapplied. In this statement it is requested, that it may be specified at what times interest commenced on the several sums obtained, and at what times it was stopt, by the several payments made.]

To this order the Secretary reported on the 3d of January following that 18,678,000 florins, equal to 7,471,200 dollars, had been borrowed. That of this sum 4,029,217 dollars had been paid to France, about 3,000,000 dols. drawn into America, 2,304,369 of which by bills upon our bankers, and between 6 and 700,000 dollars by a diversion of that amount to the payment of the interest of the foreign debt, and that the residue of the sum borrowed (except about 160,000 dollars still on hand) had been, *or were to be* applied to different purposes abroad+.[It would be highly satisfactory to know with certainty that this money is really on hand; the prevailing and probable opinion is, that it has been turned to the actual service of the bank, and of those who have speculated on its discounts—The suspicions on this subject are strongest with those who are best acquainted with the late transactions and present conditions of that institution: And when large sums have been taken without necessity, and put in a situation which admits of abuses with scarce a possibility of detection, it affords sufficient ground for the strongest suspicion, that every thing is not as it ought to be.]

But the question still remained to be answered, Why had this money been drawn here? where was it, if on hand, or how disbursed? The report threw no light on these important points, but rather increased the obscurity with which it had been inveloped. There was therefore an obvious impropriety in proceeding further upon either of the bills, which were depending at this time, one before each house, until the real state of the public finances should be thoroughly understood. To vote the foreign money improperly drawn here to the bank, thereby preventing its possible application to any object for which it was originally intended, or to complicate our affairs further by another loan from that institution, were by no means desireable objects, at least with those who had commenced the inquiry. Correspondent efforts were therefore made in each house to dispel the clouds which covered these transactions, and orders were accordingly issued from each, for more correct information in every necessary particular*.[In the Senate of the United States, The 15th of January, 1793. *Ordered*, That the Secretary of the Treasury lay before the Senate, the account of the United States with the bank of the United States; specifying the precise funds, with the dates of the debits and credits, from the institution of the bank to the day the return is made.

That the Secretary of the Treasury also lay before the Senate, an account of the surplus of revenue appropriated to the purchase of the public debt, to the same period; specifying the sums and dates.

That he lay before the Senate, a statement of the monies borrowed by virtue of the law passed the 4th of August, 1790, with the appropriation of the amount, and the precise dates.

That he lay before the Senate, the amount and application of the money borrowed by virtue of the law of August the 12th, 1790.

And that he also lay before the Senate, an account exhibiting the probable surplus, and unappropriated revenue of the year 1792, stating, as far as possible, the dates and the sums.

The 23d of January, 1793.

Ordered, That the Secretary of the Treasury, lay before the Senate, a general account, exhibiting the amount of all the public funds and monies (loans included) up to the end of the last year, and what remains of each appropriation, either in cash, bonds, certificates, or other securities, and stating where the balances are deposited, as far as the same can at present be done.

That he particularly state the amount which has been drawn into the United States, of the monies borrowed in Europe, under the acts of the 4th and 12th of August, 1790, the purposes for which drawn, how any part thereof hath been applied, with the balance now on hand, and where deposited.

In the House of Representatives of the United States,

November 21st, 1792.

Resolved, That measures ought to be taken for the redemption of so much of the public debt, as by the act, entitled, "An act making provision for the debt of the United States," the United States have reserved the right to redeem; and that the Secretary of the Treasury be directed to report a plan for that purpose.

November 22d.

Resolved, That the Secretary of the Treasury be directed to report the plan of a provision for the reimbursement of the loan made of the bank of the United States, pursuant to the eleventh section of the act, entitled, "An act to incorporate the subscribers to the bank of the United States."

December 24th.

Resolved, That the Secretary of the Treasury be directed to lay before this House, an account of the application of the monies borrowed in Antwerp and Amsterdam, for the United States, within the present year.

December 27th

Resolved, That the President of the United States be requested to cause this house to be furnished with a particular account of the several sums borrowed under his authority, by the United States; the terms on which each loan has been obtained; the applications to which any of the monies have been made, agreeable to appropriations; and the balances, if any, which remain unapplied. In this statement, it is requested, that it may be specified at what times interest commenced on the several sums obtained, and at what times it was stopped by the several payments made.

January 23d, 1793.

Resolved, That the President of the United States be requested to cause to be laid before this House, copies of the authorities, under which loans have been negociated, pursuant to the acts of the 4th and 12th of August, 1790; together with copies of the authorities directing the application of the monies borrowed.

Resolved, That the President of the United States be requested to cause this House to be furnished with the names of the persons, by whom, and to whom, the respective payments of the French debt have been made in France, pursuant to the act for that purpose, specifying the dates of the respective drafts upon the commissioners in Holland, and the dates of the respective payments of the debt. A similar statement is requested respecting the debts to Spain and Holland.

Resolved, That the Secretary of the Treasury be directed to lay before this House, an account, exhibiting half monthly, the balances between the United States, and the bank of the United States, including the several branch banks, from the commencement of those institutions to the end of the year 1792.

Resolved, That the Secretary of the Treasury be directed to lay before this House, an account of all monies which may have come into the sinking fund, from the commencement of that institution to the present time, specifying the particular fund from which they have accrued, and exhibiting half yearly, the sums uninvested, and where deposited.

Resolved, That the Secretary of the Treasury be directed to report to this House, the balance of all unapplied revenues, at the end of the year 1792, specifying, whether in money or bonds, and noting where the money is deposited; that he also make a report of all unapplied monies, which may have been obtained, by the several loans authorized by law, and where such monies are now deposited.]

To these orders the Secretary reported, not a plain statement of the public finances, but a free criticism upon the conduct of one of the members of the House of Representatives, highly disrespectful to the House, and a series of elaborate essays illustrative principally of the policy of our institutions, relative to which no information had been required, and of which certainly no panegyric from him was necessary. They contained likewise a vindication of his conduct in certain particulars, relative to which no charge had been brought forward. These reports too were protracted, and detailed, in such manner, as to occupy the whole of the session, except a few days before its close.

It is scarcely necessary in this stage, and after the subject has been, so fully and ably, discussed before the public, to mention the nature, extent, and objects of those funds which the Secretary had to disburse, with the extent of his authority over them. A brief statement, may, however, make it more explicit, and intelligible. The following then is the outline: Upon the domestic revenues consisting of impost, tonnage, and excise, the current expences of the government, with the interest upon the sovereign and domestic debt, were solely chargeable. Two foreign loans were authorized by law, the first of 12,000,000 dollars of the 4th of August 1790, and the second of 2,000,000 of the 12th ensuing of the same month, destined for different purposes, and established on different funds. The first was deemed commensurate with the whole foreign debt, and was suggested as well from the necessity of providing for the installments as they became due, and which it was concluded could not otherwise be satisfied, as by the consideration that as the debt itself was contracted in the course of the late war, under very inauspicious circumstances, and whilst the fate of those strenuous and manly exertions, then making for our independence, was uncertain, it were possible in the present more prosperous state of our affairs, to obtain a remodification of it to advantage. The second was intended in aid of the sum of 1,374,656 dollars, being the surplus of revenue at the end of 1790, appropriated for the sinking fund; and for this latter purpose only, if required, could any foreign money be drawn here. The power over these loans, was given in every respect, exclusively to the President. In regard to them, the Secretary acted by his instruction, and under his authority, only.

In discharge of the ordinary duties of the Secretary of the Treasury, and which I never considered as being very difficult or important, otherwise than as the care and application of great sums of public money make it so, the course appears to me to be both simple and obvious. If the revenue should at any time prove inadequate, the deficiency could not be attributed to him nor the executive, unless indeed fallacious statements had been given as the ground for additional charges, assumptions, increase of the military establishment, and the like. In such event it became his duty to state the fact simply and correctly to the legislature, that they might in time supply such additional funds, as should be necessary; and if the domestic resources of the sinking fund were exhausted, to state the fact to the President, that he might determine whether he would avail himself of a foreign loan.

In the foreign transaction, and which was committed to the President, two considerations were to be principally regarded—the first, not to borrow at all, unless, in relation to the object for which the money was designed, it might be done with advantage—and the second, so to arrange the business, that the money borrowed should, immediately after it was received, be paid over to those for whom it was procured, otherwise we would be subjected to the payment of double interest. For this latter purpose, an accurate arrangement became necessary with France, and the money lenders in Holland, that the amount necessary to be borrowed, might be ascertained with precision.

It appeared, however, by these reports that he had violated the instructions of the President, in the first instance, by borrowing upon the two million loan, though expressly confined by them to the other, and for the purpose of foreign debt only, precluding all idea of drawing any part of the monies borrowed into this country*. [Clerks printed instructions of the President, dated 28th August 1790]

That he had violated the law by blending the two loans together, whereby a door was opened for a free use of the whole amount of the foreign money in domestic expenditures, except so much as should be paid to France, under this single restraint, that upon the final adjustment of the accounts of his administration, two millions only should be credited to the sinking fund, in case they were used*. [See the acts of the 4th and 12th of August, 1790; and a continuation of his report on foreign loans, page 4th.]

That by virtue of this arrangement, and upon the pretence of the sinking fund, or, to use his own words, by way of *instrumentality* to it, although in fact, by his own shewing, not a single farthing stands thus accounted for, (the domestic resources having been adequate, except occasionally and under particular pressures, and which it is to be presumed any of the banks would have accommodated) he had drawn into this country directly and indirectly, as above mentioned, about 3,000,000 of dollars, of the foreign money, near 1,000,000 more than was authorized for the sinking fund, in the utmost extent.+ [No notice is here taken of the payments to St. Domingo, because a part only of the money has been even yet paid, and because the Secretary himself does not seem willing to rest much upon this contingent item in his statement.]

That he had exposed the United States to considerable loss, arising from the loss of interest for the time these monies have been thus afloat, and which must have produced, from the period the drafts were furnished the bank, a correspondence benefit to those instructions++. [This remark needs no particular proof. The degree of loss to the public may be calculated, by any one who will consult the dates and sums in the transaction necessary. It may however further be remarked, that the sums deposited in the bank of the United States remain yet to be accounted for, amounting to between 12 and 1,300,000 dollars.]

That he had borrowed money from the bank when there was no occasion, for such loans, except upon the idea that there ought to be, beyond the pressure of current demands, to guard against the contingencies of war, and other fanciful dangers, at least five or six hundred thousand dollars always on hand*. [See pages 12 and 13 of said report.]

That he had occasioned a violation of our faith with France, in not paying the money borrowed in the amount, and at the times stipulated.

And lastly, that the whole of these transactions had been carried on without the knowledge of the legislature or the President.

That all these facts are literally and strictly true, will appear by his own reports, and to which I have referred, except that respecting the failure in our payments to France, and this I have taken from a view of the debt in possession of every one, in any degree conversant with public affairs. We owed to that nation up to the end of 1792, 5,498,697 dollars; the actual payments amounted to 4,473,480 dollars only, leaving due on the 1st of January last, the sum of 1,025,216 dollars+. [The debt from the United States to France calculated to the end of 1791, computing the livre at 5 and 4–10ths to a dollar, amounted to the sum of

		dols. 4,814,814
The instalment due in 1792 amounted to		683,888
		5,498,702
The payments made, computing the florin at 2 and 1/2 to a dollar were, in 1791	3,372,717	
In 1792 paid to Europe	656,500	
In 1792, paid at the Treasury of the United States for the relief of St. Domingo	444,263	
		4,473,480
Balance due to France on the 1st day of January, 1793,		dols. 1,025,222

This statement being taken from the Secretary's own reports to Congress, must be admitted to be true.]

These charges are of a high and serious import; and which require the severest reprehension. Nor has any satisfactory explanation been given, to justify even the motive, in any one respect. Who shall violate the law, and trample under foot the boundary of appropriations, especially in the extent and manner herein shewn? Shall the President himself? Does an invading enemy approach your coast and threaten the public safety? And if in case of extraordinary emergencies, he had authorised it, would he not have announced it to the legislature at their next meeting? Those who are acquainted with the respect always entertained and shewn, to the constitution and the laws, by the present chief magistrate, in every station he has filled, will give the answer. But not only to violate the law, but likewise the President's instructions, pointing out the mode of its execution, and on the day they were given, to withdraw the money from France, in derogation of our national faith, and at a time she most required our aid, with the other circumstances of misconduct alledged, are not to be palliated whilst they are acknowledged to exist.

When none are furnished, the mind naturally ranges at large, to seek for motives to account for a conduct so subversive of all legal and other obligations of public duty. The character of the man, and his known political principles, must lay the foundation for conjecture, if indeed, when the facts are apparent, there can exist any doubt of the motive. Would this money have aided the republican cause in France, and contributed to enable that gallant and generous people, to repel the invasion under the Duke of Brunswick? 'Tis well known that the pulse of the whole party beat in unison with him, as he advanced towards Paris, and that with him they were covered with shame and mortification as he retreated*. [It is an important and well known fact, that the success of the Duke of Brunswick, was most earnestly wished for by the principal agents of this aristocratic and fiscal party, who had not even the decency to conceal their sentiments upon the subject. Is it possible that men of such principles can be friends to republican government any where, and that their influence should not be exerted to give a contrary tendency to the administration of our own?] Or was it intended solely to aid the bank here, and those speculators his political associates, pressed it is true by difficulties, and which were sufficient to excite his sympathy? Was it one or both of these objects which influenced his measures, for both were answered? Let facts speak to an impartial and discerning public!

The very respectable and independent member, who had been most active in pressing this enquiry, considered it his duty to make known his sentiments of these transactions. Although the last of the long series of reports furnished, was not presented more than four or five days before the close of the session, yet he deemed it incumbent on him, and consistent with that candour which has always marked his character, to shew in that stage, the extent of his objections to this gentleman's official conduct. With this view he laid on the table, and subject to the disposition of the house, several resolutions specifying these objections. It was to be inferred, that on account of the short time intervening before the adjournment, and of course, the impossibility of examining, and thoroughly comprehending, all the various documents relating to the subject, and of giving it that full and free discussion its importance required, it was his wish the consideration should be postponed to the next session. Upon this point, however, he appeared to be indifferent, because he well knew the subject was now before another tribunal, who would do justice to it. But the conduct of the house which I deem important in the scale of these observations, shall now be noticed.

The fiscal corps appeared to consider themselves more critically circumstanced than this member. They were obviously struck with consternation. To get rid of it altogether, they could not hope. To postpone it to the next session, was what of all things they dreaded. It was before the public, who were interested in the result, and who would force a trial at one time or other. They therefore laid hold of it with avidity, and a strong hand. If we now decide upon it, perhaps it may be deemed satisfactory, and with us who are his friends, no danger need be apprehended. They say day and night upon the resolutions, until they got through them; and although they complained there was not sufficient time for the investigation, yet they hurried the decision, in half the time remaining. The free latitude of discussion, practiced upon other occasions was refused; the smallest departure was censured; and whenever, in particular, an approach was made toward the bank, the whole party tumultuously crying to order, and, with the directors at their head, rose in arms to defend it.

The character of the vote itself, which constituted this majority, is easily given, by every person acquainted with that of the House, or with public transactions in general. Of the thirty five, twenty one were stockholders, or dealers in the funds, and three of these latter bank directors, and whose degree of zeal was obviously in the ratio above stated, as their relative profits; the bank directors, being considerably more active and zealous than the other members of the corps. That the fact, of this number being bank directors, is true, can it is be believed, be satisfactorily shewn. The public books however must contained the evidence, unless entered in fictitious names, and by them let it be tested* of. [The books of transfer at the Treasury, and the books at the bank, are held secret under the obligation of an oath, on all persons who use or inspect them, not to reveal the names or amount of stock-holders. But from information obtained through other sources, the following members of C—g—ss, are known to be stock-holders in the bank of the United States, or in the public funds.

        N—w H—pshire.

Mr. G—m—n* [*Nicholas Gilman*][5]
    L—gd—n* [*John Langdon*]
    M—ssa—s—tts.

Mr. C—b—t* [*George Cabot*]
    St—g [*Caleb Strong*]
    A—s* [*Fisher Ames*]
    G—y* [*Elbridge Gerry*]
    S—dg—k. [*Theodore Sedgwick*]
    Rh—Isl—d.

Mr. B—n* [*Benjamin Bourn*]
    F—st—r. [*Theodore Foster*]
    Conn—t—t.

Mr. T—b—ll* [*Jonathan Trumbull*]
    S—rm—n* [*Roger Sherman*]
    E—sw—th* [*Oliver Ellsworth*]
    W—sw—th* [*Jeremiah Wadsworth*]
    H—llh—se* [*James Hillhouse*]
    L—n—d* [*Amasa Learned*]
    N—w Y—k.

Mr. L—r—ce* [*John Laurance*]
    K—g* [*Rufus King*]
    N—w J—r—y.

Mr. B—di—t [*Elias Boudinot*]
    D—yt—n* [*Jonathan Dayton*]

R—hf—d. [*John Rutherford*]
P—ns—v—a.
Mr. M—rr—s* [*Robert Morris*]
F—zs—s* [*Thomas FitzSimons*]
H—st—r [*Daniel Heister*]
D—la—re.
Mr. R—d. [*George Read*]
M—yl—d.
Mr. M—rr—y* [*William Vans Murray*]
K—y [*Philip Key*]
N—th C—l—a.
Mr. J—ns—n* [*Samuel Johnston*]
W—ms—n [*Hugh Williamson*]
St—le. [*John Steele*]
S—th C—l—a
Mr. Iz—d* [*Ralph Izard*]
S—th* [*William L. Smith*]
T—k—r. [*Thomas Tudor Tucker*]
G—g—a.
Mr. F—w* [*William Few*]

Those marked thus *, are believed to be stock holders in the bank.

For the motive of their vote, sufficient cause has already been assigned. But for that of the other members, candour furnishes an apology. The short space of time allowed for the discussion, to those who had not previously examined the subject, rendered it impossible for them to understand it: and in that situation it became their duty to vote on the favourable side. Besides, this was an affirmative proposition of censure; had one of approbation been proposed to sanctify these proceedings, it would have been resisted by those thus circumstanced, with equal force, and most probably have turned the majority, in like degree, the other way.

I have given a summary of the above proceedings, to evince the solidity of these observations, and to demonstrate that a combination has been formed of a powerful faction, in two departments of the government, and upon principles dangerous to the rights and interests of the community. That being founded on the basis of private interest, embracing a very extensive circle of society, and which must acquire additional strength, in proportion as the public debt shall be accumulated, its activity and force are the more to be dreaded. That is progress in undermining the great pillars of the government, by the establishment of an institution, in express violation of its powers, and capable, as an engine of corruption, of sapping the foundation of public virtue, and polluting all its measures, has been already great. And that the consequences to be justly apprehended, unless a speedy and efficacious remedy shall be applied, are really of the most alarming kind. In contemplation of the pernicious tendency of these measures, with

James Monroe. Stipple engraving by Goodman and Piggot of painting by C. B. King, published by W. H. Morgan (1817).
LC–USZ62–16956.

the astonishing success which had attended them, and their probable future extent, there was a period not far back, when I considered the cause of liberty itself in danger, and trembled for the public safety. I feared that the glorious fruits of the revolution, had been thrown away, by the blind confidence and temerity, of a generous and unsuspicious people. But I trust that our day of trial has passed, and that we may yet be secure. To the manly efforts and disinterested patriotism, of those who maintained the conflict, against such a combination of interests, and checked its rapid career, much praise is due. America is sensible of their services, and will remember their virtues. Thanks, illustrious patriots, your country greets you well, and will enroll your names upon the immortal record of fame!

By marking the extent of the evil, the cure is in a great measure designated. With the legislature should the correction commence, for "whilst that branch preserves its independence and integrity, we are safe." Let us cast from it then, whatever impurities, tend to impair these qualities, or lessen its responsiblity to the people. Let the public creditors stand apart, not as a class of men to be branded with reproach and infamy, but as constituting an interest, which, without due restraint, may endanger the general welfare; and if admissible at all into that branch, let them be inhibited under the severest penalties, from a profanation of its functions afterwards, by any traffic in the public funds. Let the law establishing the bank, as a violation of the principles of the constitution, be declared null and void, or at least let the establishment be repudiated from its present impure connection with the government. Let the whole system of the treasury department undergo a thorough reform and the most effectual guards be provided against those liberties and abuses, which have been charged, upon its present administration. Let it be completely subjected to the supreme head of the executive, against which it seems to have revolted, and let its communication with the legislature be put on a footing, more consistent with the constitution, and the dignity and independence of the representatives of the people. Renovations of this kind, will not violate public credit, but establish it in the public confidence; will not impair the energy of the constitution, but restore it to its pristine health, and proper functions, will not stain our national character, but exhibit it, in its legitimate features, of a dignified simplicity, and genuine republicanism.

1. Beckley and Monroe began their collaboration on this pamphlet during the political turmoil surrounding Congressional debate on the resolutions of William Branch Giles censuring Secretary of the Treasury Hamilton. The defeat of the Giles Resolutions on March 2 left the Republicans frustrated and bitter. Monroe's mid-March departure from Philadelphia for Virginia left Beckley to complete the pamphlet and see to its publication and distribution. Although scholars have often attributed authorship of this work to John Taylor of Caroline, recent examination of contemporary documents has demonstrated the clear authorship of Beckley with the probable assistance of Monroe. The pamphlet made its first appearance in Philadelphia on April 9, and quickly went through several printings. Beckley and other republican leaders saw to its wide dissemination throughout the country in their efforts to discredit Hamilton and his congressional supporters. See Beckley to Monroe, April 10, 1793, and Edmund and Dorothy Smith Berkeley, " 'The Piece Left Behind' Monroe's Authorship of a Political Pamphlet Revealed," *Virginia Magazine of History and Biography*, 75 (April 1967): 175–180.

2. Monroe had introduced a bill in late February 1791 to open the Senate debates to the public, but it had been rejected by a vote of 17 to 9. The Senate continued to reject a policy of open-door deliberations until February 20, 1794, when it adopted a resolution of Alexander Martin of North Carolina to hold open and public deliberations unless specifically deciding otherwise. *Debates and Proceedings, Third Congress*, pp. 33, 46–47.

3. Notes keyed to specific words in the text and printed at the bottom of the page in the pamphlet have been inserted in the text in roman letters within brackets at the spot to which they were keyed.

4. That is, Theodore Sedgwick.

5. Names in brackets and italic typeface are explications of abreviations in the text. See the next document for a similar but slightly variant list of members of Congress, that Beckley provided to Jefferson.

JOHN BECKLEY LIST OF PAPER-MEN
COMMUNICATED TO THOMAS JEFFERSON

March 23–25, 1793

Mar. 23, 1793. The following list of paper-men is communicated to me by Beckley.[1]

Gilman* S.H.

Gerry.*+ S.H.

Sedgewick.

Ames.* S.H. Goodhue.* S.H.

Bourne.R.I. suspected only.

Trumbul.* S.H.

Wadsworth.* S.H.

Hillhouse.* S.H.

Learned. S.H.

Laurence. S.H. & Director.

Gordon.

Boudinot.+ S.H.

Dayton.* S.H.

Fitzsimmons.* S.H. & Director.

D. Heister.* S.H.

Sterret.

Murray. S.H.

Williamson.*+ S.H.

Smith. S.H. & Director for himself & his proxies, his vote is near 1/5 of the whole.

Cabot.* S.H. & Director.

Sherman.* S.H.

Elsworth. qu.

King.* S.H. & Director.

Dickinson.

		H.Repr.	Senate.
Morris.* S.H.	Stockholders	16	5
Johnson.*	Other paper	3	2
		19	7
Izard. * S.H.			
	Suspected	2	1

Mar. 25. Beckley says he has this day discovered that Benson is a stockholder. Also Bourne of Rhode Island and Key. T.J.

* These are known to Beckley.

+ These avowed it in the presence of T.J.

MS (JEFFERSON PAPERS, LIBRARY OF CONGRESS). IN THE HAND OF JEFFERSON.

1. Beckley had given this information to Jefferson in the midst of preparing the pamphlet, *An Examination of the Late Proceedings in Congress*, which is printed as the preceding document. In his pamphlet Beckley included a similar but slightly longer (34 names) list of members of Congress whom he believed to be holders of Bank of the United States stock or other public securities certficates. Jefferson recorded the information provided by Beckley on March 23 and 25 and added comments and emendations of his own. For an analysis of Jefferson's recording of Beckley's information, see Catanzarini, ed., *Jefferson Papers*, 25:517–19, 534.

Beckley's interest in the "moneyed men" of Congress had surfaced as early as August 27, 1792, when he told Benjamin Rush "that a member of Congress had examined the Register's books and found 26 members of the House of Representatives and 8 of the Senate certificate holders." George W. Corner, ed., *The Autobiography of Benjamin Rush. His "Travels Through Life" together with His Commonplace Book for 1789–1813* (Princeton: Princeton University Press, 1948), p. 227.

JOHN BECKLEY REPORT TO THOMAS JEFFERSON

March 31, 1793

Mar. 31. Mr. Beckley tells me, that the merchants' bonds for duties on 6 mo. credit became due the 1st instant to a very great amount, that Hamilton went to the bank on that day, and directed the bank to discount for those merchts. all their bonds at 30 days, and that he would have the collectors credited for the money at the Treasury. Hence, the Treasury lumping its receipts by the month in it's printed accts. these sums will be considered by the public as only recd. on the last day; conseqly. the bank makes the month's interest out of it. Beckley had this from a mercht. who hd a bond discounted, & supposes a million dollars were discounted at the bank here. Mr. Brown got the same information from another mercht. who supposed only 600,000 D discounted here. But they suppose the same orders went to all the branch banks to a great amount.[1]

MS (JEFFERSON PAPERS, LIBRARY OF CONGRESS). IN THE HAND OF JEFFERSON.

1. For Secretary Hamilton's instructions to the collectors of the customs and to the officers of the Bank of the United States concerning the merchants' "bonds for duties," see Syrett, ed., *Hamilton Papers*, 14:128, 136–38, and 183.

JOHN BECKLEY REPORT TO THOMAS JEFFERSON

April 7, 1793

Apr.7.93 . . . . Eod. die. Mr. Beckley tells me that a gentleman,[1] heartily a fiscalist, called on him yesterday, told him he had been to N. York. & into the Prison with Duer, with whom he had much conversation. That Pintard,[2] Duer's agent has about 100,000 D. worth of property in his hands & bids defiance: that this embarrasses Duer much, who declares that if certain persons do not relieve him shortly, he will unfold such a scene of villiany as will astonish the world.

MS (JEFFERSON PAPERS, LIBRARY OF CONGRESS). IN THE HAND OF JEFFERSON.

1. Not identified.
2. John Pintard, formerly a clerk for Jefferson in the State Department, was a loan procurement agent for William Duer, New York merchant and speculator in funds and land. Cullen, ed., *Jefferson Papers*, 23:447–52.

JOHN BECKLEY TO JAMES MONROE

Dear Sir,   Philadelphia, 10th April 1793.

I received your several favours from Wilmington & Frederg, their contents were duly attended to. The pamphlet[1] is out, and I think merits all the attention bestowed upon it—altho' it only appeared yesterday the demand has nearly exhausted the 250 copies reserved for this place. 200 go with us tomorrow to New York, and will be scattered there, at Albany, in Connecticut & Vermont—200 go to Boston—100 to Charleston—100 to Augusta, 100 to Petersburg—100 to Richmond—100 to Frederg. I have also ordered by water two parcels of 20 each, one for Mr. Madison, the other for you—to be made into one packet and addressed to Mr. James Blair at Fredg. The whole expense is only about £57—this money, which, at the price demanded 3/16th of a dollar will be defrayed by the 250 copies sold here. <*this cost is exclusive of the paper*> The Assembly of this State adjourns to morrow, and I have taken care to scatter it pretty well among them, thro' the means of Dallas. They have impeached Nicholson their Comptroller[2] and it is confidently said, that another nefarious connection of H's with him, will be laid open.

The continuance of the business yo. hint at, will be steadily pursued in various ways. Every day evinces the propriety of so doing.[3] Burr accompanies us to N. York. I will write you more fully from there. War in Europe, now rages, its effects on us are yet uncertain, and I think our situation Critical—at present grain is up and Stocks down—but no money in the treasury to purchase with. Be so good as to bear me in mind respecting the British business, should yo. see Mr. Henry, it might be serviceable to speak to him. I have removed all difficulty here, by having qualified in the Supreme Court & shall do so, in course, in the fœderal Courts. Present me respectfully to Mr. Madison—.your good lady &c.

I am, most sincerely, Dear Sir, Your friend & Servt.

John Beckley

RC (JAMES MONROE MUSEUM AND MEMORIAL LIBRARY, FREDERICKSBURG, VA.).

1. Beckley is referring to the pamphlet, *An Examination of the Late Proceedings in Congress, Respecting the Official Conduct of the Secretary of the Treasury*, which was jointly authored with Monroe and is printed above under March 8, 1793.

2. That is, John Nicholson, comptroller of Pennsylvania, who was impeached by the legislature for improper expenditures. He resigned in April 1794 owing the state $100,000. Kline, ed., *Burr Papers*, 1:53–57.

3. Beckley was probably referring to continuing Republican plans to discredit Secretary of the Treasury Hamilton, which involved attacks on Hamilton both in Congress and the public press. The "Reynolds Affair," the Giles Resolutions, Beckley and Monroe's pamphlet, and the soon to be made public charges of Andrew G. Fraunces were all key elements in this campaign to discredit Hamilton and his congressional supporters. Beckley knew that Monroe, who had been one of a three-man committee of congressmen (Frederick Muhlenberg and Abraham B. Venable completed the trio.) to investigate the accusations of James Reynolds and Jacob Clingman against Hamilton in December 1792, would have a continuing interest in Beckley's efforts to ferret out further information. See Beckley and Monroe, *An Examination of the Late Proceedings in Congress*, March 8, 1793, Beckley's Report to Jefferson, June 12, 1793, and Beckley to Unknown, June 22, 1793.

For further information on Beckley's involvement in the public revelation of this scandal, see Beckley to Tench Coxe, October 10, 1796.

JOHN BECKLEY TO UNKNOWN[1]

Sir, New York. 29th April 1793.

Presuming that the subject of the present communication, is most properly addressed to you, I take the liberty to suggest such provision, in the alteration of the building for the accomodation of Congress, as, it appears to me, is indispensably necessary for the House of Representatives. Three Committee rooms, and a Lobby room, of equal size with the present Committee rooms, two rooms for the Clerks Office, and one for a library and Speakers Chamber, of equal size with the room now used as a Clerks Office, are in my opinion, the least that will be wanting, and could a fourth Committee room be had, or one of the three made half as large again as the others, it would not be more than the <u>necessary</u> accomodation of that House, in the dispatch of public business, will require.

I do not mean this provision as additional to, but inclusive of that, which now exists, for the like purpose, and trust that the Gentlemen to whom may be confided the superintendance of the business, will find the less difficulty in Effecting it, within the means which the Legislature of Pennsylvania have assigned for the purpose.

I do not presume to offer any plan or Sketch of the accomodation I have suggested, which more properly falls within the province of the Commissioners, and will therefore only add that the Office rooms & library, ought to be as contiguous to the Representatives Chamber as possible.

Relying, Sir, that you will submit the subject of this Letter, in such manner as will best ensure it Success, I remain, with great regard and Esteem, Sir, Your most obedient & very humble Servant, John Beckley.

RC (STAUFFER COLLECTION, HISTORICAL SOCIETY OF PENNSYLVANIA).

1. The recipient of this letter has not been identified, but perhaps it was Miers Fisher, a Philadelphia lawyer and member of the Pennsylvania assembly, whom Beckley had addressed on November 17, 1790, concerning the original spacial requirements of the House of Representatives in Congress Hall, located on the northwest corner of State House Square, and the nearby State House, where the clerk of the House had an office in the west wing. The stated need of additional space for the members of the House of Representatives was a result of the enlargement of the House from 65 to 105 based on reapportionment following the 1790 census. Congress Hall underwent a major renovation in 1793, including the addition of a large extension to the south. See Bickford, ed., *Documentary History of the First Federal Congress*, 9: 78n. 19, and 337n. 9.

JOHN BECKLEY REPORT TO THOMAS JEFFERSON

June 7, 1793

June. 7. 93. Mr. Beckley, who is returned from N. York within a few days tells me that while he was there, Sr. John Temple, Consul General of the Northern States for Gr. Br., showed him a letter from Sr. Gregory Page Turner, a member of Parliament for a borough in Yorkshire, who he said, had been a member for 25 years, and always confidential for the ministers, in which he permitted him to read particular passages of the following purport "that the government were well apprized of the predominancy of the British interest in the US. that they considered Colo. Hamilton, Mr. King, and Mr. W. Smith, of South Carolina, as the main supports of that interest; that particularly, they considered Colo. Hamilton, & not Mr. Hammond, as their effective minister here; that if the Anti-federal interest (that was his term), at the head of which they considered Mr. Jefferson to be, should prevail, these gentlemen had secured an asylum to themselves in England." Beckley could not understand whether they had secured it themselves[*1]

or whether they were only notified that it was secured to them. So that they understand that they may go on boldly in their machinations to change the government, and if they should be overset and choose to withdraw, they will be secure of a pension in England, as Arnold, Deane &c.,

had. Sr. John, was to retain the whole salary. (By this it would seem, as if, wanting to use Bond, they had covered his employment with this cloak.) Mr. Beckley says that Sr. John Temple is a strong republican. I had a proof of his intimacy with Sr. John in this circumstance. Sr. John received his new Commission of Consul for the Northern department, and instead of sending it thro Mr. Hammond, got Beckley to enclose it to me for his Exequatur. I wrote to Sr. John that it must come thro' Mr. Hammond, inclosing it back to him. He accordingly then sent it to Mr. Hammond . . . . . [2]

Eodem die. (June 7.) Beckley tells me that he has the followg fact from Govr. Clinton. That before the proposition for the present general govmt, i.e. a little before Hamilton conceived a plan for establishing a monarchical govmt in the US. he wrote a draught of a circular letter, which was to be sent to about[3] persons, to bring it about. One of these letters, in Hamilton's handwriting, is now in possn of an old Militia genl. up the North river, who, at that time, was though orthodox enough to be entrusted in the execution. This General has given notice to Govr. Clinton that he has this paper, and that he will deliver it into his hands, and no one's else. Clinton intends the first interval of leisure, to go for it, and he will bring it to Philadelphia.[4] Beckley is a man of perfect truth as to what he affirms of his own knolege, but too credulous as to what he hears from others.[5]

MS (JEFFERSON PAPERS, LIBRARY OF CONGRESS). IN THE HAND OF JEFFERSON.

1. In the margin Jefferson wrote with a different pen and ink than the body of the June 7 entry: "Impossible as to Hamilton; he was far above that."
2. Sir John Temple, American loyalist and British consul general in New York, was a Cortland Street neighbor of Beckley's in-laws, the Princes. Sir Gregory Page Turner was an administration supporter who had served eight years in Parliament. Catanzarini, ed., *Jefferson Papers*, 26:220. For a related supportive report by Beckley, see Beckley to Madison, May 25, 1795.
3. Blank in MS.
4. Beckley was reporting a story of Federalist support for a restored monarchy which often had been bruited about by Republican leaders, such as Clinton, Samuel Adams, Elbridge Gerry, and James Monroe. This particular one concerned Hamilton, John Adams and "an old Militia genl.," William Malcom. This was just one of many reports of monarchical leanings involving Federalist leaders, such as Hamilton, Adams, Rufus King, Nathaniel Gorham, and John Armstrong. Written testimony concerning Hamilton's involvement was not made until 1804. Syrett, ed., *Hamilton Papers*, 26:198–99, 202–3, 209–10; Catanzarini, ed., *Jefferson Papers*, 26:220–21; Louise B. Dunbar, *A Study of Monarchical Tendencies in the United States from 1776 to 1801* (Urbana, Ill.: University of Illinois Press, 1922), pp. 60–75.
5. This last sentence as well as the marginalia were added by Jefferson at a later date and written with a different pen and ink than body of the June 7 entry.

JOHN BECKLEY REPORT TO THOMAS JEFFERSON

June 12, 1793

June 12. Beckley tells me that Klingham[1] has been with him to-day, & relates to him the following fact. A certificate of the old Congress had been offered at the treasury & refused payment, & so indorsed in red ink as usual. This certificate came to the hand of Francis,[2] (the quondam clerk of the treasury, who, on account of his being dipped in the famous case of the Baron Glaubec, Hamilton had been obliged to dismiss, to save appearances, but with an assurance of all future service, and he accordingly got him establd. in New York.) Francis wrote to Hamilton that such a ticket was offered him, but he could not buy it unless he would inform him and give him his certificate that it was good. Hamilton wrote him a most friendly letter, and sent him the certificate. He bot. the paper, & came on here. & got it recognized, whereby he made 2500 dollars. Klingham saw both the letter and certificate.

MS (JEFFERSON PAPERS, LIBRARY OF CONGRESS). IN THE HAND OF JEFFERSON.

1. Jacob Clingman, former clerk of House Speaker Frederick A. C. Muhlenberg, an indicted co-conspirator of James Reynolds, and a principal accuser of Hamilton in the "Reynolds Affair," provided Beckley with information on the charges of Andrew G. Fraunces, whom Hamilton had dismissed as a treasury clerk in March, 1793 for his alledged involvement in personal trading in treasury claims. Specifically, Fraunces accused Hamilton of personally profiting from the sale of claims against the U. S. government belonging to Peter William Joseph Ludwig, Baron de Glaubeck, a foreign officer who had served in the U.S. army during the American Revolution. For a detailed examination of this complex affair, see Syrett, ed., *Hamilton Papers*, 13:115–16, 14:460–71. For Clingman's testimony see the next document.
2. That is, Andrew G. Fraunces.

JOHN BECKLEY TO UNKNOWN[1]

Dear Sir,   Philadephia, 22d June 1793

Some information, which I have received from Mr. Clingman[2] seems to be so connected with what you already possess in relation to Mr. Hamilton, that I cannot withhold communicating it. He says that Andrew J. Fraunces was here, about ten days ago, with letters from Duer to Hamilton, and carried back answers. That Fraunces brought with him and received payment, at the Treasury, for two Warrants issued by the old Board of Treasury, which he purchased in New York on speculation, and by which he cleared fifteen hundred dollars, that before he purchased those warrants, and when they were offered to him they were indorsed on the back with red ink, in a date which he did not then recollect "presented at the Treasury of the United States, and refused payment—Jos. Nourse Regr."—Whereupon that he, Fraunces, wrote to Hamilton to know whether they would be paid, and if so, to send him a Certificate under his hand to that effect; which Hamilton did—and Clingman says that he has seen both Fraunces's letter, and Hamilton's answer and certificate.[3]

Clingman also says that Fraunces told him he could, if he pleased hang Hamilton. And altho' he considers Fraunces as a man of no principle yet he is sure that he is privy to the whole connection with Duer and is the agent between them, for supplying the latter with money, and that he saw him when last in New York, pay money to Duer's Clerk (who brought a note to him for it) and took his receipt. He tells me too, that Fraunces is fond of drink and very avaricious, and that a judicious appeal to either of those passions, would induce him to deliver up Hamilton's and Duer's letters, and tell all he knows.

Clingman further informs me that Mrs. Reynolds has obtained a divorce from her husband, in consequence of his intrigue with Hamilton to her prejudice and that Colonel Burr obtained it for her: he adds too that she is thoroughly disposed to attest all she knows of the connections between Hamilton and Reynolds. This, if true, is important.

Clingman has been sent for by Hamilton, and had an interview with him this week, in which he used every artifice to make a friend of him and asked many leading questions about who were his friends? What he would do to serve him &c &c &c. He is to be with him again tonight and has promised to call on me tomorrow morning, and inform me of all that passes. If he should, I will add it to this letter.

June 25th. The proposed interview did not take place till today; it was to the following effect.

1st. Was he (Clingman) intimate with Mr. A. G. Fraunces of New York?
    Answer. He knew him.
2nd. Did he ever board at his house?
    Answer. He never did.
3d. Did he not frequently dine and sup with him?
    Answer. He had once dined with him at a Stranger's house.
4th. Did he not frequently visit Mr. Fraunces's office?
    Answer. He had been there several times.
5th. Did he not visit Mr. Beckley sometimes?
    Answer. He knew Mr. Beckley, as he had seen him at Mr. Muhlenberg's.

Mr. Hamilton then observed that Clingman did not put that confidence in him that he ought, as every thing that he (Clingman) said, was as secret as the grave.

Mr. Hamilton then asked if Mr. Beckley did not visit at Mr. Muhlenberg's, and what other persons frequented Mr. Muhlenberg's house.

Mr. Hamilton said that Clingman should not mind what Fraunces said, as he spoke much at random and drank.

June 27th. Mr. Clingman left this yesterday morning for New York and I expect will, as well as Fraunces, be well watched by Hamilton's Spies. I do not think it will be advisable that Clingman should be applied to, or in any manner, made acquainted with any thing here communicated respecting Fraunces or Hamilton, as he will continue to give me every information, or evidence, he can collect respecting them. You will make such a confidential use of the contents of this letter, as you may deem proper, and believe me to be with great regard, Dear Sir, Your most obedient Servant.

John Beckley

P.S. July 1st. I had closed this letter, when I received the letter from Clingman, of which a copy is inclosed.[4] A. G. Fraunces is now here, and, I am told in treaty with Hamilton for delivering up to him all such letters and papers as he (Fraunces) may be possessed of in relation to Hamilton's speculations and connection with Duer; and for which, Hamilton is to pay him two thousand dollars. I have written to Clingman and expect him here this night. Should he come, I think it probable, he may so far counterwork Hamilton, as to possess himself of some further, and corroborating evidence to that of Fraunces's. If he does not come this evening, or by tomorrow night at farthest, I shall conclude that he has declined it, and shall therefore set off the next day with my family for the Virginia Springs, and expect to be absent from this, until the tenth of September. In the mean time, I hope it will be in your power, from the information now given you, so to manage Fraunces thro' the influence of Clingman (whom I now think it will be advisable for you to confide in, seeing how far he has committed himself in his letter to me) as to obtain some decisive proof, during my absence. When I return, should it be necessary, and you will drop me a line thro' our common friend, Melancton Smith, I will come on to New York, and aid, with my best endeavors, to unravel this scene of iniquity.

Perhaps the following hints may be worth attentions.

1st. To urge Clingman to get from Fraunces the power of Attorney for Glaubeck's pay with Hamilton's correction.

2d. To obtain Bazel's[5] deposition respecting that transaction.

3d. To get Fraunces's letter to Hamilton, and Hamilton's answer respecting the two Treasury Warrants, mentioned in the beginning of this letter.

4th. To obtain the original or copies of any receipts of Duer's, for monies paid to him by Fraunces.

5th. To enquire respecting Mrs. Reynolds's divorce, and to obtain her certificate or affidavit of all she knows.

6th. To make like enquiry and obtain like evidence from Mr. Reynolds.

7th. To obtain some corroborating evidence from Fraunces besides his own, of Hamilton's having purchased public stock on his private account.

8th. To obtain any like corroborating evidence respecting the connection with Duer.

9th. To obtain Fraunces's certificate or affidavit of all that passed at his late and present interview with Hamilton.

The instrumentality of Clingman in this business, you see, will be highly important; but in your communications with him I do not wish that he should see any thing that I have written to you. Altho' you must necessarily acquaint him with the sources of your information. My own opinion is, that he may be fully depended on; but you know human nature too well, not to observe every proper caution. Nor can I forbear to hint, how quickly Hamilton will take an alarm, at the remotest appearance of your concern in the business.

Tuesday evening. 2nd July. Clingman is not come, and I therefore close this letter.   JB.

FC (FEINSTONE COLLECTION, MICROFILM, LIBRARY OF CONGRESS). IN THE HAND OF BECKLEY'S CLERK, BERNARD WEBB.

1. Not identified, but perhaps DeWitt Clinton, a New York opponent of Hamilton and correspondent of Beckley.

2. See the preceding document, note 1.

3. For Andrew G. Fraunces's correspondence with Hamilton, see Syrett, ed., *Hamilton Papers*, 14:460–71, 476, 15:45, 52–53, 164–65, 171–72, 177, 354–55.

4. Beckley enclosed a copy of Clingman's June 27, 1793, letter to Beckley, in the hand of Bernard Webb, which is also in the Feinstone Collection, microfilm, Library of Congress.

"I got to York only late last night and this morning called on Mr. A. G. Fraunces, who is just a going to Philada. Mr. A. G. Fraunces seems to be vexed with Col. H—— and shewed me a power of Attorney of his own writing corrected by Colo. H—— and which correction is in his handwriting for the purchase of the Baron De Glaubeck's pay which he the said Fraunces purchased for Colo. H—— and D—er , from one Bazel, and for which they gave him fifty dollars for doing the business. He further told me, that Colo. H—— had agents in Philada. who purchased stock for him, and in a few days after the stock was sold to the Commissioner of the United States, which was appointed to purchase Stock, at a higher price, which agents name he mentioned to me; and further said, that he had carried checks to the said agents from Colo. H—— and he hath promised me, that, the moment he gets to Philadephia, to get a certficate from one of those agents, to certify that he had transacted such business and that he had received money from him, A. G. Fraunces, for that business: and further told me, that he could prove and was known to a connection in speculation with D—er. All which A. G. Fraunces is willing to swear to and can bring other witnesses beside himself.

Now, my dear Sir, if you think that these facts will be sufficient to do his business, I would wish you to stay in Philada. and write me word and I will come on immediately.

I am somewhat afraid, that Fraunces will fall back from what he has said, but he declares, that he will stick to what he has told me, and that beside his own oath, he can bring proof to support it—and as to the power of Attorney, I have seen it myself, and know that the correction is in Colo. H—— own handwriting."

5. Thomas Bazen, New York storekeeper and merchant.

JOHN BECKLEY TO JAMES MADISON

Dear Sir,   Philadelphia, 20th November 1793.

I drop a line to inform you, that I returned to this place with all my family, on Saturday last, and that there is now as perfect safety from contagion
of any kind as was ever known here; there is not known a single case of the
yellow fever in the City or its suburbs; the Citizens have returned almost
universally, the public Offices are all opened, as well as all the public & private seminaries, business of every kind is resumed, the Markets as fully
attended & supplied as ever, and in short no vestige of the late calamity
remaining, except in the mournful remembrances of those whose friends &
relatives have fallen victims to it. Doctor Rush, assured me last evening that
a greater degree of health had never prevailed in this City than at present. A
general fumigation of houses, apparel, bedding &c. has taken place by order
of the Corporation, and the lodging houses in particular will be as safe as
ever, or perhaps the safest of any from their peculiar purifications &c. I
mention these things & hope this may meet yo. at Fredericksburg, that yo.
may rely on my assurance that there is not the smallest possible danger of
proceeding immediately into the City, and that as far as this short notice
may enable yo. to do so, it may be communicated to others of the Southern
Members, as I find great pains has been taken to bring on the Eastern &
Pennsylva. Members to decide the choice of a speaker &c.[1]

With great regard, I am, Dear Sir, Yr. mo. obedt. Servant,

John Beckley

[*P.S.*] R. B. Lee, is arrived.[2]

RC (MADISON PAPERS, LIBRARY OF CONGRESS).

1. Muhlenberg was elected speaker of the House succeeding Jonathan Trumbull and Beckley was uanimously returned as clerk, when the House of Representatives reached a
quorum on December 2 after the abatement of the Yellow Fever epidemic in Philadelphia. *The Journal of the House of Representatives, . . . Third Congress* (Washington, D.C.:
Gales and Seaton, 1826), p. 4.
2. That is, Richard Bland Lee (1761–1827), who served as a U.S. representative from Virginia, 1789–95.

JOHN BECKLEY REPORT TO THOMAS JEFFERSON

December 1, 1793

Dec. 1. 93. Beckley tells me that he had the following fact from Lear. Langdon, Cabot[1] and some others of the Senate, standing in a knot before the fire after the Senate had adjourned, & growling together about some measure which they had just lost, "Ah!" said Cabot, "things will never go right till you have a President for life, and an hereditary Senate." Langdon told this to Lear, who mentioned it to the President. The Presidt. seemed struck with it & declared he had not supposed there was a man in the US. who could have entertained such an idea.

MS (JEFFERSON PAPERS, LIBRARY OF CONGRESS). IN THE HAND OF JEFFERSON.

1. Tobias Lear of New Hampshire was personal secretary to Washington. John Langdon of New Hampshire and George Cabot of Massachusetts were Federalist U.S. senators. See also Beckley to Tench Coxe, October 30 and November 3, 1800.

JOHN BECKLEY AS A CALM OBSERVER[1]

New-York March 1795

The following succinct and accurate account of the endeavour used in the Session of Congress before the last to establish a standing army, is furnished by the Journal of the two houses and the debates in Congress, as published in the newspapers.[2]

The Session commenced the second day of Decr. 1793 and terminated the 9th day of June 1794. On the 11th day of Decr. a bill was ordered into the house of Representatives for completing the military Establishment; it appearing by returns from the War-Office that out of 5,000 effective men of which, by Law, the establishment ought to consist, not more than 3,000 were then in the field, the deficiency of 2,000 not having been enlisted. On the 23d January this Bill was passed and sent to the Senate, the provisions of it being to grant an additional pay of one dollar per month to each Soldier then in Service, or who should enlist for three Years, and a bounty of two hundred acres of Land, with some increase of the ration of provisions. On the 31st January, this Bill was rejected by the Senate, in toto, without amendment, modification. message, or conference.

So much for the first attempt to <u>complete</u>, the exisiting military Establishment. The next attempt was made in the house of Representatives on the 20th March when a Bill was ordered in, to encourage the Recruiting Service, being nothing more than the first attempt to complete the military establishment, revised with the same provisions of pay and bounty under a new title. On the 4th of April this Bill was passed and sent to the Senate, on the 25th April, this Bill was returned by the Senate with the amendment to strike out the additional pay of one Dollar per month and the bounty in lands and to allow only an additional bounty on enlistment, of four dollars to each recruit. This was disagreed to by the Representatives, who adhered to their Bill. The Senate also adhered to their amendment, the Bill was lost on the Sixth of May, and thus failed the second attempt to <u>complete</u> the existing military Establishment.

Whilst the last Bill was depending to wit on the 12th March, a motion was brought into the house of Representatives by Mr. Sedgwick of Massachusetts, to increase the military establishment of 5,000 men by an addition of fifteen Regiments of 1,000 men each. On the first of April a Bill was brought in by a Committee of which the same Gentleman was Chairman, to make the augmentation 25,000 men, instead of 15,000 men the first motion. On the 19th May this Bill was fully discussed, and the 25,000 men being struck out, a motion was made for 15,000 men, which being lost a motion was made for 10,000 men, which, being also lost, the Bill itself was totally rejected, upon a division of fifty ayes, against thirty nays—and thus failed the first attempt to augment the military force.

It will be observed that those members who thus defeated this attempt, had uniformly supported both the attempts that had been made as before recited, to complete the military establishment to its legal complement of 5,000 men. They had also supported and voted for the various measures of fortifying the post and harbours of the United States; of raising a corps of 800 artillerists and Engineers to garrison the fortifications, of providing money for repairing, completing, and filling with sufficient stores of arms and ammunition the magazines and arsenals; and of calling upon the states to provide 80,000 militia in readiness to march at a moments warning. These measures in addition to the necessary and proper reliance upon the whole body of the militia, in case of war, being deemed by them fully adequate to the defence of the United States, they therefore opposed every attempt to augment the military Force.[3]

The second attempt to augment the military Force was made in the Senate on the 24th day of May, five days after the failure of the first attempt in the other house, a committee was appointed to report further measures for the defence of the United States. On the 26th May, that Committee reported an increase of 10,000 men to the military Establishment, On the 29th May this Bill passed the Senate, and was sent to the other house for concurrence, On the 30th of May at the first reading of the Bill in the house of Representatives, it was opposed, and on the question, rejected upon a division of 50 Yeas to thirty two nays. Thus failed the second attempt to augment the military force.

A Third attempt to augment the Military force was also made in the Senate and arose in consequence of a Bill which passed the house of Representatives on the 29th May, for the defence of the South western frontier, and was sent to the Senate for concurrence. This Bill was occasion'd by a message from the president, stating the imminent danger of a war with the Creek and Cherokee Nations of Indians. It provided a plan of defence by posts, to be garrison'd by militia with constant patrols or scouting parties of militia to ply between the posts, and to be relieved at stated periods. This Bill went to the Senate and received one reading, before and on the same day on which they passed their Bill for adding 10,000 men to the military establishment. As soon as their Bill was rejected as before shewn, they immediately laid hold of the Bill for the South Western defence, as a fit means to enforce their favorite object of an augmentation of the military force, and totally changing the Bill from the plan of a defence by posts to be garrison'd by militia, to the simple expedient of raising and adding an entire new legion of 1,200 men to the military establishment with the extra-ordinary bounty of twenty dollars to each recruit they sent back the Bill thus amended to the house of Representatives on the sixth of June—That house the next day disagreed to the amendments of the Senate, the Senate adhered, and asked for a conference, which was had, which still not being able to agree with the Senate, a majority of the house of Representatives adhered on their part, and the Bill was lost on the 8th June upon a division of 30 yeas and 28 nays; Thus failed the third attempt to augment the military force,—altho' in this instance several of the Southern members, from an apprehension of being left without any means of defence, were influenced to vote for the amendments to the Bill, as proposed by the Senate, and many others had sett off on their return home, Congress being to adjourn the next day.

The fourth and last attempt to augment the military force was also made in the Senate on the very last day of the Session, by Mr. Rufus King of New York, who brought in a Bill "to authorize the president, in case he should not deem it expedient to employ any part of the then military establishment in the defence of the South western frontier, to raise, equip, and officer a new legion of 1,200 men for that purpose, to be rais'd for three years, at the same pay and emoluments of the other Troops, but with the extraordinary bounty of 20 dollars to each recruit"—This Bill was read twice, but on the question for its third and last reading, Mr. Burr of New York, the colleague of Mr. King, enforced the rule of the Senate, that no Bill shall be read three times on the same day without unanimous consent; and putting his Veto on it, the Bill was lost, And thus failed the fourth attempt in the same Session to augment the military force.

It is difficult to view the preceeding state of facts, without being impressed with some of the remarkable circumstances it presents, on the one side is seen an earnest, persevering and systematic attempt to encrease the military force by augmenting the existing establishment, or by creating and establishing a new Army on the pretext of foreign danger, or of a defence for the South Western Frontier, and to this end, the various propositions of 25,000, 20,000, 15,000, 10,000, and 5,000 men, and finally a new legion of 1,200 men, additional to the military establishment. On the other-side is seen a firm, decided, and successful opposition to all these repeated and various attempts, whilst the former pursue their object without disguise or palliation, the latter acting merely defensively, maintain their ground, with temper, moderation and consistency—of the respective merit of the two parties, the public will be enabled to decide, recurring only to a few of the facts herein before stated, with the obvious reflections resulting from them, propositions to complete the existing military Establishment to the legal complement of 5,000 men by additions of pay and bounty, are made by the opponents of an augmentation of the Army, with a view to prevent that augmentation, on the ground, that 5,000 men, in addition to those other means of defence, hereinbefore referred to, were fully competent to the exigencies of the United States; Three propositions are opposed and defeated by the supporters of an augmentation of the military force, who refuse to give any additional pay, or even more than the small additional bounty of four Dollars per man for the purpose of completing the existing establishment; whilst at the same time they strenuously urged their own multiplied propositions, of augmenting the military force from 25,000 men, down to a simple additional Legion of 1,200 men, under a grant of the extraordinary and increased bounty of twenty Dollars per man, nor was this all, more alarming consequences were involved in the propositions of augmentation, as they went to authorize the president, in case war should break out between the United States and any foreign nation, to raise during the next recess of Congress, 25,000 regular Troops, or any intermediate number, to organize them as they might see fit, to appoint the proper officers, according to the grades in the existing military establishment, and to borrow 800,000 dollars to defray the present expence, In fine, that the great questions of War and peace of the time and occasion for raising armies; of the power to raise armies, and of the creation of officers, which by the constitution are exclusively vested in Congress, should by a single vote be transplanted to the Executive, Or as was emphatically said by a member from Virginia, that the Executive should by act of Congress be authorized to pass a law to raise armies, precedents so dangerous are thus established by the proposition and may be seen at large in the Journal of the house of Representatives of that Session, pages 187, 188, 233, 343, and of the Senate pages 159, 161.

It is observable, that amongst those who supported the propositions in the house of Representatives are to be found the names of Ames, Bourne, Fitzsimons, Goodhue, Richard Bland Lee, Sedgwick, Smith of South Carolina, Hartley, Gordon, Thatcher, Trumbull, Ward, and Jeremiah Wadsworth, And in the Senate, Cabot, Ellsworth, Henry, Izard, King, Morris, and Vining, all of whom were members of the first Congress, have continued in Congress ever since, and who, it will appear by the Journal of the two houses, were among the original proposers, and most strenuous supporters of the Funding System, Assumption, Excise, irredeemability of public debt, mortgage of public revenues, the Bank, increase of the military Force, Titles, Loans of Money, and other great and extraordinary grants of power and discretion to the Executive and heads of departments, So true it is that in some minds the Idea of governing thro' the medium of a public debt, a standing army, and great and Energetic powers in the Executive magistrate forms the only rule of political conduct, paramount to every consideration of the feelings, affections, and Interests of a great and generous people, and subversive no less of the principles of the federal Constitution than of the general and sacred principles of liberty and republicanism.

So far as the foregoing review, and the reflections accompanying it, may assist the Citizens of this State,[4] and our Eastern brethren to make an estimate of the respective Merits of their own immediate representatives, it will be seen in the Journals of Congress that Gilbert, Gordon, Glen, Talbot, Van Allen, Gaasbeck, and Watts of this State, Ames, Cobb, Coffin, Dexter, Foster,[5] Goodhue, Sedgwick, Thatcher, Ward, and Wadsworth of Massachusetts, Bourne and Malbone of Rhode Island, and Hillhouse, Learned, Swift, Tracey, Trumbull, and Wadsworth of Connecticut constantly voted for the propositions, to augment and increase the military force.

Whilst on the other hand, Bailey, Van Cortland, and Treadwill of this State, Dearborn and Lyman of Massachusetts, Sherburne and Gilman of New Hampshire, Joshua Coit of Connecticut and Smith and Niles of Vermont, as consistently voted against them.

A CALM OBSERVER

MS (KIRBY PAPERS, DUKE UNIVERSITY). IN THE HAND OF BECKLEY.

1. Beckley's essay addressed to publisher Thomas Greenleaf, was published in the May 12, 1795, issue of *The Argus, or Greenleaf's New Daily Advertiser,* a New York newspaper sympathetic to the Jeffersonian Republicans. The essay is reprinted here from the copy in Beckley's hand enclosed in Beckley's August 6, 1800, letter to Ephraim Kirby soliciting Kirby to have the essay updated and reprinted in Connecticut. See Beckley to Kirby, August 6, 1800.

2. Further information on the actions of Congress described by Beckley can be found under the appropriate dates provided by Beckley, in *Journal of the House, Third Congress* and *Debates and Proceedings, Third Congress.*

3. When this essay was published in Greenleaf's newspaper the following phrase continued this sentence: "as most of them did, in all its progress, the law for building and equipping the frigates; although in the latter instance, their opposition failed of success." This was the only major difference in the text of the essay between Beckley's manuscript copy and the published version.

4. That is, New York.

5. The name of Foster was omitted in the published essay.

JOHN BECKLEY TO F. W. LECOMTE

Sir,[1]   Philadelphia. 8th April 1795.

Availing myself of your obliging Overture for an interchange of such public documents as may conduce to mutual information of the general as well as relative interests of our respective countries, and solicitous, on my part, to improve every occasion of cementing, not less the obligations of private friendship between individuals than that cordial union and good understanding, which, for the benefit of mankind, has arisen and ought ever to exist between the two republics of France and America, only and effectually to be promoted by free communications thro' the channels of truth. I have the pleasure now to possess you with a sett of the Journals of the first American Congress from the Year 1774 to the Year 1788 inclusive, Also of a sett of the Journal of the House of Representatives of Congress under the present fœderal Government of the United States from the year 1789, inclusive to the termination of the late Session on the 3d of March last, with such of the Official reports of the Executive departments as have been made during the same period. The public disposition which, in our conversation of yesterday, you proposed to make of these documents, will be highly agreeable to me and in return, it is my wish to obtain, in the mode you also then expressed, such documents as may from time to time be published in France in relation to Agriculture, Manufactures, Commerce, improvements or discoveries in the Arts and Sciences, or on any subject whatever within the Sphere of political Œconomy. I prefer not to make a specification on any particular subject for fear of Error or mistake, and will only add that I know of no exception to the general enumeration I have made within the amount of a small annual fund of about 600 dollars, committed to my disposal for these purposes by Congress.[2]

With true regard, I am, Sir, yr. most obedt. Servt.

FC (BECKLEY FAMILY PAPERS, LIBRARY OF CONGRESS). UNSIGNED, BUT IN THE HAND OF BECKLEY.

1. LeCompte was one of the many mysterious French "agents" at work in the United States in the 1790s purchasing supplies and ships often in violation of American laws and regulations for the French revolutionary government. The French minister Fauchet described him as "un caratere trop orginal pur que je ne t'en parle pas" and went on to describe how LeCompte had traveled through the northern states procuring supplies and ships and acquiring information about American manufacturing and mercantile activities. Frederick J. Turner, ed., *Correspondence of the French Ministers to the United States, 1791–1797* (Washington: American Historical Association, 1904), pp. 426–27. See Beckley to James Monroe, September 23, 1795.

2. Beckley was undoubtedly planning to make these purchases from the newspapers, journals, and stationery part of the contingent fund of the House of Representatives, which Beckley, as clerk of the House, oversaw. Syrett, ed., *Hamilton Papers,* 5:388, 9:463, 13:71, 15:510, and 18:508.

   Beckley's efforts to obtain the journals and statutes of other countries represents part of his continuing effort to establish a library of important books and documents for Congress.

JOHN BECKLEY TO JAMES MADISON

Dear Sir,   New York, 20th April 1795.

I was detained by bad weather & other causes, so that I did not reach this until friday evening. The next day I saw Mr. Dorhman, who promises fairly, altho' at the same time he talks of the scarcity of Money, his distresses &c. I expect to see him again to day, and you may be assured nothing in my power shall be omitted to obtain of him a full and satisfactory settlement.[1]

I have not seen General Lamb, long enough to know any thing of the issue of the letters committed to his care.

There has been no late arrival and is therefore no foreign News. The Election of Governor & Lt. Governor comes on to day, and the great probability is that Yates and Floyd will succeed.[2]

In Massachusetts Varnum is 50 votes a head of Dexter, and within three of gaining his Election. Another trial must now be had, in which it is thought his success is certain.[3] In this State, Havens, Livingston, Van Cortlandt, Bailey, Hawthorn, & Williams are on the republican side,[4] and since the issue of the Virginia Elections is known, no doubt can be entertained of a decided Majority of the same Character in the next H. Rs. By the bye, they talk of a republican from Connecticut, whose name I have forgotten, in room of Trumbull.[5]

I hope you reached home in safety & without accident or injury. Be pleased to present my best regards to the ladies & accept them yourself, from, Dear Sir, Your friend & Servt.

John Beckley.

RC (MADISON PAPERS, LIBRARY OF CONGRESS).

1. Madison had enlisted Beckley's aid in securing payment of an outstanding debt owed to Philip Mazzei (1730–1816), a republican from Tuscany and neighbor of Jefferson, by Arnold Henry Dohrman (1749–1813), a former merchant and American agent in Lisbon. Madison held a mortgage on the debt. See Rutland, ed., *Madison Papers*, 2:34n. 4, 10:31n. 6, and 16:285. See also Beckley to Madison, May 4 and 25, and September 10, 1795.
2. That is, the elections for New York governor and lieutenant governor. The Republican candidates Robert Yates and William Floyd, lost to Federalists John Jay and Stephen Van Rensselaer.
3. James B. Varnum was elected to the House of Representatives in a contested election.
4. Theodorus Bailey, John Hathorn, Jonathan N. Havens, Edward Livingston, Philip Van-Cortlandt, and John Williams were elected to the House from New York.
5. Jonathan Trumbull moved from the House to the Senate, but he resigned from the Senate on June 10, 1796.

James Madison. Stipple engraving by D. Edwin of portrait by T. Sully, published (1810) by W. H. Morgan.
LC–USZ62–16960.

JOHN BECKLEY TO JAMES MADISON

Dear Sir,   Monday Morning, 4th May 1795. (Phila.)

I wrote you on this day week from New York, stating the causes which had induced a postponement of the settlement with Mr. Dohrman, until I could hear from you on the subject. I returned from New York on Friday evening and have been very unwell ever since, with the fever & Ague, occasioned by a cold caught in travelling, and I drop you this line merely to request as speedy an Answer to my former as possible. There is nothing new either here[1] or at N York, but what the Newspapers contain; the president returned on Saturday. With my best respects to the ladies, I am Dear Sir, Yrs.

J. Beckley.

[*P.S.*] The papers brought from N.Y. shall be forwarded the first opportunity. Shall write yo. fully as soon as I am able.

RC (MADISON PAPERS, LIBRARY OF CONGRESS).

1. That is, Philadelphia.

JOHN BECKLEY TO JAMES MADISON

Dear Sir,   Philadelphia 25th May 1795.

I have written you twice by post, once from New York and once since my return, but being without any acknowledgment of their receipt, am fearful of some miscarriage or failure thro' the post Office. I stated to you very fully the reasons that delayed the settlement with Mr. Dohrman, and shall now repeat them; By the Mortgage to you of Novemr. 1788, the debt is specified and acknowledged to be £2000. New York Currency, with Interest thereon at seven per Centum from the date of the Mortgage; this he insists, was an Arbitrary sum put in the Mortgage, solely, to cover the bona fide amount of the debt, as the same should afterwards on a final settlement appear, on a recurrence to the Original Bill, with the Interest and damages thereon, according to the laws & custom of Virginia, and that it was impossible by any fair rule of settlement that his Bill drawn in March 1785 for 2700 dollars, could in November 1788 amount to 5000 dollars=£2000 York Currency. How far these suggestions are found in fact you can best decide. On the one hand, the original Bill and papers remaining with you after the Mortgage was given, seemed to favor the Idea that no definitive liquidation of the debt was then made, whilst, on the other hand it was impossible for me to determine, how far the Interest, damages and difference of Exchange, between the date of the Bill and the date of the Mortgage, might have operated to the prejudice of Mr. Dohrman in producing such an amount of debt when the latter was given. Thus circumstanced I proposed a settlement on his principle, retaining the Mortgage in my possession and giving him a conditional acquittance until I heard from you, but to this he demurred proposing that the matter should rest until I could write to you, and that by your answer he would be governed, and immediately authorise & empower his correspondent in this City to make a final settlement and payment of the debt to me. He produced two acknowledgments of Mr. Mazzei, in part payment, since the date of Mortgage, amounting as well [as] I recollect to about 1400 dollars, but as we made no settlement I omitted to take a memorandum of them. His mode of payment will be in negotiable notes at 90 days with an approved endorser. Be pleased to favor me with your earliest answer on this subject.

This letter will be delivered you by Mr. Preston, and I enclose eight copies of the `Political Reflections.'[1] I brought two dozen from New York and have distributed them all. I expect 50 more in a day or two, and shall scatter them also—they were bought and dispersed in great numbers there, and are eagerly enquired after by numbers here. It will be republished in Boston, Portsmouth, Vermont, and at Richmond. Some careless delay has attended the little statement of facts by `A Calm Observer.'[2] But I have written to Colo. Burr and expect to see it shortly, and will forward a copy. The election of Governor is still in dubio. Great bets are depending on both sides, but I understand, thro' a very direct channel (Knox civedant Secy.) that King & Hamilton despair. In my last, I hinted at a fact respecting Hamilton, which, knowing the security of the present conveyance, I will now fully state. About six or eight weeks ago, whilst Hamilton was in N. York, Commodore Nicholson in conversation with a friend of Hamiltons stated that he had authentic information on which he knew he could rely, that Hamilton had vested £100,000 Sterling in the British funds, whilst he was Secretary of the Treasury, which sum was still held by a Banking house in London, to his use and Interest. H's friend took fire, declared it a base calumny, and that it should be immediately investigated, demanding Nicholsons authority— Nicholson replied that he would be ready at any time & place when called on by Hamilton, to produce his Author, with the proofs he possessed. No call has however been made from that time to this. Nicholson informed me of these particulars himself, and added that if Hamiltons name is at any time brought up as a candidate for any public office; he will instantly publish the circumstance.[3]

Dispatches from Monroe were lately intercepted by the British in the Pomona, and opened by the Kings Atto. General, in the Admiralty Court at Halifax, notwithstanding Mr. Purveiance the Supercargo of the Ship and bearer of the dispatches produced Monroes passport to him under the same official Seal—this has produced a warm correspondence between Mr. Randolph and Hammond.[4]

Intelligence to several commercial houses here particularly Willings, Bing-hams or Lewis's, Swanwicks &c. from their correspondents in France &c. state most decidedly that a seperate peace was signed the 26th March between France, Prussia, Spain, & Portugal. The Aristocrats here beleive it to be true, but I anxiously wish a confirmation. In a late conversation with Mr. Ran-dolph he disclosed many corrobating particulars in the correspondence from Spain, evidencing that they were eagerly seeking for peace, even thro' the gen-erals of the Armies. In the same conversation too, he hinted very directly at you as the Author of 'Political reflections.' I discover in him, a great anxiety for Jay's election, and conclude that it is equally desireable by the President.

Mr. Pinckney's departure for Madrid,[5] is delayed for a short time, in con-sequence of some circumstances which Mr. Jay is to explain; he may be expected daily. A new frigate, the Agricola, was preparing at Rochfort to bring out Mr. Adet the new French Minister & two Commissioners, Mem-bers of Convention, they are expected every hour. These arrivals and the seperate peace, if true, will probably have an influence on the ratification of Mr. Jays treaty. This Moment, by an arrival from Guadaloupe in 14 days, we have the intelligence of the arrival there of a fleet from Brest of Eleven sail of the line with eight or ten thousand troops on board; this force will prob-ably sweep all the West India Islands, before any assistance can be afforded from Gt Britain, for so completely are the Ministry engrossed with the apprehension of an invasion that they have no idea of breaking the force of their channel fleet, wholly trusting to the force now in the West Indies and to the hope that the French would not risk a division of their Marine force; besides no fleet can now be obtained from England before the Hurricane Months, after which, it will be October or November before the Season for action commences again, by which time the complete conquest of all the leward islands may be expected, as also the recovery of Saint Domingo. Another crisis appears to be approaching between the contending factions at Paris of the Moderates & Jacobins; the trial of Barrere & his Associates will probably decide it, but in whatever way it terminates, little benefit can be expected to result from it to the cause of the revolution.

Mr. Brown,[6] is returned from his excursion to the Southward, he has not received the two letters yo. took on for him to Geo. town. If you carried them on to Orange, be so good as to forward them here by Post. Be pleased to present the best respects of all our family to Mrs. Madison & her Sister & accept them yrself, from Dear Sir, Yrs. truly.

John Beckley.

RC (MADISON PAPERS, NEW YORK PUBLIC LIBRARY).

1. That is Madison's anonymously published pamphlet, *Political Observations*, which is dated April 20, 1795, and is published in Rutland, ed., *Madison Papers*, 15:511–34.
2. See Beckley's essay as A Calm Observer, March, 1795, which was published on May 12, 1795, in the *New York Argus; or, Greenleaf's New Daily Advertiser*.

3. Hamilton and James Nicholson, head of the Democratic Society of New York, nearly fought a duel over the reports of Nicholson's allegations. See Syrett, ed., *Hamilton Papers*, 18:471n. 1.

4. The illegal British seizure of Monroe's papers from his private secretary John Henry Purviance of Baltimore led to a sharp exchange of correspondence between Secretary of State Randolph and British Minister George Hammond in May and June of 1795. Rutland, ed., *Madison Papers*, 15:404. This was quickly overshadowed by subsequent events, such as the debate over the Jay Treaty and Randolph's forced resignation.

5. That is, Thomas Pinckney (1750–1828), minister to Great Britain, who was appointed envoy extraordinary to Spain in April 1795. He ultimately negotiated the advantageous treaty of San Lorenzo with Spain. He was the unsuccessful Federalist candidate for vice–president with John Adams in 1796.

6. That is, Senator John Brown of Kentucky.

JOHN BECKLEY TO JAMES MONROE

My dear Sir,   Philadelphia, 1st June 1795.

This letter will be delivered you by Mr. Cummings,[1] a young Gentleman, native of Maryland, of respectable family in Frederick Town, and himself of very, amiable character & manners; permit me to recommend him to your civilities & attention. He comes out under the auspices of one of the first mercantile houses in this City, with design to settle at St. Petersburg in Russia; his intelligence, ability and discretion, may possibly render him, in some way, a useful correspondent to you, but of this, you will be the better judge, after knowing and conversing with him.

I wrote you a very long letter in March and confided it to the department of State, which I hope you received, as also a number of communications & documents of a public nature, which accompanied it. Mr. Cummings will hand you a pamphlet by our friend Madison & a copy of Tench Coxes Book or compilation stiled "A View of the UStates",[2] containing as usual, a great deal of useful matter blended with much Egotism and more of the clanism of a Pennsylvanian.

The theme of domestic politics was never so barren as at present, every thing suspended on the event of Jays treaty & the approaching meeting of Senate.[3] Unfortunately, should there be any thing unsound in it, every circumstance seems to conspire in favor of the probability of its ratification— Jay arrived from England on thursday last, just in time to prepare the government junto, and give them their previous cues, while every doubtful man will be kept in total ignorance until the day. The anxiety for his arrival and joy thereupon, teach me to suspect that great fears prevailed with the Executive for its final success, without his aid, & presence, ergo there must be something rotten in it. The non arrival of Fauchetts successor,[4] and of any communications from yo. later than 17th March, will also conduce to facilitate its adoption. Besides, my good Sir, unhappily for the interests of

France, a system of Colony administration is adopted and became universal in all the French W India possessions, without a single exception, subversive at once of all treaty, Union or Connection whatsoever between the U.S. & France, and violative of every principle of national & neutral right, faith, justice and common Liberty. The system is this, Invitations are held out to the Americans to bring their supplies of provisions &c. which being done, at no little risque and hazard, in most cases, the Cargo is taken for Government use, a prohibition to trade with the inhabitants for any part of it or for any produce of the Colony is imposed, Arbitrary prices allowed on the Cargo, greatly below what might be obtained from the inhabitants, an increased price on the produce which the administration may please to give in Exchange, tho' often it pleases them to give nothing but written acknowledgments for a sum fixed by their own arbitrary decisions, or to detain the unfortunate adventurer many months before he can obtain written ackonwledgement, or produce. To the shameful abuse and monopoly on the part of the colony administrators, it is well known they add the infamous cupidity of charging the mother country, with fifty to a hundred per cent on the prices of the Articles thus dishonestly obtained.

You can readily conceive what effect these things are calculated to produce, and what use the Enemies of France & her glorious revolution will make of them. I will take the libery to suggest to you a mode by which this evil may be pressed to the bottom, and the villainous impositions of the Colony administrators upon the Mother Country, exposed and prevented. Suppose two Commissioners authorized for the purpose come out, first to the United States, and publish an invitation to the merchants here to furnish authentic accounts of sales of cargoes delivered to or taken by the adminstrators of any French Colony, within a given period, and of the mode of payment and prices imposed for the same. Let them then proceed to the Colonies, and ascertain the mode, manner & amount of Supplies there, with all the administrative accounts respecting the same, and transmit the whole to France for final examination and report. The desire such a measure would manifest on the part of France to do justice to the injured Citizens of the U.S. and to detect & punish the infamous peculations and shameful abuses of her Colony administrators would insure to the Commissioners the most full, complete & authentic information on the part of the American merchants, and a better check could not be devised.

In respect to one of the French Colonies, Cayenne, I am possessed with the clearest information and proof, that the administrators there have imposed upon the mother Country to the amount of several millions of livres—Nor am I entre nous without strong suspicions that the whole business is well known to and for doubtful reasons, connived at by Fauchett. I mean so far as respects Cayenne.

I regret most sincerely that the friendly dispositions which the Government of France are manifesting towards us in Europe, should then be in danger of losing its effect thro' the wicked system of Colony administration at which I have glanced. My hope is that the evil will be temporary and the cure effectual.

In my first letter I gave you a full view of the complection of our next Legislature, and in the late Elections, except as to Virginia, where three changes only have been made, namely Cabell in room of Walker, Brent in room of Lee, and Clopton in room of Griffin.[5] Dexter too, has lost his election in Massachusetts & Varnum (said to be a good republican) comes in his place on the 4th trial.

Since yo. left us the New Hampshire Senators[6] have both joined the republican party and zealously adhere to them—Livermore, will never forgive their giving the vacant Judgeship of N.Hampshire to another person.

Randolph stil continues at windy buffettings with Hammond & Van Berkle and complains much of the toilsome labors of his station, hinting now & then at retiring. Hamilton sinks fast into obscurity, he has not yet commenced his law career, nor is it believed he ever will but merely as a blind.

It is probable that Jay is elected Governor of NYork—the votes are now canvassing—Burr declined, & the contest was between Yates or Jay. If the latter succeeds, a new Ch. Justice must be [chosen] perhaps Hamilton, or Randolph.[7]

It is generally suspected that the president will decline for another election. If he does, and nothing turns up greatly to change the present temper of the public mind, Jefferson will undoubtedly succeed him.

We have strong report, by private letters from France, of a separate peace with Spain, Portugal, and Prussia, signed the 26th March, and anxiously await its confirmation or contradiction. We are also made uneasy of accounts and appearances of great dissention in the Convention, and the fear of another concussion and massacre. Can yo. spare a moment to me, on the state & prospect of the internal government & the speedy and final establishment of a republican Constitution?

I shall omit, no favorable opportunity of supplying yo. with every information, within my limited sphere of observation. As soon as the decision of Senate is known you shall have it.

Mr. Randolph writes yo. by another opportunity (Mr. Grubb) who sails today. He transports yo. the newspapers of the last month, and I presume will give yo. a history of the manner in which your dispatches by the Pomona were intercepted, carried to Halifax, and opened by the British advocate there, as also of the unwarrantable conduct of Consul Fenwick at Bourdeaux &c. &c.

Make my respectful compliments to your amiable lady & to friend Skipwith, and accept yourself, the best regards of, dear Sir, Your friend & Servant.

John Beckley

RC (MONROE PAPERS, NEW YORK PUBLIC LIBRARY).

Tench Coxe. Engraving by Samuel Sartain of a 1795 painting by J. Paul. LC–USZ62–887.

1. William Cummings, son of William, an attorney in Frederick, Maryland.
2. For Madison's pamphlet, *Political Observations,* see Beckley to Madison, May 25, 1795. Beckley also included Tench Coxe, *A View of the United States of America, in a Series of Papers. . . .* (Philadelphia: 1794).
3. On May 28, John Jay, special envoy to Great Britain, returned to New York from London. President Washington had recalled the Senate for a special session on June 8 to consider the treaty.
4. Pierre August Adet, successor to Jean Antoine Joseph Fauchet as French minister to the United States, arrived in Philadelphia on June 12.
5. Richard Brent, Samuel J. Cabell, and John Clopton had been elected to the House of Representatives from Virginia replacing Samuel Griffin, Richard Bland Lee, and Francis Walker.
6. That is, John Langdon and Samuel Livermore.
7. John Rutledge of South Carolina was nominated by Washington to succeed Jay as chief justice of the United States Supreme Court but he was rejected by the Senate. After William Cushing declined a promotion from associate justice, Oliver Ellsworth of Connecticut was nominated and confirmed as chief justice in 1796.

JOHN BECKLEY AS A CALM OBSERVER[1]

West-Chester July 7, 1795.

For the Minerva.

In a free government, every individual has a right to express his sentiments on public measures, provided they do not infringe any law, and are delivered with moderation. Under this impression a few remarks will be made on the Treaty of Commerce, &c. lately published, between America and Great-Britain, in which some notice will be taken of, "A candid explanation of that treaty" lately published.[2] It is not the intention of the author of these remarks to make any strictures on the views of those members of the Senate, who were for or against the treaty, his sole object being to treat the subject as an American, guided solely by patriotic views, but shackled by no party. On a subject of such magnitude to the commercial views of this country it is a matter of astonishment, that no one has appeared to expose the details of the treaty, by which the agricultural as well as mercantile interest, will probably be essentially impaired even if no political injury should arise therefrom.

By the treaty of peace we have liberty to cure our fish on the uninhabited shores of Nova Scotia, from which by the 4th article of the treaty of Commerce we are excluded without assigning any reason, or receiving an equivalent. We are not admitted by that article, into even any of the bays of his Britannic Majesty's possessions in America on the Atlantic Ocean. By the 6th article, the United States agree to compensate the British merchants for any equitable demand, to which there had been heretofore any legal impediment. Would it not therefore have been reasonable that the British government should have made compensation for the negroes carried away contrary to the treaty of peace, instead of making it an object of future demand on that government? The 12th article being considered as ruinous to the trade of this country and consequently rejected. I shall make no other remark on it than that it is impossible to carry on the trade to the West-Indies to advantage in vessels of 70 tons. Vessels of 120 tons are too small for the European trade and are very useful for the West Indies, being of a proper burthen for the transportation of lumber and livestock. Should this article therefore be discussed hereafter every true American must wish attention might be paid to this particular. No injury can arise to Great Britain by admitting vessels of this size, but ruinous consequences to the American merchants concerned in the transportation of lumber, horses and cattle in vessels of 70 tons.

By article 13th we are deprived of the carrying trade from India to China and elsewhere except to America. The author of "candid explanation of the treaty" has taken no notice of this instance, nor of the want of provisions for the compensation of the negroes carried off in 1783; America has a right to expect to receive an equivalent, for what they may part with in the way of compromise. Admitting Great Britain to have the right to keep her colonial ports shut to us except under certain restrictions advantagious to herself, what true friend to his country does not think we give more than is given in return, when the vessels of Britain can freely by the treaty import India and China goods at the same duties as American ships, or if not, can balance it by equivalent duties in Britain, while American ships can transport no goods from India or China or any part of the world. except first to America, at the same time British vessels have the liberty to carry provisions and lumber from that country to the West Indies, on the same terms as our own ships. Is this reciprocal? Would it not have been more proper if they restricted us to the transporting of goods from India to America only, than we should have insisted on being our own carriers of American produce to the West Indies. The West India Islands according to a report of the British planters, cannot subsist without us, would it not therefore have been more equitable, as well as liberal, to have opened all their ports to us in India and America, on the same liberal terms as they have free access to all our ports. In the 17th article it is agreed, among other objects that "pitch, tar and ship timber, shall be considered contraband." This is indeed signing our own death warrant. Great Britain produces none of these articles to any quantity and consequently the injury will be sustained by us alone; Georgia, North Carolina, New-York, and New-Hampshire are essentially injured by this article.

Would it not have been more prudent to have trusted to events, and had the subject decided as cases might occur, and according to our future wishes by the law of nations: Vattel is almost the only author who is of opinion that naval stores are contraband, while the greater number of authors are opposed to this opinion. Besides which, all the northern powers of Europe have decided them not to be contraband, and we recognize them not to be so in our Treaty with France, & if I recollect with Holland and Prussia also. All true friends of America must sincerely wish that we may never consent to admit provisions to be contraband, but it appears by article the 18th, that Britain intends to endeavor that we may hereafter agree to it in certain cases, that that nation may capture our provision vessels when it pleases without any regard to the damages which may arise, by reason of the loss attending the return voyage. In article the 21st it is agreed, "that subjects or citizens of either party shall be treated as pirates, if they accept continuous commissions in the service of the enemy of either." This article is the same in our treaty with France, &, in itself, perhaps just. It was adopted before the adoption of the constitution. That instrument declares that Congress shall define piracy. The only objection to this article in the case before us is, that it appears to militate against the constitution and therefore to that account ought to have been treated differently.

It appears to be the decided opinion of those merchants whom the author of these remarks has consulted on the occasion, that the treaty will operate very injuriously on the carrying trade of this country, if ratified in its present form, it therefore behoves every well wisher to the rising prosperity of America, to offer his mite on this momentous subject. From this source, the great man the President of the United States will be the better able to judge of the treaty in a commercial view, and may perhaps suspend his signature, till it is so modified, as to appear before us in a more pleasing form, and on terms of *reciprocity* between the two nations.

A CALM OBSERVER

TR (*AMERICAN MINERVA* (NEW YORK), JULY 14, 1795).

1. For Beckley's authorship of the Calm Observer essays, see Beckley as A Calm Observer, March, 1795, and Beckley to Madison, September 10, 1795.

2. President Washington had laid the so-called Jay Treaty with Great Britain before the Senate on June 8, 1795, and had ordered that the treaty text be kept secret until the Senate acted on the treaty. Benjamin Franklin Bache subsequently abstracted it in his Republican newspaper *Aurora* on June 29 and published it in its entirety in a separate pamphlet on July 1. After the treaty received provisional Senate approval on June 24 it was officially printed in *The Philadelphia Gazette,* July 1, 1795. This essay marks Beckley's emergence as a leader in the Republican fight in the House and the public forum against implementing the treaty. Syrett, ed., *Hamilton Papers,* 18:388–92; *Debates and Proceedings, Third Congress,* pp. 854–68; and John C. Carroll and Mary Wells Ashworth, *George Washington: First in Peace* (New York: Charles Scribner's Sons, 1957), pp. 214–99.

JOHN BECKLEY TO DEWITT CLINTON

Sir,[1]   Philadelphia, 24 July. 1795.

Expecting Mr. Woolcots return from Virginia, I deferred thus long, answering your favour by that Gentleman, hoping for the pleasure of congratulating you on the successful termination of that business: It afforded me great pleasure, to give him an immediate introduction to Mr. Brown, one of the Senators from Kentucky, who has relations in the County in which his enquiries lay, and furnished him with recommendatory letters to Gentlemen of the first character and influence there.

Yesterday, we followed the good example of our Sister towns Boston and New York, and held a general town Meeting in the State house Yard, on the subject of Mr. Jays British Treaty, particulars of which you'l see in the Aurora of this morning; there were present about 5000 Citizens, and perhaps no occasion of an equal assemblage of people ever presented so orderly, peaceful and dignified a Conduct. With one Voice and one Mind the Treaty was utterly condemned, and altho' every Resolution was deliberately read, and the question thereon taken and reversed by the show of hands, not a single hand was raised of all the numerous concourse, either in favour of the treaty, or in opposition to the resolutions. On Saturday, a Memorial to the president will be presented, which if adopted, will be carried thro' the different Wards of the City and offered for the signature of the individual Citizens, by which means we shall discover the names and numbers of the British adherents, Old tories, and Aristocrats, who modestly assume the title of faederalists, and stile themselves the best friends of our beloved president & At the same time it will effectually shew the Major and decided sense of the great Commercial City of Philadelphia.[2] Is it not a painful reflection, my friend, that the machinations and intrigues of a British faction in our Country, should place our good old president in the distressing situation of singly opposing himself to the almost unanimous voice of his fellow Citizens, and of endangering the peace, happiness and Union of America, as well as destroying his own tranquility, peace of mind, good name and fame? But I trust in heaven to enlighten his mind and give him wisdom and firmness to turn away the evil cup, so insidiously prepared for him.

Present me respectfully to your Worthy Uncle, our friend General Lamb, Colonel Burr, Sir John Temple &c—and believe me, respectfully, Yours,

John Beckley

RC (CLINTON PAPERS, COLUMBIA UNIVERSITY).

1. DeWitt Clinton (1769–1828), nephew of New York Governor George Clinton, was already a leader of the Republicans in New York State. When the Jeffersonian party attained national dominance in 1800, Clinton's Republican Party returned to power in New York. Clinton influenced state politics through the assembly and his control of the council of appointment.
2. At the July 23 meeting a committee of leading Republicans was appointed to memorialize the president and Congress in opposition to the treaty. At a mass meeting on July 25 the crowd rioted and attacked the homes of the British minister George Hammond and treaty advocate William Bingham. Tinkcom, *Republicans and Federalists in Pennsylvania*, pp. 88–90.

JOHN BECKLEY TO JAMES MADISON

Dear Sir,   Philadelphia, 10th September 1795.

I have purposely delayed answering your favor of the 10th. Ulto. until now, because of some political events here of a nature the most extraordinary, and in which you, as well as others, stand particularly involved and named; they stand connected with the causes of Mr. Randolphs resignation,[1] and will be fully explained to you by Mr. Nicholas. To that Gentleman I must also refer you for all other news foreign & domestic, and he will hand you a packet containing Smiths pamphlet in favor of the treaty and three numbers of Cary's remembrancer.[2] I have been and am still much occupied in a removal from my late residence to a new house in 8th Street South of Walnut, which I have purchased, besides I am at this moment confined to my room by a tumour on the leg. I do not however omit any endeavor to assist the common cause of republicanism & our country as endangered by the impending treaty. A select few, move in concert with friends at New York; a regular correspondence and union of effort is maintained and we have already dispersed in Circular letters, all over the States a petition to the H. of Represents.[3] without, as yet, the smallest suspicion from our opponents: All our movements are kept secret until they have reached their ultimate destination, and we now meditate an address to the people[4] in the same mode, developeing, as far as may be proper, the insidious plan that effect a ratification of the treaty. Dallas the reputed author & actual penman of the Features,[5] we do not confide in, neither in Swanwick[6]—the former, since the ratification has manifested a disposition to trim. You can have no idea, how deeply the public confidence is withdrawing itself from the president, and with what avidity Strictures on his conduct are received; sensible of this, his friends are redoubling their efforts to exalt his name and exaggerate his past services. But all in vain, the vital blow aimed at the Independence & best Interests of his country, by the impending treaty, mark him in indelible character as the head of a British faction, and gratitude no longer blinds the public mind. I have not yet rescued the calm observer from the negligence of Melancton smith, but have writen to Dewit Clinton to do it for me.[7] Dohrman seems determined to maintain silence, notwithstanding a triplicate of my last letter put into his own hand by my friend Mr. shippey. Would it not be advisable for you to write him?

Maria, joins me in best regards to Mrs. Madison & the Ldies and I remain, Dear Sir, Yrs. sincerely.

John Beckley

RC (MADISON PAPERS, NEW YORK PUBLIC LIBRARY).

1. Edmund Randolph resigned as secretary of state on August 19 when confronted by President Washington with a translated dispatch of the French minister, Fauchet, suggesting that Randolph had solicited bribes from the French government. Madison, Jefferson and Monroe were named by Fauchet as leaders of the group of "honest" men who were supporting the French government and resisting the subversion of the United States constitution. John J. Reardon, *Edmund Randolph: A Biography* (New York: Macmillan Co., 1974), pp. 307–34, 367–80; and Moncure D. Conway, *Omitted Chapters of History Disclosed in the Life and Papers of Edmund Randolph* (New York: G.P. Putnam's Sons, 1888), pp. 270–369; and George Gibbs, ed., *Memoirs of the Administrations of Washington and John Adams edited from the Papers of Oliver Wolcott, Secretary of the Treasury*, 2 vols. (New York: reprint Burt Franklin, 1971), 1:232–80.

2. John Nicholas, U.S. representative from Virginia, undoubtedly carried William Loughton Smith's, *A Candid Examination of the Objections to the Treaty of Amity, Commerce, and Navigation, between the United States and Great Britain. . . .* (Charleston, 1795); and copies of the first three issues of volume one of the *American Remembrancer*, which had been published by Matthew Carey on August 20, 27, and September 4, 1795.

3. Perhaps, the broadside, *To The Speaker and Members of the House of Representatives of the United States of America. . . .* (Philadephia, 1795), which opposed the Jay Treaty.

4. This "address to the people" could not be clearly identified, but there is an "Address to the Citizens of New York" arguing for rejection of the Jay Treaty in Mathew Carey, *The American Remembrancer: or, An Impartial Collection of Essays, Resolves, Speeches, etc. Relative, or Having Affinity to the Treaty with Great Britain* which was published in Philadelphia in December 1795. See also Beckley to Clinton, September 13, 1795.

5. Alexander J. Dallas was the author of *Features of Mr. Jay's Treaty....* (Philadelphia: Mathew Carey, 1795).

6. John Swanwick was the author of *A Rub from Snub...addressed to Peter Porcupine...* (Philadelphia: 1795), an attack on Federalist writer William Cobbett.

7. Beckley's letter to Clinton has not been found, but the essays written by Beckley over the pseudonym, A Calm Observer, resumed publication on October 23, 1795, in the Philadephia *Aurora* with a bold attack on President Washington. This statement of Beckley indicates that he had to retrieve the essays from New York, where he had published two earlier essays of A Calm Observer, which are printed in this volume under dates March 1795 and July 7, 1795.

JOHN BECKLEY TO DEWITT CLINTON

Dear Sir,   Philadelphia, 13th September 1795.

I have been prevented by sickness, from making an earlier acknowledgment of your favor of the 3d instant. Its contents were communicated at our Select Meeting on thursday last. We perfectly accord with you in sentiment and are adopting measures on our part in furtherance of your ideas. A change in the public sentiment, now so universally manifested against the treaty, is the great desideratum of our opponents, as the means to influence a Majority of the Representatives in his favor, at the ensuing meeting of Congress; to this object all their efforts will be pointed, and to frustrate them We have concluded on An Address to the people of the U.S. to be printed and dispersed in hand bills in the same Mode and subject to the same rules of Secrecy that we observed in the case of the petition respecting which not a suspicion is yet excited here. By this means, we hope to give the first effectual blow, and to make it as impressive as possible, we shall incorporate into it, as far as may be politic, a history of the late intrigues in the Cabinet, connected with the causes of Mr. Randolphs resignation, which produced the presidents Ratification of the treaty and a revocation of his first determination, officially made known to Hammond, not to ratify—for this purpose, we have waited Mr. Randolphs return that we may obtain from him more full & complete information—he arrived yesterday, and the moment I am able, I will give yo. the particulars, altho' my present hope and belief is that he will lay it before the public.[1] Have you seen Hancock, Valerias, Belisarias &c.[2] and are they republished with you? Every where to the Southward they are republished with avidity. I know not the writers. Who is Cato? Decius &c. if it be a fair question. Poor Wilenks began to squeak out of tune and I suppose will be silenced. Rely on every effort &

cooperation here in pursuit of what, we religiously think our Countrys political salvation rests on the defeat of the treaty.

Yours truly, John Beckley

RC (CLINTON PAPERS, COLUMBIA UNIVERSITY).

1. See note 4 to the preceding document. Randolph published a lengthy pamphlet in his own defense, *A Vindication of Mr. Randolph's Resignation* (Philadelphia: Samuel H. Smith, 1795).
2. Essays by Hancock, Valerius, and Belisarius were direct attacks on the treaty and Washington and they first appeared in the *Aurora*. For a discussion of these and the hundreds of other essays concerning the Jay Treaty, see Donald H. Stewart, *The Opposition Press of the Federalist Period* (Albany: State University Press of New York, l969), pp. 177–236.

JOHN BECKLEY TO JAMES MONROE

My dear friend,   Philadelphia 23rd September 1795.

I received and thank you for your acceptable favour of the 13th June[1]—all its requests were duly complied with. This letter & an accompanying packet containing Careys remembrancer &c &c will be delivered you by Mr. Le Compte[2] who has been in our Country a considerable time and will be able to give you much useful information.

The British treaty occupies the whole attention of America. It was ratified on the 14th August by the president with the condition only of suspending the 12th Article, as recommended by the Senate, and Hammond, the British Minister, sailed with it in the Thisle frigate from New York on the 17th August. It may be expected back by the meeting of Congress. Still however I do not believe it will ever become a treaty, or any thing more than a mere inexecuted instrument. The opposition is universal, and petitions from every State and district with more general signatures than ever was known, are on foot to the House of Reps. against it. But my friend a deeper cause will finally defeat it. A wicked scene of Cabinet intrigue is just discovered, by which alone it has progressed to its present dangerous State.[3]

Mr. Randolph has resigned his Office as Secretary of State—Bradford Atto. General is dead.[4] Both offices have now been vacant a month, and no suggestion who is to supply them. Mr. R's resignation—the Senate ratification; and lastly the president are the effect of this intrigue. On the 19th August two days after Hammond sailed, and when there was also every reason to believe that Fauchett who had been visiting at Rhodeisland upwards of a month for the sailing of the Medusa was gone, an intercepted letter of Fauchetts to the Committee of Exterior Relations, dated in October last, was communicated by US presidt <by Wolcott, Pickering and Bradford. His letter to> to Randolph. It had been made known to the president a week before. Hammond, who says it was transmitted to him by Greenville, shewed it to Woolcot, he to Pickering, they two to Bradford, and the three to Washington. Its effect was this, that the president on Randolphs advice having before made known in a formal & official manner to Hamond that he would not ratify the Treaty, without an explicit disavowal on the part of G.B. of any right or claim to seize our provision Vessels bound to France and an absolute repeal of their existing Orders of Seizure, was now influenced without Randolph's privity, to rescind that determination & to ratify & forward the treaty by Hammond in the manner I have stated. But you are anxious for the tenor of Fauchetts letter and I hasten to give it you. Fauchett, in a confidential dispatch of ten or a dozen sheets of paper, gives to his Government a full view of parties, politics & opinion in America—in many particulars he is perfectly right, in others, as might be expected mistaken & misinformed. His view of the British party & their politics is pretty just, and the president he supposes, as we do, to be an honest man, well disposed to France, but wickedly misled & deceived. In speaking of the Republican & antiBritish party, he appears to be jealous of Randolph, as not well disposed to France, and mentions Jefferson, Madison, yourself, Mifflin, Clinton & Dallas as the Republican leaders, but as honest men contrasted with their opponents. He speaks also of Randolphs previous Confessions to him, and of an overture he made to him to employ the money of his nation thro' the uses of proper agents to procure useful intelligence of the British movements. This last circumstance is stated somewhat ambiguously, but he refers to reference papers No. 3 and 6 for more full explanation. Critically, for the views of the british faction, neither of these references accompany the intercepted letter; whether they had them & for obvious reasons withheld them, or not? is not known, tho' the president acknowledges he never saw them. Sufficient however for their purposes the president was worked up into a suspicion that Randolph had either previously received, or manifested a disposition to receive French Money. Accordingly on the 19th August he sent for him and under all the strange circumstance I have stated, most abruptly delivered him the letter demanding an explanation of it. R— behaved very properly and Woolcot & Pickering being present declined any particular answer, except signifying his determination to resign and immediately to proceed to Rhode Island in quest of Fauchett for the requisite explanation. He executed both purposes, and a few days since returned from Rh Island, the unexpected sailing of the Medusa, the day after he reached Newport, had nearly deprived him of his object but Fauchett, with whom in presence of a third person he held a full interview the evening before, sent a dispatch from on board the Medusa by the pilot, addressed to Mr. Adet, which covered a full & explicit explanation & exoneration of Mr. R added to which Adet has, found the reference papers No. 3 & 6—from all which it results that there is not a shadow of suspicion agst Randolph. The president is now absent at Mount Vernon, but on Saturday Mr. R. published in Browns Gazette a letter to him concerning his return & possession of proofs sufficient to satisfy every impartial mind that his resignation was dictated by considerations that ought not to have been resisted for a moment & stands upon a footing perfectly honorable to himself—and further that he was digesting into order & should shortly forward him a full view of the subject. In this situation the business now stands, but that it must fully come before the public is inevitable. The attempts to assassinate R's character during his trip to Rh. island were base and infamous to a degree—the final effect of this pretty intrigue you may readily conceive. I ought not however to omit that Fauchett declares the letter never was intercepted, but stolen from him last winter when in New York. You will probably have seen Fauchett before this reaches you, as also the letter itself, or a copy of it.[5]

I have endeavored to give you the outlines of this bagatelle business, and would to God, my friend, there were not better ground to suspect the application of British Money in our country, than this letter or any thing else can give for a suspicion of the application of French money. In the mean time, however, the true friends of our Country, among which I may without vanity class myself, feel deeply anxious to see what will be the conduct of France respecting the treaty—Whatever step she takes, will be critically applied as it relates to the next session of Congress—that it may not be hostile I rather hope than expect—that it might be temperate, but firm & decisive I could wish, and that as far as relates to an effectual check on British intrigues in American, it should be the policy of France to repossess herself of Louisiana and the Floridas, I fervently wish as an American, a republican & a friend to Liberty. It may be satisfactory to add that the paragraphs of Fauchetts letter respecting Mr. R's previous confessions, and the overture to apply French Money, are thus explained—the previous confession was, the shewing to Fauchett so much of Jays intelligence as inhibited him from agreeing to any stipulations injurious to France—the overture for applying French money was to obtain from Fauchett, without his knowing it, a concert of operation in ferreting out British machinations to foment the insurrection then at its height.

I have nothing farther to add on the State of public affairs—Every thing will remain probably in statu quo, until the meeting of Congress on the 3d December. All friends in Virginia are well and that state is unanimously opposed to the treaty. Accept of what I have now written as an earnest of my purpose not to let any important occasion of possessing you of useful & necessary information, to pass away unimproved. I shall hope early in the next Session to have your acknowledgement of the receipt of this letter, with such interesting particulars as you can with propriety communicate.

Make my best respects acceptable to your amiable Lady, and believe me, most truly, My dear Sir, Yr. affect. friend,

John Beckley

RC (MONROE PAPERS, LIBRARY OF CONGRESS).

1. Certainly Monroe's letter of June 23, copies of which were also sent to Jefferson, Burr, George Logan, and Robert R. Livingston. Monroe Papers, Library of Congress.
2. See Beckley to LeCompte, April 8, 1795.
3. For further information on the Randolph resignation and its relationship to the ratification of the Jay Treaty, see Beckley to Madison, September 10, 1795 and note 1.
4. Attorney General William Bradford had died on August 23, 1795. Washington first attempted to appoint John Marshall in his place, put when he declined he appointed Charles Lee of Virginia. Carroll and Ashworth, *Washington*, pp. 299, 300, 311–12, and 326.
5. For Randolph's published personal defense, see note 1 to the preceding document.

JOHN BECKLEY AS A CALM OBSERVER[1]

October 23, 1795

TO OLIVER WOLCOTT ESQ. LATE COMPTROLLER,
NOW SECRETARY OF THE TREASURY OF THE UNITED STATES.[2]

SIR,

When a man who has been advanced from an inferior to a superior station in the Government and called upon to exercise a high and responsible public office, deliberately violates every obligation of duty, overleaps the barriers of the constitution, and breaks down the fences of the law, contemning and despising every principle which the People have established for the security of their rights and to restrain the arbitrary encroachments of power, what, I ask, Sir, is the degree of guilt of such a man? And to you, is the enquiry particularly addressed, for as Nathan said unto David "*Thou art the man,*" and by your own acts shall you be condemned.

Attend then, Sir, to the following particulars and state of facts.[3]

On the 30th day of April 1789, the President of the United States qualified into office and took the following oath: "I do solemnly swear that I will faithful[ly] execute the office of President of the United States; and will to the best of my ability, preserve, protect and defend the Constitution of the United States."

By a clause in the 1st section of the 2nd article of the Constitution, it is declared, "that the President shall, *at stated times*, receive, for his services, a compensation, which shall neither be encreased nor diminished during the period for which he shall have been elected, and he shall not receive, within that period, any other emolument from the United States, or any of them."

By the 3d Section of the same Article it is directed "that the President of the United States shall take care that the laws be faithfully executed."

By a clause in the 9th Section of the first Article it is declared "that no money shall be drawn from the Treasury, but in consequence of appropriations made by law."

By the act of Congress to establish the Treasury department passed the 2d of September 1789 it is made the duty of the Secretary of the Treasury "to grant under the limitations therein established or thereafter to be established, all warrants for money to be issued from the Treasury *in pursuance of appropriations by law.*"

By the act of Congress, supplemental to the act establishing the Treasury department, passed the 3d day of March 1791, it is directed that every officer in the said department shall take an oath "well and faithfully to execute the trust committed to him."

By the act of Congress for allowing a compensation to the President, passed the 24th of September 1789, there is allowed to the President *at the rate of 25,000* dollars per annum, *for his services* to commence with the time of entering on the duties of his office, to continue as long as he should remain in office, and to be paid *quarterly* out of the treasury of the United States.

By an annual act of Congress, provision is made for the President's compensation by a specific appropriation of the sum of 25,000 dollars and no more.

Between the 30th of April 1789, the day on which the President qualified into office and the 30th of April 1790, which completed the first year of his Presidency he drew by warrants from the late Secretary of the Treasury countersigned by the Comptroller the sum of 25,000 dollars and no more.* [Mr. Eveleigh was the Comptroller]

Between the 30th of April 1790 and the 30th April 1791 being the second year of his service the President drew by like warrants the sum of 30,150 dollars, being an excess beyond annual compensation made by law and the appropriation thereof by Congress of 5,150 dollars.

Between the 30th of April 1791 and the 30th of April 1792, being the third year of his service the President drew by like warrants the sum of 24,000 dollars which being l000 less than his annual compensation reduced the excess that he received the year before to 4,150 dollars.

Between the 30th of April 1792 and the 30th of April 1793 being the fourth year of his service the President drew by like warrants the sum of 26,000 dollars which again made up the excess of his second year's compensation to 5,150 dollars more than the law allows.

On the 4th of March 1793 when the first term of four years for which the President was elected into office expired, he had drawn from the public Treasury by warrants from the late Secretary of the Treasury, countersigned by the Comptroller, the sum of 1037 dollars beyond the compensation allowed him by law estimating from the day he qualified into office.

The evidence of the sums drawn and of the truth of the facts here stated, will be seen in the official reports made to Congress of the annual receipts and expenditures of the public monies, signed by you as Comptroller of the Treasury, and which have been published for the information of the people.

But, sir, as it had been determined by the late Secretary of the Treasury, and yourself as Comptroller, to set at defiance all law and authority, and to exhibit the completest evidence of servile submission and compliance with the lawless will and pleasure of a President, attend to the following facts:

On the 4th of March 1793, the President qualified into office and commenced the second term of four years for which he was re-elected.

On the 18th February 1793 Congress passed an act providing "that from and after the 3d day of March in the present year (1793) the compensation of the President of the United States shall be *at the rate of 25,000 dollars per annum, in full for his services, to be paid QUARTER YEARLY at the Treasury.*"

Between the 4th day of March 1793, and the 4th day of June following, being the first quarter after the passing of the last mentioned act, there was paid to the President out of the public treasury by warrants from the late Secretary of the Treasury, countersigned by you as Comptroller, the sum of eleven thousand dollars, being an excess of 4750 dollars in one quarter beyond the compensation allowed by law, and making at the same rate a compensation of 44,000 dollars per annum instead of the 25,000 dollars, fixed by Congress.

Upon you, Sir, the late Secretary of the Treasury and the President must rest the responsibility of these extraordinary outrages upon the laws and constitution of our country; since it remains to be seen how far the independent & impartial justice of the National Legislature will be exercised in punishment of the offence already committed as well as to prevent the repetition of it hereafter. In vain, Sir, are all the obligations of oaths and duty, and in vain will be all future precautions of the Legislature to guard the chastity of the public treasury from lawless violation and abuse, if one man can exalt himself above the law and with impunity disregard those high restraints which the people have ordained.

Is there any other man in the government of the United States who would have dared to ask, or to whom you and your predecessor in office would have presumed to grant the like favour?* [It will hereafter be seen whether the excess of compensation has been continued up to the present time, and to what amount?]

Is it or is it not a small favour to receive 4750 dollars of the public money in one quarter beyond the amount of legal salary, and in addition to the former excess of 1037 dollars, already in hand and not refunded?

If the precedent which this donation from the treasury furnished, were to be followed in favour of other public officers, how many hundred thousand dollars per annum would thus be lawlessly taken from the public treasury and saddled upon the people? Was it or was it not the duty of the late Secretary of the Treasury and of yourself as comptroller to have checked and restrained the abuse of power that has been stated, and why, instead of doing so, did you become, obedient like, the servile and submissive instruments of it?

Can the people feel respect for the constituted authorities of their country, when those very constituted authorities are the first to trample upon the laws and constitution of their country?

What will posterity say to the man who has acted in the manner I have stated, after having thus solemnly addressed the Legislature of his country: "When I was first honoured with a call into the service of my country, then on the eve of an arduous struggle for its liberties, the light in which I contemplated my duty required that I should renounce every pecuniary compensation. From this resolution I have in no instance departed; and, being still under the impressions which produced it, I must decline as inapplicable to myself any share in the personal emoluments which may be indispensably included in a permanent provision for the executive department, and must accordingly pray that the pecuniary estimates for the station in which I am placed, may, during my continuance in it, be limited to such actual expenditures, as the public good may be thought to require"? Will not the world be led to conclude that the mark of political hypocrisy has been alike worn by a *CESAR, a CROMWELL and a WASHINGTON*?

A CALM OBSERVER

Alexander Hamilton. Mural painting by Constantino Brumidi in U.S. capitol. LC–USA7–25904.

TR (*AURORA* (PHILADELPHIA), OCTOBER 23, 1795).

1. Beckley was identified as one of the authors of the Calm Observer series, by Oliver Wolcott in a November 19, 1795, letter to Oliver Wolcott, Sr.: "I am well satisfied that the 'Calm Observer' is a joint work of certain patriots. Randolph was doubtless an adviser, and Beckley, Clerk of the House of Representatives, the writer. I think I cannot be mistaken." Gibbs, ed., *Memoirs of Oliver Wolcott*, 1:268

2. Beckley's attack on Washington was one of the first direct and open political attacks on the president. Although shocked by the personal nature of the partisan attack, supporters of the president, such as Wolcott and Hamilton, quickly responded to the essays of A Calm Observer in the newspapers. Wolcott was the first to reply in a public letter to Benjamin Franklin Bache of October 24, 1795, which was published in the *Aurora*, October 26, 1795, and then again on October 28, following the publication of A Calm Observer's letter on October 27. Hamilton's public reply was published in the *Daily Advertiser* (New York), November 20, 1795. For further information and copies of Wolcott's and Hamilton's essays, see Syrett, ed., *Hamilton Papers*, 19:350–426; and Gibbs, ed., *Memoirs of Oliver Wolcott*, 1:257–61.

3. References in the essays by A Calm Observer to specific acts of Congress can be located by date in the relevant volumes of the *Journal of the House of Representatives* and *The Debates and Proceedings in the Congress of the United States*.

JOHN BECKLEY AS A CALM OBSERVER

October 27, 1795

TO OLIVER WOLCOTT, ESQ. LATE COMPTROLLER,
NOW SECRETARY OF THE TREASURY OF THE UNITED STATES.

SIR,

The Calm Observer desires to claim the benefit of your testimony with the public, that he was neither party or privy to the defence you have exhibited before them.[1] Whatever confession, the cunning or contrivance of a professed enemy, had such a man been one of your advisers, might have counselled you to make, so complete an acknowledgment of guilt could not have been expected, as the result of your own deliberate act, after long and previous consultation with the President, had not conviction forced it.

Had you, Sir, commenced your defence under the influence of the just reflection, that evasion belongs only to a bad cause, and that the language of indecent invective is the usual resort of conscious guilt, you had spared yourself all the preliminary remarks, with which you introduce yourself to the public.

The Calm Observer exhibited a direct charge against you, which, it is true, equally involves the late Secretary of the Treasury and the President, of having violated the laws and constitution of your country—But he did not as you have done, deal in affection without proof. His charge was accompanied by a citation of the various clauses of the constitution and of the laws, which had been violated, & by a reference to your own official acts and reports, to prove by dates, sums and amount, every fact there stated. You, Sir, have not, in a single instance, excepted to, denied, or controverted those facts, as, in truth, you could not; they therefore stand fully acknowledged and admitted, on your part, before the public.

Your defence, Sir, is a flimsy attempt at an apology for misconduct, fraught with contradiction and evasion. It would disgrace a Tyro of the schools; and reflects nothing but shame and dishonour on yourself and all concerned. The honor of the invidious endeavor, to place in front of a public accusaion against the President, his private Secretaries, in order that they may receive the full weight of public censure, on his behalf, has been reserved for you, and is in perfect character with all your conduct in this business.

The idle tale about the President's *household expences* is wholly inapplicable to a just defence, and directly in the face of the *Constitution* and the laws; neither of which say one word about *expences. They* have fixed compensation for *services* at the rate of 25,000 dollars per annum, payable at *stated times*, that is, *quarter yearly. They* have forbidden the President to receive *any increase* of that compensation, or *other emoluments, within the period*, for which he was elected—And an annual act of Congress appropriates, for payment of the President's compensation, the sum of 25,000 dollars in each year, and no more. Upon these authorities, I submit the following propositions to the opinion of any legal counsel within the United States:

1st. If the President has received in any one quarter, more than at the rate of 25,000 dollars per annum, unless it included some arrearage due him for a preceding quarter, has he not violated the Laws and Constitution of his country?

2dly. If the President has received in any one year, more than 25,000 dollars, unless it included an arrearage due him for a preceding year, has he not violated the Laws and Constitution of his country?

3dly. If the President has received, within the period of four years, for which he was first elected, more than at the rate of 25,000 dollars per annum, computing from the time of entering on the duties of his office, has he not violated the Laws and Constitution of his country?

I presume, sir, that you have admitted the truth of the fact, that the President has so received more than he was intitled to, in each of the preceding instances.

And now, sir, for your novel doctrine of agency and responsibility—you say, that the advances from the Treasury have been uniformly made on the *application*, and in the name of one of the *private Secretaries*, and without the *special order* of the President—And you thence conclude, "that *if there has been an error* in advancing monies, *the President* is not responsible for it, he is merely accountable, in a pecuniary view, for the act of his agent; as a matter affecting personal *character*, he is, in no manner concerned." In what relation, then, sir, has the President stood in this business; As a mere private citizen, or as President of the United States? Is he not responsible in both characters; as a private citizen to refund to the public, whatever monies he has received in his public charcter, more than he was legally entitled to; —as President of the United States, in his personal and public character, for having in so receiving, violated the laws and Constitution of his country? In what manner, does his acting by an agent vary the question? That agent received the money *on his behalf, to his use,* and in virtue of *some* authority from the President so to do.

As unavailing too, sir, is the merit of your claim to the entire responsibility of this business upon the Treasury Department, which you *so readily assume.*— There have been three actors in it—the President of the United States, the late Secretary of the Treasury and yourself, as Comptroller. You are all three equally amenable, in your several public characters, for your respective parts therein contrary to the laws and Constitution of your country. The President was the receiver, the late Secretary of the Treasury, and yourself, the payers; neither, therefore, can assume an entire responsiblity, in exoneration of the other.

Your affirmation, sir, that not one dollar has been advanced, at any time, for which there was not an existing appropriation by law, is an evasion unworthy of you; it is no more than saying, that all the money in the treasury is covered by legal appropriations. But a fair application of what you affirm, more strongly confirms your guile;—since, if there be not, at any time, any money in the Treasury, but what is appropriated by law to some given object; and you have, at any time, taken money not appropriated to the payment of the President's compensation, and advanced it on account of such compensation, you have, in so doing, violated an appropriation of Congress; and this you have not pretended to say, has not been done.

Your concluding sentence, being an apostrophe to Mr. Bache,[2] on the conduct of his paper, would pass wholly unnoticed by me, were it not to expose the hypocritical cant of alarm and danger to the government, and the solemn farce of denominating yourself and your coadjutors in this business *the government*. What, sir? Cannot one, two or three public officers be detested and exposed, for a violation of the laws and Constitution of their country, but the government is attacked, the government is in danger, and the constitution is to be destroyed? No, sir, you well, know, that, in this case, the constitution is supported, the cause of good government maintained; and that the conduct of the Calm Observer will receive the approbation of all good citizens.

Upon the whole, sir, I cheerfully appeal to an enlightened public, to decide between you and me, on which side, lie the truth, reason and law of the case, and on which side, sophistry and evasion.

A CALM OBSERVER

TR (*AURORA* (PHILADELPHIA), OCTOBER 27, 1795).

1. Wolcott's quick response of October 24, appeared in the October 26 issue of the *Aurora*. Wolcott argued that "advances from the treasury" had been made "on the application, and in the name of some one of the private secretaries" and thus Washington was not responsible for any "error in advancing monies." The treasury was responsible for dispensing money, but no errors had been made, according to Wolcott. Gibbs, ed., *Memoirs of Oliver Wolcott*, 1:259.

2. Wolcott accused Benjamin Franklin Bache, publisher of the *Aurora*, of being part of "a confederacy whose nefarious object it is, by calumny and misrepresentation, to induce the people to believe that those who manage their public concerns are utterly destitute of integrity." Gibbs, ed., *Memoirs of Oliver Wolcott*, 1:260.

JOHN BECKLEY AS A CALM OBSERVER

October 29, 1795

TO OLIVER WOLCOTT, ESQ. LATE COMPTROLLER,
NOW SECRETARY OF THE TREASURY OF THE UNITED STATES.

Sir,

A very short statement will be sufficient to expose the new evasion you are guilty of in a second attempt to justify against the charges of the CALM OBSERVER.[1]

On the 3d day of March 1793, the day on which the first term of four years for which the President was elected into office, expired, he had received 1037 dollars on account of compensation *more than the law allows*, estimating from the day he entered on the duties of his office, to wit, the 30th of April 1789. Now, sir, let me ask whether the acts of appropriation by Congress justified the payment of this excess; and if they did not, whether the appropriation has not been violated, and what becomes of your repeated declarations "that not one dollar has been *at any time* advanced for the use of the President for which there was not an *existing* appropriation."

You surely, sir, do not mean to insinuate, that if Congress at any time make an appropriation for any given object, for a greater amount than that object can *legally* demand or claim, the officers of the Treasury are justified in paying the whole sum, so appropriated to that given object. For instance, sir, you will not pretend to say that the President's whole salary of 25,000 dollars can be paid him, on the first day or within the first quarter of his year of service; or that if it were so paid him and he was immediately thereafter either to die or resign, the appropriation by Congress would not in such case be violated. Let me then ask you to point out what difference there is between the case of death and resignation, and the case of the expiration of the President's first term of service before stated, which can exonerate you from the charge of having violated the appropriation laws of Congress in favor of the President, by paying him more money than he was legally entitled to for his first term of service.

A CALM OBSERVER

TR (*AURORA* (PHILADELPHIA), OCTOBER 29, 1795).

1. Wolcott had responded in the *Aurora*, October 28, 1795, to Calm Observer's October 27 essay, repeating his argument that the president had never received any more compensation than Congress had appropriated or allowed.

JOHN BECKLEY AS A CALM OBSERVER

November 2, 1795.

TO OLIVER WOLCOTT, ESQ. LATE COMPTROLLER,
NOW SECRETARY OF THE TREASURY OF THE UNITED STATES.

SIR,

That the most incontrovertible evidence may be given to the public, of your guilt and evasion, under the charges of the Calm Observer, and that your reiterated assertion "that not one dollar has been *at any time*, advanced for the use of the President, for which there was not an existing appropriation," may be proved to be totally destitute of foundation, I now subjoin the following facts and remarks, in adition to my short statement of Thursday last.

On the 29th of September 1789, Congress passed an act appropriating 25,000 dollars for payment of one year's compensation to the President of the United States.

On the 16th of March 1790, Congress passed an act appropriating 25,000 dollars for payment of another year's compensation to the President of the United States.

On the 11th of February 1791, Congress passed an act, appropriating 25,000 dollars for payment of a third year's compensation to the President of the United States.

On the 23d of December 1791, Congress passed an act, appropriating 25,000 dollars, for payment of the fourth year's compensation to the President of the United States.

These are the only acts, that were, at any time, passed by Congress, making appropriation for the President's compensation, during his first four year's term of service.

These acts were subject, at the Treasury, to one of the following rules of construction, and no other.

1st. That the appropriation of each year was to be considered as operating by the *Calendar year,* that is, from the 1st day of January to the 1st day of January succeeding; or

2dly. That the appropriation of each year was to be considered as operating by the *Congressional year,* that is, from the 4th day of March to the 4th day of March succeeding;—or

3dly. That the appropriation of each year was to be considered as operating by the *Presidential year,* that is, from the 30th day of April, when the President qualified into office, and commenced his services, to the 30th of April following;—or

4thly. That these four several acts of appropriation were to be taken together, and considered as forming an *aggregate appropriation* for payment of the President's legal compensation, during the whole of his first term of service.

And yet, sir, it is no less remarkable than true, that by every one of these rules construction, you have violated the appropriation acts of Congress, and paid to the President, money out of the public treasury, for which, *at the time of payment,* there was not *an existing appropriation* to authorize the same; and thus I prove it.

On the 31st of December 1790, taking it by the *Calendar year,* your official report to Congress of the receipts and expenditures of the public money ; pages 16 and 17, shew that you had then paid to the President, 4264 dollars, more than he was legally entitled to, up to the day, and consequently, that by this rule of construction, the appropriation was violated.

On the 4th of March 1791, taking it by the *Congressional year,* the same official reports shew, that you had then paid to the President, 5537 dollars, more than he was legally entitled to, up to that day; and, consequently, that by this rule of construction, the appropriation was violated.

On the 30th of April 1791, taking it by the *Presidential year,* the same official reports shew, that you had then paid to the President, 5150 dollars, more than he was legally entitled to, up to that day; and, consequently, that by this rule of construction, the appropriation was violated.

On the day the President's first term of service expired, viz. the 3d day of March 1793, taking the several acts together, and as forming *one aggregate appropriation,* it will be seen by the same official report, that you had then paid to the President 1037 dollars more than he was legally entitled to, up to this day; and, consequently, that by this rule of construction, the appropriation was violated.

But, sir, if it were possible, for the most blind and devoted apologist of your conduct, to possess a remaining doubt of your guilt, let him attend to the further facts and remarks following:

Between the 4th of April 1793, and the 4th of June 1793, being the first quarter of the President's re-election into office under his present term, there was paid to him for compensation 11,000 dollars;—

By the act fixing the President's compensation, passed the 18th of February, 1793, there is allowed to him, *at the rate of* 25,000 dollars per annum, *in full for his services,* to be paid at the Treasury *quarter yearly.*

By the act of appropriation for the support of government for the year 1793, there is appropriated 25,000 dollars "for the compensation *granted by law* to the President of the United States."

Now, sir, the compensation *granted by law* was at the rate of 25,000 dollars per annum, in *full for services,* payable at the Treasury *quarter yearly;* and, consequently, the appropriation of 25,000 dollars, which was made for a whole year's services, could not be paid otherwise than *quarter yearly,* as the services accrued; that is, 6250 dollars, at the end of each quarter, and no more. When, therefore, sir, you paid to the President 11,000 dollars, *in one quarter,* you expressly and positively violated the appropriation of Congress, and actually paid to the President, 4750 dollars on account of compensation, for which, *at the time of payment*, there was not an *existing appropriation* to justify it.

Further, sir, the compensation of all the executive and judicial officers of the government are provided for in the same act of appropriation, which provides for the President, and are, by law *expressly ordered* to be paid at the Treasury *quarter yearly*; that is, at the end of each quarter, *after, and not before* the services have been rendered; And you know, that the constant, uniform and invariable practice, at the Treasury, has been *except in the case of the President*, to pay them in that manner, and not otherwise.

Indeed, sir, it would look like insult, under any other circumstances than the present, to remind the head of the Treasury Department, that a contrary conduct, such as you have adopted in the case of the President, would not only be in violation of the laws of compensation and appropriation, but, moreover, productive of confusion, distress and bankruptcy at the treasury: Since the appropriation for the support of government is made payable out of the accruing duties of each year; and an established right in the officers of government to claim their compensations which amount to several hundred dollars per annum, either on the first day of the year, or on the first day of a quarter, before the services were rendered, would create a demand at a time, when there might not, and possibly would not be, a single shilling in the Treasury, arising out of that appropriation to satisfy it.

The foregoing facts and reflections, sir, are addressed to you; and altho' I believe they cannot more fully confirm those convictions of your own guilt, with which you are impressed, and would, therefore, in that view, have been withheld; yet, sir, respect for the public opinion, to which the verity of the charges against you is submitted, has induced me to offer them.

Nor, sir, can I close the correspondence with you on this subject, without remarking that the charges which I have adduced against the President, the late Secretary of the Treasury and yourself, are of solemn and serious import; that they were not lightly and trivially made, nor are, or will be, lightly and trivially supported before any tribunal, which jointly or severally you dare appeal to; that, specifically repeated, they stand as follows:

1st. A violation of the laws of appropriation by Congress;

2dly. A violation of the laws granting compensation to the President, for his services;

3dly. A violation of the Constitution of the United States, in various parts and clauses of it; and

4thly. A violation of your several and respective oaths of office.

Finally, sir, whilst, I know of no *crime or misdemeanor* against the Constitution and the laws, *greater or higher* than that which you have severally committed, I confide in the paramount justice of my country, and the perfect integrity of those constituted authorities, with whom the power of impeachment resides, that the 4th section of the second article of the Constitution, which provides "that the *President*, Vice President, and all civil officers of the United States, shall be removed from office, on *impeachment for*, and *conviction of*, treason, bribery, *or other high crimes and misde-meanors*," was not made in vain, or is to be regarded by the people of the United States, as a mere dead letter.

A CALM OBSERVER.
November 2, 1795.

TR (*AURORA* (PHILADELPHIA), NOVEMBER 5, 1795).

JOHN BECKLEY TO JAMES MONROE

My Dear Sir,   Philadelphia, 14th December 1795.

I take occasion to introduce to you my friend Mr. James Smith,[1] who has been about two years in our Western Country in pursuit of Lands, and now visits Europe in search of a good Market. He will come to Paris first, and then proceed to the Low Countries and Elsewhere as circumstances may direct. Any notice or countenance you can consistently afford him will be an obligation to me.

Congress commenced its Session on Monday last and my reelection as Clerk of the HRepts. was the first essay of party, and in the absence of 23 of my friends a vote was taken, of 30 against me, and 48 in my favor.[2] Mr. Tazewell, who lives with me during the Session, writes you very fully by an opportunity that offers thro' Mr. Adet, and I refer you to him for explana-tion generally, as also for Randolph's vindication &c. &c.

The bearer hereof is an agent from Ireland In whom you may confide. His object is to obtain of France aid in favor of his distressed country. What that aid shod. be & the manner of giving it he will mention. The French I am told will aid the business by a secret donation to his nation. You will act in this man as you deem best. His name is Teobald Wolfetone. He is the friend of Hamilton, Randolph, and a person in [*whom*] his countrymen fully confide.[3]

Decypher this by our friend Madisons cypher.

Yours truly & sincerely,
John Beckley

RC (MONROE PAPERS, NEW YORK PUBLIC LIBRARY).

1. The bearer, James Smith, was identified by Beckley in the encyphered section of this letter as the Irish revolutionary leader, Theobald Wolfe Tone, who as founder of the outlawed Society of the United Irish had been exiled from Dublin. Upon reaching Paris, Tone quickly presented this letter to Monroe, who according to Tone's later testimony assisted him in the early preparations for his failed attempt to invade Ireland. See the postscript to the next document; Berkeley, *Beckley*, pp. 130–31; and Ammon, *Monroe*, p. 135.

2. *Journal of the House of Representatives, Fourth Congress* (Washington: Gales and Seaton, 1826), p. 365 and *Debates and Proceedings, Fourth Congress*, p. 126.

3. This paragraph was written by Beckley in cypher, and decoded in the hand of Monroe.

JOHN BECKLEY TO JAMES MONROE

My dear Sir,   Philadelphia 2d April 1796.

I snatch a moment to enclose you a few papers and drop a line, per favor of an opportunity this moment communicated to be by Mr. Gernon. On the 24th ulto. our house requested the correspondence, Instructions &c. as to British treaty by a vote of 62 to 37—and you will see the presidents refusal & <u>reasons</u> for it among the enclosed—his Message is committed to Wednesday next and also a motion of Kitchell enclosed. What will be the result I know not; you know the force of Executive influence united with British, fiscal &c. I <u>fear</u> the B. Treaty will be carried into effect; it will not, however, without some vote asserting the Constitutional power of the House.[1] Fitzsimons & Innes (of Virga.) are appd. commissioners under the 6th Article—Knox for the 5th—and Gore of Boston & Pinckney of Maryland for the 7th.[2]

A meeting of the republicans will be had this evening to consider what is best to be done; there appears a disposition to make a firm stand, and I think that should the treaty take effect <u>at all</u>, it will be by a very small majority. I cannot add more at present for fear of losing the present opportunity. Mr. Madison has recd. yours of 26th Jany. but one preceeding that & to which you refer is not come to hand. Be pleased to acknowledge rect. of this as it will serve to regulate my future transmission of papers &c.

Yrs. Sincerely,
J. Beckley.

[*P.S.*] We have just heard of Smith alias T——s[3] arrival at Harve the 1st February.

RC (MONROE PAPERS, NEW YORK PUBLIC LIBRARY).

1. Washington's message of March 30 rejecting the House request for all documents related to the Jay Treaty and Aaron Kitchell's resolutions asserting the constitutional right of the House of Representatives to approve all laws implementing treaties were focal points of the debate on the Jay Treaty which occupied the representatives for part of nearly every day of the first session of the Fourth Congress. See *Debates and Proceedings, Fourth Congress*, pp. 428 ffl; *Journal of the House, Fourth Congress*, pp. 487ffl; and Carroll and Ashworth, *Washington*, pp. 345–85.

2. For commissioners required by the treaty, Washington nominated Henry Knox of Massachusetts for Article 5, Thomas FitzSimons of Pennsylvania and James Innes of Virginia for Article 6, and Christopher Gore of Massachusetts and William Pinkney of Maryland for Article 7. Carroll and Ashworth, *Washington*, p. 357n.120.

3. That is, Theobold Wolfe Tone; for Beckley's introduction of the Irish revolutionary to Monroe, see the preceding document.

JOHN BECKLEY TO DEWITT CLINTON

Dear Sir,   Philadelphia, 11th April 1796.

Altho not among the first I am not among the least sincere of those who offer you their congratulations on the late happy change in your condition of life,[1] and you will permit me to add, that should any circumstance of business or of pleasure induce Mrs. Clinton & yourself to visit our City, it will afford Mrs. Beckley and myself much happiness to welcome you at our habitation during your stay with the best accomodation we have at No. 96 South Eighth Street.

The interruption to our past correspondence has had <u>sufficient cause</u> on your part, and on mine has resulted more from sickness and the recent interruptions of my public avocations than from choice or the remotest wish to discontinue it.[2]

In seeking how to renew it, you will perceive in the delicacy of the present communication my <u>undiminished</u> confidence in your good disposition to cooperate with me <u>in all things pro bono publico</u> and for promoting the best interests of the common cause of republicanism. Hitherto all has gone well with us, and the firm, but temperate conduct of the H. of Rpts. reflects dignity whilst it ensures success to the Republican cause. Still, however, much remains to do, and when we rejoice at the failure and misconduct of our officials, we must not cease our exertions in a case where "nought is done, while ought remains to do." The questions of adopting, rejecting or suspending the British treaty are still unacted upon. The object of the republicans appears to be to resolve explicitly "that it is inexpedient to pass the necessary laws for giving it effect" and by way of inducement to recite some of the most weighty objections to it. Such a proposition will certainly be offered, and I think obtain by a Majority. But we are not without fears that some of our republican friends may want the necessary stamina to carry them thro' and more particularly from your State; hence, my previous hint of the delicacy of my present communication, since I know not another person, but yourself, to whom I would suggest a doubt as to our friends Bailey, Van Cortlandt, and Havens on the final question—And yet my friend, such doubts do strongly exist, resulting as I have understood more from their respective situation in their districts than from any other cause. Elected by small majorities, and doubtful from the present circumstances of your state how the political scale will preponderate at another Election, they perhaps wish to steer that course which will best ensure their reelection. So often & so fatally my friend do personal, supersede public considerations.

You can best judge of, and will I am sure pursue <u>the most Earnest</u> means to keep our three friends in the true course. If they go right, the British treaty will infallibly be rejected. But remember whatever is done, <u>must be</u>

done quickly. You possibly know their political characters, and from whence they can be best encouraged and supported.[3]

Another object that requires immediate attention is the appointment of Electors in your State and in this—Here we are pursuing it with pointed attention. With you I understand it must wholly depend on the complection of your next legislature; the Elections to which are now depending. Mr. Washington has at length publicly declared at his own house, that he will not serve again; and I find that State politicks is now the last hope of the Hamilton faction in the choice of a new president. This, they will endeavor to play off, with all possible art and intrigue. It may be truly considered as their forlorn hope. If the Treaty is rejected, it will doubtless operate well in those States where the appointment of Electors is given to the people and does not come on speedily. In other cases, the friends of republicanism must redouble their exertions to counteract their opponents. The British treaty defeated, and a republican president to succeed Mr. Washington, and our Country is yet safe, prosperous and happy.

The State of Europe seems to render another campaign inevitable, and thus we devise an argument in answer to the terrors of a British War held out by the Treaty faction. It would seem as if France was decreed to fight our battles for us, for if England was disentangled from her war with the Republic she might in reality hold up the terms of it to frighten us into the adoption of her detestable treaty.

How does the public sentiment progress in your State—since the presidents' unmasked claim of absolute & unlimitted power, as set forth in his refusal of the papers? Think you not, that reflecting men will universally protest against it? And if so, that the effect of it both on him and his administration, will be, however "slow, sure & inevitable."

I shall promise myself the pleasure of an early answer to this letter, and must request you to bear my warm respects to your Uncle, Governor Clinton, and to our friends Mr. Osgood, General Lamb & Commodore Nicholson—being with great regard, dear Sir, Your friend & Servt.   John Beckley

RC (CLINTON PAPERS, COLUMBIA UNIVERSITY).

1. On February 13, 1796, Clinton had married Maria Franklin, daughter of New York merchant Walter Franklin.
2. The last letter of Beckley to Clinton, which has been found is dated September 13, 1795.
3. On the key vote on April 30, 1796, "that it is expedient to pass the laws necessary for carrying into effect the treaty lately negotiated between the United States and Great Britain," New York representatives Theodorus Bailey and Philip Van Cortland voted to carry the treaty into effect, while Jonathan Havens voted with the Republican opposition. *Debates and Proceedings, Fourth Congress*, p. 1291; *Journal of the House, Fourth Congress*, pp. 530–31.

JOHN BECKLEY TO DEWITT CLINTON

Dear Sir,   Philadelphia, 21st April. 1796.

Your acceptable favour of the 16th came to hand yesterday, and I feel myself indebted for the communication it contains. Our three friends are certainly wavering, and I sincerely wish may acquire the requisite firmness. I think it probable that there will be a majority without them, but you know how desirable it is to have that Majority as large and respectable as possible. Every means to intimidate and take off from that majority is in operation and I confess I do not approve of procrastinating the question, delays are always dangerous and in a case like the present give too much opportunity for cabel and intrigue. We have passed the Spanish and Indian Treaties in two seperate bills and sent them to the Senate, who, it is well known, intend to keep them until the decision of the British treaty is had, when, if that be rejected, they mean to consolidate all the Treaties into one Bill and send it down in that form by Way of amendment—they also mean to keep the Bill for sale of Western lands, the Bill for a loan to the City of Washington, the pay bill, appropriation for the Army &c. by way of hostage to coerce the House into an adoption of the B. treaty. I think however that a Major. vote, once obtained & recorded vs. the treaty, it will be extremely difficult to change, and in this view, your elections which I am told come next tuesday will be greatly important, if favorable to the republican side, in confirming the timid & wavering. Doubtless every exertion will be made by the true friends of republicanism and of the treaty, the crisis is deeply important, and from the influence it must have as well upon the treaty, as upon the future choice of a president, it will I hope and trust call forth all the energies of patriotism. It will be Sir not less encouraging than worthy of example in your city, that we have exhibited such strength and patriotism here on this day, the monocrats prin[ciple pet]itions in favor of the treaty, which you will See in the Gazettes of the Day, and after . . . [1] artifice, and influence with the clamour of War, disunion &c. and the aid of . . . [2] our part. Exhibited about 600 of all descriptions of Character and the other including Clerks, draymen, tide waiters &c &c 800 making together 1400—and the same Moment one of the opposition petitions praying to reject the treaty was presented with upwards of 1500 signers, and another will be presented to morrow with about 2000 more. Thus, if the voice of the people can influence, we have or shall have at least three to one. I hope your City will not be behind us in exertion on this occasion. I think it probable a question on the treaty will be taken tomorrow, I will immediately apprise you of the event. In the Interim, I shall be glad of any thing from yo. worth communicating, and am, with great respect, Dr. Sir. Yrs. Sincerely,

John Beckley

RC (CLINTON PAPERS, COLUMBIA UNIVERSITY).

1. Manuscript torn, one word missing.
2. Manuscript torn, one word missing.

JOHN BECKLEY TO EPHRAIM KIRBY

Sir,[1]   Philadelphia 10 June 1796.

Your favor of the 5th this Moment came to hand. Inclosed is a certificate which I hope will answer your purpose; Mr. Lee, the Attorney General is absent on a trip to Virginia.

The continuance of the European War and the certainty of its extension among the Northern powers, will, it is said, divert large sums of money & Goods, from Hamburg & other places, to this Country, for investitures in our Lands. Advices of this nature, by the last arrivals, have stated good lands here 10 cents per acre.

Yrs. with regard,   John Beckley

RC (KIRBY PAPERS, DUKE UNIVERSITY). ADDRESSED: "EPHRAIM KIRBY, ESQUIRE, COUNSELLOR AT LAW, LITCHFIELD, CONNECTICUT. (FREE, J. BECKLEY)"

1. Ephraim Kirby (1757–1804) practiced law and republican politics in Litchfield, Connecticut to 1803. He collaborated with Beckley in land speculation and support for Jeffersonian Republicans. Beckley had written letters of May 7 and June 3, 1796, to Kirby concerning his acting as agent for the sale of Beckley's 37,952 acres in Kentucky and 5,558 acres in Greenbriar, Virginia. (Kirby Papers, Duke University).

JOHN BECKLEY TO JAMES MADISON

Dear Sir,   Philadephia, 20th June 1796.

A few days ago a barrel of hams arrived to your address, which I immediately took into possession and had them opened—there were twelve apparently sound hams, which I have had hung up to dry & smoke. If it is agreeable to you, as I think it doubtful that they would keep 'till the winter, I will take them for my familys use and pay you the price of them, when we meet again, or in any other way you may advise. They came in a Vessel from Norfolk, the name I could not discover.

The president left this on Monday last for Mount Vernon. When Hamilton was here, he lodged at Francis's Hotel, and our friend Brown extracted from him, that the president does not mean to resign, but merely to decline a reelection, and that to make known this intention, he designs about the Month of August to publish an address to the People. We may presume whose pen will indite it, and what views & principles it will be designed to propagate;[1] happily however the controul of events is less within the power than the wish of the American Catiline, and I shall not be surprised to see the address predicated on an anticipated State of things at the time of the Election, which taking a contrary issue in the event, may wholly frustrate a well-scheemed object. In Massachusetts the attempt to appoint Electors by the Legislature has failed & it is to be as heretofore, one in each Congressional district to be elected by the people, and two (for the Senators) by the Legislature. Mr. Jefferson, is already in nomination, and Swan who is now here, says that one half will vote for Mr. Jefferson, along with Mr. Adams, on the true Yankee ground, that the former will make an unexceptionable Vice president. Swan, seems very earnest & sanguine, and says that before the election he intends to publish with his name, certain damning proofs, now in his possession, of Adams's Monarchism & Aristocratism. It is also an idea strongly urged by Swan, to play off Chancellor Livingston for V. p. upon New York & Jersey, as the most likely means of a successful diversion there. He is however strongly in favor of Burrs election. In this State, Gallatin, Rittenhouse the Ch. Justice,[2] General Irvine (who was here a few days ago) and in short the whole body of Republicans are decided in favor of Burr. Mr. Brown has carried the same impression to Kentuckey, and Blount & Cocke to Tennessee. No. Carolina & Georgia you know to be fixed. Colo. Hampton says the treatment of Rutledge & the obnoxious idea of nominating Pinkney by the Aristocrats, will he thinks ensure the vote of the lower districts of S. C. for the republican ticket & the upper districts he never doubted. Maryland, I have little hope from, as their Assembly will appoint the Electors. Upon the whole however, if no great Schism happens in Virginia, I think it morally certain that Mr. Jefferson and Colo. Burr will be elected. Indeed, as Hamilton admitted to Brown, there may be a state of things in which it would be desirable that Mr. J. should be elected without opposition, an idea which I beleive to be founded on the Presidents firm persuasion, that the Southern States will never consent to a War with France, and that in such an event on the Part of France, which they admit they beleive to be inevitable, Mr. J's influence could alone preserve the Union, and produce a favorable termination of the breach. I discover too, that whilst the resentful & even hostile temper of the French Government, is beleived by our Executive to have taken deep root, they think, & most probably with truth, that France will choose & await, the most favorable moment for herself, amidst the events of Europe, for speaking to us in a Style suitable to her views & intentions. What the state of Europe really is, seems uncertain from our last advices, altho' the probability of a peace between France & Austria, and of a Union in the War between Spain & France *vs* Britain, strengthens every hour. A junction of the Spanish, Dutch & French Marines, will be extremely formidable, & most probably too powerful for England. It is beleived here, that Jamaica will certainly be attacked, wch. fully corrobates the idea of Spains union with France. At Saint Lucia, the British have sustained a third defeat with the loss of 1400 men; in the three attempts we may fairly estimate their loss at 4 to 5000 killed & wounded; thus exhausting their force in an immaterial conquest, will completely disable them from any great or effectual operations; besides the reinforcements France has sent out & which have all safely arrived at St. Domingo, forbid all further hope of success on the part of England in the W. Indies—she can only act, hereafter, on the defensive.

In Massachusetts, Strong & Cabot have both resigned, and Goodhue & Sedgwick are elected in their room until the 4th of March next. A Mr. Robbins was elected in preference to both, but refused to serve.[3] New York Assembly is wholly Jayite. Wadsworth is to succeed Trumbull—they talk of Harrison to succeed King, and Watts to Burr.[4]

I have delivered the packets for Mr. Monroe as you desired.

I omitted to mention before, the arrival of a Dutch fleet in the West Indies, which on their passage captured a large proportion of the outward bound Cork fleet, and are now said to be retaking the Dutch islands seized on by the British.

Pickering has received a letter from Monroe of 21st March,[5] announcing that he had been officially notified by the Executive directory, that they had relinquished their determination to send a Special Commissioner: this I learn thro' Mr. Adet, to whom it was indirectly communicated by Pickering, and as Adet has no late dispatches, he supposes something may have been done to pacify & divert Monroes suspicions & fears in consequence of their first notification. He still thinks they mean to act with great decision, altho' their demands will not be immoderate.

The president returned to town suddenly last night, supposed, to receive the Spanish Minister plenipotentiary.[6] Mr. Adet, designs to visit Mr. Jefferson this Summer and will set off in a few weeks. I will apprise you when.

Quere—May not Strong & Cabot design to become Electors, and if a suitable Election prevail thro' Massachusetts, to suddenly nominate & by their influence carry Hamilton in that State? Rh. island, Vermont, Connecticut, New York, Jersey, & Maryland, would all probably follow very unanimously. Some late indications seem to warrant the Suspicion. Hamilton himself industriously propagates that Adams & Pinckney are their choice. In any event, every precaution should be used to prevent a Schism in Virginia, where every effort will be made to produce it. Even the presidents personal influence I doubt not will be used, and his residence at Mount Vernon thro' the Summer will conduce not a little to the object. Every effort, and all possible industry of the true friends of republicanism will be requisite. The presidents cast of temper may be collected from this, a few days ago, Governor Blount offered to shew him letters from Paris stating the hostile disposition of the French Government towards us; he answered with great Asperity "I am informed of & beleive your information to be true, but if War comes, it originated here, not there. The people of this Country it would seem, will never be satisfied until they become a department of France: It shall be my business to prevent it."

I guess I have sufficiently tired you with my desultory scrawl, and being at the bottom of my paper, bid you adieu—being very sincerely, dear Sir, Yours,

John Beckley

[*P.S.*] Mrs. B. & all this family desire best regards to Mrs. Madison & Miss Payne.

RC (MADISON PAPERS, NEW YORK PUBLIC LIBRARY).

1. For the role of Madison, as well as the predominant role of Hamilton, in the drafting of Washington's "Farewell Address," see Syrett, ed., *Hamilton Papers*, 20:169–83; and Stagg, ed., *Madison Papers*, 16: 355–56, 373n. 2.

2. That is, Thomas McKean. For a detailed discussion of the 1796 campaign for presidential electors in Pennsylvania, see Tinkcom, *Republicans and Federalists in Pennsylvania*, pp. 159–74; and Cunningham, *Jeffersonian Republicans*, pp. 89–115.

3. Theodore Sedgwick and Benjamin Goodhue, members of the House from Massachusetts, were elected by the Massachusetts legislature to the Senate in the place of Caleb Strong and George Cabot.

4. In Connecticut Uriah Tracy, rather than Jeremiah Wadsworth was chosen to replace Jonathan Trumbull in the Senate.

In New York John Laurance was elected to the Senate in the place of Rufus King, minister to Great Britain. Aaron Burr retained his seat in the Senate, but neither Richard Harrison nor John Watts was chosen by the legislature.

5. Although Beckley was repeating the report of Adet, the French minister, that Secretary Pickering had received "lettres de Mr. Monroe en date du 21 Mars," it is clear from Adet's report that he was referring to Monroe's March 10 letter in which Monroe had announced the French decision not to send an envoy extraordinary. Monroe Papers, Library of Congress, and Turner, ed. *Correspondence of the French Ministers to the United States, 1791–1797*, p. 922.

6. Carlos Fernando de Yrujo (1763–1824) was the newly arrived minister from Spain.

JOHN BECKLEY TO WILLIAM IRVINE

Dear General,[1]   Philadelphia 15th September 1796.

I was disappointed in writing you by the last post, by an entire mistake of the post day. We reached home on Monday the 5th; after a very fatiguing Journey, and happily had our anxiety relieved by finding all our friends well. Maria, wrote to Mrs. Irvin, by the way of Harrisburg on Monday last, enclosing some lace & other Matters, but I told her then that I greatly feared it would not come to hand. I very much regretted not having the pleasure of seeing you before we left Carlisle, but the uncertainty of your return and in great anxiety at not hearing from home for two posts, must apologize for our abrupt departure, since it was impossible that any body could be happier than we were with Mrs. Irvin and all your amiable family. I am informed that nothing farther can be traced from the Virginia records, respecting your claim to the Island. If you think of any farther enquiry I will cheerfully pursue it for you.

The president has at last concluded to decline a reelection, and has forwarded on to the Governor of each State a notification thereof, to be published in each State at the same time, so that we may expect to see it published here about the 1st of next month.[2] You will readily perceive that this short Notice is designed to prevent a fair Election, and the consequent choice of Mr. Jefferson. It will not however produce that effect, if your State make but a reasonable exertion—the general sentiment is in favor of Jefferson, and I think a little exertion by a few good active republicans in each county would bring the people out, and defeat the influence of your little rotten towns such as Carlisle, Lancaster, York &c. A Silent, but certain Cooperation among the country people may do much. In my next I will send you a list of the republican Electors, that have been agreed upon for this State, and hope you will be able to scatter a few copies thro' some proper hands. It will not be forgotten that no ticket must be printed.[3] From Georgia, No. Carolina, South Carolina, Virginia, Kentuckey, & Tennessee we expect a unanimous Vote—half Maryland, & Delaware—some in New Jersey, and several to the Eastward. So that if Pennsylvania do well the Election is safe. In the City & County we expect to carry the republican ticket by a large Majority. Have you any western friends that you can drop a line to, to assist us? What seemed to be the sentiment, if any, in the Country you passed thro'? Cannot an effectual Exertion be made? It is now or never for the republican cause. We have no foreign news of late date. Our joint love to all your family. Your sincere friend,   John Beckley

RC (IRVINE PAPERS, HISTORICAL SOCIETY OF PENNSYLVANIA).

1. See Beckley to Madison, August 1, 1792, note 7.
2. Washington's Farewell Address was first published on September 19 in *Claypoole's American Daily Advertiser* (Philadelphia).
3. Under the state law adopted April 1, 1796, each voter was required to write in the names of up to 15 electors.

JOHN BECKLEY TO WILLIAM IRVINE

Dear General,   Philadelphia, 22d September 1796.

Since my last I am particularly desired by Doctor Jackson, to inform you that the Comptroller General of the State has advised him that there will probably arise a considerable ballance against John Nicholson, late Comptroller for arrearages in that Office, due to the public, and that as one of his securities you stand responsible. The Doctor thinks that if you contemplate a trip down here shortly, the sooner you make it the better. I lose no time in giving you the information as Nicholson is in a situation at least to indemnify you.[1]

By this mail you will receive the presidents address of declension to serve again, and I enclose you a list of the Electors agreed to here, just before the Assembly adjourned. Governor Mifflin's name being added in the room of Mr. Rittenhouse, deceased; the Governor is as fully eligible as Judge McKean, and it is believed his name will greatly assist the ticket. I shall decline, until I have the pleasure to see you, any remarks on the presidents address, and only say that we have every assurance of success in favour of Mr. Jefferson to the Southward. How it will be to the Eastward I am not yet informed. Your state must decide it, and I hope every exertion will be made. A few copies of the lists of the Electors with the names plainly written, dispersed in a few judicious hands in the Country, and copies of them scattered about in different neighbourhoods, would do great good, if the people are warned of the day, and a few popular men will endeavor to bring them out. By next post I will endeavor to send you some handbills, by way of address to the people of Pennsylvania, shewing the strong reasons there is for this States having a Southern rather than an Eastern president.

There is a report that the King of England is dead, and that England has sent overtures to France to make an immediate peace with her.

Maria joins me in affectionate regards to Mrs. Irvine, Nancy &c. all your family, as do all of ours. With the truest regard, I am, dear General, Yr. friend & Servant   John Beckley

P.S. The Governor declines being put on the ticket of Electors. No name is yet concluded on in his room; it will be either Charles Biddle, or Thomas Barclay. tomorrow it will be decided & by tuesday mail I will inform you.

Thomas McKean, Cheif Justice	William Irvine, Cumberland
Jacob Morgan, County of Philadelphia	Abraham Smith, Franklin
Jonas Hartsell, Northampton	William Brown, Mifflin
Peter Muhlenberg, Montgomery	John Piper, Bedford
Joseph Heister, Berks	John Smilie, Fayette
William McClay, Dauphin	James Edgar, Washington
James Hanna, Bucks	
John Whitehill, Lancaster	

RC (IRVINE PAPERS, HISTORICAL SOCIETY OF PENNSYLVANIA).

1. See Beckley to Irvine, October 4, 1796.

JOHN BECKLEY TO WILLIAM IRVINE

Dear Sir,   Philadelphia, 30th September 1796.

I enclose you a complete list of the ticket for Electors, and by next mail or before, I will forward you a dozen or two hand bills on the same subject. By every information we can get Mr. Jefferson will have a unanimous Vote in every Southern State, except Maryland, and there about half. To the East-ward of the North river, we count certain on Eight votes, perhaps more. Rhode Island will be with us, two in New Hampshire—three or 4 in Massa-chusetts, and one or two in Vermont and Connecticut. If Pennsylvania stirs the business is safe. It was not possible to get a character of the two tickets as you suggested, but I think something as good will be done. We shall elect to Congress Swanwick for the City, and General Morgan for the City. Fred. Muhlenberg will be dropped as he richly merits. Pet. Muhlenberg will be elected for Montgomery. It will be a hard race between Sitgreaves and Richards. Further up the country I am not informed.[1]

I have heard nothing from Virginia. Mr. Lewis, has been absent from the City, when he returns I will inquire of him as you request. Maria will pur-chase the Quilt for Mrs. Irwin, and will write her as soon as it is procured. With our joint regards. We are dear Sir,   Yours truly,

                                                    J Beckley

RC (IRVINE PAPERS, HISTORICAL SOCIETY OF PENNSYLVANIA).

1. For the results of the congressional elections in Pennsylvania, see Beckley to Madison, October 15, 1796, note 4 and to Irvine, October 17, 1796, note 2.

JOHN BECKLEY TO WILLIAM IRVINE

Dear General,   Philadelphia, 4th October 1796.

I am very happy to contradict the Idea of your having been one of John Nicholsons Securities, I went as you desired to Dallas's Office and find that James and Mathew Irwin are the names of two of his Securities, along with Doctor Jackson, Doctor Binney & two others, but your name does not appear.

Inclosed are 6 copies of an address to the people of Pennsylvania—by next mail on friday, or by first certain opportunity will forward you 100 more. It would be most advisable however to push them on over the Moun-tain, before they are circulated below, which will prevent any counter address—1000 Copies are struck & will be dispersed in such manner that they may appear first above, before they can come back to the City. Mr. Jef-

View of federal edifice (New York) 1789.
LC–USZ62–45577.

ferson, has explicitly declared that if elected he will serve, and Mr. Patrick Henry, of Virginia, has as explicitly that he neither wishes nor would accept the office. I am this moment advised by a Letter from New York, that Mr. Hamilton publickly declares, that he thinks it would be best on the score of conciliation & expediency to elect Mr. Jefferson, president, since he is the only man in America that could secure us the affections of the French republic. Will it not be advisable to throw this paragraph into the Carlisle paper?

It is too late now to make a change in the Electors. The Aristocrats say themselves that the Republican ticket is by far the best, and believe it will carry. Many of them prefer Pinkney to Adams, and there will be great Schism amongst them. Our accounts South & East, look Well, and we have hopes in New Jersey. By Fridays mail I will write you again. Maria has purchased Mrs. Irvines quilt and will write her fully on friday. Our affectionate regards to every body.   Yours truly,   John Beckley

RC (IRVINE PAPERS, HISTORICAL SOCIETY OF PENNSYLVANIA).

JOHN BECKLEY TO TENCH COXE[1]

10th Octor. 96

Enclosed are Hamiltons precious confessions.[2] Be pleased to preserve every scrap; they are <u>truly</u> original and <u>authenticated</u> by himself. Yrs. J.B.

RC (COXE PAPERS, HISTORICAL SOCIETY OF PENNSYLVANIA).

1. Tench Coxe (1755–1824), a Philadelphia merchant, land speculator, and assistant secretary of the treasury, was a recent convert to Republicanism from the ranks of Federalist officeholders. Coxe was a frequent author of pamphlets and newspaper essays on the American economy and American politics.

2. "Hamiltons precious confessions" were undoubtedly part of the group of documents acquired by House Speaker Muhlenberg, Senator Monroe, and Representative Venable in the December 1792 investigation of Hamilton's involvment in the "Reynolds affair" and intended to be transmitted to President Washington. Beckley and his clerk Bernard Webb had been employed by these congressional investigators to make copies of the documents they acquired. Obviously Beckley had retained a copy.

These papers implicating Hamilton in this finance and sex scandal were kept out of the public prints for nearly five years, but in June 1797 James Thomson Callender published several of them in Number V of his *History of the United States in 1796*. Contemporaries and recent scholars have generally seen the hand of Beckley in their release. This brief note indicates that Beckley probably used Coxe as the conduit for their release to Callender.

Perhaps the most direct contemporary evidence of Beckley's responsiblity for the release of the scandalous documents, beyond Beckley's own note and the fact that the documents were in Webb's hand, is in a December 1, 1797, letter of Monroe, who narrowly had avoided a duel with Hamilton over his refusal to deny a role in the release of these documents, to Aaron Burr, who had served as his representative in replying to Hamilton's challenge. Refering to the papers regarding the Reynolds Affair, Monroe wrote: "You know I presume that Beckley published the papers in question. By his clerk they were copied for us. It was his clerk who carried a copy to H. who asked (as B. says) whether others were privy to the affr.—the clerk replied that B. was, upon wh. H. desired him to tell B. he considered him bound not to disclose it. B. replied by the same clerk that he considered himself under no injunction whatever—that if H. had any thing to say to him it must be in writing. This from B.—most certain however it is that after our interview with H. I requested B. to say nothing abt. it & keep it secret—& most certain it is that I never heard of it afterwards till my arrival when it was published." Kline, ed., *Burr Papers*, 1:319.

For a detailed examination of the Reynolds' Affair see Syrett, ed., *Hamilton Papers*, 21:121–285; Boyd, ed., *Jefferson Papers*, 18:611–88; Cooke, *Coxe*, pp. 283–84; and Berkeley, *Beckley*, pp. 161–73.

JOHN BECKLEY TO JAMES MADISON

Dear Sir,   Philadelphia, 15th October 1796.

I received your favor of the 1st instant, covering one for Colo. M.[1] which I shall forward to morrow; the mystery of his recall is not developed here, and can only be resolved into the personal hatred of Hamilton to Mr. M. and Mr. J.—and the intrigue of enlisting the interest of the Pinckney family, in the appointment of the president; and you may be assured that neither Hamilton or Jay, wish the appointment of Adams, tho' this is a card they are constrained to play with great caution. In last evenings Gazettee (Fenno) Hamilton[2] makes his first appearance under signature of *Phocion* No. 1, in a systematic attack on Mr. Jefferson; one or two Numbers more will unfold his plan more fully; but you will observe a marked caution in the first number not to aid the pretensions of Adams; a military character is declared essential. I do not think this effort will produce any great public impression in this State, for which it is intended; whilst at the same time I consider it as an Evidence of fear on their part. Great exertions are making in this state by the republicans to carry their Electoral ticket for J. & B.[3] and we are very sanguine of Success. Indeed our late victory in Swanwicks reelection, the putting out Muhlenberg and electing B. McClanahan in his room inspires us with confidence.[4] Three weeks hence we will tell you more about it. I cannot discover much from the Eastward, we are however told that 6 votes at least will be had East of Jersey. Burr has been out electioneering these six weeks in Connecticut, Vermont, R. Island & Massachts., but I doubt his efforts are more directed to himself than any body else. You well know him; would it not be prudent to vote one half of Virga. for Clinton? Consider this. If we succeed in our ticket in this State, every vote will be right, and we have very great hopes. 30,000 tickets are gone thro' the State, by Express, into every County.

Respecting foreign news, the prospect of Spanish War encreases every hour. The decree of the Executive directory to seize all neutrals bound to or from British ports, has created universal consternation. Insurance houses are all shut up. Flour fell three dollars a barrel. Upwards of 50 seizures in the W. Indies, and several in Europe. No bills on Europe or England to be bought, one half those last drawn returned. No Money. Every body crying distress.

I have endeavored with great industry to procure you a house, but find it absolutely impossible. Mr. Habersham, post master, had partly promised me his, but finds it impracticable to procure another. Rents are advanced 50 per cent, and before a house is finished, or an old one given up, it is taken. I do not think a house of any description can be got. I have assayed in at least a dozen instances without success.[5]

RC (MADISON PAPERS, NEW YORK PUBLIC LIBRARY).

1. That is, James Monroe, who had been recalled as minister to France by Washington in August because of his outspoken opposition to the Jay Treaty. Charles Cotesworthy Pinckney of South Carolina was his replacement, and was a Federalist candidate for president or vice-president in 1800.

2. Hamilton was not the author of the 25 essay series over the pseudonym "Phocion" in John Fenno's *Gazette of the United States*, but rather the author was William Loughton Smith (1758–1812), Federalist representative from South Carolina (1789–97). Beckley responded to "Phocion" over the pseudonym "A Subscriber" in an essay dated October 26, 1796, in Fenno's *Gazette* of October 29.

3. Jefferson and Burr.

4. Beckley was referring to the October 11 congressional elections in Pennsylvania, in which Republican John Swanwick won reelection and Republican Blair McClenahan captured the seat formerly held by Frederick Augustus Conrad Muhlenberg, who as Speaker of the U.S. House had cast several critical tie-breaking votes on April 30, 1796, on resolutions to implement the Jay Treaty to the House floor. See the next document, *Debates and Proceedings, Fourth Congress*, pp. 1281–92, and Baumann, "John Swanwick," pp. 167–74.

5. MS damaged; closing and signature missing.

JOHN BECKLEY TO WILLIAM IRVINE

Dear General,   Philadelphia, 17th October 1796.

By old Doctor Nesbit, I have forwarded to you a packet with hand bills, which I must tax your goodness to put under way for the Western Country, so as to reach it before the Election for Electors. You best know what characters to address them to. In a few days a select republican friend from the City will call upon you with a parcel of tickets to be distributed in your County. Any assistance and advice you can furnish him with, as to suitable district & characters, will I am sure be rendered. He is one of two republican friends, who have undertaken to ride thro' all the middle & lower counties on this business, and bring with them 6 or 8 thousand tickets. It is necessary at the same time to aid the common object by getting all our friends to write as many tickets as they can, in their respective families, before the Election. The great victory obtained here, over the united & combined force of the British & Aristocrats, gives us great confidence, and is a presage of success in the choice of Electors; to rule out Muhlenberg, who gave the casting vote for the British treaty, and elect Blair McClanahan, in his room, who recommended to kick the treaty to hell, and to reelect Swanwick against the most violent exertions ever made in this City, are sufficient to Shew that republicanism [remains][1] firm here. I hope you are and will be as firm and zealous in Cumberland. I [received] letters from Virginia which assure me that notwithstanding every Exertion of the Aristo[crats the] republicans count with certainty on an unanimous vote in favor of Jefferson [there]. Have you heard of Findley & Gallatins Elections, how did they go? Who succeeded in Cumberland? I hope they trimmed the trimmer Gregg, as they did Christie in Maryland.[2] We continue in great hopes of several Votes in the Eastern States for Jefferson, since it begins to be suspected that Pinkney & not Adams is designed by Hamilton for president. Perhaps their intrigues may benefit us.[3]

I enclose you a few copies of the ticket to disperse among such good friends, as will exert themselves, to get as many copies before the Election, as they can. I shall hope to hear from you by next mail. Mrs. B. wrote Mrs. Irvine a few days ago, when she forwarded the quilt. She & her Mother unite with me, in affectionate [regards] to Mrs. I and Miss Nancy, and I am most . . . dear General, Yrs. [truly].   John Beckley

RC (IRVINE PAPERS, HISTORICAL SOCIETY OF PENNSYLVANIA).

1. Manuscript damaged here and below. Conjectured words are in brackets.
2. William Findley, Albert Gallatin, and Andrew Gregg were all elected members of the House from Pennsylvania for the Fifth Congress. Gabriel Christie of Maryland was defeated for the Fifth Congress, but returned to the Sixth.
3. See Hamiton to Unknown, November 8, 1796, in Syrett, ed., *Hamilton Papers*, 20:376–77.

JOHN BECKLEY TO JAMES MONROE

Dear Sir,   Philadelphia, 17th October 1796.

This covers a letter from our friend Mr. M.[1] I cannot pass it on to you without a line. Your recall has been matter of surprise to us all; we do not penetrate the mystery it involves, and can only account for it from a few obvious causes, to wit, Hamiltons tenderness for you, and attachment to Jefferson; his desire to enlist Pinkney & that family interest in the intrigue of electing a Successor to old W. and a determination to render the last moments of the old Automatons public life subservient to his private resentment & personal views.[2] Of this also rest assured that Adams, if Hamilton can prevent it, without danger, is not designed as Ws.[3] Successor—Pinkney from London is the man, altho' this card they are well aware must be dexterously played. Jefferson & Adams are the only candidates publicly held up for president. Burr & Pinkney for V.P. The probability is that it will be a very close election & that this State must decide it, accordingly our republican ticket is pushing with infinite zeal & earnestness. Should it come to a choice by the H Rns—we are sure.

Our news from France is to 1st Sepr.—the late decree of the directory has agitated our British folks extremely, and greatly affected insurance & the price of provisions, the former cannot be done at all to W. Indies below 25 per cent, and the latter falls rapidly, an Embargo is talked of—our situation is extremely unpleasant, and if as is yet doubted here, the decree is rigidly to operate against us, I know not what will be done. It has been said that your remonstrance has not been successful. I believe that a general indisposition prevails to enter into any hostility with France, and that America would be happy to sever the connection with G.B. Still however I do not think we can be forced to form a new, exclusive, or disadvantagious connection with France. One principle seems to be, to have political connection in Europe, to be free to direct our commerce on terms of reciprocity with all nations, to do justice to all our past obligations of gratitude & friendship to France, and to manifest to the world that as a people we will be impartial, just, and generous.

The events of Europe succeed with such astonishing rapidity that it is no less difficult to pursue them, than to conjecture their probable consequences—peace with Germany—war between G.B. & Spain, and another campaign between France & G.B.—will add to the dilemmas of that situation in which the British politics of an un wise & perfidious President have placed the US—on the wisdom & moderation of France we shall have principally to rely.

I shall be greatly indebted, if in your power, to favour me with a line in acknowledgment of this. It will reach me in the midst of our next Congressional Session, and be greatly satisfactory to many of yr. friends. Mrs. B— desires her affectionate remembrance to your amiable lady & daughter, and may it please heaven to waft you back in peace & safety, to the bosom of a country that loves & respects you, beyond the stormy scene of political Strife & Warfare.

Your sincere friend,   John Beckley

RC (MONROE PAPERS, NEW YORK PUBLIC LIBRARY).

1. That is, James Madison. See Stagg, ed., *Madison Papers*, 16:403–4.
2. See Beckley to Madison, October 15, 1796.
3. That is, Washington's successor as president.

JOHN BECKLEY AS A SUBSCRIBER[1]

FOR THE GAZETTE OF THE UNITED STATES   26th October, 1796.
Mr. Fenno,

I observed some shamefull mis-statements of the writer in your Gazette under the signature of *Phocion*, respecting the conduct of Mr. Jefferson while governor of Virginia in the year 1781, and having been personally present, in actual service, through all the active scenes of that year, from its commencement, and before, until after the termination of the siege of York, I can state what that conduct really was, with more truth and certainty than either Phocion or his friend Charles Simms, neither of whom, appear to know much about what they have written, and were certainly neither of them in Virginia at the period referred to.[2] First then, it is not true that "Mr. Jefferson *abandoned his trust at the moment of invasion.*" Arnold's invasion took place in January, 1781. Mr. Jefferson remained in his station through the whole period of that invasion. Cornwallis' invasion took place in May, 1781, and he continued to advance into the country until the beginning of June, when he commenced his retreat before the Marquis Fayette into the lower country, on the sea-bord, the Marquis having taken the command about two months before. Mr. Jefferson did not resign at all, or abandon his station, he remained in office until after Cornwallis' retreat, and until the time for which he was constitutionally elected, had expired, to wit, the 12th of June, 1781. Before he left office, however, Mr. Jefferson demanded of the legislature, a full enquiry into the conduct of the executive for the last twelve months, which was accordingly granted by the resolution of the 12th of June, 1781, and the 26th of November following appointed for the enquiry, being a period of near six months allowed to bring forward any charges or proofs against Mr. Jefferson. On the 26th of December, 1781, the assembly proceeded to take up the enquiry at large, on the report of a committee of their own body, and having just voted that *no charge* or accusation, whatever, appeared against Mr. Jefferson, and "*that there never was any cause for the enquiry, but some vague and groundless rumours,*" they unanimously passed the resolution of the 12th December, 1781, already published in your gazette, Mr. Fenno, and which if Phocion's candour will permit him again to read, he will find not merely an acknowledgment of Mr. Jefferson's ability and integrity, and *altogether silent on the want of firmness*, but containing express thanks for "*his attentive administration of the powers of the executive while in office.*"

Secondly, Mr. Fenno, It is not true that Mr. Jefferson at any time fled before a few light-horsemen, and shamefully abandoned his trust, or, as suggested by Charles Simms, contributed by his conduct to the loss and distress which accrued to the state, in the destruction of the public records, and vouchers for general expenditures. Let facts speak. In a few days after the arrival of Arnold's fleet, the enemy proceeded 150 miles up James's River, and landed his troops within 24 miles of Richmond, the night before his march to that place. All the militia of the state, which could be armed being then out, under the command of General Nelson, about sixty miles distant, in the neighborhood of Williamsburgh, and no defence at hand for the security of Richmond, but about 200 half-armed militia, under the command of Baron Steuben, who would do nothing more than cover the removal of the records and military stores across James River, from Richmond to Manchester, and secure the boats and batteaus on the Manchester side, to prevent the enemy's passing; the writer of this remained in Richmond with the last detachment of militia that passed the river with records and stores, and until the enemy (about 9 oclock in the morning) had entered the lower part of the town, and began to flank it with their light-horse he saw Mr. Jefferson, as active as man could be, as well the night before, as that morning, issuing his orders and using every exertion to remove the records and stores. He afterwards saw him at Westham, five miles above Richmond, where Arnold pushed a detachment to destroy the stores at that place, and which thro' Mr. Jefferson's exertions were almost entirely saved. The next day, when the enemy evacuated Richmond, the first man he the writer of this saw, as he entered the town, was Mr. Jefferson. Let a candid public then determine whether conduct like this, to which the writer hereof was an eye-witness, manifested want of firmness, or an abandonment of trust. The situation of the State was at that time peculiarly distressing, the whole of the Continental quota of troops were then acting in South Carolina; many thousand stand of arms had been supplied for the defence of North Carolina, and Arnold's invasion found the State, almost totally defenceless. The state of things was little better in a few months afterward when Cornwallis' invasion happened, and the Marquis Fayette took the command, since it is well known, that thro' the whole of that campaign, the Marquis' thro' want of arms, never had more than three or four thousand militia badly armed, in aid of the few continental troops that were detached from the Northern Army to Virginia, such was the deplorable situation both of the State and Continent, for want of arms. In respect to Tarleton's sudden march to Charlottesville, during that campaign, in order to surprise the Governor and Assembly, it will be remembered, that the Marquis' Army was inferior to Cornwallis', and had few or no cavalry attached to it, that at Charlottesville there was not even a single company of militia, and that Tarleton made a rapid march of about 60 miles thro' the country at the head of about 500 cavalry. The writer of this was also present at Charlottesville at the time, and saw Mr. Jefferson, and his Executive Council attending their duty at that place with the Assembly; it will not be pretended then, under the circumstances stated, that Mr. Jefferson "*fled before a few light horsemen, and shamefully abandoned his trust*," as is falsely asserted by Phocion.

But, Mr. Fenno, why do the enemies of Mr. Jefferson, cavil at his honourable acquittal alone by the Assembly of Virginia, from the groundless and unfounded charges; they well know that at the end of that very year, his brave and gallant successor in office, General Nelson, was subjected to public accusation and impeachment before the Assembly for supposed misconduct in office, and honourably acquited by the same body, in the same manner precisely, and with an unanimous vote of thanks, as in the case of Mr. Jefferson. No proof appeared against either, the accusation in each case was declared to be groundless, and the honourable reputation of both, stand or fall by the verdict of the same body. I leave it with a candid public to form their own reflections.   A SUBSCRIBER

TR (*GAZETTE OF THE UNITED STATES; AND PHILADELPHIA DAILY ADVERTISER*, OCTOBER 29, 1796).

1. Beckley asserted authorship of this essay in a June 28, 1805, letter to William A. Burwell, then serving as Jefferson's private secretary. In explaining an enclosed copy of his July 4, 1800 pamphlet, *Address to the People of the United States; with an Epitome and Vindica-*

tion of the Public Life and Character of Thomas Jefferson, Beckley stated in reference to a reprint of the essay by A Subscriber "In pages 12, 13, 14 & 15, you will observe a full statement of my testimony in the cases of Arnolds & Cornwallis's invasions, as I delivered it to Fenno for publication in the Year 1796." In his pamphlet, Beckley attributed authorship to "an officer in the army and an eye witness of all Mr. Jefferson's conduct." Both of these documents are printed in this volume.

    This essay was written as a response to charges leveled by William Loughton Smith, in a series of essays over the pseudonym, Phocion. Beckley had mistakenly thought that Hamilton was Phocion. See Beckley to Madison, October 15, 1796.

2. For a detailed examination of these charges against Jefferson by Smith and Charles Simms, Lieutenant Colonel of the Second Virginia Regiment during the Revolution, see Boyd, ed., *Jefferson Papers*, 4:256–78.

JOHN BECKLEY TO WILLIAM IRVINE

Dear General,   Philadelphia, 2d November 1796.

I received your favour by Wm. Taylor, and am happy it was in my power to assist him in his enquiries after the sharper who it appears intended to have Kidnapped his son.

We are all busily engaged in the Election and are sanguine in our hopes of success for Jefferson. The other side are equally active and equally sanguine. I think however that including the City and County of Philadelphia, we shall carry a Majority for the Jefferson ticket. We hope the Counties below the Mountains will be nearly divided and that the Western Counties will carry the Election for us. I send yo. a copy of the last Address of the Republicans to the people. Cumberland & Mifflin we rely will be generally in our favor. As soon as the result of our poll is known I will inform yo. of it, and beg the same favour from you.[1]

Shall we have the pleasure of a visit from yo. after the Election and at what time? We earnestly hope that Mrs. Irvines situation will permit your absence from home, and that Nancy will accompany you. Maria expects Miss Mason the 15th of the Month, and nothing would make us more happy than Nancy's joining our party this winter when we hope to be as happy & merry as the last. We shall also have a spare bed for you. Maria received the money for the quilt and is happy Mrs. Irvine approved of it. With our joint & affectionate regards, I am dear General, Yrs. sincerely,   John Beckley

[*P.S.*] I am sorry that Wm. Taylor has been again disappointed about his Boy. I shall employ a lawyer for him to morrow & use every Exertion I can to recover his Son. He leaves 30 dollars with me to defray any Expences of the business, which I will take due care of.   J.B.

RC (IRVINE PAPERS, HISTORICAL SOCIETY OF PENNSYLVANIA).

1. Through the efforts of Beckley and other supporters of Jefferson, thirteen of the fifteen electors chosen in Pennsylvania were pledged to the Jefferson-Burr ticket. When they voted on December 7, Jefferson received 14 votes, Burr received 12, Pinckney received 3, and Adams received 1. Tinkcom, *Republicans and Federalists in Pennsylvania*, pp. 171–72.

JOHN BECKLEY TO WILLIAM IRVINE

Dear General,   Philadelphia 16th December 1796.

I received your favour of the 13th instant. I was disappointed in an opportunity by Judge McKean and have delayed until now the sending Taylors 30 dollars, hoping for a certain private conveyance. You will receive the 30 dollars inclosed.

We shall be very happy in the promised visit from Nancy, and if you can come yourself we shall be additionally so.

After all our Exertions I fear Jefferson will fail altogether, and that Adams & Pinkney will be, one of them president, the other Vice president. All the New England States except Rh. Island, Vermont & NHampshire, have returned, also Pennsa. Delaware, Jersey, Maryland & Virginia, which give Adams 54. Pinkney 44. Jefferson 38. No return from the other states. As yet there may be doubt—the moment I can give you the result of the whole I will give it you.[1]

Excuse haste. We have had uncommon busy day in Congress.

Dunmores proclamation has not been received. I will enquire again of Lewis respecting the business. Accept for Mrs. Irvine & the family all our best wishes.

Yours truly,
John Beckley

RC (IRVINE PAPERS, HISTORICAL SOCIETY OF PENNSYLVANIA).

1. The final electoral vote for president and vice-president was: Adams, 71; Jefferson, 68; Washington, 2; Thomas Pinckney, 59; Burr, 30; Samuel Adams, 15; Oliver Ellsworth, 11; Samuel Johnston, 2; James Iredell, 3; John Jay, 5; George Clinton, 7; Charles Cotesworthy Pinckney, 1; John Henry, 2. *Debates and Proceedings, Fourth Congress*, pp. 2095–99, *Journal of the House, Fourth Congress*, p. 686.

JOHN BECKLEY TO TENCH COXE

Saturday 11th March 1797.

J Beckley, to his friend Mr. Coxe.

Mr. Jefferson will take a family dinner to morrow with JBeckley at 3 o'clock, and JB undertook to assure him that Mr. Coxe would join us.

RC (COXE PAPERS, HISTORICAL SOCIETY OF PENNSYLVANIA).

JOHN BECKLEY TO WILLIAM COBBETT

Mr. Cobbett,[1]   May 19, 1797

You have used an unwarrantable, I will not add base freedom with my name and character, in your gazette of Tuesday evening last.[2] Referring to the proceedings of the house of representatives of the United States on Monday last, respecting the appointment of a clerk, you remark in the following words:

"As to Mr. Beckley's ability, I can be no judge of that; but respecting his *fidelity,* the adding up of the votes on the important question respecting the British treaty, by which a *point already decided*, was submitted to the decision of the chairman, was no very favourable specimen."

The following facts of which you Could not be ignorant, will prove that the injurious insinuation which your remarks are calculated to convey, is totally unfounded in truth:

On the 30th day of April, 1796, when the resolution for making an appropriation to carry into effect the British treaty, was depending in the house of representatives of the United States, a motion was made by Mr. Dearborne to prefix to the resolution a preamble, stating certain objections to the treaty; on this motion the yeas and nays were called for. In taking the yeas and nays on every question, the mode of proceeding is known to be this: A record book lays on the clerk's table, in which the names of all the members are alphabetically entered, with a column on each side of the name, one for the yeas, the other for the nays, in this form:

Yeas	Names	Nays
x	A.B.	
	C.D.	x
x	E.F.	
	G.H.	x
	J.K.	x

As soon as the call is over, the clerk reads aloud the names of all the members as they voted, whether yea or nay, so that if any member's vote has been omitted to be entered in the record, or afterwards to be read aloud by the clerk, the error is instantly discovered and corrected. Now in the case to which you refer on Mr. Dearborne's motion, it happened that there were 49 yeas and 49 nays, when the speaker being about to give, or having actually given, his casting vote, a member suggested that the clerk had made a mistake in counting the numbers; I instantly recurred to the record book, and reported to the chair, that it appeared that there were 50 nays entered on the question; and having previously read aloud to the house the names of those 50 members without having omitted a single vote either in entering the votes or reading the names, the mistake in calling up the numbers was so obviously a casual and unintentional one in the view of the whole house, that the proceeding was instantly put right, and the decision of the question on Mr. Dearborne's motion entered on the minutes and journal of the day, by a vote of 50 nays against 49 yeas, *without the decision of the chair*, and contrary to your assertion, as will appear by a reference to the printed journal of the house, page 380.[3]

This explanation will, I presume, satisfy the most tortured suggestions of malice; but to remove all possibility of doubt, I subjoin the then speaker, Mr. Dayton's certificate on the subject.

John Beckley

This may certify, that the statement of facts herein before made by Mr. Beckley, both as to the method of taking, entering and announcing the yeas and nays generally, and as to the error in casting up the votes on Mr. Dearborne's motion particularly, is accurate and just. This I can declare with the greater freedom and confidence, because I recollect precisely my having marked with my pen the number of fifty nays as Mr. Beckley read and announced them from his entry.   Jona. Dayton

TR (*PORCUPINE'S GAZETTE AND DAILY ADVERTISER* (PHILADEPHIA), MAY 20, 1797).

1. William Cobbett (1763–1835), an English author and political refugee in America, 1792–1800 and 1817–19, settled in Philadelphia where he delighted the Federalists and enraged Republicans with his vituperative political writings over the pseudonym Peter Porcupine. On March 4, 1797, he began his own newspaper, *Porcupine's Gazette and Daily Advertiser*, which featured political criticism of the Republicans. Mary E. Clark, *Peter Porcupine in America: The Career of William Cobbett, 1792–1800* (Norwood, Pa.: Norwood Edition, 1975).

2. On May 15 Beckley had lost his clerkship in the House of Representatives by one vote to the Federalist candidate Jonathan Williams Condy. A debate in the House over the propriety of accepting nominations for this office from the House floor preceded the vote, but there was no recorded mention of Beckley's political affiliation nor his job performance. *The Debates and Proceedings in the Congress of the United States,... Fifth Congress* (Washington: Gales and Seaton, 1851), pp. 51–52. Beckley became angry when Cobbett not only delighted in Beckley's defeat but charged that Beckley had deliberately miscounted votes during the Jay Treaty confrontation in the hope of manipulating the out-

come. When Beckley demanded that Cobbett print his refutation, the two political partisans nearly became embroiled in a brawl. Cobbett agreed to print Beckley's statement in his newspaper of May 20, but printed his own account of the Cobbett-Beckley "fracas" in the May 19 issue of *Porcupine's Gazette*.

COBBETT'S ACCOUNT:

Fracas

As various reports will get abroad respecting the *fracas*, that took place at my shop this morning between me and Beckley, late clerk to the house of representatives, I think proper to give the public a faithful account of it.

Beckley put a paper into my hands, containing something about a defence of his conduct on a particular occasion, while clerk. I read it. When I had done so, he told me he should expect to see it in my paper *this evening*; to which I replied, that things of greater consequence would engross the whole of the paper this day; that therefore, it could not appear, and if it *could*, it *should* not: but, that *to-morrow*, it *could* and *should* appear.

As no objection could be made to this, Beckley made none; but he had the assurance to tell me, that if I took any more *liberties with his name, he would horsewhip me!* This he accompanied with a posture as menacing as his poor emaciated frame could possibly assume. I replied, that I was resolved to take just what liberties with his name I thought proper, and invited him to come immediately into the street, and put his threat of chastisement into execution. Finding him hang back, it struck me, that he might be ashamed to show his bare bones to the populace, which were gathering about the house, I therefore proposed to him to go back into my garden and bring his friend with him. He now bethought himself (for the first time) that I was a "*scoundrel beneath his notice.*" To this I replied that he was "*a damned scoundrel,*" and dared him (which I now do again) to a *comparison between our characters*, adding, that I *owed nobody any thing*. The rest of the conversation would be very unedifying, as it consisted almost entirely of abusive names and epithets of high toned threats on his part and of contemptuous defiance on mine.

It will be observed (and the number of witnesses precludes the possiblity of a denial) that Beckley was the *aggressor*, both in threats of violence and in abusive language. I am fully persuaded that his intention was to provoke me to strike him, and this opinion is corroborated by his having two or three persons with him. I certainly did feel an almost irresistible temptation to kick him into the street; but I luckily forebore, and he went off with no other satisfaction than the miserable one of being called "*a damned scoundrel.*"

See Clark, *Peter Porcupine*, pp. 97–98.

3. See *Journal of the House, Fourth Congress*, pp. 529–31 and *Debates and Proceedings, Fourth Congress*, pp. 1281–92.

JOHN BECKLEY TO LITTLETON TAZEWELL

Dear Sir,[1]   Philadelphia 16th June, 1797

When your father arrived he informed me, that you expected soon to receive payment of Mr. Kings debt. I am therefore induced to request you to urge him to speedy payment, if not already paid. He will not I am sure beleive, that the late deprivation of my Public Office has rendered my family circumstances more comfortable than they were, nor can he now be without a motive for requiting an act of generous friendship on my part, by a

Speedy discharge of the debt and interest, which may afford a releif I now stand in need of.

With true regard, I am, dear Sir, Yr. Obedt. Servt.

LB (BECKLEY FAMILY PAPERS, LIBRARY OF CONGRESS). UNSIGNED, BUT IN THE HAND OF BECKLEY.

1. Littleton Waller Tazewell (1774–1860), son of Henry Tazewell (1753–99), served in the House of Representatives (1800–1801) from Virginia filling the seat vacated by John Marshall. The elder Tazewell served as a U.S. senator, 1794–99 and when in Philadelphia resided with the Beckleys. See Beckley to Jefferson, January 24, 1799, and Norma Lois Peterson, *Littleton Waller Tazewell* (Charlottesville: University of Virginia Press, 1983).

Washington, 1801.
C. Cartwright.
LC–USZ62–4702.

JOHN BECKLEY TO GEORGE THOMPSON

My good old friend,[1]   Philadelphia, 18th December 1797.

After a lapse of ten years, we can at least greet each other by letter, since no time will, on my part, ever efface the remembrance of our former intimacy. When your friendly favour of last spring, by Mr. Davis reached me, I was very ill in bed and so continued for three Months; after my recovery I was directed by my physicians to travel, and thus, until my return home about a month ago, with my health perfectly restored, have I been engaged. One of my first employments is to recognize my old friend, and to thank him with a heart full of sincerity for his affectionate letter. Happy indeed should I be to come among you, and to acquire and merit the estimable character of a Citizen of Kentuckey; but to accomplish this with more certainty I must rely on a little of your assistance in answer to this letter. Inclosed is the copy of 3 surveys of Land in your state, now my property, but formerly belonging to our late worthy old friend George Webb, deceased, which were patented to me in 1790. Will you my dear Sir, give me a full description of this property as far as you can and as speedily as possible, that I may make immediate arrangements to come out.

You understand so much better than myself every circumstance necessary to be mentioned respecting them, that I will not be particular. In general I could wish to know their situation, value per acre or per hundred, how near to public roads, stations or settlements, if there be any & how many settlers upon them, and if any & what interfering claims natural advantages, Waters, Salt licks &c. &c. Whatever description or account you can give me of them, be so good as to annex it to the enclosed copy of the Surveys and return that to me by mail under cover to Mr. Davis.

Congress have as yet done nothing. No news from Europe or from our Commissioners at Paris—dull, hard times in this part of the World. I shall be anxious indeed until I hear from you in answer to this letter that I may with all possible speed emancipate myself from it.

With sincere affection, I am, dear Thompson, Yr. friend.

J. Beckley

LB (BECKLEY FAMILY PAPERS, LIBRARY OF CONGRESS).

1. George Thompson (d. 1834), colonel in the Virginia militia and former planter in Fluvanna County, Virginia, was the owner of "Pleasant Fields," a large plantation near Harrodsburg, and a magistrate of Mercer County, Kentucky.

JOHN BECKLEY TO ISAAC POLOCK

Dear Sir,[1]   Philadelphia 17th January 1798.

I received your favor of the 8th instant, and thank you for your attention to my land concern. Neither Morris nor Nicholson have gone, or intend to go to Jail, if they can avoid it, and I rather suppose they will avoid it.[2] I do not think their paper ever will be lower than it now is, indeed it seems rather to look up; since judgment paper could be purchased here, at less than 1/6 or 2/ in the pound.

You may be assured, that we shall no[t] war with France, unless our Government declare it: and as Congress only have the power, you may rest easy that it will not be done. No insult has been offered to our Commissioners. It has been demanded of them, if they have power to treat upon the basis of the modern law of nations, and a fulfilment of the guaranty in our treaty of 1778 with France. Their answer is not known; but as they have certainly no such power, it will of necessity, result, that they must retire to Holland, or elsewhere, and await further powers and instructions from hence.

The loan to the Fœderal City was very opportune, and will, I trust, accelerate the object we wish; but I very much regret that the investiture in the Potowmac shares has failed.[3] Is there any perceivable rise in the value of City lots? Will you be so good as to say, what you think mine are worth at the lowest Cash rate of valuation.

I expect, in a week or two, to receive from Kentucky ample description of my property there, copy of which shall be immediately forwarded you. As soon as I obtain from General Morgan an answer to Mr. Mercer's letter, I will write him fully on that and other topics; In the interim, be pleased to make my respects to that family, being truly, with great regard, dear Sir, Yours,

John Beckley.

LB (BECKLEY FAMILY PAPERS, LIBRARY OF CONGRESS).

1. Isaac Polock was a land speculator from Georgia, who had invested heavily in the property development of the District of Columbia.
2. Beckley badly underestimated the financial problems of Robert Morris and his partner John Nicholson. Morris was imprisoned for debt in 1798 when his land speculations went sour and his partner Nicholson followed him to debtor's prison in 1800.
   Beckley and Andrew Moore, a former U.S. representative from Virginia (1789–97), were partners in land ventures of several hundred thousand acres, which they subsequently contracted to sell to Morris and Nicholson. Berkeley, *Beckley*, pp. 100–102.
3. This is apparently a reference to the second loan of $100,000. which was obtained from Maryland under Congressional authorization. The commissioners in charge of erecting the Federal City had obtained several loans from Maryland and Virginia and in 1798 obtained an appropriation from the Federal government. See Wilhelmus B. Bryan, *A History of the National Capital*, 2 vols. (New York: The Macmillan Co., 1914), 1:265–72, 299, 329; and *Debates and Proceedings, Fifth Congress*, p. 1266.

JOHN BECKLEY TO THOMAS JEFFERSON

Thursday Evening 15th March 1798.

J. Beckley returns enclosed Mr. Jefferson's parliamentary Notes.[1] On the first part he has pencilled a few remarks. On the Second part 'respecting priviledged questions' want of time now to consider it, induces a wish, that at the close of the Session Mr. Jefferson would permit him to take a copy of these, and any other notes which Mr. J. may add on the law of parliament generally, when an attentive revisal of the whole subject of will be endeavored to be made by JB—before the Succeeding Session.[2] A Copy of the notes on Conferences will be handed to Mr. Jefferson tomorrow.

Enclosure:

EXTRACTS FROM BOOK OF MINUTES ON PARLIAMENTARY PROCEEDING.[3]

1791. 29 Decemr. First instance of Sections or parts of a bill recommitted to a Select Committee, after a Commitment to the whole House, the Bill itself being before the House—post office Bill 18th and 19th Sections.

1972. 31st January. In discussing "Bill for protection of the frontiers"—after commitment and the amendments reported and agreed to, the House proceeded to consider the Bill at the Clerks table. Observe, this mode of proceeding is dangerous and should be used with great caution, because it admits amendments, new and important in principle, without due consideration—practice and rule in House of Commons that every amendment to a Bill in the House, not merely verbal or corrective shall be committed and go thro' all the previous stages of discussion which the Bill itself has undergone, before it shall be brought up to the Speakers table into the Bill.

N.B.—On 3d reading of the Excise Bill, some of the most important clauses in it were added with little or no discussion.

RC AND MS (JEFFERSON PAPERS, LIBRARY OF CONGRESS).

1. Beckley, as former clerk of the House, and Jefferson, as president of the Senate, were both compiling laws and precedents illustrative of parliamentary proceedings.

Jefferson's work was ultimately published as a two-part handbook *A Manual of Parliamentary Practice*. Beckley's compilations remained in the orginal form of a manuscript commonplace book. A portion of the notes accumulated by Beckley while he was clerk of the House of Representatives has been published in this work under the date October 26, 1791. Another fragment of his work on parliamentary practices is published as the next entry under the date March 1798.

For a discussion of Beckley's possible impact on Jefferson's parliamentary writings, see Wilbur S. Howell, ed., *Jefferson's Parliamentary Writings* in *The Papers of Thomas Jefferson*, 2nd ser. (Princeton: Princeton University Press, 1988), pp. 15–16.

2. See the next document.

3. Beckley may have enclosed these slightly variant copies of dated entries from Beckley's Book of Minutes on Parliamentary Proceedings with this note, or sent them to Jefferson on another occasion. Nevertheless, they are clearly related to this note to Jefferson and the following essay fragment written by Beckley.

For informational footnotes see the dated entries printed under the general entry, Book of Minutes on Parliamentary Proceedings, October 26, 1791.

JOHN BECKLEY ESSAY FRAGMENT

[March 1798][1]

2d: the operation of the circumstances before mentioned there is hardly a State in Empire, save England, in which the will of the prince does not hold the place of law, and even there so partial and corrupt is the present representation of the people in Parliament, that without some revolution in the Government, this exception will probably not continue long to exist. To trace the progress of the causes which have produced these effects, is not within the scope or design of the present treatise; suffice it, that in reviewing the page of history we behold the rise and termination of the Governments which have been produced by superstition and conquest in contra distinction to those which have arisen out of Society on the Social compact and that the recent examples of the American and French revolutions we are taught the great elementary principles of human power and human happiness, principles which promise soon to become as universal as the truths on which they are founded, and which by reverting to and renovating the natural order of things may produce systems capable of combining moral with political happiness and of ultimately completing the union and prosperity of Nations.

The origin of parliament being supposed to be Coeval with that of Government itself, we are next to consider its jurisdiction and power. In England, where Parliament is the great prototype of the Congress or National Legislature of the United States, this jurisdiction is thus defined (b. *Cokes Institute,* Sect. 164).[2] "The jurisdiction of this Court is so transcendent that it maketh, inlargeth, diminisheth, abrogateth, repealeth and reviveth Laws, Statutes, Acts, and Ordinances, concerning matters Eclesiastical, Civil, Martial, Marine, Capital, Criminal, and Common." (1c) *and 4th Institute Fol. 36.* "The power & jurisdiction of the parliament for making of laws in proceeding by Bill, is so transcended and absolute as it cannot be confined either for causes or persons within any bounds." Of this Court it is truly said "If you regard its original, it is most ancient; If its dignity, it is most honourable; If its jurisdiction, it is most capacious." (d).[3] A great statesman has also said "The most high & absolute power of the realm of England consisteth in the parliament; for the parliament abrogateth old laws, maketh new, giveth order for things past, and for things hereafter to be followed;

changeth the rights and possessions of private men; legitimateth bastards; corroborates religion in the civil sanctions; alters weights and measures; prescribes the right of succession to the Crown; defines doubtful rights where there is no law already made; appointeth subsidies, taxes and imposi- tions; giveth most free pardons; restoreth in Blood & name &c." (e) And by the declaratory Statute 25th Henry 8th cha. 21: it is Enacted: "Whereas this realm recognizing no superior under God but the King, hath been and is free from subjection to any mans laws, but only to such as have been devised, made, and ordained within this realm, for the wealth thereof, or to such other as the people of this realm have taken at their free liberty by their own consent, to be used amongst them; and have bound themselves by long use and custom to the observance of the same; not to the obser- vance of any foreign prince, potentate or prelate, but as to the accustomed & ancient laws of this realm, originally established as laws of the same by the said Sufferance, consent, and custom, the King, and the Lords spiritual and temporal and commons representing the whole state of the realm on the most high court of parliament, have full power and authority, to dis- pense with these and all other human laws of the realm, and with every one of them, as the quality of the persons and matter shall require; And also the said laws and every of them to abrogate, annul, amplify, or dimin- ish, as to the King, nobles, and Commons of the realm present in parlia- ment shall seem most meet & convenient for the wealth of the Nation." (f) In *the Mirror*, another authority, the power of parliament is said to be "to confer of the government of Gods people, how they may be kept from Sin, live in quiet, and have right done them according to the Customs, and laws, and more especially of wrong done by the King, Queen or their chil- dren."—than which, there is not perhaps, any where to be found, a more just and adequate idea of free Government.

Again, for making of laws and in proceeding by Bill, this Supreme Court of parliament is not confined either for causes or persons within any bounds, nor is it tied down to any certain rules or forms of law in proceed- ings & determinations. It hath power to judge in matters of law; and redress grievances that happen, especially such as have no ordinary remedy; to examine into the corruption of Magistrates and illegal proceedings of other Courts; to redress errors & determine on petitions and appeals &c. and from this high Court there lies no appeal. Affairs of parliament are to be deter- mined by the parliament; tho' the parliament err it is not reversible: and not only what is done in the House of Commons, but what relates to the Com- mons during the parliament, and sitting the parliament, is no where else to be punished but by themselves, or a succeeding parliament. (g.).

Every Court of justice having laws and Customs for its direction, the high Court of parliament hath its own proper laws & customs called the laws & customs of parliament, insomuch that no judge ought to give any opinion of matters done in parliament, because they are not to be decided by the Common law (h). But the parliament in their judicial capacity, are governed by the common & statute laws as well as the Courts in Westminster hall (j). The Lords and Commons in their respected houses have power of judicature, and so have both houses together. And in former times both houses sat together in one house of parliament. (k) The King, cannot take notice of any thing said to be done in the House of Commons but by the report of the House; and every Member of the House of parliament has a judicial place and can be no witness (l) When Charles lst being in the House of Commons, and sitting in the Speakers chair, asked the then speaker, whether certain members, whom the King named were present? The Speaker, from a presence of mind which arose from the genius of that house, readily answered, that "he had neither Eyes to See, nor tongue to speak, but as the House was pleased to direct him." (m) Henry 8th having commanded Sir Thoms Gaudy, (one of the Judges of the Kings bench) to attend the chief justices and have their opinion, whether a man might be attainted of high treason by parliament and never called to answer; the judges declared that it was a dangerous question, and that the high Court of parliament ought to give Examples to inferior Courts for proceeding according to justice, and no inferior Court could do the like (n). The House of Lords is a distinct Court from the Commons to several purposes and is the sovereign Court of justice and dernier resort. They try criminal causes on impeachments of the Commons; and have an Original jurisdiction for the trial of peers upon indictments found by a grand jury: They also try causes upon appeals from the Court of chancery or upon writs of Error to reverse judgments in the Kings Bench &c. And all their decrees are as judgments, and judgments given in parliament may be executed by the Lord Chancellor (o). It is said that the judicial power of parliaments is in the Lords; but that the House of Lords hath no jurisdiction over original causes, which would deprive the subject of the benefit of appeal (p). Also the House of Commons is a distinct Court to many purposes; they examine the rights of Elections, expel their own Members, and commit them to prison, and sometimes other persons &c. and the book of the Clerk of the House of Commons is a record (q). The Commons coming from all parts are the grand inquest of the realm to present public grievances and delinquents to the King and Lords, to be punished by them: and any member of the House of Commons has the privilege of impeaching the highest lord in the Kingdom (r).

From the review of the jurisdiction & power of parliament we are necessarily led to enquire how far the general principles from which it is derived are applicable either to any of the specified & enumerated powers of Congress or to the general nature and design of those Legislative and judicial functions with the execution of which, it is entrusted, as the supreme power of the Union. In pursuing this enquiry it will be proper, first, to ascertain what are the specified & enumerated powers of Congress in its Legislative capacity? Secondly, what are the express or implied limitations to those powers? and thirdly, In what is the judicial power of Congress consists?

1. What are the specified & enumerated powers of Congress in its Legislative capacity? By the 8th section of the first articles of the Constitution of the United States, it is provided that Congress shall have power,

To lay and collect taxes, duties, imports & excises, to pay the debts & provide for the common defence and general welfare of the United States; but all duties, imposts and excises shall be uniform throughout the United States:

To borrow Money on the Credit of the United States:

To regulate Commerce with foreign Nations & among the Several States, and with the Indian tribes:

To establish an uniform rule of Naturalization, and uniform laws on the subject of Bankruptcies throughout the United States:

To Coin Money, regulate the value thereof, and of foreign Coin, and fix the standard of weights & measures:

To provide for the punishment of counterfeiting the Securities & Current Coin of the United States:

To establish Post Offices & Post roads:

To promote the progress of Science & useful arts, by securing for limited times to authors & inventors the exclusive right to their respective Writings and discoveries:

To constitute tribunals inferior to the Supreme Court:

To define & punish piracies & felonies committed on the high seas, and offences against the laws of nations:

To declare War, grant letters of Marque and reprisal, and make rules concerning captures on land and Water:

To raise and support Armies, but no appropriation of Money to that use shall be for a longer term than two years:

To provide and maintain a Navy:

To make rules for the Government & regulation of the land & naval forces:

To provide for calling forth the Militia to execute the laws of the Union, suppress insurrection and repel invasions:

To provide for Organizing, Arming, and disciplining the Militia, and for governing such part of them as may be employed in the service of the United States, reserving to the States respectively, the appointment of the Officers, and the authority of training the Militia, according to the discipline prescribed by Congress:

To exercise exclusive legislation in all cases whatsoever, over such district, (not exceeding ten miles square) as may by Cession of particular States & the acceptance of Congress, become the seat of the Government of the United States, and to exercise like authority over all places purchased by consent of the legislature of the State in which the same shall be for the erection of forts, magazines, arsenals, dockyards and other needful buildings:

By various other clauses of the Constitution, it is moreover provided that Congress shall have power,

To apportion representatives & direct taxes among the several States, according to their respective numbers, which shall be determined by adding to the whole number.....

Footnotes:
f. The Mirror Chap. 2. Section 18.[4]
g. 1st Instit. 110.
h. 4 Instit. 14.15.
j. State trials Volo. 2 pa. 735.[5]
k. 4th Instit. 23.
l. 4th Institute 15.
m. Atkins antiquity & jurisdiction of Ho. of Commons.[6]
n. Lex Constitution 161.[7]
o. 4th Inst. 21. First 233. 1 Lev. 165.[8]
p. 2 Salk 510.[9]
q. 2 Inst. 531. 4 Inst. 23.
r. Woods Instit. 455.[10]

MS (BECKLEY FAMILY PAPERS, LIBRARY OF CONGRESS). IN THE HAND OF JOHN BECKLEY.

How many pages of this essay are now missing can not be determined. The fragment printed here begins with numbered page "2d" and ends with numbered page "5." Footnote labeled "a" is missing and was evidently on page one. Footnotes labeled "b" through "e" were incorporated into the text. The footnotes labeled "f" through "r" were written on the verso of the manuscript pages.

1. Although this document fragment is undated, it may be the "attentive revisal of the whole subject" of "parliament generally" which Beckley stated in the preceding document he was currently undertaking "before the Succeeding Session" of Congress. Therefore, it has been tentatively dated March 1798.

2. It was not determined which editions of the cited works were actually used by Beckley. Edward Coke, *Institutes of the Laws of England*, 4 parts (London, 1628–44). Also cited in Beckley's notes c, g, h, k, l, o, and q.

3. Beckley's citations to notes d and e were not found.

4. Andrew Horn, *The Mirrour of Justices*.... (London, 1646).

5. *A Collection of State-Trials, and Proceedings, upon High Treason, and other Crimes*.... 10 vols. (London, 1766).

6. Robert Atkyns, *The Power, Jurisdiction and Priviledge of Parliament; and the Antiquity of the House of Commons Asserted*.... (London, 1689).

7. Giles Jacob, *Lex Constitutionis: or, the Gentleman's Law, Being a... Treatise of All the Laws and Statutes relating to the King, and the Prerogative of the Crown, the Nobility, and House of Lords, House of Commons* (London, 1719).

8. Creswell Levinz, *Reports of Cases in the Court of Kings Bench and Common Pleas*.... (London, 1702).

9. William Salkeld, *Reports of Cases Adjudged in the Court of Kings Bench*. 3 parts (London, 1721–1724).

10. Thomas Wood, *An Institute of the Laws of England*.... 4 vols. (London, 1720).

JOHN BECKLEY TO PETER GALLINE

My Dear Sir,[1]   Philadelphia 8th June 1798.

Illness and the extreme confinement to business occasioned by the constant sitting of our Courts of Law have prevented my writing before this. Congress is still in Session and I beleive will not rise earlier than the middle of July and to meet again the lst of October. Further dispatches have been recd. from our Commissrs. and Our Executives have published as late as the 9th of March altho' it is said they have them as late as the 4th April and that a Schism prevails among our Commissrs. of which you'l probably be better informed than we are. A phrenzy seems still to prevail in the public mind in consequence of the publication of the first dispatches and War measures, short of an actual declaration of it, are continued to be persued, altho' the last proposition made for granting letters of Marque & reprisal was postponed for a fortnight and it is thought will be rejected. An Act to raise a provisional Army of 10,000 men has however passed—also an Act to prohibit intercourse with the french republic after the 1st July until she desists from her spoliations. An Alien Bill and a Sedition Bill are also depending, and in my judgment nothing will save us from an actual War, but the state of Affairs in Europe and the moderation of France both being alike unpropitious to the views of our ruling faction. An Act has also passed authorizing Armed Vessels of US to return Vessels captured by French Cruizers & to bring in all such Cruizers if taken within 4 leagues of our Coast. If however we have the misfortune to be brought into war, I do not believe it can long exist, since if the people discover that they have been deceived, they will displace their present rulers & command Government to make peace, Or should France really prove unjust and untrue to her own as well as our real interest and continue to reject our overtures, the united energies of this Country will compel her to speedy peace.[2]

In any event, my dear Sir, I do not abate in my confidence in your Success and the reliance I place in your talents & abilities to accomplish our object, if at all attainable. The State of Europe, particularly of Switzerland & Great Britain have so materially changed since yo. left us, and as in moral certainty it must continue to do so, I doubt not an opportunity will be presented either in one or other of these countries, Or in Holland, of effecting a Sale. I have forwarded duplicates of my letter & power to Mr. Skipwith,[3] so that if he should not have retired from France, he may lend every cooperation in his power. Mr. Coxe has written you several letters and as opportunity occurs I shall repeat mine until I hear from you, which I am Sure will be as early as it is in your power. I enclose half a dozen of Bache's latest papers. Mrs. Beckley and our two families continue well, and with Messrs. Blount & Tazewell desire their affectionate regards. Prince is not yet arrived, but we look for him hourly. With the most fervent wishes for your health, prosperity and happiness I am, My dear Sir, Your sincerely affect. friend.

John Beckley

LB (BECKLEY FAMILY PAPERS, LIBRARY OF CONGRESS). ADDRESSED: "MR. PETER GALLINE, AT MESSRS. BELLAMI, RICCE & CO., MERCHANTS-HAMBURG. OR AU CITOYEN P. GALLINE, CHEZ LE CITOYEN BONTEMS, BANQUIER, RUE DU MONT BLAN. NO. 18. A PARIS."

1. Peter Galline, a nephew of Mallet Prevost, a self-styled former banker from Switzerland who was living in Alexandria, New Jersey, while arranging several large land purchases on behalf of European investors. There is no evidence that Galline had any success in selling land for Beckley. See Beckley to Galline, July 18, 1798; Beckley to Coxe, October 25, November 12, 1798, and Berkeley, *Beckley*, pp. 179–80, 188.
2. For a discussion of the diplomatic and domestic ramifications of the diplomatic crisis with France, known as the XYZ Affair, which contributed to the undeclared naval warfare between France and the United States, see William Stinchcombe, *The XYZ Affair* (Westport, Conn.: Greenwood Press, 1980) and George A. Billias, *Elbridge Gerry. Founding Father and Republican Statesman* (New York: McGraw-Hill Book Co., 1976), pp. 245–308.
3. See Beckley to Fulwar Skipwith, U.S. consul in Paris, April 12, 1798, Beckley Family Papers, Library of Congress.

JOHN BECKLEY TO JAMES PRINCE

My dear friend,[1]   Philadelphia June 18th. 1798.

In the moment of ruin, and with a mind borne down by anguish, I acknowledge the receipt of the only letter received from you, since you left us, under date 28th May by the Schooner Three Sisters. Anxiously hoping some aid from you, and finding by letters to Hollingsworth that the Schooner brought a full cargo and that laid in at a low price, I have felt all the force of that disappointment, which a man cou'd feel, who, in the hour of distress, looked for a friend, and found him not. I mean not, however, to reproach or wound your feelings; you have had difficulties on your part, and I can rejoice that Powers has behaved generously and paid you all he owed. A few words will exhibit my unhappy case. Every attempt to sell any kind of property fails, from the alarming state of public afairs, and the dread of approaching war; my House sacrified for 6000 dollars, and my family compelled, in a few days, to leave it and disperse; your mother to seek an asylum with the benevolent Shippey,[2] where our dear Isaac still remains, without any ability on my part to assist him; your Sister heavy with child to lodgings; myself at mercy of exonoretur to Carmick and Thunn, both of whom I have with difficulty prevailed to wait the arrival of the schooner, and who, with the aid of 1000 dollars only I could have obtained 3 or 4 months indulgence from; Tatem has sued in the Circuit Court Mr. S.[3] for your part of the land, and at present mine will not sell at any price. Galline was detained by unforeseen causes, until the 10th of May, and if not taken, can hardly have yet arrived. He sailed in the Dominick Terry for Hamburg, and I do not expect to hear from him till all Sept. By aid of the late act of Assembly, I can protect my person until the 1st Monday in September next. My property, however, all that can be got at, must go, and in September without it should please God to send me some releif, I must submit to go to jail, or surrender every thing I hold to be sacrificed for nothing and left at my time of life to begin the world anew. This, without disguise or exaggeration, is my situation. If it be possible, you will assist me. You cannot see the total ruin of our family, which was one fortunate to afford an asylum, in the hour of its distress, without an effort to prevent it. Professions signify nothing; Actions only are the test of sincerity; and with ability to perform. I must believe that your heart is made of different materials, than ever to be indifferent to the last distress of a mother, brother, sister, and friend, whatever may be your distance of time or place from these objects of just affection. This letter comes by the pilot boat bound from New York, which sails on the 20th, and will, I hope, be with you in three weeks. Hollinsworth writes you also by her. He will dispatch Shallcross to Surinam in a fast sailing vessel, and explain to you the necessity for so doing. If by her, or any other vessel, you can remit any thing, or thro' Powers, or any other friend, or by any other means, procure a bill on this place for about 2000 dollars, it may reach me by September Court, and save me from the last sad necessity. I enclose Bache's paper of yesterday, by which you'll see the State of things between us and France, and the happy prospect, that Mr. Gerry may conclude a treaty. Your mother and Sister, write in tender wishes for your health and happiness. Nancy writes you fully by this Conveyance; And with unfeigned attachment, I remain dear Prince, Yr. distressed friend.   J.B.

LB (BECKLEY FAMILY PAPERS, LIBRARY OF CONGRESS).

1. James Prince, Jr., older brother of Beckley's wife, Maria, was a ship captain engaged in the West India trade. His family resided in Philadelphia, while Prince carried merchanise to St. Eustatius, Surinam, Trinidad, and Cayenne. Soon after writing this letter, Beckley received a signed note due to Prince, which helped ease the family financial obligations. Berkeley, *Beckley*, pp. 53, 103, 183.

2. That is, Josiah Shippey, merchant in New York.

3. Perhaps, Col. John Stuart of Greenbriar County, Virginia, a partner in land speculation with Beckley and Prince. Legal entanglements with Stuart tied up the title to Beckley's Virginia land until 1835.

JOHN BECKLEY TO PETER GALLINE

My dear friend,   Philadelphia 18th July 1798.

I wrote you on the 8th of June by the Brig Ariel Captain Gallis, bound to Hamburg and I now enclose Baches paper of yesterday, by which you'l perceive that Congress adjourned yesterday and after every effort of party to produce offensive measures and a declaration of War against France a Majority of Congress have firmly resisted and confined their Legislative Acts to defensive measures only having refused either to declare War or to authorize reprisals on French Merchant Vessels. I am sanguine therefore in the hope that we may yet escape War and notwithstanding the Offensive endeavors of some among us to involve the two republics in a bloody conflict that France will display her wonted magnanimity and consult, in the sacrifice of her resentment, the best interests of the two republics and the general welfare of mankind. The first week in August the New York Legislature assemble and the first week in September the Virginia legislature. It is expected that both these Legislatures will address the president to make another effort and a <u>sincere one</u> to negotiate by sending a Known republican with sufficient powers. The Virginia Legislature will also assuredly pass an Act for the admission & protection of Emigrants and to admit aliens to hold and pass real Estate. Your efforts therefore may now be made with more certainty and I trust with full success. Congress do not meet again until the 1st Monday in December. I shall continue very anxious respecting you until I have the pleasure of a letter and permit me to repeat my request respecting my friend in London and a remittance to My Mother if your arrangments may possibly admit of it. I have a letter from Mr. Moore of the 27th ultimo in which he says that he has been offered 20/ per acre Virginia money say 3 dollars and 1/3d for a quantity of our lands to be laid off in small parcels, which of course he refused, and I mention it to shew the rapidity of its rise in value. Princes vessel arrived three weeks ago. Mr. Mallet returned but not Prince. They made a great voyage. With sincere prayers for your health, success, prosperity & happiness, I remain, yrs. &c.   JB.

JOHN BECKLEY TO JAMES MONROE

My dear Sir,   New York, 20th October 1798.

I reached this on Sunday last, my family having returned hither from New Ark, to a situation on the North River, which is esteemed safe, altho' the general state of the City is otherwise; and our friends Gilston & Provost[1] are both abroad. Eustace[2] still continues his contemptible scribbling, but promises speedily to wind up and give his name to the public. As soon as it is safe to go about and see our dear freinds I shall take effectual means in concurrence with them, on the subject. We have little foreign news that can be relied upon, as every thing is now of British character—the issue of Bonapartes Expedition is still uncertain; that Alexandria & the East Indies by the Isthmus of Suez is his object I have no doubt. A small invasion of Ireland has taken place, its fate is yet in doubt. Our Elections in Pensylvania are past—from report I believe we have 8 or 9 out of 13. In Maryland we have Smith, Christie & Seney. In New Jersey we have Kitchell, Condict, and Lyme. I cannot learn any thing from Massachusetts.[3]

Inclosed is a letter which my brother in law Mr. Gregory[4] gave me when in King William. It was written by him as addressed, but never sent. Mr. Wilson Nicholas will inform you that I gave him the Bond and a guinea to pay the lawyers fee, for which I have now Wilsons receipt. The Bond is for £30 given in or about the year 1786 for defending Turner Christian in the General Court, for Murder of his wife, on which charge he was acquitted.

If possible you will recover the Money for me—and if it can be done speedily pay it for me to our good friend Mr. Jefferson, to whom I am indebted about 250 dollars, and advise him of this request.

I shall write you again, on the subject of my coming to Virginia, in about a fortnight, Or sooner if circumstances will permit.

A letter from Mrs. B—compeled me to pass so rapidly from Fredericks-bg. that I could not call on any of our friends respecting other matters, but if I determine to proceed to Richmond, I shall do so in full time to see them all before the meeting of the Assembly. But Quere what is the precise day of your assembly's meeting? And can you forward me the leaves of a Virginia Almanack with a return of your present Members? Address to me in Philadelphia.

I deeply sympathize with Mrs. Monroe in the loss of her Sister Knox.[5] If she has not heard of it before, remember caution in the distressing communication.

Accept my cordial wishes of health and happiness, yours truly,

John Beckley

RC (MONROE PAPERS, JAMES MONROE MUSEUM AND MEMORIAL LIBRARY, FREDERICKSBURG, VA.).

1. David Gelston and Henry Prevost were New York merchants currently residing in France. Stinchcombe, *The XYZ Affair*, pp. 135 and 138.

2. John S. Eustace, a native of New York, former Revolutionary War officer and former American soldier of fortune in France. He had been expelled from Great Britain, France, and the Netherlands before coming to New York in 1798, where he wrote a series of eight newspaper articles (*The New-York Gazette*, August 22–25, 27, 31, September 1, 4, 6, 7, 1798) entitled "Embassy of Mr. Monroe" over the pseudonym "An American Soldier" which Eustace claimed were "publications of the Facts respecting Mr. Monroe" while he was minister to France "and his more shameful defence of the French Directory." Eustace wrote another series of seven anonymous articles as a letter to Timothy Pickering, in *The New-York Gazette*, October 10–13, 20, 24, 25, 1798. Syrett, ed., *Hamilton Papers*, 22: 213–216, 223–24, 253–61.

3. Overall the Republicans lost seats in the Sixth Congress, and the Federalist majority of six reportedly grew to 20. Cunningham, *Jeffersonian Republicans*, pp. 134–36. However, in Pennsylvania the Republicans picked up one spot by capturing eight of thirteen congressional seats. In Maryland only Republicans Gabriel Christie and Samuel Smith and in New Jersey John Condit and Aaron Kitchell were elected to the House.

4. Nathaniel Gregory, son of Roger Gregory of King William County was married to Beckley's sister Mary Anne.

5. That is, Maria Kortright Knox, wife of Thomas Knox, a New York merchant.

JOHN BECKLEY TO TENCH COXE

Dear sir,   New York 25 October 1798.

I am much indebted for your favour of the 23d. My only letter from Galline under date 4th July, gave no encouragement to a Sale, he says that as soon as it is certain he cannot succeed, he will advise me to remove all suspense. Have yo. any advice on this Subject, from your brother-in-law?[1] It will be best to keep to ourselves whatever communication we receive.

Foreign news of this morning states that Nelson is returned to Sicily without affecting his object, and that the french were on 9th September strongly intrenched at Castlebar. Our domestic concerns afford little matter except on the Subject of Elections. I am happy to see your result in Pennsylvania., and am glad that we keep our own as to members, and still hope Burd has succeeded.[2] As yet we stand on the ground of advantage—lost is it? Connecticut 4 gained, in N York—2, in Jersey 3, in Maryland 1-In Virginia I think we shall at least be where we were as to numbers, altho' it is too soon to calculate with certainty. Events between this & March next may greatly change the present sentiment of the public mind. I doubt not that the ensuing Session will be played off entirely to influence Virginia, encouraged as they are by their success in N. Carolina. Apropos to this, have yo. seen Lyon's persecution & sentence?[3] it will certainly do good in Virginia. I cannot hear a word from Massachusetts—not from Gerry or Pinkney. Our friends of this City are all in the Country, as soon as they return to town I shall be able to gather some information as to the state of things Eastern.

You say Duane begins in a few days, who I presume is to be Editor for it?. The argus also commences here in a few days. I think it probable I shall be here two or three weeks and shall be happy to receive your further communications. Mine shall supply you as matter seems—But you must take it, desultory as it comes.

I think that the death blow to the British Empire in Asia, is struck. Respecting Ireland you'l perceive the paucity and caution with which Governmt. speak of the state of things there, whence I argue, that there is <u>yet</u> no termination of the rebellion. Radstat Congress is certainly broken up and renewed hostilities commenced between France & Austria—Prussia and the Northern powers will be neutral, while Russia & the porte are actually engaged.

Have you any thing from So. Carolina & Georgia on the sense of Elections? Will Harper be excluded?[4] Mr. Brown writes me of 15th Septr. that our mind pervades Kentucky and that their members will be reelected. Mrs. B. joins me in best wishes to Mrs. Coxe and your family. <u>She</u> is, according to matronly phrase, '<u>still up</u>'.—but well and in high spirits. My affectionate regards to my good & worthy friend Duponceau & his amiable lady. Yours most sincerely,

John Beckley

RC (COXE PAPERS, HISTORICAL SOCIETY OF PENNSYLVANIA).

1. That is, Andrew Allen, husband of Sarah Coxe, former attorney general of Pennsylvania, and loyalist refugee in London.
2. Republicans increased their majority in the Pennsylvania delegation to the House of Representatives from 1 to 3 (8 Republicans and 5 Federalists). Edward Burd was not a successful candidate. Tinkcom, *Republicans and Federalists in Pennsylvania*, pp. 187–89.
3. On October 9, 1798, Matthew Lyon (1750–1822), Republican member of the House of Representatives from Vermont, had been found guilty of violating the Sedition Law and sentenced to four months in jail and a fine of $1000.
4. Robert Goodloe Harper was returned as a Federalist representative from South Carolina to the House of Representatives, but was defeated in the election of 1800 and subsequently moved to Maryland.

JOHN BECKLEY TO TENCH COXE

Dear sir,   New York 12th November 1798.

Your favour of the 8th instant, was handed me too late to answer by the next mail. I sincerely congratulate you on the return of yourself and neighbours to the City, and am happy that our friend Duponceau[1] is of the number. My continual expectation has been to join you myself, but Mrs. Bs. situation, and a variety of causes have interposed to prevent me; the birth of our daughter is not among the least, and I received with thankfulness your congratulations on the happy event. In a few days I hope to be with you.

I am equally with you without advice from Galline since the 4th July— from the tenor of his letter of that date I am indeed to hope that he has been partially successful since in the event of no prospect presenting itself within a month, it was his purpose to return immediately.

The summary view you have taken of British and European affairs, is highly satisfactory. Ireland appears to be irrecoverably lost to the British Empire for every future and useful purpose. I have seen and conversed with several well informed Irish Emigrants only 8 weeks from Cove of Cork, who all concur that a deep spirit of disaffection prevails in all the loyalist Corps, ready to manifest itself in the whole kingdom, whenever a body of six to eight thousand french can maintain a landing. Events in the West Indies, and probably, 'ere this, in the East Indies, are not less inauspicious to the interests of the most favored nation. Nor do I see that the earnestly designed alliance with those republican states, can be, ultimately, one jot more propitious to the cause of Monarchy.

I perceive that the Aurora has arisen with poison (to Aristocracy) under its wings. The argus is also awakened and will I am told, under the direction of Mr. Meigs a professor of New Haven College,[2] extend its enlightened vigil thro' this & other Eastern States. You have seen and can now truly appreciate the merit of the persecution vs. Lyons. It is my opinion, that the friends of the rights of the people, should unite in an application, without reference to the man, for a writ of Error from the Supreme Court to obtain a reversal of the sentence vs. him, Or compel the Supreme Judiciary to record, in its affirmation of the sentence, its own voluntary submission to an oppressive and unconstitutional law. On this & other topics, I have much to say to you when we meet. I fear the next Congress will be too nearly divided to express much change of system. Not a word yet of the Massachusetts Elections.

Accept the united regards of our ladies & myself to Mrs. Coxe and yourself, and may I ask you to make them acceptable to my friend Mr. Duponceau & his lady. Within a week I hope personally to salute you. Yrs. as ever,

John Beckley

RC (COXE PAPERS, HISTORICAL SOCIETY OF PENNSYLVANIA).

1. Pierre E. DuPonceau (1760–1844), a native of France and a veteran of the American Revolution, was a lawyer in Philadelphia, who specialized in estate managment for Republicans, such as Coxe and Beckley.
2. Josiah Meigs, lawyer and professor of mathematics and natural philosophy at Yale University, had established the *New Haven Gazette* in 1784. Thomas Greenleaf, who had been publisher of the Republican New York *Argus* since 1795 had died on September 14, 1798, but was succeeded by his wife, Ann.

JOHN BECKLEY TO THOMAS JEFFERSON

Sir,   24 January 1799. 12 o'clock A.M.

Mr. Tazewell is no more—he this moment departed.[1]
Will you be pleased to make this melancholy event known to the Members of the Senate.
I have taken immediate preparatory measures for his funeral.
In great distress, I am, Sir, yrs.   John Beckley

RC (JEFFERSON PAPERS, LIBRARY OF CONGRESS).

> 1. The death of Henry Tazeweil, U.S. senator from Virginia since 1794 and boarder in the Beckley household while Congress was in session, was a deep personal loss to Beckley and during the next year he spent much of his time settling Tazewell's affairs and advising his son, Littleton Waller Tazewell after "the melancholy event" of the death of a friend "founded on an acquaintance of upwards of twenty Years." Beckley to Littleton Waller Tazewell, January 27, 1799, and eight additional personal letters of Beckley to the younger Tazewell are in the Virginia State Library.

JOHN BECKLEY TO JOHN MILLEDGE

My Dr. sir,[1]   Philadelphia. March 9th. 1799.

Your favor of the 5th January, with our deed from David Allison, duly recorded, were delivered me by Colo. Tatnall;[2] and I feel myself under great obligation to you for them, and for the accompanying letter and certificate from Mr. McGillis, the tax collector. I have written to Peirce Butler esqr. to pay Mr. McGillis 305 dollars and 23 cents, my one half of the tax, and Mr. Wescott has taken measures for the payment of his also. I now forward by Colo. Tatnall the original deed from John Ware Hunter to Mr. Allison, which ought to have been forwarded, at the time our was; but thro' mistake of Mr. Wescott was omitted. Mr. Allison being now dead and not possibility of any intermediate or interfering deed, either between Hunter & him or between him and any person other than Mr. Wescott and myself, I trust, not difficulty will occur in admitting it also to record; to which end, I solicit the aid of your professional efforts if necessary; remarking that Allison's deed to us being recorded, this would seem to go on record as of course.[3]

It is an old remark, that having once created an obligation to a friend, you thereby establish a fund for future similar demands on him: I am about to verify the remark, tho' not without a hope, that I may, as some time in my life be enabled to place myself a creditor to this fund. Colo. Tatnall advices me to request of you to procure for us from the Surveyor of the County, a complete draft of our lands, on a scale not too large or expensive,

155

but sufficient to exhibit a full view of the lines and courses; the rivers, creeks, and watercourses, swamps &c. &c. and to annex thereto, a special Certificate from the Surveyor, on these several points, to wit:

1st. At what distance from the Sea, do these land lay?

2d. Do they adjoin or lay on either or both the rivers, Satilla and St. Marys?

3d. What is the general or particular quality of them?

4th. What proportion of them may be called Hammock lands?

5th. What, or is any proportion, rice swamp, or capable of being made so?

6th. What is the general, or particular timber growth?

7th. Is the timber generally large and of lofty growth?

8th. What useful general purposes can the timber be applied to?

9th. What is the general value of Hammock lands?

10. Can vessels of any, and what burthen, approach the lands, and how near?

11th. What distance are those lands from Savanna and Charleston? And every other information he may think useful or necessary.

We request the favor of you to draw on John Beckley and George Wescott, at seven days sight, for amount of the Surveyor's charges and all other expenses of recording the deeds &c. &c. which shall be duly accepted and honored: And we solicit your friendly attention for as early an answer as can possibly be obtained from the Surveyor, referring it to your discretion to forward it to our address, either by the land or water mail.

And now, my good friend, permit me to request your attention to another subject more particularly interesting to myself; and which, I confide in your sympathetic efforts to serve me in, having seen the unmerited treatment I received from the late H.Reps. of the U.S. My intention is to be a candidate at the next Congress for my former station, and, when I shall receive from you the necessary information to address by letter, and commit to your care, my applications to Mr. Taliaferro and Mr. Jones, both of whom, I am, I believe a personal stranger.[4] Their characters place them beyond the influence of any improper brass, and to their candor and justice only shall I appeal. If you know the gentlemen sufficiently to appraise them of my purpose, and can conveniently do so, I will ask it of you and also to advise me of any thing you may think necessary or proper for me to do on the occasion.

Mrs. Beckley and our little daughter write with me in our best wishes for your health and happiness, and with a heart full of grateful acknowledgment for your friendly exertions to serve me, I remain, my dear Sir, Yrs. ec.   JB.

PS: It is designed by Mr. Wescott and myself to offer our land to the Commissioner or Secretary of the Navy, at such a valuation as, upon a view and examination of it, indifferent men may fix. In our proposition we have taken the liberty to name you as our friend, to whom the Agent of the navy may apply for directions to find the Survey of the County to shew the land; referring it to you also, to name any suitable man of character and fitness as the viewer on our part, whose charges and reasonable expenses we will pay, and who in case of disagreement with the Agent of the Navy, shall agree on an Umpire. We presume that the timber growth of the land is fit for most naval purposes in ship building. JB.

LB (BECKLEY FAMILY PAPERS, LIBRARY OF CONGRESS).

1. John Milledge (1757–1818) served as a representative from Georgia in the 3rd, 4th, 5th, and 7th Congresses.
2. Josiah Tattnall (1764–1803) was a U.S. senator from Georgia (1796–99) and governor of Georgia (1799–1802).
3. Beckley and George Wescott had acquired by default the murky claim of David Allison to approximately 200,000 acres in Camden County, Georgia. Beckley spent much of 1799 trying to determine the status of the grant, which was later listed as involved in the Yazoo Land Grant scandal. Berkeley, *Beckley*, p. 188 and Beckley Letterbook, Library of Congress.
4. James Jones and Benjamin Taliaferro were Georgia's newly elected representatives to Congress, replacing Milledge and Abraham Baldwin. Beckley did not regain his House clerkship in the Sixth Congress, losing to Jonathan W. Condy, 47 to 39. *Debates and Proceedings, Sixth Congress*, p. 186.

JOHN BECKLEY TO WILLIAM IRVINE

Dear General, Philadelphia, 22 March 1799

I conclude since the mail has arrived without a line from you that the bad roads detained you on the way until [it was] too late, or your reaching home to write. We are all very anxious to know the situation of the family but I will continue to hope that you found them better than your fears had anticipated. It affords me great pleasure to inform you that your bill has passed the Senate without opposition and is this day gone to the Governor for his approbation. My information is from Mr. Morgan.[1]

Our entire family remains as you left us—the erruption on the Childs face has almost entirely disappeared. Have you any farther news of Nancy. I send off today duplicate of my letter to Major Butler, in which I request the favour of his interesting himself respecting the mode of her return.

Mr. Coxe has placed the Committee business on the footing he promised. Nothing is to be done for two or three months and before that time you can determine what course it will be advisable to pursue.[2]

We have no foreign news. Of domestic our accounts to day say that full and entire submission has taken place in Northampton. Notwithstanding, General Hamilton is arrived, and it is said an effective force of 2000 men, must march.[3]

With the best wishes of all this family to all of yours, I remain, dear Sir, Your affect. friend John Beckley[4]

RC (IRVINE PAPERS, HISTORICAL SOCIETY OF PENNSYLVANIA).

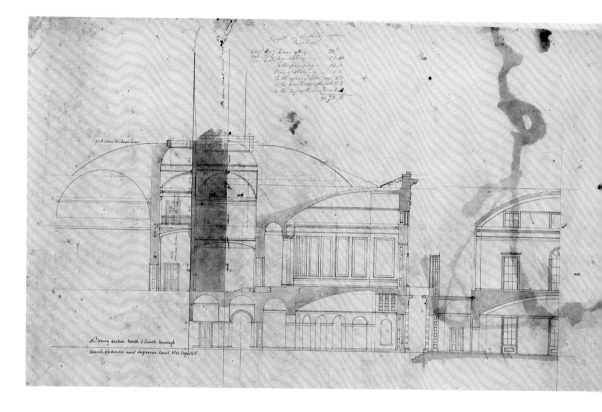

1. Benjamin Morgan, Federalist member of Pennsylvania state senate or Jacob Morgan, a sugar refiner, director of the Bank of Pennsylvania, and a member of the Pennsylvania Democratic Society. Tinkcom, *Republicans and Federalists in Pennsylvania*, pp. 84–86, 176–79, 201, and 307.

2. The "committee business" was the Republican committee of correspondence appointed at a March 1, 1799, meeting in Philadelphia to direct the party campaign on behalf of Thomas McKean in the governor's race. Coxe was chairman of the seven-man committee and Irvine was one of the members, but Irvine played little role in the campaign and was even accused by some Republicans of supporting the Federalist candidate, James Ross. Nevertheless, McKean did appoint Irvine superintendent of military stores at Philadelphia. See Beckley to Irvine, August 23 and November 8, 1799; Cooke, *Tench Coxe*, pp. 348–70 and Tinkcom, *Republicans and Federalists in Pennsylvania*, pp. 221–41.

3. In the face of a second anti-tax revolt within five years in Pennsylvania, President Adams issued a proclamation on March 12, 1799, ordering the dispersal of the rebels and on March 20, the administration directed General Hamilton to call out the militia to suppress the rebellion. Hamilton, who commanded the federal forces called to service in the quasi-war with France, used federal troops to suppress the rebellion. Capt. John Fries, the suspected leader of the rebellion was arrested, convicted of treason, sentenced to be hung, and later pardoned by Adams. Tinkcom, *The Republicans and Federalists in Pennsylvania*, pp. 217–19, and relevant documents in Syrett, ed., *Hamilton Papers*, vols. 22 and 23.

4. Beckley wrote personal letters to Irvine on April 12 and 26. In that of April 26, Beckley remarked to Irvine that:"The full tide of success to Republicanism in Europe and the removal of the state government to Lancaster, have reanimated the hopes of the friends of Liberty here." Irvine Papers, Historical Society of Pennsylvania.

JOHN BECKLEY TO WILLIAM IRVINE

Dear General,   Philadelphia 10th May 1799.

Your favour by Doctor McCroskey came to hand to day, and we are all happy to know that the family in general is well and Callender[1] no worse. Nancy is recovered of her passage and appears in confirmed good health. We think that it will be too inconvenient for her to take a seat in Doctor McCroskeys Phaeton, and have concluded to her taking a seat in the mail Stage on Saturday morning the 18th when, if it will procure the best escort for her that I can. She writes you fully by this days Mail. Our family all continues well and little Miss grows finely.

There are about 12 or 13 democrats returned for Virginia and the rest of the worst sort, altho I count fewer enemies than before.[2]

Fries is convicted of High treason and I presume must hang if it were only to prove the infallibility of presidential proclamation. O tempore. O Mores.

God bless you. Adieu, Yours sincerely,   John Beckley

RC (IRVINE PAPERS, HISTORICAL SOCIETY OF PENNSYLVANIA).

1. Capt. Callender Irvine, son of William, recovered and was appointed by Jefferson to succeed his father as superintendent of military stores in 1804.
2. Beckley was referring to the Virginia congressional delegation for the Sixth Congress. Washington and Jefferson estimated that eight of Virginia's nineteen representatives were Federalists. Cunningham, *Jeffersonian Republicans*, p. 134.

JOHN BECKLEY TO WILLIAM IRVINE

Dear General,   Philadephia, 17th May 1799.

Your favour of the 14th found us all well last evening Setting round the tea table, and we were made happy to know that it was all equally well with you. Nancy will hand you this, She leaves us in the Morning-Neither Mr. Duncan or Major Henderson return so soon, but a young Gentleman from Lancaster, Who knows her, is a fellow passenger as far as there. I regret on her account, that it now rains so hard as I fear she will have a disagreeable Journey. Tell my little friend Armstrong that I have laid by for him a drum and equipments to be sent by first opportunity, Sister Nancy not being able to take them along.

I remind you again of Callenders Case. Our James is absolutely restored and several other equally unlooked for cures have been made.

I am sorry I cannot answer your enquires about Mr. Orr, only to say I believe he is uncle to the young man and a Contractor to the Army and consequently in the receipt of Monies. Why he neglects his kinsman and leaves you in the lurch I cannot account. But you don't mention his first name or what part of Kentucky he lives in. There are many of the name of Orr in that Country as well as Virginia. In case you are like to suffer by him, a more particular description from the young man, might Enable me to pursue some useful enquiry for you or for him.

Nancy will tell you all our family news. Club law has commenced here. You will see by the Aurora the gallant alihnment of 15 cavalry officers against the Editor of that paper. But as I am called on to prosecute them, I shall forbear to animadvert here. Yesterday however the victorious sons of Order, were content to walk away untriumphant—the democrats assembled, and the Macedonian heroes vanished in the Shade, after having collected avowedly to tar and feather Duane. The discretion of one or two Kept off the Northern Liberty boys and prevented a scene of bloodshed. I am happy that the affair is not like to pass off judicially.[1]

Accept all our best wishes to every body—and believe me, dear General, very truly, Yours,   John Beckley

RC (IRVINE PAPERS, HISTORICAL SOCIETY OF PENNSYLVANIA).

1. William Duane, editor of the *Aurora*, was attacked by cavalrymen angered by critical reports of military actions in Fries Rebellion appearing in the newspaper. Duane retained Beckley as attorney in a planned civil suit against the attackers. Tinkcom, *Republicans and Federalists in Pennsylvania*, p. 218.

JOHN BECKLEY TO WILLIAM IRVINE

Dear General,   Philadelphia 2d August 1799.

As the promised time of our intended Visit approaches I begin to be apprehensive of farther delays. I have sold a tract of my Kentuckey land for 12,000 dollrs payable 19th January next, and am endeavouring to convert the contract into Money at a discount; the delay and difficulty of this operation, and its importance to me, will I am sure be admitted, by all your good family, as a sufficient cause for delay, or, should it so happen of failure until another Season—or perhaps a flying visit for a few days from your humble servant. Our City continues uncommonly healthy, not a single case of yellow fever known. You have not mentioned for some time the state of our friend Captain Irvines health, from whence I conclude that it progresses well. We all continue well—little Mary improves daily—the Browns are at Morristown, and Nancy Prince and Sally near Germantown.

If we should be finally defeated in our proposed visit, Mrs. Irvines Commission to Maria, will be nevertheless duly executed & forwarded by some safe hand. We do not however by any means dismiss the hope of seeing you in all this Month.

How comes on Election for Governor with you. It engrosses all conversation here. I suspect it will be a...[1] no foreign news but what the paper [contains]... have begun again to move forward....

With our united regards... dear Sir, Yrs. Sincerely.   John Beckley

RC (IRVINE PAPERS, HISTORICAL SOCIETY OF PENNSYLVANIA).

1. Manuscript damaged here and below; an unknown number of words in three lines are illegible.

JOHN BECKLEY TO WILLIAM IRVINE

Dear General   Philadelphia 23d Augst 1799.

I write you in a state of Convalescence from a sickbed, to which I have been confined one week, by a severe cold which fell into my loins & kidneys, attended with fever and symptoms of inflammation. Dr. Rush, by dint of depletion, has once more restored me, and, save weakness, I am as well as ever—and trust on Saturday the 31st to set off for Carlisle. Our City is again alarmed—the fever has burst forth again like a volcano which has been somewhile smothered, and death or desertion is the only alternative. Imperious circumstances detain me till the time I mention, but principally my health & present weakness, however, we hold no communication down town, and the sickness is yet principally confined to Spruce and Pine streets near the water. Should next month prove hot & dry the desolation will be complete, and I fear that instead of a short visit, we shall be compelled to shelter with you much longer. We may hope however, that as it has begun late it will cease early.

Your favour of the 13th has this moment been handed to me. I am far too weak to answer it fully. As soon as I am able I will see Mr. Dallas and communicate your ideas to him. Your situation is to be sure as undesirable as I know it was unsought for on your part, and therefore highly unmerited. Cuffed at by both parties, and counted an Enemy by both, It only remains to act with that consistent firmness which has so conspicuously marked your Character and conduct, by Evidencing that without being, in the present tumult of struggle for the Chair of Government, a partyman, you are undeviatingly devoted to republican principles.[1] We are happy in Callenders recovery. Accept all our best wishes, and believe me, dear General, Yours sincerely,   John Beckley

RC (IRVINE PAPERS, HISTORICAL SOCIETY OF PENNSYLVANIA).

1. See Beckley to Irvine, March 22, 1799, note 1.

JOHN BECKLEY TO WILLIAM IRVINE

Dear General,   Philadelphia, 8th November 1799.

Your favour of the 4th is just received. On Monday last, I delivered to Mr. Dunwoody the Medicine & directions from Doctor Howell for Captain Irvine. He (Dunwoody) gave me the most solemn promise to send it by Thursday with a safe & certain conveyance, and I flatter myself it has come to hand 'ere this—I feel great concern at the unremitting severity of your sons case, but have great confidence of his speedy cure.

F. Muhlenberg[1] is certainly appointed by Mifflin in place of Johnson. Dallas left this yesterday for Lancaster and will be there a Week. I called several times to converse privately with him but always found company, and could therefore only glance generally at your Views, but I shall see Mifflin, in a day or two, and if I find him in a proper mood, will be very unreserved with him. You will see our Republican Address to the Cheif,[2] and his resolute answer. It fell upon me at the public meeting to harangue for the proper. . .[3] a right and orderly direction to the proceedings. . . the Excess of popular feeling. You'l see that. . . Every thing passed off with decency & moderation.

I am happy that you saw & conversed with Colo. Hartley and think it may be important for me to write to him & advise that he attend the first day at all events, even if he should return home immediately. Had I known his wishes to dispose of Land, I think I could have served him, and probably can yet do so. At all events I should be very happy to do it, if I can.

I will write to Dawson at New York. If you can drop a line to Gregg, it may be very serviceable. I fear that nothing can be done with Woods. If his Neutrality can be obtained it is all I can expect. Should the Southern Men attend, I do not fear Success.[4]

I will see the Chief in a day or two & discover how your letter Works. I think he is at present very favorably disposed towards you. Occasionally, I will keep you informed. Accept to all the good family, our United best wishes.

Most sincerely, dear General, Yours   John Beckley

RC (IRVINE PAPERS, HISTORICAL SOCIETY OF PENNSYLVANIA).

1. Governor Thomas Mifflin had appointed Frederick A. C. Muhlenberg as receiver-general of the Pennsylvania Land Office.
2. That is Chief Justice McKean, who had just been elected governor of Pennsylvania. Irvine's efforts to regain McKean's favor, despite his opposition to his candidacy, resulted in his appointment as superintendent of military stores at Philadelphia. Tinkcom, *Republicans and Federalists in Pennsylvania*, pp. 220–24; and Berkeley, *Beckley*, p. 195.
3. Manuscript damaged, one word missing here and in three subsequent lines of text.

4. Thomas Hartley, Andrew Gregg and Henry Woods were representatives from Pennsylvania, and John Dawson was a representative from Virginia. Beckley was trying to enlist support for his second attempt to regain the clerkship of the House, which he subsequently lost to Condy 47 to 39. He attributed his loss to the absence of 16 southern members including 8 from Virginia. Hartley was among the absent members of Congress. *Debates and Proceedings, Sixth Congress*, p. 184 and Beckley to Andrew Moore, December 12, 1799, quoted in Berkeley, *Beckley*, p. 193.

JOHN BECKLEY TO TENCH COXE

Dear Sir,   Philadelphia 7th January 1800.

Mr. Brown takes a <u>sudden</u> trip to Lancaster, on business, and I cannot omit the opportunity of addressing you, altho' I have nothing particular to say, more than to enquire after your health and situation since you left us. We are without any occurrence foreign or domestic, and the severity with which the weather has set in, would seem to forbid for some days at least, the hope of any foreign arrival. Mr. B— will hand to the Governor a line from Mr. Jefferson on my behalf,[1] which I thought might produce no harm at least, even if it should be too late for any <u>immediate</u> arrangement that the Governor has contemplated. On your friendship and goodness I will equally rely and trust that if no disposition of the office of Register of Wills, adverse to my views, has been conclusively made, you will not cease to bear in mind the anxious wishes of a fellow sufferer with you.

It will afford me great pleasure to interchange with you whilst at Lancaster, such communications as our respective situations may afford. And with my best wishes and warmest regard, I am, dear Sir, sincerely yours,

John Beckley

RC (COXE PAPERS, HISTORICAL SOCIETY OF PENNSYLVANIA).

1. Jefferson praised Beckley in a January 9, 1800, letter to McKean: "Mr. Beckley informs he has proposed himself to your notice in the disposal of offices in this state. His long residence here has given you such opportunities of personal knowledge of him that it is unnecessary to supply that: otherwise I should add with pleasure & truth my testimony of the talents, diligence & integrity with which he has conducted himself in office, and of his zealous attachment to good principles in government, but all this has been under your own eye, and my putting pen to paper on the subject is only because he has set some value on my evidence."

In response McKean informed Jefferson on March 7, that he had appointed Beckley as clerk of the Mayor's Court for Philadelphia and clerk of the Orphans Court "which will amount to an Equivalent for the Clerkship of the House of Representatives which he was unjustly deprived of by a party, who place Mr. Condy (married to a sister of Mr. Joseph Hopkinson & my niece) in his stead." Jefferson Papers, Library of Congress.

JOHN BECKLEY TO TENCH COXE

Dear Sir,   Philadelphia, 24th January 1800.

Having little worth communicating and occupied by a number of Engagements of business, I have thus long delayed to acknowledge and thank you for your friendly favour by Mr. Brown. Concerns foreign & domestic thicken apace—those from France respecting Bonnaparte's Counter revolution are highly interesting, but until the entire Scheme is developed we must suspend any opinion of its ultimate effect on the republican cause, unless it be in adventuring to predict that the restoration of royalty is not the object.

On state affairs, I have forwarded to Virginia such a full view of our situation, and the necessity of their Assembly acting decidedly on the great questions of standing army, alien & sedition laws, assumption of common law, and a general ticket for Electors, that our friends have written me that every one of the Measures is or will be adopted, besides a corresponding change in their law for summoning Jurors, with the one contemplated in our Assembly. Mr. Madison has sent me a Copy of his resolutions which I would have forwarded to you, but understand that a Copy has been sent you by another friend.

I am now busily engaged in pursuit of a full collection of facts to establish on the part of the fœderal Government the creation of the prescriptive principle of disqualification to office and the application of it in each State, connected with Mr. Hamiltons original scheme to a System of Espoinage and Mr. Adams's recognition of the Jersey principle, of sending their opponents into the Enemys lines. My view is, by a temperate appeal to facts to vindicate in a full & satisfactory manner, to the Citizens of Pennsylvania, Mr. McKeans late course of proceeding, and the truth of the principles on which his administration is predicated. The late infuriate address of the senate affords him a golden opportunity to vindicate himself, and I Expect must favor his well known talents and soundness of mind. It strikes my recollection, that sometime ago I lent you (to copy) Mr. Hamilton's original proposition to the late president for an organized System of Espoinage thro' the medium of Revenue offices, with Mr. Jeffersons objections thereto, as stated to president Washington. If you have, or can point to where I can get it again, you will feel how critical it is for me now to be possessed with it.[1]

A deadly blow has been this day aimed at us in the Senate of the U.S. by our Senator Ross, who has laid on the table a Motion to appoint a Committee to enquire whether any and what provision is necessary by Congress to Explain the directions of the Constitution respecting the choice of Electors &c. &c. and to report by Bill or otherwise—avowed as intended to take away the right of any state to choose by general ticket.[2]

You will see in the papers the strange proceeding in the H.R. of Congress, respecting the Standing Army and the Sedition law. Marshall of Virginia, has played a deep, insidious game of intrigue with Bayard to defeat the repeal of the Sedition law, which feeling himself constrained to Vote for, he obtained of Bayard to introduce his common law amendment, which produced a rejection of the first proposition to repeal altho' it had been carried by a majority of two— but this 'entre nous'.[3]

In respect to myself, I am anxiously awaiting Mr. McKeans pleasure, as to office or employment. Mr. Jefferson has written him on my behalf, a very interesting letter, and I am equally sure of your zealous cooperation, but I am not acquainted Sufficiently with Joseph B. McKean, and Dallas had before promised to further my views. I confess however, that I am perhaps too little qualified in necessary assurance, to further effectually my own views. Nor have I ever been able to express to any one but yourself & our friend Duponceau my wish, if Campbell is removed, to occupy that Station. I think it probable that Mr. Findley, Mr. McClay, Mr. Barton, &c. might be useful auxiliaries to promote my wishes. If they can, I am sure you will not be unmindful of their aid. If that office is not yet absolutely fixed for another, it would enable me effectually, to serve our common cause, with my fullest exertion. I cannot however, remain a long time in my present uncertain State. My Virginia friend (Monroe) has offered me too small Stations worth together about 1200 dollars per annum and I must accept them if I cannot do better here—but is at this time inconvenient and injurious to remove, and I will not do it, but in the last resort.[4]

Accept my best wishes for your health & happiness and believe me, most sincerely, dear Sir, Your obliged friend   John Beckley.

RC (COXE PAPERS, HISTORICAL SOCIETY OF PENNSYLVANIA).

1. Beckley was referring to a draft circular to federal customs collectors prepared by Hamilton in May 1793, which included a paragraph directing these officials to report all violations of American neutrality directly to the Secretary of the Treasury. Following advice received from Jefferson and Attorney General Randolph, Washington directed Hamilton to amend the circular letter so that the customs officials were to report violations to the U.S. district attorneys instead of to the Secretary of the Treasury. No copy of Hamilton's original draft circular has been found by historians. Syrett, ed., *Hamilton Papers*, 25:666–67.
2. U.S. Senator James Ross of Pennsylvania had proposed the appointment of a committee to consider what "provisions ought to be made by law for deciding elections of President and Vice President of the United States, and for determining the legality or illegality of the votes given for those officers." *Debates and Proceedings, Sixth Congress*, pp. 28–31.
3. After a debate of nearly two weeks the House of Representatives voted not to repeal the acts of 1798 and 1799 providing for augmentations of the army. After another lengthy and spirited debate, the House voted not to repeal the "Sedition Act," which was due to expire in March 1801, and replace it with common law regulation of seditious actions. James A. Bayard of Delaware and Nathaniel Macon of North Carolina were the outspoken proponents of this action. *Debates and Proceedings, Sixth Congress*, pp. 247–425.
4. The nature of Monroe's offer has not been identified.

John Beckley's Address to the People of the United States with An Epitome and Vindication of the Public Life and Character of Thomas Jefferson. Philadelphia: Printed by James Carey, 1800.[1]

To the People of the United States.
Fellow-Citizens,   Pennsylvania, 4 July, 1800.

Auspicious to the best hopes of Americans, for the universal success of Republican liberty, the revolving year, 1800, presents you with the periodical right of suffrage in the election of a President of the U. States.

The magnitude of this right, and the deep interests it involves for the fate and happiness of our common country, demand your immediate, vigilant, unceasing and deliberate attention. Impartial, firm and independent, it remains with you to vindicate the rights of Republican liberty, and to crown with success the noblest and fairest experiment the world has ever yet seen, attempted by freemen, to establish self-government.

The probationary period of ten years, since the institution of a fœderal government, affords much ground to hope and fear, amidst that continued concussion of nations which still agitates the European world, and threatens to involve our western hemisphere in its ruinous vortex. Your sacrifices for peace and the virtuous efforts of your republican sons, have, hitherto preserved you from the fatal curse and calamity of war.

Pursuing, with misled confidence, the measures of men, whose hostility to the fundamental principles of your government, conceived the only hope of success, amidst scenes of war and confusion, you have been placed, more than once, on the precipice of destruction. Seceding from the principles avowed to the world as the basis of your republican institutions, the pillars of aristocracy have arisen, and in the direlection of American truths, the world has been astonished at your *retrograde* turn and rapid advance to monarchy.

A review of past events will but present the painful spectacle of political apostacy, amidst the wreck of principle: and the creation of systems equally subversive of liberty, peace and happiness—Suffice it to say, that new and unheard of doctrines have been advanced, precedents established, and laws enacted, which go to sap the very foundations of public liberty—Hence we have seen, in the abandonment of constitutional truth and principle, constructive treason avowed, and the right of trial by jury of the vicinage exploded in our courts of justice, whilst our legislative acts have begotten new and arbitrary principles of alienism and sedition, with an extended and boundless system of common law, adopted by a foreign nation, and never yet incorporated into any American code. And our executive functionaries have not been slothful in pursuing, under colour of law, persecutions and proscriptions of personal disqualifications for political opinions, and restraints on the liberty of the press—Or in promoting, by every faculty they possessed, systems of extended influence and wasteful expenditure, to the creation of heavy and oppressive public burdens, in numerous and unnecessary appointments to office, a standing army, a permanent navy, augmentation of public debt, loans at excessive and exorbitant interest, and finally additional and aggravated impost duties, excises, salt tax and land tax.

But, fellow-citizens, if in addition to this dark catalogue of public evils, you are told from the mouth of the now President of the U.S. that "*REPUBLICAN GOVERNMENT MAY BE INTERPRETED TO MEAN ANY THING,*" that "*THE BRITISH CONSTITUTION IS, IN THE STRICTEST SENSE, A REPUBLIC,*" that "*AN HEREDITARY PRESIDENT AND SENATE FOR LIFE, CAN ALONE SECURE YOU HAPPINESS;*" and that in the conflict of political opinions which prevail in our country, "*IT IS ADMISSIBLE FOR ONE FACTION TO SEIZE THE PERSONS OF THESE OPPONENTS AND TRANSFER THEM WITHIN THE LINE OF AN INVADING ENEMY;*"—*When* and *where* will you look for relief? Heaven has wisely ordered, that on your own virtuous efforts alone, shall it depend, to disavow the principles, revoke the measures, and discard the men, that have thus afflicted you. Happy, in the possession of a citizen, to whom, under God, American is principally indebted for the share of political well-being she now enjoys—*JEFFERSON*, mild, amiable, and philanthropic, refined in manners as enlightened in mind, the philosopher of the world, whose name adds lustre to our national character, and as a legislator and statesman, stands second to no man's—*Jefferson, yet lives*. On him then concentre your present views and your future hopes.

Illustrious by an active life, of great and consistent efforts to promote the universal establishment of republican liberty, and the permanent happiness of the great family of mankind, he will neither disappoint your hopes nor defeat your wishes. Look into his past life, examine all his conduct, and if you can discover one instance of political apostacy, or the direlection of a republican principle, then withhold from him your confidence and your suffrages.

Neither suffer yourselves to be deceived by the calumnious efforts of electioneering partizans, the real enemies of America, to depreciate the moral and political character of the man whose name should be dear to every republican heart. It is through the turpitude of those enemies that the pure virtues and pre-eminent talents of Jefferson stand reflected, with undiminished lustre, and present him to the world as the friend and benefactor of the human race. See the testimony of the venerable judge Pendleton, president of the Virginia convention, as recorded in the debates of that convention, page 100 and 101, on the question for adopting the fœderal constitution, who speaks in the following emphatic words: "I know and highly respect the great abilities of Mr. Jefferson—Providence has, for the happiness of mankind, accompanied those abilities with a disposition to make use of them for the good of his fellow-being."[2] Honourable testimonial of an aged and veteran statesman, who could contemplate with pleasure the support and patronage he had yeilded to the youthful virtues and rising talents of Jefferson, in early life—a testimonial as honourable to him that gave, as to him that received it.

But, resting on the same high and respected authority of judge Pendleton, see what he further says in the same debate, in reply to the artful insinuation then made, that Mr. Jefferson, who was at that time absent as minister of the United States in France, had written sentiments hostile to the adoption of the fœderal constitution, and advising the rejection.—"I have seen, says Mr. Pendleton, the letter in which Mr. Jefferson has written his opinion upon this subject.—It appears that he is possessed of that constitution, and has in his mind the idea of amending it—He has in his mind the very question of subsequent or previous amendments, which is now under consideration. His sentiments, on this subject are as follow: 'I wish with all my soul that the first nine conventions may accept the new constitution, because it will secure to us the good it contains, which I think great and important. I wish the four latest, whichever they be, may refuse to accede to it, 'till amendments are secured.' He then enumerates the amendments which he wishes to be secured, and adds—'We must take care however that neither this, nor any other objection to the form, produce a schism in our union. That would be an incurable evil; because friends falling out never cordially reunite.' Are these sentiments, (asks Mr. Pendleton) in favour of those who wish to prevent its adoption by previous amendment? He wishes the first nine states to adopt it—What are his reasons? Because it will secure to us the good it contains, which he thinks great and important, and he wishes the other four may refuse it, because he thinks it will tend to obtain necessary amendments—But he would not wish that a schism take place in the union *on any consideration*. If then we are to be influenced by his opinion at all, we will ratify it, and secure thereby the good it contains."

Republican citizens of America, will you believe it, and shall the groundless calumny yet find currency in our land, that Jefferson is an antifederalist and enemy to the constitution of the U. States? Reflect, and ask yourselves, whether, if in the prophetic spirit that dictated his remarks to the constitution, as before quoted, the convention of four states had refused to accede to it, until amendments were obtained, you would probably now have cause to regret the existence in your country of an alien and sedition law, of the lately adopted doctrine of constructive treason, and above all, of the ruinous and disgraceful treaty with Great-Britain?

Equally repulsive to the malign suggestion that Mr. Jefferson is an enemy to religion, the public records of his native state, present to the world in the statute book of their laws, the celebrated act "for establishing religious freedom"—drawn by the pen, and offered to the assembly of Virginia, by the hand of their enlightened and illustrious fellow-citizen: Read, ye fanatics, bigots, and religious hypocrites, of whatsoever clime or country ye be—and you, base calumniators, whose efforts to traduce are the involuntary tribute of envy to a character more pure and perfect than your own, read, learn, and practise the *RELIGION OF JEFFERSON*, as displayed in the sublime truths and inspired language of *HIS* ever memorable "Act for establishing religious freedom," thus:— [3]

"*WELL* aware that Almighty God hath created the mind free; that all attempts to influence it by temporal punishments or burdens, or by civil incapacitations, tend only to beget habits of hyopcrisy and meanness, and are a departure from the plan of the Holy Author of our religion, who being Lord both of body and mind, yet chose not to propagate it by coercions on either, as was in his Almighty power to do, that the impious presumption of legislators and rulers, civil as well as ecclesiastical, who, being themselves but fallible and uninspired men, have assumed dominion over the faith of others, setting up their own opinions and modes of thinking as the only true and infallible, and as such endeavouring to impose them on others, hath established and maintained false religions over the greatest part of the world, and through all time; that to compel a man to furnish contributions of money for the propagation of opinions which he disbelieves, is sinful and tyrannical; that even the forcing him to support this or that teacher of his own religious persuasion, is depriving him of the comfortable liberty of giving his contributions to the particular pastor, whose morals he would make his pattern, and whose powers he feels most persuasive to righteousness, and is withdrawing from the ministry those temporary rewards, which proceeding from an approbation of their personal conduct, are an additional incitement to earnest and unremitting labours for the instruction of mankind; that our civil rights have no dependence on our religious opinion, more than our opinions in physics or geometry; that therefore the proscribing any citizen as unworthy the public confidence, by laying upon him an incapacity of being called to offices of trust and emolument, unless he profess or renounce this or that religious opinion, is depriving him injuriously of those privileges and advantages, to which, in common with fellow-citizens, he has a natural right; that it tends also to corrupt the principles of that very religion it is meant to encourage, by bribing with a monopoly of worldly honours and emoluments, those who will externally profess and conform to it; that though indeed these are criminal who do not withstand such temptation, yet neither are those innocent who lay the bait in their way; that to suffer the civil magistrate to intrude his powers into the field of opinion, and to restrain the profession or propagation of principles on supposition of their ill tendency, is a dangerous fallacy, which at once destroys all religious liberty, because he being of course judge of that tendency, will make his opinions, the rate of judgment, and approve or condemn the sentiments of others only as they shall square with or differ from his own; that it is time enough for the rightful purposes of civil government, for its officers to interfere when principles break out into overt acts against peace and good order; and finally, that truth is great, and will prevail if left to herself: that she is the proper, and sufficient antagonist to error, and has nothing to fear from the conflict, unless by human interposition, disarmed of her nat-

ural weapons, free argument and debate, errors ceasing to be dangerous when it is permitted freely to contradict them:

"Be it therefore enacted by the General Assembly—That, no man shall be compelled to frequent or support any religious worship, place, or ministry whatsoever, nor shall be enforced, restrained, molested or burdened in his body or goods, nor shall otherwise suffer on account of his religious opinions or belief; but that all men shall be free to profess, and by argument to maintain, their opinions in matters of religion, and that the same shall in no wise diminish, enlarge, or affect their civil capacities.

"And though we well know that this assembly elected by the people for the ordinary purposes of legislation only, have no power to restrain the acts of succeeding assemblies, constituted with powers equal to our own, and that therefore to declare this act to be Irrevocable, would be of no effect in law; yet we are free to declare, and do declare, that the rights hereby asserted, are of the natural rights of mankind, and that if any act shall be hereafter passed to repeal the present; or to narrow its operation such act will be an infringement of natural right."

Further, if the opponents of Mr. Jefferson require additional proof of the *ardent piety* and *religious fervour* of his mind, let them read in his "Notes on Virginia," page 237,[4] his reflections on the subject of slavery, expressive of his wishes for a *gradual* emancipation, which are concluded by the following pious apostrophe. "Can the liberties of a nation be thought secure when

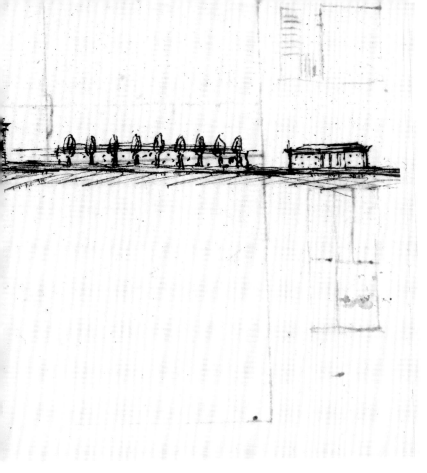

Sketch of White House south front showing War and Treasury Department buildings. Attributed to William Thornton, 1793–1805. LC–USZ62–37199.

we have removed their only firm basis, a conviction in the minds of the people *that these liberties are of the gift of God?* That they are not to be violated but with *his* wrath! *Indeed I tremble for my country when I reflect God is just: that his justice cannot sleep forever*: that considering numbers, nature and natural means only, a revolution of the wheel of fortune, an exchange of situation is among possible events: that it may become probable by supernatural interferrence! *The Almighty* has no attribute which can take side with us in such a contest. But it is impossible to be temperate and to pursue this subject through the various considerations of policy, of morals, of history, natural and civil. We must be contented to hope they will force their way into every one's mind. I think a change already perceptible since the origin of the present [American] revolution. The spirit of the master is abating, that of the slave rising from the dust; his condition mollifying, *the way I hope preparing, under the auspices of heaven,* for a total emancipation, and that this is disposed in the *order of events,* to be with *the consent of the masters, rather* than by their *extirpation.*"

Again, in the same Notes, page 240, evincing his anxiety to cultivate a spirit of genuine virtue in the public mind, as the sure preservative of republican liberty, he expresses a no less exalted sentiment of the cultivators of the soil, the yeomanry of our country, than a just confidence in the order of providence to perpetuate, through them, the sacred flame of moral and religious virtue.

"Those," says Jefferson, "who labour in the earth are the chosen people of God; if ever he had a chosen people, whose breasts he has made his peculiar deposit for substantial and genuine virtue. It is the focus in which he keeps alive that sacred fire, which otherwise might escape from the face of the earth. Corruption of morals in the mass of cultivators is a phenomenon of which no age nor nation has furnished an example. It is the mark set on those, who *not looking up to heaven*, to their own soil and industry, *as does the husbandman*, for their subsistance, depend for it on the casualties and caprice of customers, Dependance begets subservience and venality, suffocates the germ of virtue, and prepares fit tools for the designs of ambition—It is the manners and spirit of a people which preserve a republic in vigour. A degeneracy in these is a canker which soon eats to the heart of its laws and constitution."

But is there not yet another accusation produced by the *calumniators* of this good man, which the recorded testimonial of his country's approbation, also refutes? Namely, that while he was governor of Virginia, in the year 1781, during Arnold's invasion of that state, he shamefully fled before a handful of light horse, and left the capital of the state, Richmond, to be pillaged and plundered by the enemy. If indeed it were true that Mr. Jefferson had been thus timid and faithless to his public trust, no man will believe that the Legislature of Virginia were ignorant of the circumstances, or unmindful of his conduct. Accordingly it will be found in the proceedings of the Virginia Legislature of the 12th of December, 1781, that that assembly, having all the circumstances of Mr. Jefferson's conduct before them and within their knowledge, respecting that invasion, *unanimously* resolves, "That the thanks of the General Assembly be given to Thomas Jefferson, Esq. for his *attentive administration* of the powers of the Executive, whilst in office."

In addition, if the *unanimous* testimony of the Legislature be not, in the opinion of his caluminators, most conclusive, it will be seen in the Gazette of the United States, published at Philadelphia, by John Fenno, that on the 26th of October, 1796, when the same groundless calumny was brought forward in that gazette, against Mr. Jefferson, for the same purpose that it is now used, a gentleman, who then gave his name to the printer, and who had been an officer in the army and an eye witness of all Mr. Jefferson's conduct during the invasion of Virginia, in the year 1781, published in that gazette the following testimonial of that conduct, which was never either answered or controverted; to wit,[5]

Mr. Fenno,

I observe some shameful mistatements of the writer in your Gazette under the signature of Phocion, respecting the conduct of Mr. Jefferson, while governor of Virginia, in the year 1781, and having been personally present, in actual service, through all the active scenes of that year, from its commencement and before, until after the termination of the siege of York, I can state what that conduct really was, with more truth and certainty than either Phocion or his friend Charles Simms, neither of whom appear to know much about what they have written, and were, to my knowledge, neither of them in Virginia at the period referred to. First, then it is not true that "Mr. Jefferson *abandoned his trust at the moment of invasion.*" Arnold's invasion took place in January, 1781: Mr. Jefferson remained in his station through the whole period of that invasion. Cornwallis's invasion took place in April, 1781, and he continued to advance into the country until the beginning of June, when he commenced his retreat before the marquis Fayette, into the lower country, on the seaboard; the marquis having taken the command about two months before. Mr. Jefferson did not resign at all, or abandon his station; he remained in office until after Cornwallis's retreat, and until the time for which he was constitutionally elected had expired; to wit, the 12th of June, 1781. Before he left this office, however, Mr. Jefferson demanded of the Legislature, a full enquiry into the conduct of the Executive for the last twelve months; which was accordingly granted by their resolution of the 12th of June, 1781; and the 26th of November following appointed for the enquiry—being a period of near six months allowed to bring forward any charges or proofs against Mr. Jefferson, and that there never was any cause for the enquiry but some vague and groundless rumours, they passed the resolution of the 12th December, 1781, already published in your paper (Mr. Fenno), and which if Phocion's candour will permit him again to read, he will find not merely an acknowledgment of Mr. Jefferson's ability and integrity, and *altogether silent on the want of firmness,* but containing an unanimous and express vote of thanks for *his attentive administration of the powers of the Executive, whilst in office.*

Secondly, Mr. Fenno, it is not true that Mr. Jefferson at any time fled before a few light horsemen, and shamefully abandoned his trust, or, as suggested by Charles Simms, contributed by his conduct to the loss and distress which accrued to the state, in the destruction of public records and vouchers for general expenditure. Let facts speak: In four days from the arrival of Arnold's fleet, he proceeded 150 miles up James river, and landed his troops within 24 miles of Richmond, the night before his march to that place: all the militia of the state, which could be armed, being then out under the command of general Nelson, in the neighbourhood of Williamsburg, and no defence at hand for the security of Richmond but about 200 half-armed militia, under the command of baron Steuben, who could do nothing more than cover the removal of the records and military forces across James river, from Richmond to Manchester, and secure the boats and batteaus on the Manchester side, to prevent the enemy's passing. The writer of this remained in Richmond with the last detachment of militia that passed the river with records and stores, and until the enemy, about 9 o'clock in the morning, had entered the lower part of the town and began to flank it with their light horse, he saw Mr. Jefferson as active as man could be, as well the night before as that morning, issuing his orders and using every exertion to remove the records and stores. He afterwards saw him at Westham, five miles above Richmond, where Arnold pushed a detachment to destroy the stores at that place, and which, through Mr. Jefferson's exertions, were almost entirely saved. The next day, when the enemy evacuated Richmond, the first man the writer saw, as he entered the town, was Mr. Jefferson. Let a candid public then determine whether conduct like this, to which the writer hereof was an eye witness, manifested want of firmness or an abandonment of trust. The situation of the state was at that time peculiarly distressing; the whole quota of its continental troops were then acting in South-Carolina; many thousand stand of arms had been supplied for the defence of North-Carolina, and Arnold's invasion found the state almost totally defenceless. The state of things was little better a few months afterwards, when Cornwallis's invasion happened, and the marquis Fayette took the command; since it is well known that through the whole of that campaign the marquis could never muster more than three or four thousand militia, badly armed, in aid of the few continental troops that were detached from the northern army, to Virginia. Such was the deplorable situation both of the state and continent, for want of arms. In respect to Tarleton's sudden march to Charlottesville, during that campaign, in order to surprise the governor and assembly, it will be remembered, that the marquis's army was inferior to Cornwallis's, and had few or no cavalry attached to it; that at Charlottesville there was not even a single company of militia, and that Tarleton made a rapid march, of about 60 miles through the country, at the head of about 500 cavalry. The writer of this was also present at Charlottesville at the time, and saw Mr. Jefferson and his executive Council attending their duty at that place, with the Assembly: it will not be pretended then, under the circumstances stated, that Mr. Jefferson "*fled before a few light horsemen, and shamefully abandoned his trust,*" as *shamefully* asserted by Phocion.

But, Mr. Fenno, why do the enemies of Mr. Jefferson cavil *alone* at his honourable acquittal by the Assembly of Virginia, from groundless and unfounded charges? they well know that at the end of that very year, his brave and gallant successor to public accusation and impeachment before the Assembly, for supposed misconduct in office, and honourably acquited by the same body, in the same precise manner, and with an unanimous vote of thanks, as in the case of Mr. Jefferson. No proof appeared against either; the accusation in each was declared to be groundless, and the honourable reputation of both stand or fall by the verdict of the same body. I leave it with a candid public to form their own reflections.

26th October, 1796. A SUBSCRIBER.

There yet remain two other calumnies against the much-abused character of Mr. Jefferson, which require notice. They were both suggested in the year 1792, on the eve of a presidential election, and again in the year 1796, on a similar occasion, and are now revived; to wit,

1st, That when minister of the United States to France, in the year 1787, he made a dishonourable proposition to Congress, respecting a transfer of the debt due by the United States to France, to a Dutch company.[6]

2dly, That he was a debtor to British merchants before the revolutionary war, and pursued measures to defraud his creditors.[7]

Unhappily for his calumniators, both these charges have been proved to be perfectly groundless, and to have originated only in the wickedness and malice of his enemies.

The first charge was published in the year 1792, in Fenno's Gazette, and given, as believed, from the treasury department of the United States, on whose books Mr. Jefferson's letter to Congress respecting the French debt, was recorded. The then head of that department was roundly accused, in the public prints of that year, with misrepresentation and the breach of an official duty, in causing or permitting to be published from the treasury books, for the purpose of aiding the calumny against Mr. Jefferson, a mutilated copy of his letter to Congress, leaving out two entire paragraphs of it, and changing the sense of the part published, by substituting words not in the original. This accusation was evaded, but never disproved before the public, and it remains a solemn and incontrovertible truth, that the letter was published, so mutilated.

The facts in relation to that letter are briefly these: Mr. Jefferson informs congress, that an offer had been made by a speculating Dutch company to the French court, to purchase the American debt due to that nation, at a discount of six or eight million of livres; to which offer, when communicated by the French minister, to Mr. Jefferson, for his approbation, he replied that he had no power to approve or disapprove; to the agent of the Dutch company, who made the same application, he returned a similar answer; and in his letter to congress, presuming that the Dutch agent would made application to that body, he states the reflection, "how far, if congress apprehended any future danger of the punctuality of payment, it might be adviseable to transfer the discontents arising from that source, from the French court, whose friendship we ought to cultivate, to the breasts of a *private company* of *adventuring speculators*, who foreseeing the possible delays of payment, had calculated the probable loss, and were willing to encounter the hazard."

Two other paragraphs follow; to wit, "That in his (Mr. Jefferson's) opinion, however, the honour and credit of the United States may be preserved inviolate: that the French debt may be discharged *without discount* or *loss* to that nation, and the stipulations of the United States be complied with, to all its creditors." And he then suggests to congress the mode of doing it.

The enemies of Mr. Jefferson published this letter, leaving out the two last paragraphs, and changing the sense of the first in the manner that had been stated.

On the whole letter a single reflection is submitted, Whether in any instance of public conduct Mr. Jefferson could have more justly appreciated the duty of a public minister, or more happily combined it with the conscientious and moral sense of public and private integrity?

The second charge, "That Mr. Jefferson was a debtor to British merchants, before the revolutionary war, and pursued measures to defraud his creditors," is refuted and disproved, in a manner highly honourable to Mr. Jefferson's reputation, by a publication of the 5th of April last, made in Philadelphia, by a gentleman who took particular pains to investigate the subject; and is as followeth:

ACCOUNT OF MR. JEFFERSON'S BRITISH DEBTS.

It is the fate of every man whose virtue and talents have elevated him in society, to excite the envy and hatred of many; among persons thus disposed, some are imperceptibly carried into error, others are designedly criminal. The steady industry displayed by the assailants of virtue exceeds infinitely that of its defenders; and unfortunately, the meditated injury has its full effect before the person accused is aware of it, and instead of parrying the blow he has the wound to heal. In this situation of things, so rare is benevolence to be found amongst us, so little interest do we generally take in the welfare of our fellow-men, that we are apt to imagine we have discharged our duty when we declare our belief of the innocence of the accused, and content ourselves under the self-approbation, that we have done nothing to injure the feelings of the sufferer.

The evils to society which we permit to remain, without our utmost exertions to remove, may answer well enough with people who are *negatively good*, or who believe that virtue consists in abstaining from evil: I think differently: and thinking as I do, will never permit the people to be duped by false accusations levelled against their most meritorious and deserving servants. If in the charges, which, from my best judgment, I am obliged to make against public characters, I pass into error, the principle which governs me, ought also to draw forth an advocate for truth and virtue, on the opposite side of the question.

For some time past, a great clamour has been made through the United States, respecting debts due from Mr. Jefferson, to British merchants: I have taken some trouble to inform myself upon this subject, and I confess, that although I did not believe the charge to be correct, as to the idea which it was intended to convey of that gentleman's honour; I had no conception, that his enemies would be driven to attack him upon a subject, which, if fairly examined, would add so considerably to the lustre of his character.

In the year 1774, before a shilling of paper money had been issued, Mr. Jefferson sold about five thousand acres of land in Cumberland and Bedford counties, to pay his proportion of a debt due from the estate of Mr. Wayles to Farrel and Jones. He offered the bonds to their agent immediately, who refused to take them. The money was paid to Mr. Jefferson in 1779 and 1780, and he carried it to the treasury of Virginia, as the laws pressed on all to do, who owed money to British subjects; declaring that the public would pay it over, dollar for dollar. This delusion soon passed away, and it became evident, that the public neither could nor ought to pay according to the nominal value. The reader will perceive the loss which Mr. Jefferson sustained, and that if he had been disposed to quibble, no event could have afforded him a more plausible pretext: But it appears that this gentleman considered himself still answerable to Farrel and Jones, and therefore settled with their agent otherwise.

The next debt in succession, was one due to Kippen and company, for whom Mr. Lyle, of Manchester, was agent. I called upon that gentleman for information respecting Mr. Jefferson's conduct in the settlement of this claim, who assured me that it was strictly honourable. Mr. Lyle told me that as soon as the Vice President returned from his mission to France, he waited upon him, and made immediate arrangements for payment, deducting the 8 years war interest.

Concerning the war interest, I think the annexed letter from Mr. Jefferson, will be quite satisfactory. But exclusive of his particular situation, and the losses which he sustained, probably from his conspicuous services during the revolutionary contest; I know of not a solitary instance in which the eight years interest has been paid, if objected to by the defendant's counsel; and I fancy it was the opinion of the federal judges assembled in Philadelphia, that the war interest ought to be deducted, if a special reason for avoiding it could be assigned—and surely no reason could be assigned with more forcible propriety, than that the British themselves had destroyed the means. But, to my mind, there is the best evidence of the equity of withholding the eight years interest; the juries have uniformly deducted it, although the counsel for the plaintiff has often assigned peculiar and strong reasons, springing from the manner in which the debt originated, why it should be allowed.

The following letter from Mr. Jefferson, while in Paris, is now submitted to the public. It was not procured from him, but having been produced in court by Jones's agent, in another case, twas by the counsel of that agent candidly and honourably read in court as an act of justice to Mr. Jefferson; got thus into the press, and has since been used by the advocates for the payment of British debts and by them, very much complimented.* [We add, from unquestionable authority, that soon after Mr. Jefferson's return from France, arrangements were made with the agent of Farrel and Jones, and a deposit placed in his hands, to the amount of the claim against Mr. Jefferson.]

————

SIR.   Paris. January 5, 1787.

When I had the pleasure of seeing you in London, I mentioned to you that the affairs of Mr. Wayles's estate, were left to be ultimately settled by Mr. Eppes, the only acting executor; that I have left in his hands also, and in those of a Mr. Lewis, the part of Mr. Wayles's estate which came to me, together with my own: that they were first to clear off some debts which had been ncessary contracted during the war, and would after that apply the whole profits to the payment of my part of Mr. Wayles's debt to you, and to a debt of mine to Kippen and company of Glasgow.—Being anxious to begin the payment of these two debts, and finding that it would be too long postponed if the residuary ones were to be paid merely from the annual profits of the estate; a number of slaves have been sold, and I have lately received information from Messrs. Eppes and Lewis, that the proceeds of that sale, with the profits of the estate to the end of 1781, would pay off the whole of the residuary debts. As we are now, therefore, clear of embarassment to pursue our principal object; I am desirous of arranging with you, such just and practicable conditions, as will ascertain to you, the terms at which you will receive my part of your debt, and give me the satisfaction of knowing that you are contented. What the laws of Virginia are, or may be will in no wise influence my conduct. Substantial justice is my object, as decided by reason, and not by authority or compulsion.

The first question which arises, is, as to the article of interest. For all the time preceding the war and all subsequent to it, I think it reasonable that interest should be paid; but equally unreasonable during the war. Interest is a compensation for the use of money. Your money in my hands, is in the form of lands and negroes. From these during the war, no use, no profits, could be derived. Tobacco is the article they produce, that only can be turned into money at a foreign market. But the moment it went out of our ports for that purpose, it was captured either by the king's ships, or by those of individuals. The consequence was, that tobacco worth from twenty to thirty shillings the hundred, sold generally in Virginia, during the war, for five shillings—this price it is known will not maintain the labourer and pay his taxes. There was no surplus of profit then to pay an interest. In the mean while we stood insurers of the lives of the labourers, and of the ultimate issue of the war. He who attempted during the war to remit either his principal or interest, must have expected to remit three times, to make one payment; because it is supposed, that two out of three parts of the shipments were taken. It was not possible then for the debtor, to derive any profit from the money which might enable him to pay an interest, nor yet to get rid of the principal by remitting it to his creditor. With respect to creditors in Great Britain, they turned their attention to privateering, and arming the vessels they had before employed in trading with us; they captured on the seas, not only the produce of the farms of their debtors, but of those of the whole state. They thus paid themselves by capture more than their annual interest; and we lost more. Some merchants indeed did not engage in privateering; these lost their interest, but *we* did not gain it; it fell into the hands of their countrymen. It cannot therefore be demanded of us. As between these merchants and their debtors, it is the case where, a loss being incurred, each party may justifiably endeavour to shift it from himself; each has an equal right to avoid it; one party can never expect the other to yield a thing, to which he has as good a right as the demander: we even think he has a better right than the demander in the present instance. This loss has been occasioned by the fault of the nation which was the creditor. Our right to avoid it then stands on less exceptionable ground than theirs. But it will be said, that each party thought the other the aggressor—in these disputes, there is but one umpire, and that has decided the question, where the world in general thought the right lay.

Besides these reasons in favour of the general mass of debtors, I have some peculiar to my own case. In the year 1776, before a shilling of paper money was issued I sold lands to the amount of £4,200, in order to pay these two debts. I offered the bond of the purchasers to your agent, Mr. Evans, if he would acquit me, and accept of the purchasers as debtors, in my place. They were as sure as myself; had he done it, these debts being turned over to you, would have been saved to you by the treaty of peace. But he declined it. Great sums of paper money were afterwards issued; this depreciated, and payment was made me in this money, when it was but a shadow. Our laws do not entitle their own fellow citizens to require re-payment in these cases, though the treaty authorises the British creditor to do it. Here then I lost the principal and interest once. Again, Lord Cornwallis encamped ten days on an estate of mine at Elk Island, having his headquarters in my house. He burned all the tobacco houses and barns on the farm, with the produce of the former year in them; he burnt all the enclosures, and wasted the fields in which the crop of that year was growing (it was in the month of June): he killed or carried off every living animal, cutting the throats of those which were too young for service. Of the slaves, he carried away thirty. The useless and barbarous injury he did me in that instance, was more than would have paid your debt, principal and interest: Thus I lost it a second time. Still I will lay my shoulders assiduously to the payment of it a third time; in doing this, however, I think yourself will be of opinion, I am authorized, in justice, to clear it of every article not demandable in strict right: of this nature I consider interest during the war.

Another question is, as to the paper money I deposited in the treasury of Virginia, towards the discharge of this debt. I before observed, that I had sold lands to the amount of £4,200 before a shilling of paper money was emitted, with a view to pay this debt. I received this money in depreciated paper. The state was then calling on those who owed money to British subjects to bring it into the treasury, engaging to pay a like sum to the creditor at the end of the war. I carried the identical money therefore to the treasury, where it was applied, as all the money of the same description was, to the support of the war. Subsequent events have been such, that the state cannot, and ought not to pay the same nominal sum in gold or silver, which they received in paper: nor is it certain what they will do. My intention being, and having always been, that whatever the state decides, you shall receive my part of your debt fully. I am ready to remove all difficulty arising from this deposit, to take back to myself the demand against the state, and to consider the deposit as originally made for myself, and not for you.

These two articles of interest and paper money, being thus settled, I would propose to divide the clear proceeds of the estate (in which there are from eighty to one hundred labouring slaves) between yourself and Kippen and Co., two-thirds to you, and one-third to them; and that the crop of this present year, 1787, shall constitute the first payment. That crop, you know, cannot be got to the warehouse completely till May, of the next year; and I suppose that three months more will be little enough to send it to Europe; or to sell it in Virginia, and remit the money—so that I could not safely answer for placing the proceeds in your hands, till the month of August; and annually every August afterwards, till the debt shall be paid. It will always be my interest, and my wish, to get it to you as much sooner as possible, and probably a part of it may always be paid some months sooner. If the assigning the profits, in general terms, may seem to you too vague, I am willing to fix the annual payment at a certain sum. But that I may not fall short of my engagement, I shall name it somewhat less than I suppose may be counted on. I shall fix your part at four hundred-pounds sterling annually; and as you know our crops of tobacco to be uncertain, I should reserve a right, if they fell short one year, to make it up the ensuing one, without being supposed to have failed in any engagements—but every other year, at least, all arrearages shall be fully paid up.

My part of this debt of Mr. Wayles's estate being one-third. I should require that in proportion as I pay my third, I shall stand discharged as to the other two-thirds; so that the payment of every hundred pounds shall discharge me as to three hundred of the undivided debt. The other gentlemen have equal means of paying, equal desires, and more skill in such affairs. Their parts of the debt, therefore, are at least as sure as mine, and my great object is, in case of any accident to myself, not to leave my family involved with any matters whatever.

I do not know what the balance of this debt is; the last account current I saw, was before the war, making the whole balance, principal and interest, somewhat about nine thousand pounds; and after this, there were upwards of four hundred hogsheads of tobacco, and some payments in money, to be credited. However, this settlement can admit of no difficulty: and in the mean time the payments may proceed, without affecting the right of either party to have a just settlement.

Upon the whole, then, I propose, that, on your part, you relinquish the claim to interest during the war; say from the commencement of hostilities, April 19, 1775, to their cessation, April 19, 1783, being exactly eight years: and that in proportion as I pay my third, I shall be acquitted as to the other two-thirds. On my part, I take on myself the loss of the papermoney deposited in the treasury. I agree to pay interest previous and subsequent to the war, and oblige myself to remit to you, for that and the principal, four hundred pounds sterling annually, till my third of the whole debt shall be fully paid; and I will begin these payments in August of the next year. If you think proper to accede to these propositions, be so good as to say so, at the foot of a copy of this letter. On my receipt of that, I will send you an acknowledgment of it, which will render this present letter obligatory on me; in which case, you may count on my faithful execution of this undertaking.

I have the honour to be, With great respect, Sir, Your most obedient, And most humble servant,   THOMAS JEFFERSON.

It will be observed that the preceding letter is dated at Paris, in 1787. Mr. *Jones*, to who it is addressed, awaited Mr. Jefferson's return to America, and authorized his agent to settle with him there. Immediately after his arrival in Virginia, in the fall of 1789, he procured a meeting with the agent and gentlemen interested, and an amicable settlement was made in writing, on the principles of this letter.——Mr. Jefferson immediately sold property again to the *whole amount of the debt*, and in the course of the first and second years delivered over the obligations received for it to the agent, who took on himself the collection of the money; so that now it is seven or eight years since he has paid up this debt. From the foregoing facts it appears that Mr. Jefferson, before the present government existed, before he could have known that it was thought of, and at a time when there was no power to compel him to payment on account of Mr. Wayles's debts to British merchants, made a *voluntary* offer of Settlement, on the most favourable terms which they have obtained under the judicial system of the United States. The claim under the payment into the treasury of Virginia, was so well founded, that it received the sanction of a circuit court there, although that decision was afterwards reversed by the supreme court. Every body who attended on the court, will recollect the impressive argument of Mr. *Marshall* (now in Congress), in support of the decision of the circuit court, and it will ever remain a doubt whether it ought not to have been affirmed. It is highly honourable to Mr. Jefferson, to have waved a legal defence, which was complete at the time (as the courts of Virginia were sovereign), so specious in its general merits, and, as it respected himself, rendered perfectly just, by the sacrifice of as much property as was sufficient to pay the debt. It is enough to say, that no British creditor, even where payment could not be alleged, has ever obtained more from the federal courts than Mr. Jefferson voluntarily paid. There was another claim made by the agent of the same house, of *Farrell & Jones*, against the executors of Mr. Wayles and another, for a cargo of about £4,000 value, to be sold on commission, on account of the consignees: Mr. Wayles assisted in the sale, but died soon after; and the whole collection survived to the other consignee; who received it, wasted it, and died a bankrupt: the agent thought he would try the chance of recovering the money from the executors of Mr. Wayles, though they had not received it: but on the hearing, eleven of the jury determined at once against their liability, but the twelfth dissenting, the case was laid over to the next federal court; when a second jury concurred unanimously with the eleven of the first, gave a verdict for the executors, and agreeably to the opinions of judge *Iredell*, who had presided at one hearing, and of judge

Patterson, at the other. General *Marshall*, and judge *Washington*, then of the bar, were the council for the executors. Palpably unfounded as this claim was, the trumpet of calumny, swelled it, when it suited a particular purpose, from one-third of £4,000 to £40,000; and from a groundless claim, to an unquestionable debt, which was to swallow up Mr. Jefferson's fortune!

————

HAVING NOW, fellow citizens, reviewed in their order, the whole of the combined calumnies which the political enemies of Mr. Jefferson have produced against him, and exposed their falsehood and malice, it would be doing equal injustice to you, and to the honourable reputation of this distinguished native citizen of America, not to present to your view, an Epitome of his public life and services, and thereby possess you with a fuller knowledge of the laborious efforts and eminent usefulness by which he has so greatly contributed to promote the best good of our common country and the general happiness of man: It will moreover afford the most effectual antidote to all the poisonous effusions of slander, and enable you to judge for yourselves; uninfluenced by party considerations, whether a life hitherto so zealously and successfully devoted to the pursuit and accomplishment of so many great and good principles for the common benefit of mankind, shall by your suffrages to him, be rendered more eminently useful to America, in the all important office and character of *Chief Magistrate and President of the United States.*

THOMAS JEFFERSON

Was born in the year 1743, in the County of Albemarle in Virginia, where he now resides. His father was a reputable landholder of that County, and gave *this*, his eldest son, a college education at the university of William and Mary, in the city of Williamsburg. After passing his degrees, being designed for the bar, Mr. Jefferson commenced a student at law, under the guidance of George Wythe, now the venerable judge and sole chancellor of Virginia.

In 1766, Mr. Jefferson came to the bar of the supreme court of his native state, and continued to practise therein with great success and reputation, until the commencement of the American revolution in 1775, and the consequent occlusion of the courts of justice; during this period of actice practice, the industrious mind of Jefferson found time to digest the first volume of Reports of Adjudged Cases in the Supreme Courts of Virginia, which were ever exhibited in that state, and, to this day, are admitted authority in those courts, remaining a monument of his early labours and useful talents.

In 1774, when all America were roused into action by the aggravated wrongs of the British government, Mr. Jefferson stepped forward a bold and able champion of his country's rights, and published his much admired pamphlet, "A Summary View of the Rights of British America," *addressed to the King,* which brought forward against the author, threats of prosecution for treason, by Lord Dunmore, then governor of Virginia; threats which produced no other effect on the independent mind of Jefferson, than publicly to avow himself the author, prepared to meet all consequences.

About this time Mr. Jefferson married the daughter[8] of Mr. Wayles an eminent counsellor at law, and continued to enjoy uninterrupted domestic felicity in the society of one of the most amiable of women, until the year 1780, when by her death he became the mourner of her virtues, and the guardian of their two daughters and surviving issue,[9] to whose education and settlement in life, and the service of his country, he has ever since faithfully devoted himself, still remaining a widower.

In the year 1775, Mr. Jefferson was elected a member of the Virginia Convention, and on the 4th of August, in the same year, one of the members to represent the state, then colony, of Virginia, in Congress.

In that memorable year 1776, the natal year of American emancipation from British tyranny, and of the independence and sovereignty of the United States, Mr. Jefferson was one of a committee of five, to wit, Thomas Jefferson, John Adams, Benjamin Franklin, Roger Sherman and R.R. Livingston; appointed by Congress to draught the Declaration of Independence, and it was from the pen and enlightened mind of Jefferson, first named of the committee, that that glorious instrument proceeded, which was reported by the committee, and unanimously adopted by Congress, entitled, "*The Declaration of Independence &c.*" An instrument which, so long as the records of time shall endure, will perpetuate the fame of its author, and preserve, in the American mind, *forever* and *inseparable*, the names of *Independence* and *Jefferson*.

In the same year, 1776, the ardent mind of Jefferson, eagerly pursuing the glorious principles of the revolution, and foreseeing that so long as the corruptions of British systems existed, we were independent in name not in fact, produced for the adoption of the legislature of his native state, the four following important acts, to wit;

1st. An Act establishing religious freedom, published in this essay.

2. An act to regulate descents, to prevent estates entail and the rights of primogeniture.

3. An act for the apportionment of crimes and punishments.

4th. An act to establish public schools.

The influence of these acts upon the relative principles they embrace will be universally seen and felt by those who prize civil liberty as a primary blessing, and regard the preservation of it as among the first behests of God to man—whilst systems of universal toleration in matters of religion; for an equal distribution of property, and insubversion of the aristocratic and unnatural principle of entail and primogeniture right; for ameliorating the sanguinary code of criminal law; and for extending to the poorest class of citizens, the benefits of education at public expense, will be viewed as the emanations of a great and good mind, zealously endeavouring to promote the happiness and improve the condition of his fellow beings.[10]

Equally evincive of watchful regard to the rights of his countrymen, was the scheme and suggestion made by Mr. Jefferson for the formation and adoption of the Constitution of Virginia, in the same year, for prefixing thereto "A Bill of Rights, declaratory of the natural and unalienable rights of man" which was accordingly done.[11]

In the year 1778, Mr. Jefferson being then a member of the Virginia Legislature, presented to that body the act "to prevent the importation of slaves" which was enacted into a law in the month of October in the same year, and was shortly after followed by another act "to authorise manumissions," being the commencement of a system of gradual emancipation, also proposed by him.[12]

In the year 1779, Mr. Jefferson, at the age of 36, was chosen governor of Virginia, and continued in that office until June 1781—during which the state experienced three invasions, and was also brought into a critical state of collision respecting its boundary lines with two neighbouring states, North-Carolina and Pennsylvania. His conduct in that station amidst the jarring conflicts and trying difficulties of foreign invasion and domestic disquietude, was such, as secured to him, 6 months after he left the office, and upon the fullest public enquiry, the *unanimous* vote of thanks of the Legislature, consisting of 180 members, "for his attentive administration of the powers of the executive whilst in office."

It was during the same year, 1781, amidst the cares of government and scenes of private affliction, that Mr. Jefferson prepared his celebrated work, afterwards published in France, and which he modestly stiled "*Notes on Virginia.*" In this work, so justly admired by all the learned world, for its philosophical research, ingenious theory, and able disquisition, equally evidencing an enlarged, liberal and pious mind, the author, in a superior style of eloquence, boldly attacks and fully refutes the fallacious theories of Mr. Buffon and the Abbe Raynal, which tend to disparage the animal and its species, both man and beast, of the American world, and reduce them to a scale smaller that those of Europe; vindicating with truth and intelligence the equal distribution of nature's blessings to America.

In the year 1783, Mr. Jefferson was again appointed to a seat in Congress from his native state, and in the following year, on the 7th of May, was nominated by that honourable body minister plenipotentiary of the United States to the Court of France, as the successor of our illustrious Franklin, whither he embarked early in the same year, and remained absent from the United States, in the execution of the duties of that important trust, until the month of October, 1789; when he returned home by permission of the then president, Washington, who, upon being elected to the chief magistracy of the fœderal government, immediately destined Mr. Jefferson to fill the next most honourable and confidential station in the executive government, near his own person.

During his mission to France, Mr. Jefferson with that peculiar address, intelligence and attention to promote the essential interests of the United

States, which directs all his conduct, obtained from the French king, an arrette, highly beneficial to the American commerce, for the free admission, exempt from the customary foreign duties, of oil, fish and whalebone, the product of the American fisheries, into certain ports, and for the sale of American built ships in all the ports of France—benefits, which our Eastern brethren continued to reap the peculiar advantage of, until the commencement of the revolutionary convulsions which have agitated that nation.

About the same period also, Mr. Jefferson, in conjunction with our immortal Franklin, negociated with a minister from the court of Prussia, then at the Hague, that celebrated treaty known by the name of "*The Prussian treaty*," in which an astonished world has, for the first time, seen a public avowal and positive provision by treaty, between two sovereign and independent nations, for the establishment of those two great and glorious principles, promotive of universal peace and happiness, to wit, 1st. "*That free ships shall make free goods*;" and 2d. "*That privateering in time of war be abolished*;" principles which it were to be wished could be rendered universal and eternal. Mr. Adams, now president of the United States, was one of the commission for neogociating this treaty, and on its completion, it was sent over to London, where Mr. Adams then resided as minister of the United States, for his signature. It is greatly to be regretted that Mr. Adams could not be content to retain to himself a share of the glory which reflects on the authors of this celebrated treaty. But unhappily for our country, since he became president of the United States, we have seen him nominate his son John Quincy Adams, as minister to the court of Prussia, for the express purpose, as declared, of renewing the treaty with that nation, which having been limited to continue in force for ten years only, had expired. Accordingly another treaty has been made by his son with Prussia, which has been approved by a majority of the Senate and ratified by the president, but which, instead of renewing and continuing the old treaty, is in itself a new one, expressly abandoning and renouncing the two inestimable principles, 1st. "*That free ships make free goods*;" and 2d. "*That privateering in time of war be abolished*;" principles which, it appears, from the correspondence accompanying the negociation, laid before the senate of the United States by the president, the wise and enlightened ministers of the Prussian monarch, were brought, with great difficulty and reluctance, to abandon, on the earnest solicitation and reiterated demand of the American negociator, under the suggestion that the maritime powers, *particularly Great-Britain*, would never sanction or permit them.[13]

In the year 1789, Mr. Jefferson being returned to the United States, and appointed by president Washington, secretary to the department of state, immediately entered on the arduous duties of that important station, having previously stipulated with the president, that in consideration of the many years absence from his family and estate, he might be permitted, at the expiration of the constitutional term for which the president was elected, to retire from the public service.

The first result of the labours of Mr. Jefferson in the department of state, were exhibited to Congress in the following reports, to wit;

1st. A report, on the fisheries of the United States.

2d. A report, on coins, weights and measures.

3d. A report, on the privileges and restrictions on the commerce of the United States.

4th. A report, on the privileges and restrictions on the commerce of the United States in foreign countries.

Each of these reports displayed the usual accuracy, information, and intelligence of the writer.

But it was reserved for a more critical and delicate period in the affairs of the United States, that the preeminent talents of the American secretary should become most conspicuous, and interestingly useful to his country: The non-execution of the treaty of peace with the United States, on the part of Great-Britain, her detention of our Western posts, and the attendant spoliations on our commerce, both by Great-Britain and France, then at war with each other, added to the intrigues of the minister of the latter, Genet, all conduced to a situation difficult and perplexing. Besides which, Spain continued to withhold from us the free navigation of the Missisippi, so essential to all Western America. In this state of things, the just confidence, which, the discriminating mind of Washington, had reposed in Mr. Jefferson, was amply repaid, by that promptness, zeal and ability, with which the American secretary, contributed by his labours, to relieve the executive from embarrassment. Through a series of masterly and unequalled diplomatique correspondence, which he maintained, at the same time, with the respective ministers of Great-Britain and France, namely Hammond and Genet, he traversed and rebutted their respective causes of charge and complaint against the United States, and having fully manifested that he held no particular attachment to any foreign nation, but was equally prepared, with the decision, firmness and intelligence of a true American, to oppose and resist the aggressions of all. The recal of Genet, and appointment of his successor, with the subsequent proceedings between the United States and France, the appointment of Mr. Jay, his treaty with Great-Britain and the recal of Mr. Hammond, appointment of Mr. Liston, and subsequent proceedings with Great-Britain, are all well known. In respect to Spain, the labours of Mr. Jefferson, were more immediately effective and complete. Having possesed the commissioners of the United States then at Madrid, negociating a treaty with the court of Spain with the most ample and pointed instructions, and also of the form and provisions of a treaty, predicated on the basis of the free navigation of the Missisippi, it remained only for Mr. Thomas Pinckney, then minister from the United States at London, under special instruction from the president, and appointed envoy for the purpose, to repair to Madrid and seizing the favourable moment for effecting it, to accomplish this desirable work. This was accordingly done, with equal promptness and decision on his part, and jointly to that, and the labours of the American

Congress Hall and New Theatre, Chestnut Street, Philadelphia. Engraved by William Birch & Son, Neshaminy Bridge on Bristol Road, Pennsylvania.
LC–USZ62–56353.

secretary in the cabinet, are the United States indebted for the most liberal, honourable, and beneficial treaty, they have ever yet entered into with a foreign nation. Here the review of the public life and labours of Mr. Jefferson ceases.

About this time, having, at the pressing entreaty of the then president, Washington, remained one year longer at the head of the department of state, than he had before stipulated to do, he resigned his office, and retired with the warmest thanks and regret of the president, Washington, to his estate at Monticello, in Albemarle County, Virginia, where he continued for upwards of two years uninterruptedly to enjoy the sweets of domestic ease, and a respite from the fatigues of public life, following with avidity his favourite pursuits of philosophical research and agricultural improvement, until the voice of his country again summoned him to the more active scenes of public duty, and placed him in nomination for the presidential chair, as the successor of Washington. The issue of that election is well known, and but for a false return in one state, and the suppression of a return in another, Mr. Jefferson would have been declared president, as the returns however stood before Congress, it appeared that he had 68 votes, and Mr. Adams 71, consequently the latter was declared president, and the former vice-president of the United States.[14]

In the month of January, 1797, Mr. Jefferson was elected president of the American Philosophical Society, held at Philadelphia, as successor of the great and virtuous Rittenhouse, who was the immediate successor of our immortal Franklin, the founder of that society.

And now *for the second time*, the voice of his country has placed Mr. Jefferson in nomination for the *presidential chair*.

Fellow Citizens of the United States;

In the foregoing address you are presented with two very opposite characters of Mr. Jefferson:

The first, written by the pen of his enemies, conceived in malignity and malevolence, under the powerful influence of party feeling and political resentment, exhibits him to you as the worst of men, an enemy to his God, an enemy to his country, an enemy to the human race. It derives a momentary support from the basest fabrications and wickedest falsehoods. It cannot long deceive, since it fully betrays the jealousy, fear and anger of its authors; jealousy, of his unrivalled talents; fear, that on his elevation to the presidency, every germ of monarchy and aristocracy in our country will dissipate at the electrical touch of his republican virtues; and anger, that notwithstanding all their detractious efforts, he continues to possess the unshaken and undiminished confidence of the great body of the American people.

The latter character of Mr. Jefferson, is drawn not by the partial hand of a friend, nor under the influence of political or party prejudices: there is no need of fabrication, falsehood or deception. You see it in the faithful and unerring record of his many great and virtuous deeds; in the public usefulness and eminent services of a well spent life; in the numerous testimonials of his country's approbation, and, by the universal suffrage of the foreign world in their acknowledged tributes of respect and esteem for the talents of his head and the virtues of his heart. Its leading features present to you a man of pure, ardent and unaffected piety; of sincere and genuine virtue; of an enlightened mind and superior widsom; the adorer of our God; the patriot of his country; and the friend and benefactor of the whole human race.

And such fellow citizens, is the TRUE and REAL character of THOMAS JEFFERSON, unaided by artificial colourings or the false varnish of deceptive flattery.   AMERICANUS.

1. Beckley's Address has been called the "first of all campaign lives" by Merrill D. Peterson, *Thomas Jefferson and the New Nation* (Norwalk, Conn.: The Easton Press, 1987), p. 640.

    Beckley wrote it to counter the numerous attacks against Jefferson's character appearing in the public press. As William Duane stated: "This pamphlet is written with every evidence of conviction, and with a candor and plainness, that forms a very conspicuous contrast with the *stile* and *resorts* of writings to which it is opposed. After answering in an irrefutable manner every objection worth notice, which has been made to the *moral, religious, or political* character of Mr. Jefferson, he concludes as follows—with a very useful outline of Mr. Jefferson's history." The entire Address was reprinted several times after the initial printing of 2,000 copies by Mathew Carey of Philadelphia and the biographical section was reprinted by James Wilson in Wilmington, Delaware. Berkeley, *Beckley*, p. 202.
2. *Debates and other Proceedings of the Convention of Virginia, convened at Richmond, on Monday the second day of June, 1788....* (Petersburg, Va.: Hunter and Prentis, 1788).
3. For Jefferson's important role in the writing and passage of the Virginia act for religious freedom, which was actually passed by the Virginia Assembly while Jefferson was in Europe, see Dumas Malone, *Jefferson the Virginian* (Boston: Little, Brown and Co., 1948), pp. 277–79.

    For a discussion of Jefferson's religious beliefs, see Eugene Sheridan's introduction to Dickinson W. Adams, *Jefferson's Extracts from the Gospels* in *Jefferson Papers*, 2nd ser., 1: 3–42.
4. Thomas Jefferson, *Notes on the State of Virginia; written in the year 1781...* (Paris: 1785).
5. This essay has also been printed and annotated in this volume under the date October 26, 1796.
6. Hamilton's charges against Jefferson over the pseudonym, Catullus, appeared in Fenno's *Gazette of the United States*, September 19, 1792. For a discussion of Jefferson's letter of September 26, 1786, conveying a 1786 offer of Dutch bankers to purchase the French loan to the United States, see Boyd, ed., *Jefferson Papers*, 10: 405–6n, 519–23, 11:550n; and Malone, *Jefferson and the Rights of Man*, pp. 188–89 and 470–71.
7. For Jefferson's efforts to pay his British creditors, see Malone, *Jefferson the Virginian*, pp. 441–46.
8. That is, Martha Wayles Skelton, daughter of John Wayles and widow of Bathurst Skelton, who married Jefferson on January 1, 1772.

9. Martha and Mary were were the two surviving daughters of the Jeffersons' six children.
10. Only Jefferson's plans for public education were rejected by the Assembly, although his plans for revision of the laws proved less sweeping than initially envisioned and his act for religious freedom was not passed until 1786. See Malone, *Jefferson the Virginian*, pp. 248–85.
11. George Mason must be given the major credit for the Virginia constitution of 1776 and the declaration of rights. In fact, Jefferson's draft constitution arrived in Richmond too late to have more than a minor influence, and to provide a preamble denouncing the king, which the assembly adopted in its entirety. Malone, *Jefferson the Virginian*, pp. 235–40.
12. Jefferson's disputed authorship of the 1778 Virginia act outlawing the importation of slaves is discussed in Boyd, ed., *Jefferson Papers*, 2: 22–24.
13. The Prussian treaty of 1799 did omit the principle of free ships free goods to bring it into conformity with the provisions of Jay's Treaty with Great Britain. See *American State Papers: Foreign Relations*, 2: 244–69; and Samuel F. Bemis, *John Quincy Adams and the Foundations of American Foreign Policy* (New York: Alfred A. Knopf, 1949), pp. 93–95.
14. Beckley is referring to the delayed return of votes in two Pennsylvania counties which may have resulted in the loss of one Federalist elector, and the disputed election of Federalist electors in Vermont. On the other hand, Federalists charged that sympathetic electors chosen in Georgia were not counted and the state's four votes were not divided but cast for Jefferson and Burr. See Tinkcom, *Republicans and Federalists in Pennsylvania*, pp. 168–72; Stagg, ed., *Madison Papers*, 16: 152, 429n. 2, 461; and Syrett, ed., *Hamilton Papers*, 20: 418–19ns. 4–5.

JOHN BECKLEY TO EPHRAIM KIRBY

[July 1800]

You are requested to republish the enclosed in the pamphlet form[1]—a few dollars, <u>very few</u>, by 10 or 12 republicans, will circulate 500 of them in that form.

Be pleased to pay marked attention to the discussions & developments in the Aurora, respecting public defaulters &c. A vindication & Epitome of Jeffersons life will shortly be sent yo. in a pamphlet[2] about the size of the enclosed. Communicate the progress of things with you freely addressed to John Pollard Esqr., conveyancer, Prince Street, Philada. Col. Wade Hampton from So. Carolina assures us (he is now here) of every vote in that state. No. Carolina is safe and full one half of Maryland. Advise Mr. Granger[3] of these things.   JB

RC (KIRBY PAPERS, DUKE UNIVERSITY). ENDORSED BY KIRBY: "JULY 1800 MR. JOHN BECKLEY."

1. Not identified, but it was certainly one of the many Republican generated campaign pieces. Perhaps, it was the essay described in the next document.
2. See the preceding document.
3. Gideon Granger (1767–1822), a Suffield, Connecticut, lawyer had unsuccessfully run for Congress as a Republican in 1798. He was appointed postmaster general by Jefferson on November 28, 1801.

JOHN BECKLEY TO EPHRAIM KIRBY

Remarks   6 Augst. 1800.

This paper was published in New York March 1795[1] with a view to inform the people of that and the Eastern States, on the approach of the Congressional Elections of that Year, what the conduct of their Members had been. The remarkable coincidence between the course then pursured by the fœderal party, and that which they have lately pursued under their system of terror, to create a standing army, and to abandon the Militia, is too apparent not to strike with deep and impressive effect on the public mind. (See the remarks noted in the enclosed paper page 6 and 7). I think this paper, in connection with some of these remarks, coupled with such others as yourself and other republican friends may deem locally applicable and suitable to the temper and feelings of your people, will produce great good, and may be circulated in a very small pamphlet, or hand bills, at a trifling expense. You will receive by this mail a copy of the pamphlet in Vindication &c. of Mr. Jefferson's public life & conduct. 25 copies more are made into a packet and directed to you, forwarded to your friend in New York, to whom you can send and apply for them, if he does not immediately forward on this packet.   JB

RC AND MS (KIRBY PAPERS, DUKE UNIVERSITY). ENDORSED BY KIRBY: "AUGUST 6TH 1800 JOHN BECKLEY ESQR."

1. The essay enclosed by Beckley has been printed in this volume under the March 1795 date when it was written, rather than the May 12, 1795, date when it was published. It is not known whether Kirby had this essay reprinted as Beckley suggested.

JOHN BECKLEY TO EPHRAIM KIRBY

14 Augst. 1800

The death of an only child,[1] will apologize for the delay in forwarding the enclosed—25 copies are delivered to Mr. R.[2] in New York, addressed to you, agreeable to your request. The tide of republicanism has risen so high in Delaware & Maryland, and is become so irresistably rapid that you may rely with absolute certainty on all Delaware and six at least in Maryland, but more likely the whole. In No. Carolina, we advance with Equal prospect of success 9 votes are the least that even fœderalists allow us. In New Jersey, our prospects also encrease and our Efforts there as well as in this State, are unceasing. You may rely on a Vote in this State, by the Assembly, and we think 10 votes certain, if not all will be obtained.[3]

RC (KIRBY PAPERS, DUKE UNIVERSITY). IN BECKLEY'S HAND THOUGH NOT SIGNED. ENDORSED BY KIRBY: "AUGUST 14TH 1800 JOHN BECKLEY ESQ."

1. Beckley's daughter Mary died before her second birthday.
2. Not identified.
3. Despite Beckley's optimism, the method of selecting Pennsylvania's electoral votes, which concerned parties knew would have the effect of determining the outcome, was not decided until December 1, 1800. The Federalist senate and the Republican assembly each nominated eight electors and a joint vote produced eight Republican electors and seven Federalist electors. Tinkcom, *Republicans and Federalists in Pennsylvania*, pp. 243–52.

JOHN BECKLEY TO JAMES MONROE

My dear Sir,   Philadelphia, 26th August 1800.

Mr. Peters will deliver you this letter and an accompanying packet. He is a foreigner, by birth a Switz. of respectable commercial connections, persuing Commercial views in the U.S. and you will find him a Man of honor, superior intelligence and a confirmed republican. I have assured him of your Civilities and attention whilst he remains in Richmond, and ncessary directions to Monticello, should he prosecute his present purpose of visiting that place.

The packet contains 1 doz. copies of an Epitome of the life of Mr. Jefferson to be distributed as you see proper. 2d. Gallatins view of the public debt, and 3d 1/2 doz. copies of Mr. Adams's letter to Tench Coxe.[1] To you, as a friend, I must apologize for the inaccuracies & insufficiencies of the 'Epitome'—destitute of materials, oppressed by sickness myself and the death of an only child, having only designed a breif newspaper essay, and being urged by friends to give it its present form, and beleiving that it is materially founded in fact, I determined to send it forth—1000 copies were struck for me, 1000 more by the printer—1000 at New York, 1000 in Connecticut & 1000 in Maryland, have since been struck, and imperfect as it is, it will I trust do some good. The author need not be named.

Gallatins on the public debt is very interesting. An analysis of it is [appearing] in detail thro' the Aurorra, which I presume the Examiner will pass on.

Doctor [Linn][2] of New York has published a pamphlet entitled "Serious Considerations on the Election of a president &c." which in an assumed garb of moderation, virulently attacks Mr. Jefferson as an Athiest and Deist. You will see my reply to it in a series of numbers in the Aurora, disguised in stile & manner from the Epitome. when finished, it will be dispensed in pamphlet form, and I will forward you a number of Copies.

Adams's letter to Tench Coxe is a full sett off vs. the letter to Mazzei—set if it were not Fenno's pamphlet which I send you a copy of, is abundantly so. This last is working infinite good.

Our prospect of success in the pending Election, encreases hourly. Colo. Wade Hampton, will be with you in a few days. He has been thro' Connecticut, Rh. Island, Vermont & part of Massachusetts and will fully inform you of the state of things in that Quarter. In the interim, my advices from Connecticut, for shine several votes. In New Jersey and Delaware we have every degree of certainty of Success. In Maryland we are not less certain of 5 votes. Our advices from No. Carolina lead us to expect 8. In S. Carolina, Colo. Hampton & Major Butler[3] say 8 certain for Jeff. but doubt as to Pinkney's getting 8 also. Do you ever correspond with Major Butler, who is now here with his family, but purposes to be in S.C. and to be an Elector? Or with Charles Pinkney, the Senator, now at Charleston? If you do, or ever did, a line in season, suited to the respective character of the Men, might do great good—they are very important in the Carolina Election, and require, in different views, to be attended to.

I have letters from Georgia, Kentucky & Tennesse, advising of the perfect soundness of those States. In Pennsylvania, we have every reasonable assurance of a vote exclusively republican. Our efforts are pointed to the State elections to the Legislature, on the 2d Tuesday in October. In one branch (Reprsents.) we are sure of a decided majority. In the other, we calculate on an even vote, say 12 and 12, with a great chance of 13 to 11.[4]

You can hardly conceive the progressive increase of republicanism in this part of the Union. The direct tax, and the exposure of the public difficulties operate inevitably, and events in Europe are in happy coincidence with domestic concerns.

Wayne, the Successor of Fenno, & Brown & Relf[5] are republishing the lying stuff, fabricated by Wm. Smith,[6] minister to portugal under the signature of phocion—but we are prepared to expose it, that we do not apprehend any ill effect from it.

When convenient, I shall be happy to receive a line from you. Mrs. Beckley joins me in affectionate regards to Mrs. Monore, and I remain, My dear Sir, Your unchangeable friend, John Beckley

RC (MONROE PAPERS, NEW YORK PUBLIC LIBRARY).

1. Beckley's *Epitome* has been printed above under the date July 4, 1800; Albert Gallatin's *Views of the Public Debt, Receipts and Expenditures of the United States* was published on August 19; and John Adams's letter of 1792 to Coxe, alledgedly demonstrating the monarchical nature of Adams's political philosophy, which was reprinted in the August 28 as well as subsequent issues of the *Aurora*.

2. Manuscript damaged. William Linn, graduate of Princeton College, a minister in the Dutch Reformed Church, son-in-law of Bishop William White, and a neighbor of the Prince family in New York who had performed the Beckleys' marriage in 1790, was the author of *Serious Considerations on the Election of a President: Addressed to the Citizens of the United States* (New York: John Furman Printer, 1800).

For Beckley's response over the pseudonym Senex, see the next entry and those of September 2, 5, and 27, 1800.

3. William Butler (1759–1821) served as a Republican representative (1801–13) from South Carolina and Wade Hampton (1752–1835) served as a Republican representative (1795–97, 1803–5) from South Carolina.

4. For further information on the Pennsylvania elections, which resulted in Federalist control of the Senate and Republican control of the Assembly, see Tinkcom, *Republicans and Federalists in Pennsylvania*, pp. 246–47.

5. Caleb P. Wayne was the publisher of the *Gazette of the United States*, and Andrew Brown, Jr. and Samuel Relf were the publishers of the *Philadelphia Gazette and Daily Advertiser*.

6. William L. Smith, former Federalist Representative (1789–97) from South Carolina was appointed minister to Portugal by President Adams in July 1797. For further information on Smith as Phocion, see Beckley to Madison, October 17, 1796, Beckley as A Subscriber, October 26, 1796.

JOHN BECKLEY AS SENEX[1]

August 27, 1800

To the Author OF A PAMPHLET INTITLED, "Serious Considerations, on the election of a president, addressed to the Citizens of the United States."

No. 1.

Sir,—or Rev. Sir,[2]

FOR it is evident that preaching the gospel is your calling, or rather trade, from the liberties you take with the scriptures.

You in the beginning of your addresss, very gravely assume the garb of moderation, you assure your readers, that you are not an advocate for any particular man, that you are not actuated by motives of party, but by a *sincere desire for the public welfare*.

As to Mr. Jefferson, you declare, that you admire his talents and feel grateful for the services he has been instrumental in rendering to his country; *that it is with pain you oppose him*, and that your objection to his "being promoted to the Presidency is founded *singly* upon his disbelief of the holy scriptures; or in other words, his rejection of the Christian Religion, and open profession of deism."

From such an introduction the credulous reader, is led to look for nothing but impartiality and candor throughout your address; but he will not find one solitary instance of either, he will find nothing but the most rancorous political hatred, lurking under the veil of religion.

With a cant, truly hypocritical, you have endeavored to prove Mr. Jefferson, at one time a deist, at another an atheist. You have substituted assertions, for facts, sophistry for argument, and you have impiously made the sacred scriptures subservient to your malignant purposes. But my dear sir, in the heat of your political zeal, you have on two or three occasions, suffered your own infidelity to peep through the curtain. Atheism is a doctrine so monstrously absurd, so shocking to human nature, so totally at variance with all kinds of religion, and the common sense of mankind, that it never can prevail, unless among mad men. A man's religion must hang but loosely about him, before he can believe in such depravity. I have never known a pious christian to believe in the existence of Atheists. Yet because Mr. Jefferson observed to a gentleman, (as you say, and we have only your authority for it) that "he wished to see a government in which no religious opinions were held, and where the security for property and social order, rested entirely upon the force of the law," you very modestly conclude, that he must be an atheist, and that the people under such a government, would be a nation of atheists. In this conversation we are not favored with what went before or followed after the sentence quoted, not whether the gentleman to whom it was addressed, noted it down immediately in his pocket-book, so as to be certain of the words and meaning. Such is the evidence of Mr. Jefferson's atheism.

To make him a deist, you endeavor to prove-That he has advanced philosophical opinions apparently inconsistent with the holy scriptures. That in comparing the negroes with the whites, he says there are physical distinctions proving a difference of race, and that they are inferior to whites, in reason and imagination.

That, in different conversations, he has suffered expressions of contempt for our saviour and his holy religion, and for the sacred scriptures, to escape him; which expressions were heard by somebody, who told somebody, who told you.

Mr. Jefferson in his notes on the state of Virginia has these observations.[3] "It is said that shells are found in the Andes fifteen thousand feet above the level of the ocean. This is considered by many, both of the learned and unlearned as proof of an universal deluge." He then adds, if the whole atmosphere were water, it would cover the globe, but 5212 feet deep. That "in Virginia this would be a very small proportion, even of the champaign country, the banks of our tide waters being frequently if not generally of a great height. Deluges beyond this extent, then, as for instance to the north mountain or to Kentucky, *seem out of the laws of nature*. But within it they may have taken place to a greater or less degree, in proportion to the combination of natural causes, which may be supposed to have produced them." Is this "a clear proof of his disrespect for divine revelation?" Do these observations express a doubt, that in the time of Noah, there was a flood sufficient to destroy the wicked *race of man, and every thing that had breath under heaven, or had life on the earth?* Mr. Jefferson is of opinion that the flood is not to be accounted for, upon the known principles of the laws of nature; that the shells found in the Andes, add nothing to the testimony of the sacred scriptures, that deluges beyond a certain extent "seem to be out of the laws of nature" that they must therefore be supernatural and miraculous, as that of Noah undoubtedly was.

But Mr. Jefferson is not satisfied that the waters rose to the height of 15,000 feet above the surface of the ocean, for he says "these three hypotheses," (viz. that the summit of the Andes, has once been the bed of the ocean, and raised to its present height by some convulsion of natures; that the waters have covered the Andes at their present height; and the hypotheses of Voltaire)" are equally unsatisfactory, and we must be contented, to acknowledge, that this great phenomemon. [The appearance of shells in the Andes, not the deluge] is yet unsolved. Ignorance is preferable to error; *and he is less remote from truth, who believes nothing, than he who believes what is wrong.*"

Do you sir, believe with all your faith, which I suspect would not remove mountains, that the flood rose so high as to cover the Andes, and remained there a sufficient time for the propagation of such quantities of shell-fish as must have existed there, if we take the shells for a proof? Is it necessary for every pious Christian to believe, that the waters rose fiften cubits above the summit of the Andes? The whole earth is often used in the scripture language, for all the inhabitants of the earth. It is not probable that at the time of the flood, there was a living creature on the American continent; for the sacred scriptures, make but eight generations from Adam to Noah. The words of Moses are "all the high hills that were under the whole heavens were covered. Fifteen cubits upwards did the waters prevail; *and the mountains were covered.* We know that many general expressions in sacred writ, are after the manner of men, and have a limited meaning. It is probable therefore, that those general expressions were meant to apply only to the old world, the inhabitants of which had incurred the displeasure of God. It is remarkable, that Moses, speaking of the high hills, says they were all covered; but speaking of the mountains he says, they were covered, omitting the word *all.* May we not from thence infer, that the waters rose only to the height of fifteen cubits above the highest mountains in the old world; that they were no higher in the new, measuring from the surface of the ocean, and of course that they fell greatly short of covering the Andes?

It is true, the Omnipotent Being could by his word, have raised the waters to that prodigious height; yet whereever we can understand the oeconomy of his divine providence, we find the means are never greatly disproportioned to the object to be effected. God is infinitely wise as well as infinitely powerful, and does nothing in vain. His object was by the deluge, to destroy the wicked race of man, and *every thing that had breath under heaven, or had life on the earth,* such only excepted as it was his pleasure to save in the ark. He did so destroy them.

But is a philosopher to desist from his researches because they lead to discoveries apparently contradicting the opinions we have formed from reading the bible? Do we not find that many such discoveries, when fully established, are perfectly reconcilable with the holy scriptures? The greatest objection to the Copernican system was, that it seemed to contradict the Mosaic account of the creation of the world. "Galileo, after having demonstrated the motion of the earth, was obliged by the rancour of the Jesuits, to go to Rome, and there solemnly to renounce it. Besides which cruel treatment he was condemned to a year's imprisonment in the inquisition, and the penance of repeating daily some penitentiary psalms,"* [Gaileo was obliged on his knees, to declare in the most solemn manner that the earth, was at rest, but as he rose from the ground he uttered in the anguish of his heart "E pur si muove"—"and yet it moves.] yet no philosopher, was he ever so pious a Christian, believes at this day, that the sun revolves round the earth.

I think, Sir, you must be a descendant of one of those Jesuits; they took care to increase and multiply exceedingly, altho' they were doomed to celibacy.

The most extraordinary part of your address is, that after citing several passages of scripture contradicting, as you would wish to have it thought, the philosophical deductions of Mr. Jefferson, you are afraid to rely upon them yourself, but say in page 8, "It is not my business at present (and I beg it may be remembered) to refute his principles; but only to shew their inconsistency with the holy scriptures." As much as if you had said "Mr. Jefferson's philosophy is inconsistent with the holy scriptures, and one of them must be false yet, mind good people, I do not pretend to confuse Mr. Jefferson, I do not pretend to deny the truth of his principles, but only wish to shew that they and the sacred scriptures are inconsistent with each other. I am a piece of a philosopher myself, and do not wish to lose my character as such, by siding with Moses on all occasions." And so much are you afraid your readers may think you possess more faith than philosophy, that in the last sentence of your essays, you observe, "Let me further repeat, that no answer is intended in this address to his (Mr. Jefferson's) philosophical and religious principles; that the single thing intended is, to shew that these principles are contrary to *what we are taught* in the holy scripture." I am afraid that in your zeal for Mr. Pinckney and Mr. Adams, you have lost all respect for Moses and the Prophets.

You say if any apparent necessity should occur, your name shall immediately become known. If you have any reputation for piety, and that reputation is of any service to you, let me take this first opportunity of advising you to keep your name back, at least until the church shall become an organized machine of government, or until political preaching shall become more fashionable, than it is at present.   SENEX

TR (*AURORA* (PHILADELPHIA), AUGUST 27, 1800).

1. For confirmation of Beckley's authorship of the four Senex essays, dated August 27, September 2, 5, and 27, 1800, see his August 26, 1800, letter to Monroe.

    Beckley had defended Jefferson against the same issues in his July 4, 1800, *Address to the People*. See the footnotes to that text for further bibliographic information on Jefferson's views on religion, education, and slavery.

2. The Reverend William Linn was the author of *Serious Considerations on the Election of a President: Addressed to the Citizens of the United States* (New York: John Purman Printer, 1800). See Beckley to Monroe, August 26, 1800, note 2, and Sheridan, "Introduction," to *Jefferson's Extracts from the Gospels*, 1:10–11.

3. Jefferson, *Notes on the State of Virginia; written in the year 1781*.

JOHN BECKLEY AS SENEX

September 2, 1800

TO THE AUTHOR
OF A PAMPHLET ENTITLED.
"Serious considerations on the Election of a President, addressed to the
Citizens of the United States."

No. 11

REVEREND SIR:

YOU give but little weight yourself to what is said in the notes on Virginia respecting the antiquity of the Americans, and the facts proving that they never emigrated from Asia. You think however they contain an insinuation, that all mankind have not descended from a single pair, that you say "every doubt will be removed as to the sentiment of Mr. Jefferson, when we consider what he asserts more plainly respecting the negroes". I shall leave you in possession of your weak ground, as not worth the contest, and take you upon that which you think, too strong to be shaken.

For the sake of appearing very candid, you grant that Mr. Jefferson is an advocate for the abolition of slavery; but your affected candour would never have induced you to make this declaration, if you had thought it could in the least degree add to the notoriety of the fact.

From his observations respecting the diversity of the human species, you consistently infer, that his opinions are repugnant to sacred history, and to the plan of salvation revealed in the gospel. Let us examine what facts you have to warrant such uncharitable conclusions.

In his notes on Virginia, page 201, comparing the blacks with the whites he says "besides those of colour, figure and hair, there are other physical distinctions proving a difference of race." You must observe however, that all those physical distinctions do not produce full conviction on the mind of Mr. Jefferson. You give great emphasis to the word *proving*, as if proof and demonstration were the same. They are different; there may be strong proofs on both sides of a question; there can be demonstration on but one. The circumstances proving the unity of the human species are perfectly satisfactory to some, while others remain in doubt. Mr. Jefferson thinks the proofs in favor of the diversity of the human species preponderate, but he does not attempt to decide, whether the blacks are "originally a distinct race" or whether they are "made distinct by time and circumstances." He says nothing expressive of a doubt, that all mankind are the descendants of Adam and Eve. Many people who have as much piety as yourself at least, believe that the descendants of Canaan have remained a distinct race, in consequence of the curse pronounced against him by Noah. Others believe that when God confounded the language of those, who impiously attempted to raise a tower whose top should reach heaven, and when he scattered them abroad upon the face of the whole earth, he adapted their constitutions, to the different climates which they were to inhabit; and that the diversity of the human species is to be attributed to this cause—Others believe that inhospitable climates and savage modes of living have produced effects upon the human frame, as well as upon the faculties of the mind, so permanent, as never to be removed by any other climates or any other mode of living. These opinions with several others upon the same subject, are no ways repugnant to sacred history, or to the plan of salvation revealed in the gospel.

For my own part I believe with Dr. Smith of Princeton,[1] in the unity of the human race. I have no doubt, that the descendants of the blackest negroes, brought into our climate, & adopting in every respect our modes of living, would after a number of successive generations, without the least intermixture with the whites, loose all those characteristics which distinguish the savage African, from the civilized European. The greater part of mankind, however, who think upon the subject, entertain a different opinion, and you and I ought to have Christian charity enough to forgive them.

In page 209, Mr. Jefferson farther observes, "will not a lover of natural history then, one who views the gradations in all the races of animals, with the eye on philosophy, excuse an effort to keep those in the department of man, as distinct as nature has formed them? This unfortunate difference of colour, and perhaps of faculty, is a powerful obstacle to the emancipation of these people. Many of their advocates, while they wish to vindicate the liberty of human nature, are *anxious also to preserve its dignity and beauty*." "Among the Romans emancipation required but one effort. The slave might mix with, without staining the blood of his master."

A fear that our descendants may become mulattoes by mixing with the blacks, and a wish to prevent it may perhaps be a prejudice arising from weakness; but it is a prejudice from which but few of us are exempt. From the manner in which Dr. Smith speaks of the beauty of civilized nations, and the ugliness of savages, it is evident he entertains the same prejudice. It is certainly painful to think that the skins of our posterity shall be much darker than our own, particularly when we reflect that we are by no means too white.

This wish to preserve the dignity and beauty of our species, seems highly criminal in your pure eyes; but the subject which seems to have excited your highest indignation, is the *suspicion* of Mr. Jefferson, that the blacks are inferior to the whites in the faculties of reason and imagination.

Sir, if you examine with candour his observations upon this subject, you will find nothing to warrant the harshness of your censures. In page 308, he says "the opinion that they are inferior in the faculties of reason and immagination, must be hazarded with great diffidence." "Let me add too, as a circumstance of great *tenderness*, where our conclusion would degrade a whole race of men from the rank in the scale of beings which their creator may perhaps have given them." "I advance it, therefore, as a *suspicion* only, that the blacks, whether *originally a distinct race, or made distinct by time and circumstances*, are inferior to the whites in the endowments both of body and mind. It is not against reason, to suppose, that different species of the same genus or varieties of the same species, may possess different qualifications." Compare this with what Doctor Smith says upon the same subject in his elegant essay on the variety of complexion and figure in the human species; a work you mention with the highest approbation, and which is certainly an important acquisition to the science of natural history. The doctor, without the least diffidence, asserts, (in page 77) that the mental capacities of savages (for reasons which he had given before) "are usually weaker than the capacities of men in civilized society. The powers of their minds through defect of objects to employ them, lie dormant, and even become extinct." "The coarseness of their food, and the filthiness of their manners, tend to blunt their genius." In a note to the same page he adds: "The exaggerated representations which we sometimes receive of the ingenuity and profound wisdom of savages [under which term he includes the negroes of Africa] are the fruits of ignorant surprise. And savages are praised by some writers, for the same reason that a monkey is—a certain imitation of the actions of men in society, which was not expected from the rudeness of their condition. There are doubtless degrees of genius among savages, as among civilized nations; but the comparison should be made of savages among themselves; and not of the genius of a savage, with that of a polished people." And in page 94, he says, "The Hottentots seems to be a race by themselves. In their manners the most beastly, and in their persons and the *faculties of their minds* approaching nearest the brutes of any of the human species."

Now if you please, we will apply to Dr. Smith, the sentence of excommunication which you in the plenitude of your Ecclesiastical power, have pronounced against Mr. Jefferson: Thus, Your, Doctor Samuel Stanhope Smith, President of Princeton College &c. &c. &c. stand forth, you must know that "this matter is too serious to jest with. Sir, we excuse you not! you have degraded the blacks from the rank which God hath given them in the scale of being! You have advanced the strongest argument for their state of slavery! You have insulted human nature! You have contemned the word of truth, and the means of salvation! and whether you will excuse us or not, *we exclude you in your present belief." from any department among christians!*— (see serious considerations &c. page 13).

This anathema of yours, it must be confessed is very moderate, when compared with the curse of Eroulphus.

Whenever Mr. Jefferson may think of the origin, of the mental and bodily faculties of the blacks, he has uniformly been their friend. At an early period, when little had been done, even by the benevolent followers of Penn, to ameliorate the condition of this unhappy race, he appeared their advocate, and that too in the state of Virginia, where an effort for their emancipation seemed to promise but little, besides ruin and disgrace, to him who should

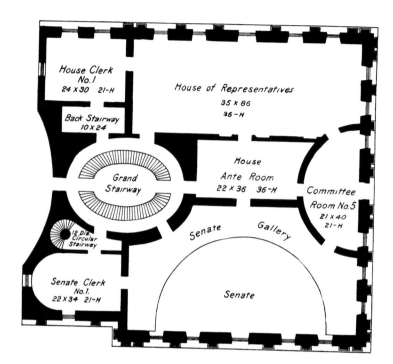

Plan of principal story of the capitol, 1800. William Dawson Johnston's History of the Library of Congress, *262, volume 1, plate 3.*

make it. Mr. Jefferson is still labouring for the abolition of slavery, and his labours have produced a very favourable impression.

What can be more philantrophic, what can be more awful, what can be more expressive of reverence for our creator, and a perfect reliance on his divine attirubtes, than the following appeal made by Mr. Jefferson, to the holders of slaves! "Can the liberties of a nation be thought secure when we have removed their only firm basis, a conviction in the minds of the people *that these liberties are the gift of God! That they are not to be violated but with his wrath! Indeed I tremble for my country when I reflect that God is just:* that considering numbers, nature, and natural means only, a revolution of the wheel of fortune, an exchange of situation is among possible events: that it may become probable by *supernatural interference! The Almighty* has no attribute which can take side with us in such a contest."* [*Notes on Virginia page 237.—For further particulars on this head see a valuable pamphlet lately published at Philadelphia intitled an "address to the people of the united States, with an epitome and indication of the public life and character of Thomas Jefferson."][2] Is this the language of an enemy to God and to our holy religion.   SENEX.

TR (*AURORA* (PHILADEPHIA), SEPTEMBER 2, 1800).

1. That is, William S. Smith, Presbyterian minister, president of Princeton, 1795–1812.

2. This pamphlet written by Beckley has been published in this volume under the date, July 4, 1800.

September 5, 1800

TO THE AUTHOR
OF A PAMPHLET INTITLED,
"Serious considerations on the Election of a President, addressed to the
Citizens of the United States."

No. III

Reverend Sir, from the first perusal of your pamphlet, I did not hesitate
to pronounce you an ambitious turbulent clergyman, prostrating your religion to answer particular purposes. It is now publicly announced that you
are a respectable clergyman of the city of New York; this information we
have from parson Abercombie[1] of this city, who is also a very respectable
clergyman, and as fit a yoke-fellow for you as is perhaps to be found in the
world. Bishop Bonner would probably have answered better, but you know
he is dead. I would therefore warmly recommend this parson Abercombie,
this intimate friend and associate of the pious Peter Porcupine, to your
polite attention, a partnership between you in temporal concerns, would be
a very desirable thing; you might labour together, to great advantage in the
political vineyard; you are a pair of kind, congenial, precious souls; *Oreades** [*Oreades, ab orco—It is a considerable time since I have looked into
Virgil—I may possibly have mistaken a word or two] *ambo et mentiri parest,
et respondere paroti.*[2]

Parson Abercombie has favoured us with your profession, but we are still
in the dark as to your name, but even that, it is probable will soon be communicated, as you say you are not ashamed to tell it; which is one proof
among many, that you are not ashamed of any thing.

Waiting your good pleasure as to these points, we will proceed to the further examination of your "Serious Considerations."

How came you to blunder upon Mr. Jefferson's plan for the institution of
schools in Virginia? A plan fully proving his high respect for religion and
virtue. You thought a part of it might be twisted into an expression of disrespect, for the holy scriptures. Mr. Jefferson thinks it would be improper to
put "the bible and testament into the hands of children *at an age when their
judgments are not sufficiently matured for religious enquiries,*" to which you
answer thus; "Had he prized the bible, and been properly acquainted with its
contents, he would have known that the facts related in that book, are the
most antient, the most authentic, the most interesting, and the most useful
in the world:*that they are above all others, level to the capacities of children.*"

Had you prized the scriptures, (no doubt you are acquainted with their
contents) you would have known, that many divine truths are there delivered in figurative language, and that our saviour commonly spoke in para-
bles, to understand which, not only a mature judgment, but often a
considerable degree of learning is required. How preposterous are the
notions formed by children, from reading the scriptures? And how danger-

ous it is, that absurd impressions, upon subjects the most sacred should be made upon their tender minds!

From an elevated situation, the objects below appear all on a level; the hillocks and little vallies, seem to form but one smooth surface; the roof of a church seen from the highest part of the steeple, appears on a level with the ground; so your exalted genius, comprehending all the divine truths of holy writ, as it were by intuition, leads you to believe there can be no possible difficulty attending them; and that they are even level to the capacities of children. But descend a little from your elevated conceptions, and you will find yourself under a gross mistake. Many men whose minds hold an intermediate rank between yours, and those of children in point of strength and maturity, have written little treatises containing in the most simple language those important moral and religious truths, which it is necessary a child should know. Among these perhaps, none is to be preferred to the shorter catechism.

Those who examine attentively will perceive that what Mr. Jefferson, in his plan for the establishment of schools in Virginia, has said of the bible and testament shews his respect rather than disrespect for those sacred volumes.

Nothing that Mr. Jefferson ever said or wrote has been more frequently quoted, or more wilfully misrepresented than the following passage (Notes on Virginia, page 231) "It does me no injury for my neighbour to say there are twenty gods, or no god. It neither picks my pockets, nor breaks my leg." From these words you say, some have ventured "to bring even the charge of atheism against him." But in your mind, where candour seems to reign with rather a tyrannic sway, those words amount only to a suspicion of Atheism. But even such a suspicion you say ought to exclude Mr. Jefferson from the Presidential chair, You declare, 'that conscience is not safe while there is a suspicion.' And you give us very timely warning that "the voice of the nation in calling a deist (Meaning Mr. Jefferson) to the first office must be construed into no less than *rebellion against God.*"

To all the objections which can be raised against the words now under consideration, I shall only answer, by quoting what Mr. Jefferson says upon the subject more at large.

Mr. Jefferson after stating that "several acts of the Virginia Assembly, of 1659, 1662, and 1693, had made it penal in parents to refuse to have their children baptized; and had prohibited the unlawful assembling of Quakers; had made it penal for any master of a vessel to bring a Quaker into the state; had ordered those already here, and such as should come heretofore, to be imprisoned till they should abjure the country; provided a milder punishment for their first and second return, *but death for their third*; had inhibited all persons from suffering their meetings in or near their houses, *entertaining them individually*, or disposing of books which supported their tenets." And after stating some religious oppressions of a later date, he adds, "This is a summary view of that religious slavery, under which a people have been willing to remain, who have lavished their lives and fortunes for the establishment of civil freedom. The error seems not sufficiently eradicated, that the operations of the mind, as well as the acts of the body, are subject to the coercion of the laws. But our rulers can have authority over such natural rights only as we have submitted to them. The rights of conscience we never submitted, we could not submit. We are answerable for them to our God. The legitimate powers of government extend to such acts only, as are injurious to others. *But it does me no injury for my neighbour to say there are twenty Gods, or no God. It neither picks my pocket nor breaks my leg.* If it be said, his testimony in a court of justice cannot be relied on, reject it then, and be the stigma on him. Constraint may make him worse by making him a hypocrite, but it can never make him a truer man. It may fix him obstinately in his errors, but it will not cure them. Reason and free enquiry are the only effectual agents against error. Give a loose to them, they will support the true religion, by bringing every false one to their tribunal, to the test of their investigation. They are the natural enemies of error, and of error only. Had not the Roman government permitted free enquiry, Christianity could never have been introduced. Had not free enquiry been indulged at the era of the reformation, the corruptions of Christianity could not have been purged away. If it be restrained now the present corruptions will be protected; and new ones encouraged. Were the government to preserve to us our medicine and diet, our bodies would be in such keeping, as our souls are now. Thus, in France the emetic was once forbidden as a medicine, and the potatoe as an article of food."

In your quotations, you discover much sagacity in avoiding such parts, as would defeat your purposes.

Sir, whenever you refer to books, it is easy to follow you and correct your misrepresentations; but when you state conversations which took place between Mr. Jefferson and a gentleman now in Europe, and which were related by a gentleman now dead, to you, who do not give your name, we have no possible check upon your malignity. Only relate consistent stories and they must be believed. Unfortunately for you however, you have failed even in this, in relating the following anecdote (page 16) "When the late Rev. Dr. John B. Smith[3] resided in Virginia, the famous Mazzei[4] happened one night to be his guest. Dr. Smith having, as usual, assembled his family for their evening devotion, the circumstance occasioned some discourse on religion, in which the Italian *made no secret of his infidel principles*. In the course of conversation he remarked to Dr. Smith, "why your great philosopher and statesman Mr. Jefferson is rather farther gone in infidelity than I am;" and related in confirmation the following anecdote; that as he was once riding with Mr. Jefferson, he expressed his surprise that the people of this country take no better care of their public buildings. What buildings? exclaimed Mr. Jefferson. Is not that a church? replied he, pointing to a decayed edifice. Yes, answered Mr. Jefferson. I am astonished said the other, they permit it to be in so ruinous a condition. It is good enough rejoined Mr. Jefferson *for him that was born in a manger!!!"*

A circumstance which perhaps did not occur to you is, that we have no proof *that Christ was born in a manger.* The probability is, that he was not. According to St. Luke, he was wrapped in swadling cloths and *laid in a manger.*

Those who are acquainted with Mr. Jefferson, know that he is extremely correct in all his expressions. He certainly knew what the evangelists say respecting the birth of our saviour; and it is rediculous to suppose that he ever expressed himself in the manner you have stated.

Mazzei was justifying his infidelity to Dr. Smith, it is highly probable he gave this story a little colouring, that it might the better answer his purpose. Dr. Smith might have forgotten some of the circumstances, and you most probably have wilfully omitted or perverted others. To suspect you of such baseness is no want of charity, when we consider the manner in which you have mangled and misrepresented several passages in the Notes on Virginia.

A very slight alteration makes the sentence perfectly harmless. Had Mr. Jefferson, to the question, why do these people suffer their Church to be in so ruinous a condition? answered, *"they perhaps think it good enough for him who lay in a manger;"* it would certainly have been a severe reflection, or sting, to use your word, upon those who had so criminally neglected their Church; but none upon the Saviour of the world. Allusions to the obscureness of his birth, the humble sphere of his life and the ignominious manner of his death, are not to be considered as sarcasms. They are the constant themes of his faithful ministers, and ought to excite our eternal love and gratitude.

Now let us suppose for a moment, a very improbable case, that you, restraining your propensity to misrepresent, have reported fairly what Dr. Smith told you; yet he got the story from Mazzei who you say "made no secret of his infidel principles." An infidel it seems is good authority when his testimony operates in your favor. Will you pretend to believe this deistical Italian, after what you have said of deists? To suspect you of such absurdity, would be doing injustice to your understanding. You have related the story, but have not declared your own belief of it. It was quite sufficient for your purpose, that others should believe it.

If such idle stories are to be taken as evidence, whose character can stand the test? Even that of Washington must fall to the dust.

In page 20, you become very witty all of a suddden; 'Some of the friends of Mr. Jefferson (you say) being ashamed that he should be reputed an infidel and wishing he had a little religion, *were it ever so little, whisper that he is a sort of christian.* Rather than give him up, they hint that he is as good a christian as Dr. Priestly, or Dr. Priestly as bad as him.'(meaning he) You had no doubt thought, that good wit and good grammar at the same time, would be too great a treat for farmers.

Now sir, is not this a hint of your own, the mere creature of your eventive imagination? Did you ever hear the friends of Mr. Jefferson, compare his religion with that of Dr. Priestly? I believe you never did.

Mr. Jefferson admires Dr. Priestly as a man of eminent virtues and of universal science, but there is no suspicion of his having subscribed to the Doctor's religious creed. It is true Mr. Jefferson went frequently to hear his lectures delivered at Philadelphia; but it must also be remembered, that Mr. Adams was a constant attendant, and that to-him, Dr. Priestly has dedicated those lectures—yet we have some strong proofs that Mr. Adams is not one of the doctor's disciples.[5]   SENEX

TR (*AURORA* (PHILADELPHIA), SEPTEMBER 5, 1800).

1. James Abercrombie, Episcopal minister at St. Peter's Church in Philadelphia, was an outspoken critic of Jefferson from his pulpit and in the press.
2. Beckley undoubtedly deliberately erred slightly in his quotation from Vergil, *Eclogues* VII, 11. 3–5. The original is "Arcades ambo, et cantare pares et respondere parati," which translated means "Arcadians both, ready in a match to sing, as well as to make reply." Beckley's verse has the Arcadians ready in a match to lie or deceive rather than to sing.
3. The Reverend John Blair Smith (1756–99), a graduate of Princeton College, had been president of Hampden-Sydney College, 1779–91.
4. Philip Mazzei, native of Tuscany and former Albemarle, Virginia, neighbor of Jefferson, was a frequent correspondent of Jefferson.
5. Dr. Joseph Priestley, author of *An History of the Corruptions of Christianity* (Birmingham: Piercy and Jones, 1786); and *History of Early Opinions Concerning Jesus Christ* (Birmingham: Pearson and Rollason, 1786), was the "basis of my own faith," Jefferson wrote to John Adams in an August 22, 1813, letter. See Sheridan, "Introduction," to *Jefferson's Extracts from the Gospels*, 1:14–16.

JOHN BECKLEY AS SENEX

September 26, 1800

TO THE AUTHOR
OF A PAMPHLET INTITLED
"Serious considerations on the Election of a President, addressed to the Citizens of the United States."

No. IV

Reverend Sir,

Do not imagine from what I have said of you and Parson Abercrombie, that I am an enemy to the clergy. I highly esteem and revere the faithful ministers of Christ, whose actions correspond with their professions, and prove the sincerity of their devotion to the cause they have espoused.

But Priests who make a *trade* of religion, for the purpose of accumulating *wealth*, who avail themselves of the sanctity attached to their characters, for the purpose of effecting political objects, with whom the cause of God, is but a secondary consideration, are the pests of society, and ought to be exhibited as such to the views of the public. The people cannot be too jealous of those ambitious and avaricious clergymen, who are incessantly labouring to bring about a union of *church* and *state*. The Jesuits had sufficient artifice to get into their hands, the most dangerous power over the persons, and property of the inhabitants of the greater part of Europe. The priests of the present day, would persuade us, that in the least as well as most important elections, the serious interests of *religion* are involved. Under this pretext, they boldly come forward as the zealous supporters of the "honnour of God," and make use of his name and his word, to exclude every candidate, whose political creed does not exactly coincide with their own. And you sir, more bold than the rest, have had the audacity to prescribe a religious test, against which the constitution of the United States has carefully guarded.

Although the great object of the clergy should be the "care of souls," yet as they are equally interested in the affairs of state with other citizens, they have an equal right to act in elections. Indeed there could be no great impropriety in their writing political pamphlets, if it did not lead them to neglect their pastoral duties; or subject them to those delusions of party so little suited to the clerical character—and, I hope, you did not compose one sermon the less, in consequence of writing your "Serious Considerations." But, Sir, whenever clergymen enter the field of politics, they should leave their *Ecclesiastical* weapons behind them; they should enter as other citizens, armed with reason alone; they should not, as you have done, come forward clothed, with the fierce garb of religion, wielding the word of God, and hurling prayers, excommunications and curses against your political opponents. This mode of warfare should be left to the Pope, who at present can resort to no other.

You discover the utmost rancour even in your prayers. What was your object in offering up the following very pious ejaculation—"Most merciful God! forgive the thoughts of the heart to take council against thee and thine anointed." It was to raise the indignation of your readers against Mr. Jefferson, and his friends, by pretending to intercede with God in their favor.

How your pious bowels seem to yearn, over the friends of Mr. Jefferson, in this goodly, little prayer, "and may even you, the unwary instruments of drawing down the calamities, be sheltered and obtain the forgiveness of God and your country." This is too forgiving in you, who have excluded Mr. Jefferson from any department among Christians, and who think his election "must be construed into no less than *rebellion against God.*"

By such hypocritical canting with which your pamphlet abounds, you were in hopes to divert the attention of your readers from the real motives which actuate your heart—with some, you might have succeeded—people long accustomed to hear divine truths of religion proved and illustrated by passages from scripture, feel a reverence for that mode of proof even when applied to objects of merely a temporal concern, and would heretofore have listened and believed; but the work has been overdone; you have done more mischief to religion than infidelity could do for you have cried out so often, where there was no danger, that the *wolves* may come hereafter with more security—such artifices have been too frequently resorted to where ambition, envy, interest, personal resentment, rancorous hatred, or any thing but the love of God, were the governing motives.

Of this reverential awe justly attached to the sacred scriptures, time-serving Priests have always availed themselves; and you, Sir, have attempted to profit by their example. It is, however, at this time a dangerous experiment, for although it may assist in effecting your immediate objects, yet it injures the cause of religion. If the positions which you have attempted to establish by the scriptures be fallacious, the confidence in the truth of those sacred volumes will be diminished. Those who under pretence of serving God, convert religion into a political machine, do indefinitely more injury to the kingdom of Christ, than those who openly profess the principles of deism. Dr. Swift says, "The scripture in time of disputes is like an open town in time of war, which serves indifferently the occasions of both parties; each makes use of it for the present time, and then resigns it to the next comer to do the same." You appear to have adopted this maxim. You have made the scriptures serve the occasions of your party, by drawing from them whatever arguments you pleased. It would be no difficult task to confute you by arguments drawn from the same source. But, Sir, I have been taught from my infancy to revere the sacred writings, and I will never prostrate them to objects of merely a political concern.

The holy zeal which you profess to feel for religion, is easily traced to its source. The ambitious, amorous little Hamilton of whom both you and general Pinckney are the humble tools, has been your oracle. By him alone have you been inspired. The marks of his hand are plainly discernable in your pamphlet, the postscript to which is evidently written by himself.

At first I was induced to believe you the friend of Mr. Adams, because you oppose Mr. Jefferson, but on a careful examination of your "Serious Considerations," I find you are not. In page 34, you say, "We have seen tokens of the divine displeasure, for several years past." This is an open censure on Mr. Adams' administration. You seem to have no objections to a change, provided it be a prudent one. In page 30, the following passage is worthy of notice, " Do you say that there has long been complaint against the measures of government; we wish for a change; and at any rate there can be no harm in trying other men? *Be it so, But let you change be wise and prudent. Have a regard for the honor of God.*" You will probably consent to have Mr. Adams, vice president, as in page 30, you name him as the second federal candidate; yet your "regard for the honor of God," induces you to support the influence of Hamilton and Pinckney, men, who if they have any kind of religion, have very carefully concealed it from the eyes of the public; not so with their follies. Hamilton has by his *previous confessions*, forced himself, and his Maria, upon the notice of the public; and the adventures of general Pinckney with *the Lady* at Paris, will be remembered 'till the ridiculous and disgraceful intrigues with X,Y, and Z, shall be forgotten.* [*Mr. Gerry ought not to be charged, with any part of the disgrace attending these transactions.][1]

For such men, have you ventured to arraign Mr. Jefferson as an enemy to the christian religion.

Mr. Jefferson has never made pretensions to extraordinary piety or religious fervour. Without doubt, he has been too negligent of those spiritual concerns, upon which his eternal happiness or misery is to depend. I fear but few of us, I have reason to feel perfectly satisfied with our conduct, on a subject of this infinite importance.

But Mr. Jefferson, although an enemy to every species of legal hierarchy, & clerical oppression, is a friend to religion.

It is true, that the church establishments in Virginia, by which the Episcopalians engrossed all offices of honor and profit to themselves; levied tythes throughout that extensive State, and enjoyed many other exclusive privileges, were destroyed by his means, soon after the termination of the revolutionary war. And it is also true, that ever since that period, he has supported, and now supports at his own expence, a very worthy episcopal clergyman, who preaches every other sabbath, at a small church within two miles of Mr. Jefferson's house, at which Mr. Jefferson and his family are constant attendants. The allowance made by Mr. Jefferson for the support of this clergyman, is equal to the amount of the tythes, to which by law he was before entitled.

In page 30, you say, "I will venture it as my serious opinion, that rather than be instrumental in the election of Mr. Jefferson, it would be more acceptable to God, and beneficial to the interest of your country, to throw away your votes." You were too modest to state this as a matter of your own knowlege, you give it merely as your "serious opinion." Is it your serious opinion, that it would be acceptable to God to throw away votes, while there are such irreproachable characters as Hamilton and Pinckney, on whom they might be bestowed? Would it not be "more acceptable to God: that the people should vote for gen. Pinckney, than that they should throw their votes away? In your next pamphlet be so good as to restrain your modestly a little, and inform us, not what you think, but what you know upon this subject; declare the whole truth fully and at large. On a matter of this delicate nature, it would perhaps be proper to consult gen. Hamilton.

It would be no strange thing if you in your pretended religious fervor, should travel through the United States, preaching up a crusade against Jefferson and his friends. "Would Jews or Mahomedans" you say "consistently with their belief elect a Christian, and *shall Christians be less active and zealous than them?*" [meaning they] Your reverence must recollect, that the Mahomedans support as well as propagate their faith by fire and sword, not merely by exclusion from office. The strong proofs of their religion are uttered from the mouths of their cannon. If a Turk should profess a belief that Christ was the son of God, he would probably be convinced of his rashness by an application of the bow-string. I hope Christians will, in this respect, be always less zealous and less active than the followers of Mohamed. You and Parson Abercrombie may possibly infuriate a few bigots with Mahomedan zeal, but your influence I trust will not be extensive.—— There is no part of your pamphlet which shews in more glaring colours the dangerous lengths to which such clergymen as you would proceed, provided you possessed the power you grasp at, than the following (page 30) "Let Mr. Jefferson only set his name to the first part of the apostles creed, I believe in God the Father Almighty, maker of heaven and earth—and in Jesus Christ his only begotten son our Lord." Can the ministers of the Gospel, who are *jealous for the glory of God* and the people to whom Christ is precious expect less?"

That you would wish to subvert the constitution of the United States, which abhors a religious test, I have no doubt. For this you have more powerful reasons than your extreme jealousy of the glory of God; one of which is, your jealousy for the glory of the clergy.

Are the clergy as a body, to assume the power of prescribing articles of faith, to the officers of government?

Can the ministers of the gospel, jealous for the glory of God expect less? Surely not, they expect a great deal more.

It is a general rule that no free native Americans have a right to vote, mediately, or immediately for President of the United States, but such as are eligible themselves to that office.

Your first step would therefore not only render the Jews ineligible, but deprive them of the privilege of voting for electors.

Your next step will probably be, to prescribe the sacrament of the Lord's supper as a test; this would exclude the Quakers. You will next oblige all candidates to office to abjure the Pope, this will exclude all Roman Catholics, which the sacramental test would not. You will then be under the necessity of establishing some regulations against occasional conformity. By this time you clergymen, so *jealous for the glory of God* will be a body far more formidable, than Mr. Ross's proposed grand committee would have been, had the plan succeeded; indeed your Reverences will have the whole election in your own hands. None but those of your church and that to which Parson Abercrombie belongs, will be eligible to office, or have a right to vote. Can the ministers of the gospel jealous of the glory of God, expect less?

If religious tests are necessary for a president, they are for a vice president, heads of departments, judges of the federal courts, members of the two houses of congress, ministers of foreign courts, &c.

It would be a subject worthy of the pencil of some modern Hogarth, to depict you and parson Abercrombie, administering the sacrament of the Lord's supper to Hamilton, Pinckney, Wolcott, Pickering, Dayton, Sedgwick, Pilot-boat Smith, and Governeur Morris, any one of who "I will venture it as my serious opinion," would, without a moment's hesitation, eat and drink damnation to himself for the sake of increasing his wealth or extending his power. "Spectatum admissi, risum teneatis amici?"[2]

Although a scene like the above, would be to the last degree impious, yet such may actually happen in this country. Many of the most vicious characters in England, who do not believe in a saviour, partake regularly once a quarter of the Lord's supper, for the sake of holding their offices. Where religious tests are established, such profanity will always take place; hypocriscy will prevail, and religion will vanish.

The general convention who framed the constitution of the United States, the different state conventions who adopted that constitution, have declared in sect. 3rd, art. 6th, that "no religious test shall ever be required as a qualification to any office or public trust under the United States," and the state legislatures who have concurred in the amendments to the constitution have said "Congress shall make no law respecting an establishment of religion, or prohibiting the free exercise thereof."

In attempting to overturn the instrument of our political union, formed by the collective wisdom of the U. States, and fixed upon so firm a basis, you and Parson Abercrombie have undertaken a task, greatly beyond the extent of your powers. SENEX

TR (*AURORA* (PHILADEPHIA), SEPTEMBER 26, 1800).

1. Charles Cotesworth Pinckney, Marshall, and Gerry were the special envoys to France in 1797, whose public rejection of a French request for an American payment to prepare the way for Franco-American negotiations led to a diplomatic crisis and a naval war between the two countries, known respectively as the XYZ Affair and the Quasi-War. Gerry was the only Republican member of the trio, while Pinckney was the Federalist candidate for vice-president, and Marshall was John Adams's secretary of state. See Beckley to Peter Galline, June 8, 1798, note 2.
2. Beckley's quotation is from Horace, Ars poetica, v. 5 [1–4]: "could you, my friends, if favoured with a private view, refrain from laughing."

JOHN BECKLEY TO TENCH COXE

My dear sir,   Philadelphia, 29th September 1800.

Your favour of the 26th is before me, and I attend to its various remarks. The Lancaster address & the letter concerning A. are both in the Aurora,[1] and you'l see a torrent of abuse against you in Brown & Rolf.[2] Dickenson and myself have forwarded many things to Jersey, Maryland & Delaware, particularly the Lancaster address. In all those States our affairs look well. Bloomfield wrote me to day that to morrow, at Kingston, a general republican meeting of that State will be held, of the result of which he will immediately after advise me. He writes in great Spirits, and I do not fail to press him by every suggestion in my view. Luther Martin is now here and says Maryland Elections will certainly be by districts, and that the fæds will have 6 to 4. Reverse the numbers & I believe he will be right. In Delaware, Doctor Tilton says we shall succeed.

I have had no letter from Connecticut altho' I have written twice, since my return. But a letter from Burr to Major Butler indicates success to a considerable degree. Granger, Kirby and about half a dozen other decided republicans are elected, but not P. Edwards—his failure will it is said benefit us, by the umbrage it has created.[3]

The Southern insurrections will not, I believe, injure us; on the contrary they will, Major Butler thinks, benefit us, by the great pains taken to make them inflammatory. That in So. Carolina has no existance in fact. In Virginia it has been serious, but I have reason to think will be found to partake more of an agency from another nation than from France. Consider this well, & say, where existed the strongest motive to convulse Virginia & deprive it of its vote on the pending Election, by internal commotion?

In So. Carolina, great exertions are making on both Sides. Our C. Pinkney is indefatigable. Major Butler thinks we are sure of 8 votes for Jefferson—the struggle will be to defeat Gen Pinkney totally or partially. One or the other will be Effected he says. Rutledge, Nott & Harper he thinks will all be superseded by Republicans.[4] His letters speak sanquinely. On Wednesday he departs and I forward by him to Hampton, Sumpter &c. many things. He promises to advise me fully and regularly. As fast as information comes you shall have it. Excuse present haste I will write again shortly. The ladies desire best respects to those of your family, and I remain, Sincerely Yrs. always,

John Beckley.

RC (COXE PAPERS, HISTORICAL SOCIETY OF PENNSYLVANIA).

1. "The Address" was a lengthy essay written by Coxe and attributed to the Lancaster Republican Committee—*To the Republican Citizens of Lancaster*. It was designed to demonstrate the "monarchical and aristocratic views" of Adams and Hamilton and appeared in the *Aurora*, September 27 as well as in pamphlet form. The reference to Adams's letter was to President Adams's 1792 letter to Coxe which had been published many times.

2. That is, the *Philadelphia Gazette and Daily Advertiser*, published by Brown and Relf. For a discussion of the Federalist attacks on Coxe for his role in the release of Adams's letter to him, see Cooke, *Coxe*, pp. 371–89.

3. Beckley is referring to the September elections in Connecticut for the state assembly, where Republicans had hoped to obtain a majority and force district-wide elections for presidential electors. On October 31, the Connecticut legislature elected men pledged to Adams and Pinckney. Kline, ed., *Burr Papers*, 1:448n. 2.

4. John Rutledge, Jr. (1766–1819), Abraham Nott (1768–1830), and Robert G. Harper (1765–1825) were Federalist representatives from South Carolina. Only Rutledge won reelection in 1800.

JOHN BECKLEY TO EPHRAIM KIRBY

Dear Sir,   Philadelphia 1st Octr 1800.

I am without any of Your favors for some weeks, and as the Elections of
Our State Legislature, have taken place it would afford me great pleasure to
Know from You, how prospects now stand, Also, if You have any recent
advices from NHampsh., Massats, R'Island & Vermont, that may be
depended upon, they will be equally acceptable.

I think You may depend upon the following Statement:
A Vote of this State entire for Jefferson. In Maryland, a vote by district
Electn. half for Jeffn. perhaps 6. In No. Car. 9 for Jeffn. In So. Car. 8 for Jeffn
and 4 for Pinkney. A General State meeting of republicans in NJersey was
held Yesterday at Princetown, my Letter advices me that we shall <u>certainly</u>
have the entire vote of that State.

In Delaware our friends are sanguine, but still I am doubtful from my
knowledge of their local divisions &c.

Kentucky, Tennesee & Georgia will be unanimous for Jefferson and Burr.

I enclose You many papers which may furnish matter of useful information. Hoping to hear from You shortly I remain.

Dr Sir, Yours sincerely,
JB

RC (KIRBY PAPERS, DUKE UNIVERSITY).

JOHN BECKLEY TO TENCH COXE

Dear Sir,   Philadelphia, 5th October 1800.

You mention in your last, that you were to take a final view of Mr. Mcs[1]
papers, and that you had already seen some strong things in his letter book.
Whatever there may be, I hope you have taken measures to secure its forth-
coming at a proper Season. Every day developes more of the original plan
and a late proclamation is strictly in raison with what <u>we</u> have seen. Mr. Ps.
successor[2] in form, adheres steadily to their System, and with more ability
possesses not less cupidity than his predecessor. The taste of diplomatic
emolument, has not, you may assure yourself, lessened his appetite for a
more lucrative speculation. Hamilton well knows in what soil to sow.

Thomas Pinkneys letter has astonished every body—[3] Even fæderalists
cry shame. Edwd. Tilghman says he made <u>A</u>'s letter known to Mr. Rutledge,
a considerable time ago, requesting him to communicate it to Mr. P. and
suggesting that he might certainly expect to see it published pending the
Election. The insinuation of forgery is base in the Extreme—to you it

belongs to make this attempt recoil on himself. There is yet full time to undeceive the Electors even in South Carolina. My information respecting E. Tilghman comes from Swift, and Mr. Dallas told me he shewed Rutledge the Original letter. You will have seen Major Butler and will have shewn him the letters or given him an attested copy. He should be well fortified on this ground.

Our ward Elections for Inspectors took place last evening, I have not heard from other wards yet, but in ours (Locust) we carried our men 2 to 1. Judge Sloane is here from the great Republican Meeting at Princeton on tuesday last. He says that he has not a remaining doubt of complete success in New Jersey. In Delaware every thing is doubtful—on tuesday next they Elect and by thursday or friday we shall probably know the result. Connecticut will do nothing, I fear altho' I am yet without any letter. Rh. Island, it is confidently said, will give us 4 votes. My letters from Maryland, by last mail, reiterate the confidence in District Elections & of 5 to 6 votes for us—they also add that for Congress 6 on the Western and 1 on the Eastern Shore may be expected. No. Carolina letters continue to assure us of 9 and a well informed Gent. from thence, now here, says he is of opinion 11 may, and probably will be got.

We had a very full and unanimous town meeting at the State house on Wednesday Evening—where our tickets were completed, all opposition & schism withdrawn, and a Mutual Solemn pledge given to pull altogether.

To morrow our Mayors Court begins, and will occupy me all the week, but if any thing occurs I will drop you a line. In the interim, let me continue to hear from you.

Be so good as to inform our friend Mr. Barton, I received his communication of friday, and have duly attended to it, but that I have not one word of advice yet concerning my Stray letters, and will be much indebted to him to write to Mr. Kelly about them, as I am very anxious to recover them.

With best wishes I remain, dear Sir, Yrs. truly,   John Beckley

RC (COXE PAPERS, HISTORICAL SOCIETY OF PENNSYLVANIA).

1. Not identified, but perhaps James McHenry, whom John Adams had dismissed as secretary of war.
2. John Marshall was Timothy Pickering's successor as secretary of state.
3. Thomas Pinckney had denounced Adams' May 1792 letter to Coxe as a forgery in a September 15, 1800, letter which was first published in Charleston, South Carolina and in the *Aurora* on October 3, 1800.

JOHN BECKLEY TO HARRY INNES

Dear sir,[1]   Philadelphia, 16th October 1800

Among other Lands advertised for sale for taxes in your State, are two tracts of mine in Lincoln County surveyed in the name of Edward Blake, to wit
One tract, Survey bearing date 10th March 1784   7952 acres
One tract, Survey bearing date 14th March 1784   10,000 acres
The taxes on them are due for one Year only, and amount, as by the advertisement, on the first tract to £1. 9.9
            on the second tract to 1.17.6

———

£ 3.7.3 Kentucky Currency

I now enclose a bank note of ten dollars, and must rely on your friendship to pay the difference for me of 7/3d. . it being impracticable to make the remittance, at present, in any other form. You will be so good as to take on my behalf, a special receipt for the payment specifying the two tracts I have described, and transmit it me by the mail, and I will pay the small difference into the hand of Mr. Brown.

There is a third tract of 10,000 acres adjoining the two former surveys, which is also surveyed in name of Edward Blake by survey bearing date 12th March 1784, and is also advertised for sale for all the taxes due thereon for 1792, 3, 4, 5, 6, 7, 8 & 9 amounting to. . .[2] upwards. This tract I sold about 3 years ago to Presly Thornton Esquire, near Fredericksburg, and I am sure he knows nothing of its danger. If there is any friend of his near you that you can discover that would interpose either to advance the tax, or purchase it on his behalf, Or if on my assurance to you of Col. Thorntons most abundant sufficiency to reimburse, and my own now positive undertaking to be responsible for him it can be saved, you will render a very high obligation to him, and also confer an additional favour on me. The tract is reported by General Knox, of Stamford, to be one half level, farming land—of course the loss to Mr. Thornton will be very great, without it is prevented by some friendly interference.[3]

I have a tract of 10,000 acres on Cumberland, deeded to me by Doctor Benjamin Say 12th August 1795, and for which I have the Sheriffs receipt of taxes for 1796 and 1797. This land has never been advertised since, nor is now—nor can I discover, at present, any thing about it. Mr. Brown paid the taxes for them two years, and gave me the receipt for it at my house when, on repaying him, I requested and he promised to take order for its annual payment thereafter. He will have left Kentucky before this letter reaches you, and as I am anxious to know its real situation I must farther trouble you to make the necessary enquiry, and advise me accordingly.

Elections in Maryland to the State Legislature, are decisive of Mr. Jeffersons receiving 6 Electoral Votes in that State. The Election of this State and New Jersey took place on tuesday last, and are equally decisive of the entire Votes of these two States. The City of Philadelphia has been decidedly republican. No. Carolina will give us 8 votes. So. Carolina 8 votes. Georgia 4 and Rhode Island 4. Mr. Jeffersons Election is considered here as inevitable.

Respecting the taxes you were so good as to negociate for the last year, by Mr. James Browns draft on me in favour of Mr. Campbell; that Gentleman's death and some other circumstances between him & our good friend Mr. John Brown, previous thereto, produced some unpleasant delay in the payment, but as Mr. B. stood indebted to me a considerable sum on his return to Kentucky this summer, he promised me and I doubt not has fully setiled the business with his brother. I mention this merely to explain to you, the cause of delay, because of your friendly exertions on my behalf.

With great regard and esteem, I am, dear Sir, Yr. obliged friend & humble Servt.   John Beckley

RC (INNES PAPERS, LIBRARY OF CONGRESS).

1. Harry Innes (1752–1816), a lawyer and legislator from Bedford County, Virginia, moved to Kentucky, where he became a federal district judge in 1789. Tainted by the Burr-Wilkinson conspiracy, Innes was embroiled in resulting civil suits for nearly a decade.
2. MS damaged one or two words illegible.
3. Six years later Beckley remained entangled in the land deal with Thornton, according to a March 17, 1806, letter from Beckley to Innes, in the Innes Papers, Library of Congress.

JOHN BECKLEY TO EPHRAIM KIRBY

Dear sir,   Philadelphia, 25th October 1800.

Your favour of the 17th came to hand yesterday, and I delay not to advise you of the State of things in this Quarter. New Jersey and Delaware are both decidedly in the Anti-republican scale, but in Maryland and this state, Our Success has been much more decided on the republican side. In Maryland, all fear of a Legislative choice of Electors is removed, by the Election of a decided Majority of republicans in to the Legislature, whereby the former law for the choice of Electors by the people, in districts, remains to operate, and we have every reason to expect 6 votes out of 10. In this state I cannot convey a better idea of our Success than to state, that last year we had only 8 out of 13 represents. in Congress, a Majority of one only in our representative branch of the State Legislature, and a majority of 6 against in the State Senate—this Year we have Eleven out of 13 represents. in Congress, two antis being chosen with great difficulty, and very small majorities—in the representative branch of the State Legislature we have 58 to 26, and in the

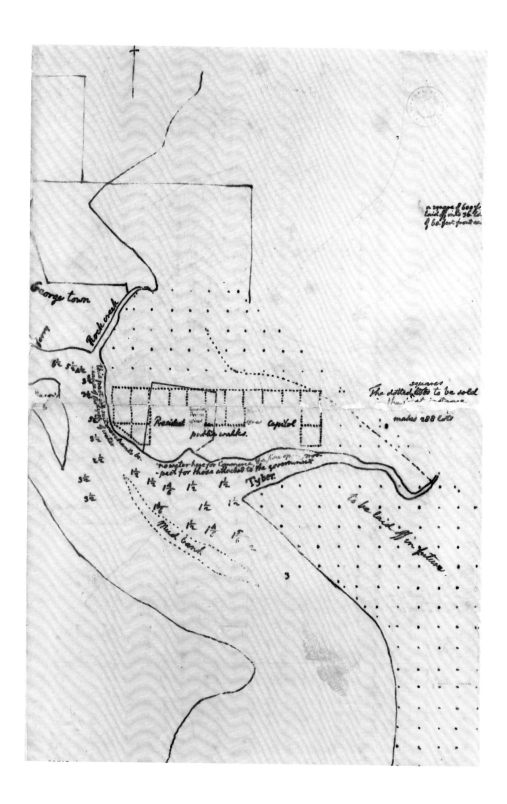

George town

Rock creek

a square of 600 f[...]
laid off into 36 [...]
of 60 feet front ea[...]

squares
The dotted lots to be sold
[...] first instance

makes 288 lots

President

public walks.

Capitol

no water here for Commerce [...] fine op[...]
-pect for those attached to the governm[...]

Tyber.

to be laid off in [...]

Mud bank

Senate 12 to 12. Our Governor has issued his proclam. to convene the Legislature on 5th Novr. and we doubt not, but a provision will be made to secure the vote of this State entire for a republican president. Indeed you may rest satisfied of this result and of the consequent election of a republican president, since very recent advices from the two Carolina's render it morally certain that we shall have 16 votes at least in those States. We do not, nor ever have counted, on aid from the Northern States. It remains for a new administration, in its development of the Maladministration of our present rulers, to convince the whole people of the U.S. of the infidelity and perfidy of those, in whom they have hitherto reposed thier confidence, and by systems of moderation, justice and equality to manifest its superior wisdom and claim to public confidence. The turbulent and intriguing spirit of Alexander Hamilton, has again Manifested itself, in an insidious publication[1] to defeat Mr. Adams's election, and in a labored effort to belittle the character of the president, he has in no small degree belittled his own. Vainly does he essay to seize the Mantle of Washington, and cloak the moral attrocities of a life spent in wickedness and which must terminate in shame and dishonor. His career of ambition is passed, and neither honor or empire will ever be his. As a political nullity, he has inflicted upon himself the sentence of 'Aut Caesar, aut nullus'.[2]

Be pleased to continue your communication of whatever you may think interesting to us, and I will continue to reciprocate from hence.

Very truly, dear Sir, Yrs "_____."

[*P.S.*] Be pleased to acknowledge this, immediately.

RC (KIRBY PAPERS, DUKE UNIVERSITY). IN BECKLEY'S HAND, THOUGH NOT SIGNED. ENDORSED BY KIRBY: "OCTOBER 25TH 1800 JOHN BECKLEY ESQR."

1. The "publication" was Hamilton's *Letter from Alexander Hamilton, Concerning the Public Conduct and Character of John Adams, Esq. President of the United States* (New York: 1800).
2. "Aut Caesar, aut nullus" was the heraldic motto of Caesar Borgia, hero of Machiavelli's *Prince*.

JOHN BECKLEY TO TENCH COXE

Dear Sir,   Philadelphia, 27th October 1800.

I received your favour of the 24th and am fully impressed with the importance of the reflections it conveys, but feel it impossible that your views can be accomplished within time to produce any effect, even if Mr. Langdon & Mr. Taylor could be immediately induced to come forward.[1]

Their respective distances are too great to write to and receive Answers to effect and before the Electors even in this State must be appointed, if at all & besides I do not now think with you that so much depends on extraneous matters. My opinion is, that the question, whether Electors be or be not appointed by our Legislature, must be decided principally under the influence of local and domestic considerations, and that a sufficient degree of Knowledge of the Character & pretensions of the respective Candidates, and of the policy and Views of the respective parties by which they are supported, is possessed by our Senators. There is one thing more important than any you have suggested, to be guarded against, if it be possible to guard against it, and that is British Gold, which I fear will be brought into action. It is sufficient to hint that Liston is now here and has his Eyes fixed upon the business at Lancaster. Every individual upon whom Seduction can be practiced, should be doubly watched. Your Senator is now here and it is said that a fœderal Caucus is to be held tonight, at which he is to attend. Bond & Liston and several of that party are uncommonly brisk and moving. Attend to this hint—it is deeply important to do so. Nothing will be left unessayed—the party are desperate & desperate means must be presumed, or they sink now to rise again. Above all, suggest to our faithful & vigilant Cheif Magistrate, the necessity of marked attention to this last and forlorn hope of the party. If the represents. of each district, would charge themselves with close and strict attention to their particular Senators, a System of observation might be established, to prevent or defeat the efforts of Seduction. I am the more solicitous on this subject, since not, more than an hour ago, I had a very interesting but deeply confidential conversation with a friend of ours from Boston, who is closely intimate with One of Listons family, and who, along with strong reasons of suspicion on his own part, entreated me to urge great caution & watchfulness on this point, accompanied with an assurance the most solemn, that if any movement towards it can be discovered, he will instantly possess me with it.

The irresistable argument, derived from the almost total change of public opinion in each of the Senatorial districts, added to the reflection that nothing is now to be expected by them from the fœderal party, must have weight with each individual Senator. Besides, what benefit has enured or is likely to enure to any of the pertinacious Senators, who, by adhering to the fœderal party, last year to defeat the Vote of Pennsylvania, have contributed to prop the hopes of that party and keep them alive, One Year longer than they could otherwise have Survived? Have themselves or their State been more particularly noticed for it? Can any looked for or expected benefit, avert the indigation and Execution of their betrayed and injured Country? Is the longer adherence to a desperate faction, supported by A Minor and opposed by the Major Sense of their Country, to be justified by any principle of public or private integrity?

I enclose you John Adams's lying, hypocritical, base letter to Thomas Pinkney.[2] You have received Hamiltons new Vindication, and will not fail to notice his assertion that Adams was a Candidate to Mr. Washington for Thomas Pinkney's appointment. Volumes, could not more fully expose the baseness of the attempt to disguise motives so apparent as those which dictated his Adams's letter to you.

Poor old hypocrite—he is now gone to displace Woolcot, in revenge for his friend Hamiltons proscription of him. Even the last act of the drama presents him a very wretch.[3]

I have two letters from Kirby and Granger—both write in assurances of the vote of Rh. Island, and possibly, nay very probably of Vermont. Israel Smith is elected in the latter State to Congress and it is expected that another republican will Succeed in the upper district.[4]

What ground of apprehension have you respecting Georgia & Tennessee ?

Let me hear from you soon and believe me, always, dear Sir, Yr. sincere friend,   John Beckley

RC (COXE PAPERS, HISTORICAL SOCIETY OF PENNSYLVANIA).

1. That is, John Langdon of New Hampshire and John Taylor of Virginia. For further information on Langdon's statement concerning Adams' "monarchism," see Beckley to Coxe, October 30, note 2.

2. That is Adams's October 27, 1800, letter to Thomas Pinckney, in which he explains his May 1792, letter to Coxe.

3. Oliver Wolcott, Jr. resigned as secretary of the treasury in a November 8, 1800, letter to Adams, and was replaced by Secretary of War Samuel Dexter. Gibbs, ed., *Memoirs of Oliver Wolcott*, 2:443–44, 462.

4. Israel Smith and Lewis R. Morris, a Federalist incumbent, were elected to the House from Vermont for the Seventh Congress. Morris withheld his vote on the thirty-sixth ballot in the House for president, thus confirming Jefferson's election. *Debates and Proceedings, Sixth Congress*, p. 1033.

JOHN BECKLEY TO TENCH COXE

Dear Sir,   Philadelphia 30th October 1800.

I have many things to say which will demand your attention, but first I will ask your indulgence on a Subject I have not, to you, hitherto touched. I mean your cause of difference with Doctor Rush.[1] Believing that you will hereafter see no occasion to refer to the Doctor on any public occasion, and observing the anguish that has been already produced to the Doctor and his family by what has already occurred, I feel too great a sympathy for him and them, arising out of those obligations of friendship which I must ever respect, not to express the wish that you may, and will, on any future occasion of publication, withhold any reference to his name. The Doctors age and situation, his past services and sacrifices, his friendship and sympathy with you in scenes of public and private feeling, urge you powerfully in conjunction with your own Sensibilites, to spare the pain which a further pursuit of him may inflict. Desirous to retreat from political collisions, I believe the Doctor is equally solicitous to be unnoticed by you, either in reference to Mr. Adams or Mr. Hamilton, farther than what is already done— And I do not conceal to you as a friend, my equal wish that this may be the case, since I am led to the conclusion, that what has already passed, is abundantly satisfactory on the score of justification to yourself.

Mr. Langdon[2] is now here and will be in Lancaster on Monday next. I have conversed with him, respecting his testimony of Mr. Adams's Monarchism, and he is fully disposed to give it to you without abatement. Mr. Bishop,[3] who hands you this, will corrobate incidentally and collaterally every thing respecting Mr. Adams's Monarchic declaration to Mr. Dana and Mr. Peirpont Edwards at New Haven. Other interesting communications Mr. Bishop will make to you, and you will find in him a powerful auxiliary to aid, all our united views & wishes at Lancaster. You must not suffer Mr. Langdon to pass on for two or three days. Indeed if a personal interview and explanation from him, to some of our doubtful Senators can possibly be effected, it may render us decisive service. If this impression comes to him from the Governor I think you will be able to detain him. I repeat it, the object is immense; his personal sacrifice not to be put in competition.

But more than all, guard against Corruption—the hint I gave you in my last, did not arise out of vague suspicion. It is a fact, which will be proved to you in a few days by our friend Duane in person, that on friday last, Liston drew out of bank 68,000 dollars, and that on Saturday and Sunday, two private dinners were given by him at old Willings, at both of which were present a cidevant Senator of our State Legislature, who will be in Lancaster on Monday. Duane will tell you his name and all other particulars.[4]

I think that a private organized Committee of Observation should be immediately instituted to consist of not less than 20 of your most active, intelligent and secret friends, whose objects shoud be:

1st: To notice & report all Strangers coming to & remaining at Lancaster, during the Sessions.

2d: To mark their persons, abodes, apparent business and intercourse.

3d: To observe the Senatorial boarding houses, their comings, goings &c. as far as may be practicable.

4th: To observe Equally our friend and our Enemy Senators, since the War may be carried into our own Country.

In addition to this, You must be prepared with a Resolve, not an Act, which in its necessary forms creates delay, "declaring, that an appointment of Electors of a president & V.P. on the part of the State of Pennsylvania Shall be made, by joint ballot of the two homes of Assembly." And this resolve should be a seperate & independent act, unconnected with any declaration about drawing this case into precedent, Or an immediate ticket or nomination of Electors, because if you can once run a resolve of the tenor I mention thro' the two houses, the Governors signature makes it an irrevocable Act to all our purposes, and the appointment which must then follow, can be made at liesure. In brief my idea is, that you should have every thing Cut and dry, as the phrase is, and be ready instanter, with a motion, plain, single, abstract and unclogged, to seize the first, precious moment of action, before delay, pause, or procrastination, can work its business of seduction. I fear only delay and corruption. It is said confidently here, that Potts, Johnson & McClellan[5] have all seperately declared that they will not oppose the public Sentiment as manifested by the late Elections—but these concessions, whether true or false, have been so much bandied about, that our Enemies are equally aware of them, and will point their Efforts accordingly. Every republican Member of the House of Reps. that belong to the districts of these three Men, should be pointedly attentive to all their Movements, and impress them unceasingly with the necessity of immediate Vote and Action. Besides that if delay arises from their holding back, Suspicion will stand justified in affixing to them the consequences of any future & apparent seduction, in whatever Other quarter it may appear.

Potts is too ill to attend immediately or perhaps at all—It behooves you therefore to seize the first favorable impulse of either of the others. In short, if it can be ascertained that one of them will immediately Act with us, I would not suffer speech or prayers to present an impediment to instance Vote—That obtained, and we will fervently pray thereafter.

My advices from Georgia, Kenty. and Tennesse are much more favorable and certain, than you appear to be. Altho' I am not sanguine of Jeff. election without our Vote, I do not despair of it. I will write you again in [a] day or two. Let me hear from you as soon as [you] can. With affectionate regard & best wishes, I am, dear Sir, truly yours,   John Beckley

[P.S.] Duane has sent you Hamilton vs. Adams.

RC (COXE PAPERS, HISTORICAL SOCIETY OF PENNSYLVANIA).

1. Coxe had stated in one of his essays that Rush, respected Founding Father and singer of the Declaration of Independence, could testify to Adams's monarchism. *Aurora*, October 9, 1800. See Cooke, *Coxe*, pp. 382–84.
2. That is, Senator John Langdon of New Hampshire, who made a statement on Adams's alleged monarchism. Cooke, *Coxe*, pp. 382–86. See also Beckley's Report to Jefferson, December 1, 1793, concerning a report of a conversation on American monarchy involving Senators Langdon and Cabot.
3. That is, Abraham Bishop (1763–1844), Republican court clerk from Connecticut, who was later appointed collector of the port of New Haven by President Jefferson.
4. That is, Benjamin R. Morgan, a former Federalist state senator. See the next letter of Beckley.
5. Thomas Johnston, Zebulon Potts, and Joseph McClellan were Federlist members of the Pennsylvania Senate. All three voted in favor of a concurrent vote of senate and assembly for presidential electors. Tinkcom, *Republicans and Federalists in Pennsylvania*, p. 322.

JOHN BECKLEY TO TENCH COXE

Dear sir,   Philadelphia, 3d. November 1800.

You will have seen Mr. Bishop & Mr. Langdon and obtained from them all the information they could furnish. This day we have received letters from Charles Pinkney & Colo. Williams[1] in North Carolina—their information destroys every remaining hope of the fœderalists that, without the aid of Pennsylva., Mr. Jefferson could not be Elected, since the former under date Charleston 22d October, says "that a decided Majority of republicans are elected to both houses of their Legislature, and that even in the City of Charleston 5 republicans are returned, whence Jefferson & Burr will have an unanimous Vote, altho' the fœderalists affect to say they expect 5 or 6 votes for Pinkney." Williams from Raleigh says that 9 to 11 votes in No. Carolina, are inevitable.

Mr. Bowen[2] direct from Rh. Island is here, he arrived last night and says that Jefferson & Adams together, will receive the Entire Vote of that State. Governor Fenner, with whom he particularly conversed, assured him of this, as a settled arrangement.

Levi Lincoln is Elected. The probability is, of 5 or 6 republicans from that State[3] in the pending Election for next Congress.

Every thing must impress the wavering fœds that Mr. Jeffersons Election, even without Pennsylva. is certain, and that further opposition whilst it must be nugatory, can only injure themselves individually. Every thinking fœderalist here, except Office incumbents, agrees in the folly of further resistance to the public Voice, Bingham, Fitzsimmons and Latimer, have unequivocally declared that the Vote of Pennsylvania must in no Event be lost, and that it is better Jefferson should be elected—so says Judge Peters.

For heavens sake, attend to British Movements—Observe the hints in my last. Ben. R. Morgan is the Cidevant Senator referred to. Is he now in Lancaster, and how long will he be there? Is his ostensible business known? Convey to our worthy Cheif, the ideas I have endeavoured to impress—rest assured, they are too important to be disregarded. British movements are more interesting at every view of this business—to day, direct advices from Cronstadt in Russian to 9th Sepr. render immediate War with G.Britain extremely probable. Liston is too well informed, not to Know what it behooves him to do, to gain an ally in us.

I have communicated to Mr. John Smith, who left this to day, and will be sometime in Lancaster, one or two ideas which he will suggest to you, but which I did not think advisable to commit to paper. They may be useful if a necessity should arise for recurring to there. I entreat a line from you to leave Lancaster on Saturday morning so that I may possess the latest information to carry on with me. I must set out on Monday morning and am obliged to go by Baltimore. Convey it, if you can by some sure hand that will deliver it at my home and if you can send an accompanying line from Mr. Jefferson under Cover to me I will deliver it to him.

I hope you have obtained, or will obtain something interesting from M. His interview with A may have been important.[4]

Duane will be up on Wednesday. He will give you a curious anecdote of papers clandestinely removed from Pickerings late office. My respects to Bishop and to Mr. Boston. Every Eye, Every tongue and every hand, must be active and unceasingly employed to accomplish our great natural object, in which are involved the peace, liberty & happiness of our Country. Your especial vigilance I rely on. When Gallatin comes on, if the business is not Settled, try to detain him a day or two. You know, the essential Services he can render from his superior Knowledge of views & Characters.

With best wishes, I am, as ever, dear Sir, Yrs. sincerely,

John Beckley.

RC (COXE PAPERS, HISTORICAL SOCIETY OF PENNSYLVANIA).
  1. Robert Williams (1773–1836) served as a Republican representative (1795–1803) from North Carolina.
  2. Jabez Bowen was Federal Commissioner of Loans in Rhode Island.
  3. That is, Massachusetts.
  4. Perhaps, Benjamin R. Morgan and John Adams.

JOHN BECKLEY TO ALEXANDER J. DALLAS

Dear Sir,[1]   Philadelphia, 7th November 1800.

I sent you yesterday by Mr. Thomson, printer, a number of petitions. I had before sent and delivered you here a number of others. I now send by Mr. Irwin the remainder for the City. The number of Signatures in these sent by Mr. Thomson and Mr. Irwin together, amount to 1648—those before sent and delivered you amounted to about 800—so that in the City the Signatures are to the Number of 2448. The petitions from the Northern liberties, Southwark and the County have received upwards of 2700 signatures. These are all independent of Delaware County, which were sent by Mr. Pearson.[2]

I have been thus particular on account of Mr. Jones,[3] one of our Senators, who publickly declared here, that if a majority of his Constituents demanded a joint Vote, he would Vote for it. A great Majority of his Constituents have done so by the Memorials sent up. It will be advisable to select them altogether and demonstrate this fact to him.

You will see the shameful resolutions of the fœderal meeting at Dunwoodys signed by Lewis, Hallowell and Milnor, but which Rawle did not sign. Indeed he is, I believe too honest to sign such a libel on the Constitution and on Common sense.[4]

223

Mr. Morton,[5] one of the Bank Directors, immediately from Rhode Island, declared yesterday to his brother directors, that Jefferson and Burr will have the unanimous vote of that State.

It may be material to mention that upwards of 60 fœderalists in one ward, signed our petitions. You see the other side were afraid to proceed by pet[ition]s. Mr. Irvine will inform you about fœderal signers—he waits for this and you will excuse haste. Respectfully, I am, dear Sir, Yrs. Sincerely,

John Beckley.

[*P.S.*] You may consider this as an official communication by me as <u>Chairman</u> of the Committee of Correspondence for the City and County.

RC (DALLAS PAPERS, HISTORICAL SOCIETY OF PENNSYLVANIA).

1. Alexander J. Dallas (1759–1817), a British immigrant and lawyer, had risen rapidly in the legal and political ranks of Philadelphia. Dallas was a founder of the Republican party in Pennsylvania and a member of the 1800 campaign committee in Philadelphia. He was rewarded in 1801 by Jefferson with an appointment as U.S. attorney for eastern Pennsylvania.

2. These petitions or memorials to the state Assembly were generated by the Republicans to prove support for a joint ballot of both houses of the Pennsylvania legislature for the election of presidential electors. Tinkcom, *Republicans and Federalists in Pennsylvania*, p. 248.

3. That is, John Jones, state senator representing Philadelphia and Delaware counties.

4. The Philadelphia Federalists meeting at Dunwoody's Tavern had resolved that it was unconstitutional for both houses of the legislature to vote in a joint–ballot for electors. Ibid., p. 248.

5. That is, James Morton of Providence, Rhode Island.

JOHN BECKLEY TO TENCH COXE

Dear sir,   City of Washington, 20th, November 1800

I could not obtain a Copy of Mr. Dawsons letter from Genl. Pinkney, in time for yesterdays mail, but now Enclose it you—in Dawsons own hand. A letter from Governor Clinton received by General J. Smith (<u>of New York</u>) now here, dated Albany 12th November, says "Governor Fenner writes me that the Votes of Rh. Island will be 4 Jefferson, 2 Burr & 2 Adams," the Governor is at the head of the republican ticket.

Further accounts of Massachusetts Elections place 6 republicans as Elected, Eustis, Lincoln, Varnum, Bishop, Bacon, Cutts.[1]

No Congress yet—Senate want 3—Mr. Jeff. not yet arrived.[2] Excuse haste—write me at this place.

Yrs. truly,   John Beckley.

1. See the next document for a variant list of Republican congresmen from Massachusetts, provided by Massachusetts Representative George Thacher.

2. Jefferson arrived in Washington on November 27.

JOHN BECKLEY TO TENCH COXE

Dear sir,   Washington 21 Novr. 1800.

Mr. *Bloodworth*[1] is this moment arrived from North Carolina—he says there are 8 districts certain in that State for Jefferson and one doubtful. He has a letter from *Wade Hampton* dated Columbia 8th November, received here, stating that every Vote in that state is <u>unquestionably</u> for Jefferson.[2] The fœderalists here are equally certain of our Success and mention it with great candor & frankness.

Mr. *Thatcher* is arrived also this morning *from Massachts.* and says that Varnum, Bishop, Eustis, Lincoln, Bacon, Dearborn, and Minturn[3] all republicans are elected *and that there will be 8 in the next Congress from that state, if speaking jocularly, you will count him as one.*

Mr. Jeff. is not yet arrived—to morrow the president addresses both houses.[4]
Yrs. truly,   John Beckley

[P.S.] *Address to me here.*

P.S. *Mr. Thatcher* <u>this moment</u> informs us that the vote of Massachusetts will be all Adams & <u>not more</u> than one half Pinkney.

1. Timothy Bloodworth was a U.S. Senator from North Carolina, 1795–1801.

2. For another similar letter from Hampton, Republican presidential elector from South Carolina, see the next document.

3. That is, Ebenezer Mattoon. See the preceding letter for a variant list of Republican congressmen from Massachusetts.

4. Jefferson arrived in Washington on November 27, too late to preside over the joint session of Congress assembled in the Senate chamber on November 22 for President Adams's final annual message to Congress. *Debates and Proceedings, Sixth Congress*, pp. 722 and 728.

JOHN BECKLEY TO TENCH COXE

Dear Sir,   Washington 22 Novr. 1800.

A letter from *Wade Hampton* is received, dated Columbia 9th November, as follows "Our Elections are over & given a decided Majority for the republican Electors of the Jefferson ticket—great Efforts will be made for admitting Genl. Pinkney to an equal Vote with Mr. Jeff. by the Charleston phalanx—But we are strong enough to prevent them, at least from a full vote, perhaps there may be 4 for Pinkney, tho' at present I doubt it—8 for Jeff., 4 Pinkney & 4 Burr I think you may set down as certain—Adams will not have a Vote."

    Yrs. in great haste   *J. Beckley*

RC (COXE PAPERS, HISTORICAL SOCIETY OF PENNSYLVANIA).
WORDS IN ITALICS WERE MARKED FOR DELETION BY AUTHOR OR RECIPIENT
IN PREPARATION FOR NEWSPAPER PUBLICATION.

JOHN BECKLEY TO TENCH COXE

Dear Sir,   Washington 24 Novr. 1800.

The enclosed is this Moment received in a letter from my friend Colo. Hoomes at the Bowling Green,[1] I have torn it from the foot of the letter, and send it you in fragments that you may have it in his own hand writing. Whether it may reach you in time for any purpose to which you can apply it, is I believe precarious-I was however unwilling to lose my chance.

Woolcot has resigned, ex necessitate, on a hint from the president—he stays until 1st January—but has this day asked, by letter to the House of Reps. for a Committee to investigate his public conduct. Ord. to lie on table.[2]

Mr. Jeff. is expected to day. Continue to address to me here.

Yrs. with great regard,   John Beckley

RC (COXE PAPERS, HISTORICAL SOCIETY OF PENNSYLVANIA).

1. Col. John Hoomes from Caroline County, Virginia was a horse breeder and holder of the stagecoach and mail contracting monopoly from Alexandria to Fredericksburg and Richmond.
2. Although Oliver Wolcott's proposal was tabled on the 24th, the next day the House appointed a committee to investigate the charges against Wolcott. *Debates and Proceedings, Sixth Congress*, pp. 787–89.

JOHN BECKLEY TO TENCH COXE

Dear sir,   Philadelphia 31st Decemr. 1800.

This year is propitious to the republican cause to its latest hour—this Moment the official returns of New Jersey Election for Congress from all the Counties of the State, have arrived from Trenton—the clear Majority is 892 for the whole republican ticket.

All the Electoral returns are in at Washington and result in an Even Vote for Jeff. & Burr 73 each.[1] You will have seen the letter of the latter to Genl Smith magnanimously declining all competition[2]—All our advices state that there will be no difficulty in Jeffs Election.

The treaty[3] continues to hang, altho' I continue to think it will be ratified. Our Merchants, are nearly unanimous for it.

Is there any movement among you about a removal back to this place? May it not be advisable in the present State of National Concerns and of the republican interest, to return for a few years, until a Central place can be permanently fixed upon? Is not the general interest of the State in the advancement of the Commercial prosperity of this City, as its Sole Emporium, better promoted by such steps, than any supposed injury of local inconvenience and travel to the western people, would counterpoise?

Accept our best wishes to Mrs. Coxe & your family & believe me truly, dear Sir, Yr. Sincere friend,   John Beckley

RC (COXE PAPERS, HISTORICAL SOCIETY OF PENNSYLVANIA).

1. In the official electoral vote, Jefferson and Burr each received 73 votes, Adams 65, Pinckney 64, and Jay 1. *Debates and Proceedings, Sixth Congress*, pp. 1023–24.
2. In a December 16, 1800, letter to Samuel Smith, Burr stated that although "It is highly improbable that I shall have an equal number of Votes with Mr. Jefferson, but if such should be the result every Man who knows me ought to know that I should utterly disclaim all competition." Kline, ed., *Burr Papers*, 1:471.
3. The "treaty" was the Convention of Mortefontaine with France, which ended the quasi-war with France. The Senate ratified the convention on February 3, 1801. *Debates and Proceedings, Sixth Congress*, pp. 1085–1207.

JOHN BECKLEY TO LITTLETON W. TAZEWELL

Dear sir,   Philadelphia, 25th January 1801.

A continued succession of Court business and after that a severe indisposition, will be my apology for the delay of writing to you, as I had promised to do on my return home. After a very diligent search for the letter I mentioned to you, written by your father, the night he was taken ill, to Bishop Madison, I cannot find it among any of my papers, and Maria informs me that she recollects my giving it to General Mason[1] to be transmitted to you. Be pleased to enquiry of the General if he recollects the circumstance.

I enclose you a minute of my account of the last disbursement of money for your fathers Estate; taken from the receipts in my hands; I beleive there was a small ballance due from me on the accot. heretofore transmitted you of the first disbursements, but must refer to you for the amount, not having retained a copy of the account.

The public mind here is much agitated by the recent accot. of the destruction of the Treasury Office, records & vouchers.[2] Altho' no very minute information is yet had of the cause & manner of the fire, still there is hardly a shade of difference between fœderalists & republicans, that something more than accident has conduced to it. It is difficult to ground a system of destruction of public accts. & Vouchers, upon two accidental burnings, each happening in a town where no other house has been subjected to similar mishap, and both taking place, at intervals, in different houses, within a few weeks of the time, when those accounts & Vouchers were to be transferred, into the hands of a new administration. Besides why were accounts & Vouchers deposited in rooms not fire proof, when there were in the house six rooms fire proof? And whence is it that the fire commenced upstairs, in Mr. Farrel the accountants room? the same trustworthy & confidential Mr. F who alone was thought worthy to receive & keep the record books which the Editor of the Aurora had access to, and from which the disclosures of public defaulters were first made to the public?

If any thing further transpires on this Subject, I shall be much obliged to you for a line respecting it, as also if there be any movements indicative of a design to interrupt or defeat the Election of a president in your house.[3] On this last point the idea of creating a president by Act of Congress, is so outrageous of all principle, propriety, or decency, that I have hardly supposed it possible any man could entertain it. A casus omissis, as flowing out of the Constitution cannot be pretended. Two cases occur, in which a president is to be chosen by the H Reps:—One, which now exists of two persons having an equality of votes of the Electors—the other, when no person having such majority, the House of Reps. must choose from the five highest on the list. The two cases are alike susceptible of a factious influence to defeat any Election at all—But the Constitution is not predicated on the Monstrous absurdity that a faction should, or could, defeat an Election, in either case. It therefore recognizes the H Reps. as voting by States, and by Ballot, in a Ministerial, not a legislative or deliberative capacity, and it uses the imperative and mandatory words "shall immediately choose One of them, by Ballot, for president". Words, which give to the HReps. no option, no discretion, no power, beyond the mere act of choosing by ballot and by

States; in the first case, one of the two persons submitted to their Choice, and, in the other Case, one of the five. In neither Case, can they exercise a discretion, or assume the power, to reject the whole, since then, the mandate of the Constitution "shall choose one of them for president", is defeated, and the Election of a president destroyed, by the very power or Body, which is expressly charged & commanded to perform it.

In no part of the Constitution can it be found that the House of Reps. have in any capacity, any other power or agency in the Election of a president, nor, as a branch of Congress any power, except to declare who shall administer the Government, in case of the removal, death, resignation, or inability of a president then last in office, and during only the remainder of the term, for which, that disqualified president, was elected.

Excuse these remarks, but as they weigh on my mind with peculiar force, I could not permit myself to withhold them.

Your Judiciary Bill has passed,[4] and if it goes thro' in the Senate, as I presume it will, a few hundred dependent fœderalists are to be pensioned 'pro bono publico.' Alas, when and where will the evils of a corrupt administration, entailed upon his Country by the wisdom of a departed Saint, terminate? Surely, mausoleums were unncessary to perpetuate their fame of blessings so transcendent.

The sudden death of your fellow lodger, Mr. Jones,[5] deeply affected me and most sincerely do I sympathise with his friends, his family and the public, in the loss of so much worth & integrity. What was the nature of his illness & supposed cause of death?

You will much oblige me by tendering my best respects to his worthy colleague Mr. Taliaferro. Accept the best wishes of my Maria & myself, and believe me, my dear Sir, ever and unalterably, Your affect. friend, John Beckley

RC (MISCELLANEOUS MANUSCRIPTS, CLEMENTS LIBRARY). ADDRESSED: "LITTLETON WALLER TAZEWELL, ESQR. IN CONGRESS, WASHINGTON."

1. Stevens T. Mason (1760–1803) served as a Republican U. S. senator (1794–1803) from Virginia.
2. For further information on the fire in the Treasury Offices, including testimony of former treasurer Oliver Wolcott, Jr. and acting treasurer Samuel Dexter, see Gibbs, ed., *Memoirs of Oliver Wolcott*, 2:478–79; and *Debates and Proceedings, Sixth Congress*, pp. 1359–76.
3. That is, the House of Representatives, where Tazewell represented Virginia in the former district of the secretary of state and the soon to be confirmed chief justice, John Marshall.
4. The bill "to provide for the more convenient organization of the Courts of the United States" passed the House (51 to 43) on January 20 and the Senate on February 7, 1800. *Debates and Proceedings, Sixth Congress*, pp. 741–42, 915, and 1534–48.
5. James Jones, first-term U. S. representative from Georgia, died on January 13, 1801.

BECKLEY TO ALBERT GALLATIN

Dear Sir,[1]   Philadelphia 4th February 1801.

Some circumstances which have come to my knowledge, and may be useful to our friends on the eve of the Presidential Election, induce me to address you.

A letter is received here from Bayard, of Delaware,[2] explicitly avowing a united Concert and intended Effort to defeat Mr. Jeffersons Election. This letter has been seen and read by Mr. Reed, the late flour Inspector, and by him communicated to a friend of mine. It does not develope the mode of defeat contemplated, but I conjecture the design is, if possibble, to elect Mr. Burr. Influential fœderalists have written to Washington in opposition to any such attempt, and advising unanimous Election of Mr. J.

But other circumstances impress me with a firm belief that mischeif is designed. I have just seen a Copy, taken by one of the Treasury Clerks, now here, of Mr. Pickerings account on the public books (and by the bye that book is preserved) containing only four heads or Items of charge, debit 1,023,000 dollars (one million twenty three thousand) and on the credit side a minute or official entry thus "Decemb 23d. 1800 No vouchers have yet been produced by Mr. P—for the disbursement of this money." Other extraordinary accounts appear in the same Book, particularly of Interest on unclaimed dividends in the Bank of the U.S. unapplied to amount of two millions of dollars.

Considering the time Mr. Pickering has been out of office, my mind is irresistably led to regard his present defalcation, as connected with the mysterious business of Saint Domingo, the supply of Touissant with Arms & ammunition, and the pay and support of his troops. Hence, the Exclamation of President Adams, to Mr. Myer the late consul, "that he had rather the whole island of St. Domingo had been engulphed in the Ocean, than that he had ever heard of the name of Touissant." Hence also Listons boast in the intercepted Correspondence by Swazey "that however disposed the haughty republicans might be to look over the capture of the Insurgents, the insults by public speeches in Congress &c &c yet that now thank God our proceedings with Touissant had rendered War inevitable." Hence further, the unceasing Efforts of Pickering & his junto to produce a declaration of War, and his marked submission, condescension, and Expressions of confidence in Liston,—and lastly, the fears expressed by Wolcot, in the hearing of this Clerk and others, particularly Farrel (if he would speak) that the Committee of Congress would call for Pickerings accounts.[3]

Again, my friend, what means the appointment of Marshall to be Chief Justice? What means Rutledges[4] boast "that they will tenant the fœderal Government with a practical Gentleman, who will have judgement, taste, and genius Enough to appreciate its usefulness, and nerve Enough to preserve its integrity." And lastly what is meant by the opprobrius stile and manner of fœderal speeches, their repeated insults, and daring measures? Is it not with the body politic, as with the body natural, desperate Cases required desperate remedies, and may not those State Empires design, rather to pull down the pillars of Government, and lay our political fabric in common ruin, than that their mis-deeds should ever be permitted to see the light.

Possessing superior lights to information, you can duly appreciate the suggestions I have made, but really the incidents of the day betray so much jiggle, intrigue, and depravity, that I can only resolve them into a settle purpose of mischief and disorder.

How far the Treasury conflagration may have set some minds at rest as to the consequences of future accounts I know not. Of the extent of the destruction we know nothing here. Or whether in Books or Vouchers the loss is greatest—But, from the Clerk now here, I discover Enough to satisfy me, that many valuable Books & papers have unexpectedly escaped—and that a number of the Clerks have seen the preparatory steps, and looked forward to the intended issue.

Mr. Duane sets off for Washington on Saturday. I think it possible he will be there on tuesday. He has collected a good deal of interesting information, and possesses confidentially the names of a number of Clerks, who are ready to communicate with him. I wish you may see him, as early as possible, on his arrival. Most probably he will seek you. The ardor of his zeal requires to be cautioned by temper and discretion.

If, as I doubt not, opposition to the Election of Mr. J—is pursued it will, I presume, depend on Jersey & Maryland. The former rests on the single vote of Mr. Linn.[5] The latter on one of four to wit Craik, Thomas, Bacher[6] and Dennis. There is the fullest confidence here in Linns vote for Mr. J—consequently it would rest with one of the four from Maryland—Craik is the brother-in-law of Harrison the creditor, and both him and Bacher voted, in the fœderal caucus, against a declaration of war with France. These are strong grounds on which to look to one of these two votes—tho' I doubt not General Smith & his republican Colleagues[7] will be fully attentive to every reasonable and proper instance that can be used on an occasion as important & delicate.

Shall I ask of you the favor of a line of what is passing, when it may be convenient to you. With sincere regard & esteem, I am, dear Sir, Yours always,

John Beckley

RC (GALLATIN PAPERS, NEW YORK HISTORICAL SOCIETY).

1. Albert Gallatin (1761–1849), Swiss-born financial expert, whose election to the U. S. Senate had been voided by the Senate in 1794 on the constitutional grounds that he had not been a citizen of the United States for nine years, was currently serving as a Republican representative from Pennsylvania. He became Jefferson's secretary of the treasury and patronage chief.

2. James A. Bayard (1767–1842), Federalist U.S. representative (1797–1803) from Delaware, was later accused of having struck a deal with the Jeffersonians—trading the nonremoval of Federalists from government offices in exchange for the withholding of his vote in the Congressional contest between Jefferson and Burr for president. Dumas Malone, *Jefferson the President: First Term, 1801–1805* (Boston: Little, Brown and Co. 1970), pp. 11–14; *Debates and Proceedings, Sixth Congress*, pp. 1028–33.

3. For further information concerning Timothy Pickering's negotiations with British minister Robert Liston concerning Toussaint L'Overture's rule in Santo Domingo, see Gerard H. Clarfield, *Timothy Pickering and American Diplomacy, 1795–1800* (Columbia, Missouri: University of Missouri Press, 1969), pp. 146–48.

4. That is, John Rutledge, Jr. (1766–1819), Federalist U.S. representative (1797–1803) from South Carolina.

5. James Linn, Aaron Kitchell, and John Condit gave Jefferson a three to two majority over Burr to carry the New Jersey vote. *Debates and Proceedings, Sixth Congress*, pp. 1028–33. Linn was later rewarded for his critical swing vote by his appointment as supervisor of the federal revenue in New Jersey. Noble E. Cunningham, Jr., *The Jeffersonian Republicans in Power: Party Operations, 1801–1809* (Chapel Hill: University of North Carolina Press, 1963), p. 16.

6. That is, George Baer, William Craik, John C. Thomas, and John Dennis, U.S. representatives from Maryland, who had cast their votes for Burr, until the final vote when they cast blanks. *Debates and Proceedings, Sixth Congress*, pp. 1032–33.

7. Samuel Smith, George Dent, Joseph A. Nicholson, and Gabriel Christie were U.S. representatives from Maryland who voted for Jefferson. *Debates and Proceedings, Sixth Congress*, pp. 1028–33.

JOHN BECKLEY TO ALBERT GALLATIN

Dear Sir,   Philadelphia 15th February 1801.

You will receive by the same Mail with this, a letter under cover to you, addressed to the republican reps. of Pennsa. in Congress.[1] It is predicated on the information public & private, that a rumour prevailed in Washington, that the republicans here had seized the public arms. The truth is, that several hundred stand of Arms and 18 pieces of Cannon, heretofore in the hands of the Militia, have lately been taken by fœderalists and removed into the public arsenals of the U.S. On this fact is the calumny founded. At no point of time, that I can remember since 1776, has there prevailed so solemn, calm and deliberate a disposition in the public mind, to await the awful issue of your present proceedings, accompanied with a firm, fixed, unalterable and universal determination that when the faction of opposition to the Voice of their Country, shall have reached that point at which opposition is a duty and obedience a crime, prompt, energetic and decisive measures shall be taken. No earthly considerations can or will induce the submission to the act of usurpation. The day such an Act passes and receives the presidents sanction, is the first day of revolution and Civil War in our Country, and irrevocable the doom of the authors of the National

Calamity, unless they can support their usurpation by superior force. I do not utter to you, my friend, a Solitary opinion, it is the sentiment of every man I see and Converse with, and it will be regarded as the first duty of the republican representatives in such an Event, to solemnly protest against the Act, appeal to their Constituents, and the world and withdraw from Congress, and that this decision should not be delayed one moment, so as to afford them any countenance to their future measures, Or by delay frustrate the immediate, prompt & necessary measures of the peoples opposition. I deprecate the crisis, but however awful the consequences, they cannot be less so to them, than to us, nor will I suppose it possible that there Exists one republican Member, that, from a fear of those consequences, will direlict the principles or abandon the ground of duty and respect to the view of his country, especially when such a direlection will only induce a state of things, possibly worse, than any other consequence he can fear. Fœderal threats can never subvert republican firmness, or if it can, there is in truth no such thing as the latter.

The call of the Senate on 4th March—the manner of that call—the refusal to accept Latimers resignation in Delaware— the movements of A. Hamilton in New York—his overtures to Colo. Burr, distainfully rejected by the latter—the appointment of John Marshall—the deceptive letter written by the federalists in Congress in favour of Jefferson—all conduce to prove a settled Conspiracy, in which J. Adams has consented to act a part. Quere therefore, ought not the republican Senators to consider previously to 4th March, the propriety of defeating, if they can, the assembling of a quorum, if that quorum cannot be found without their aid? In the progress of the business before you, this idea can be weighed.

Can you furnish us with the individual Votes of the Members on the Ballot by States, with their names? If Mr. Jefferson has 55 Votes, will it be possible to pass an Usurpation Act thro' your house, and how will the proceeding accord, of a continued Ballot agreeable to the Constitution, and an appeal from that to a Legislative choice or creation of a president? Besides can any legislative proceeding intervene without superseding and vitiating the ballot? Excuse my questions, perhaps they are already resolved & tabled. If you can spare a moment to drop a line as you progress, it will be acceptable.[2] With best wishes, I am, dear Sir, truly yours,[3]

John Beckley

RC (GALLATIN PAPERS, NEW YORK HISTORICAL SOCIETY).

1. For a discussion of preparations by Governors McKean and Monroe in Pennsylvania and Virginia to resist the election of a Federalist president by the House of Representatives, see Malone, *Jefferson the President: First Term*, pp. 8–11; and Ammon, *Monroe*, pp. 190–94.
2. Before this letter could have been reasonably expected to reach Gallatin in Washington, Jefferson had been elected president on February 17 on the 36th ballot of the House of Representatives, thus rendering moot all of Beckley's dire predictions and drastic preparations.
3. Beckley wrote in the margin "As the crisis approaches, will the mail be safe to our letters?"

JOHN BECKLEY TO TENCH COXE

Dear Sir,   18th Feby. 1801.

Our advices of this day, reduce it to a certainty that Mr. Jefferson would be Elected on Monday. The Governor received from Mr. Dallas, particulars by a letter from Gallatin.

Will you call to mind, and write me, as soon as possible, on the subject of our conversations when you were last here, respecting a comparative list or Statement of Outs and Ins in Pennsylvania. It is proper no time should be lost in a communication to Mr. J. I do not wish to lose one day, and will either carry it myself, or convey it to him thro a secure channel. In every department, it is desirable to have full information from the first to the last in office. The conduct of the feds admits not of any term of conciliation or accomodation, and none will be admitted.[1]

I shall be anxious until I hear from you. In haste, Sincerely yours,

                                          John Beckley.

RC (COXE PAPERS, HISTORICAL SOCIETY OF PENNSYLVANIA).

1. For a clear statement of Beckley's views on political patronage, see the next document.

JOHN BECKLEY TO THOMAS JEFFERSON

Dear Sir,   Philadelphia, 27th February 1801.

So inseparable, are the feelings of my mind, from a deep concern, in the welfare and happiness of our common Country, and for the success and honorable reputation, of that administration of its affairs, which you are about to commence, that I cannot permit myself to withhold the present communication. If it may in any degree conduce to aid the purposes of your own mind, or that view of things which occasion and reflection have led you to take, my wish and object will be fully answered.

In taking the helm of government at this tempestuous moment of party violence and collision, I perceive the delicacy and difficulty you will experience at the outset, from the opposite claims of firmness and decision on the one side, and of conciliation and compromise on the other. Truly to appreciate the considerations which may lead to a right decision it would seem necessary to regard,

1st: the respective Character of the republican & fœderal party.

2d: The views and policy of the late fœderal administration.

3d. the real interest and true policy of the United States, and the best means to promote it.

On the first and second points, few reflections can be offered which the superior information you possess will not have embraced. In point of fact however, I think it may be simply assumed,

> 1st: That in the proportion of numbers thro' the U.S. the republicans constitute five eights of the whole.
>
> 2d: That in like proportion is the relative degree of property and talents between the parties.
>
> 3d: That the fœderal party are, <u>strictly</u> speaking, Monarchical in their principles, views and wishes.
>
> 4th That it was the policy of Mr. <u>A</u>'s administration to approach that object, by close and intimate connection with Monarchical governmts. and by repellant or hostile measures towards those of a republican character.

On the last point, which essentially involves the conclusion to a right decision, I think it may be equally assumed on the ground of real interest and true policy,

> 1st: That all political relation, by treaty, with foreign nations should be avoided.
>
> 2d: That simple commercial connections on a basis of perfect reciprocity and the most conducive to the principles of free commerce should be pursued.
>
> 3d: That the defensive system of protecting commerce by a limitted navy, Embargo, Suspension of intercourse, and fortified ports and harbors, is the most sure, safe, cheap, and effectual.
>
> 4th: That protecting duties for the encouragement of manufactures ought to be imposed as far as revenue considerations will admit, and the Alien laws repealed.
>
> 5th: That the Agricultural interest be promoted, by repeal of Excises and Land tax, to effect which rigid Œconomy should be enforced in all the departments of Government, all unnecessary Establishments put down, sine cure offices abolished, and all speculation on the public wants, by jobs and contracts done away.
>
> 6th: That a new organization of the Executive departments of Government be made,
>
>> 1st: by a revision and amendment of the Constitution of each.
>>
>> 2d: by new, simple, and effectual interior regulations.
>>
>> 3d: by changes of men in office and new appointments so as <u>gradually</u>, but certainly & effectually, to place the executive administration in the hands of decided republicans, distinguished for talents & integrity.

The last proposition I regard as the pivot of the whole, and that on which the late happy change of the Executive was effected. So far as my opportunities of information go, and they have been considerable with men of calm, cool, reflecting minds from almost every State, there is but one opinion, and that is, that a change thorough and complete, but gradual should be

Philadelphia, 27: February 1801.

Dear Sir,

So inseparable, are the feelings of my mind, from a deep concern, in the welfare and happiness of our common Country, and for the success and honorable reputation, of that administration of its affairs, which you are about to commence, that I cannot permit myself to withhold the present communication. If it may in any degree conduce to aid the purposes of your own mind, or that view of things which occasion and reflection have led you to take, my wish and object will be fully answered.

In taking the helm of government at this tempestuous moment of party violence and collision, I perceive the delicacy and difficulty you will experience at the outset, from the opposite claims of firmness and decision on the one side, and of conciliation and compromise on the other. Truly to appreciate the considerations which may lead to a right decision it would seem necessary to regard,

1: the respective character of the republican & federal party.
2d: the views and policy of the late federal administration.
3d: the real interest and true policy of the United States, and the best means to promote it.

On the first and second points, few reflections can be offered which the superior information you possess will not have embraced. In point of fact however, I think it may be safely assumed,

1: That in the proportion of numbers thro' the U: S: the republicans constitute five eighths of the whole.
2d: That in like proportion is the relative degree of property and talents between the parties.
3d: That the federal party are, strictly speaking, Monarchical in their principles, views and wishes.
4th: That it was the policy of Mr: A's administration to approach that object, by close and intimate connection with Monarchical Governments and by repellant or hostile measures towards those of a republican character.

On the last point, which essentially involves the conclusion to a right decision, I think it may be equally assumed on the ground of real interest and true policy,

1: That all political relation, by treaty, with foreign nations should be avoided.

18801

236

made: that as no confidence can be placed in fœderal views or principles, so is there no safety in the admission or appointment of doubtful political character: that such an admission would implant jealousy, disunion and discord both in and out of the administration: that the public mind now aroused to a complete union of action in every State, to republicanize the whole, would be damped & paralized by a temporizing policy: that considering the character and conduct of the fœderal party they merit no respect, and from their numbers; wealth, or talents compared with the republicans should excite no fears of their future efforts: that future measures of Amelioration in our foreign and domestic concerns, will, aided by the present universal republican impulse, if that impulse be not unwisely counteracted, speedily put an end to the present views and wishes, and even to the very name of a fœderal party: And lastly, Sir, that a temporizing policy founded on any principle of conciliation or compromise will essentially injure your reputation and the success of your administration, since it would be difficult to remove the impression from the public mind that the reiterated charge of your supposed want of political firmness was not well grounded—an impression which would be the more indelible from the general persuasion that no principles of policy, prudence, propriety, safety, or justice, will at this time warrant any concessions to your and our political oponents.

I might add, that so far as respects the general principle of a change of men, the experience of Pennsylvania, has proved the wisdom of the policy, since, except in a few instances of intemperance and indiscretion in the execution of that principle, nothing has so much conduced, to the stability and success of republicanism in this State, and to the reputation of its government among the mass of Citizens.

There is however one modification or exception to the general rule, that merits respect, it is the case of revolutionary Whigs and Soldiers of the late Army, whose politics have not been marked by active or party exertion, and whose adherence to the fœderal side has been merely passive.[1]

Besides the general motives which have induced this letter I beg leave to offer those of my highest personal Esteem & attachment—and remain, dear Sir, Your obedt. Servt. and sincere friend,   John Beckley

RC (JEFFERSON PAPERS, LIBRARY OF CONGRESS).

1. For discussions of Jefferson's removal and appointment policies, see Malone, *Jefferson the President: First Term*, pp. 69–89; Cunningham, *Jeffersonian Republicans in Power*, pp. 12–70.

JOHN BECKLEY'S ORATION

4 March 1801

ORATION

DELIVERED BY JOHN BECKLEY, ESQ. ON THE 4TH OF MARCH, 1801
PHILADELPHIA.[1]

Friends and Fellow Citizens.

Assembled, in this holy temple, dedicated to the service of our god, let me fervently invoke his precious spirit, so to consecrate this day, and the purpose for which we are assembled, that the glad effusion of a nations joy may ascend in grateful orisons to the throne of heaven, and receive the approbation and blessing of the supreme ruler of the universe.

Assembled Citizens,

IT is no common occasion that has convened us—centuries pass and ages roll away, while, not the page of history, not the records of time, exhibit to our view, a spectacle like the present—America, rising with gigantic strength, as Hercules from his cradle, and presenting to an astonished world, the energies, wisdom and power of a great and established empire—Hail! genius of liberty, essence of power divine! thy holy inspirations have produced the scene, and spoke an empire into being.

Man, placed by the hand of his Creator in the first order of beings, was destined to be free—The organization of his body, the faculties of his mind, and the energies of his will, proclaim the great decree, whilst the influences of reason and of conscience, subserve the purposes of his destiny—In the dark ages of the world, when the human mind was held in thraldom, by ignorance, superstition, and bigotry, artifice and cunning superceded the powers of reason, and man become, but as the slave of man.

As the spark of reason progressed, the mist of ignorance was dispelled, and awakened conscience burst asunder the fetters of superstition and bigotry—A spirit of free enquiry succeeded, and the rapid improvements in arts and sciences, followed by the important discoveries of the art of printing and the use of the needle, opened to human investigation, a range, co-extensive with creation and the works of nature.

Such, fellow citizens, was the state of the old world, but particularly of modern Europe, at the commencement of that epoch, when the immortal Columbus unfolded the grandest project that human genius ever formed—the discovery of our western world—possessing the firm heart of a hero, with the enlightened mind and persevering spirit of a philosopher, that illustrious adventurer, added by his discoveries, but until then unknown half to the globe. Successive adventurers followed in the hitherto trackless path of the great Columbus, and in less than a century the north and south continents of America, with all their contiguous islands, were colonized and settled by European emigrants. Americus Vespucius whose name has been unjustly given to the discoveries of Columbus, Magellan, de Gama, de

Cabral, Raleigh, Smith, Gilbert, Cabot and Drake, were among the most distinguished navigators that led the way to those establishments on the part of the European nations, of which England, Spain, and Portugal, were the first to avail themselves. The productions and treasures of the new world were speedily laid open to the avaricious group of needy adventurers from the old, but whilst the benevolent mind views with horror and disgust those scenes of rapine and cruelty which marked the conquest of South-America, and the first European settlements in the East and West Indies, it turns with pleasure and delight to that period, in the history of this more favored part of the New World, when a great friend and benefactor of the human race, appeared in the person and character of William Penn, the founder, planner, and legislator of Pennsylvania—with a heart and mind bearing benevolence, and comprehensively embracing the combined views of the philosopher, legislator, and statesman, it was the part of Penn, to exhibit to the world the first instructive lesson of treaties of amity, peace and union, with the uncivilised and untutored aborigines of America (the wild and savage Indians, founded on the basis of equal right and mutual justice which they were soon to respect! Pursuing the same expanded policy, our American Solon devised a code of laws, wisely calculated to protect the property and interests of the settlers, and to secure the full and peaceful enjoyment of their civil and religious liberties. Auspicious systems! which gave to Pennsylvania, as an asylum to the oppressed and persecuted of European nations, early and large emigrations of useful citizens, whose descendants now form a great proportion of its population, and by their habits of industry, integrity, sobriety, and intelligence, adorn the national character of our state, and conduce to its importance in the scale of Union.

But here fellow citizens, let us pause and whilst we solemnly reflect on, admire and reverence the mysterious ways of heaven to the sons of men, Behold then, an infatuated monarch James II of England, who by the intollerant spirit of bigotry, lost his crown and kingdoms, in the religious persecution of his subjects—Behold this monarch granting to our illustrious Penn, a deed confirming the first and original charter of Pennsylvania, granted by his brother Charles II, in the year 1681, that charter which among other things contained the principle of a free and universal toleration in matters of religion. It was the germ of this principle thus obtained planted by the beneficent hand of Penn, in the then wilds of America, and followed by the *wise policy* of his systems, that has grown and progressed in the strength and majesty of truth until it has illuminated our writers world, and reflected back to Europe a portion of its original influence.

Fellow Citizens

Civil and religious liberty have thru all ages stood too intimately connected to admit the existence of the one without that of the other—they must flourish or perish together. Thus, when the spirit of commercial monopoly, succeeded to the rage of colonization and conquest among the nations of Europe, it was a leading feature in the system of oppression devised by the mother country against their colonial dependencies, to restrain alike the rights of conscience and the freedom of the press. Dark and grievous is the catalogue of ills engendered by the spirit of commercial monopoly. Human nature has been no less afflicted by its baneful effects in every quarter of the globe, than it therefore was under the reign of ignorance, superstition and bigotry, and hopeless indeed would be the condition of man, if the discovery of our western world, had only conduced to the change of one system of oppression for another. But through the influence of the causes that have been traced, the wisdom of Providence was displayed in the manifestation of the supreme decree "that man placed by the hand of his Creator was destined to be free."

Light, life, truth, and liberty, burst upon the world through the glorious event of the American revolution, and it was reserved for the youngest people upon earth, to teach the great elementary principles of human freedom and human happiness, to the first and proudest nation of the old world.

The causes and effects of that revolution so far as respect the establishment of American liberty and independence, are too well known and understood to be here enlarged upon. Coeval with the liberty was the establishment of the principle of "representative-democratic government, emanating from the people, the only legitimate source of all power," a principle hitherto unknown and unpracticed upon by any people.

It is to the operation of that principle, combined with the influence of the American revolution, that the struggles of revolutionary France may be ascribed; struggles that now agitate the whole civilised world, and over the mournful excesses of which we may be permitted to drop a tear in the cheering hope that regenerated France will in the full establishment of the principle in question shortly reach that goal of human freedom and human happiness for themselves, and the surrounding nations whose fetters they have broken, which more fortunate America now possesses in peace and safety.

But where is the American heart that does not dilate with joy at the retrospect of the glorious epoch of the 4th of July 1776? When an illustrious band of heroes and of patriots proclaimed to the world their country's independence, boldly asserted the rights of man, and nobly dared to vindicate the destiny of his nature—in arts, arms, in science and in government the American character emblasoned the world and stampt the fallacy of its supposed inferiority to the European.

WASHINGTON the shield and buckler of his country in war, and its polar star to that Temple of peace, liberty, and safety, the pillared dome of the Federal Constitution.

FRANKLIN the pride of philosophy and ornament of his country, who drew the lightening from heaven and pointed the radient steel of indignant fierceness at the breasts of tyrants.

RITTENHOUSE, illustrious astronomer, self-taught, clothed in much humility, adorned with every virtue, the patriot, philosopher and sage—Characters like these what age and nation can rival?

Happy America! favoured country! renowned at so youthful a period, in arts, in arms, philosophy and freedoms. When the historian of the day shall record thy rapid advancement to greatness, power and empire, he will not omit the unparralleled fact, that in the 21st year of independence, and the eighth from the establishment of the federal constitution, the United States of America had become the second commercial nation in the world.

Fellow Citizens,

From a review thus pleasing and scenes so bright, it is painful to turn away; but as in the physical and moral, so in the political world, there is an ebb and flow in the time of all human affairs, when by tracing the advancement to, or recession from first principles, mankind are instructed how best to fortify human freedom and perpetuate human happiness.

In the short, but eventful period of the last four years the example of the United States presents to the world a monition awful and instructive; an administration, commencing, pursuing, and ending its career in the abandonment and dereliction of all those principles, freedom and independence, and substituting those which produce dishonour, disunion, dependence, and slavery: hence arose systems of executive patronage and influence co-extensive with the creative powers of government;

Of military and naval establishments, and standing armies;

Of wasteful expenditures, oppressive public burthens and onerous taxes;

Of *alien and sedition* laws; the former to prohibit the persecuted sons of liberty in other countries from obtaining asylum in our land; the latter to restrain and punish the freedom of speech and of the press, in our own citizens;

Of new and arbitrary principles of constructive treason and common law;

Of prescription and disqualification from office, of one half the community for their political opinions;

Of unceasing efforts to legalize war and systematic murder, by hostilities against republican France; and *finally*,

Of endeavours, through the agency of foreign and domestic intrigue, to excite alarms by pretended plots, conspiracies, and treasons, thus creating a reign of terror and political delusion in which the rage of civil discord had nearly effaced the social affections, and destroyed all social intercourse, when the hand of brother against brother, and father against son, was about to be uplift each against the other, and this fair heritage of liberty imbrued in kindred blood.

But the sequel of a scene so calamitous, it was the wise order of heaven to avert; misled confidence and the influence of a name could no longer deceive—awakened to a scene of common danger, and animated to action by the guardian genius of liberty, republican America with one united voice, resolved to disavow the principles, revoke the measures, and discard the men, that had then afflicted her. It was as the decree of Heaven against the guilty Beltshazer pronounced in thunder, Mene, Mene, Tekel Upharsin![2] The inscriptive record, like the handwriting on the wall can never be effaced from the page of American history, whilst, by it, shall men through all time, be taught to reverence the principle," vox populi, vox dei".

Republican Citizens of America,

"BEHOLD YOUR TRIUMPH"

Virtue rising on the ruins of corruption—Your country emancipated, a new era of independence begotten; and the public liberty secured beyond the grasp of force, fraud or factious usurpation.

Oh! inestimable right of suffrage, first constitutional privilege, panacea, of freemen, the peaceful exercise of which has induced blessings so momentous.

Rejoice then Fellow Citizens and let your grateful Orisons ascend to and resound in the concave of heaven's high arch; render up your present triumph true, unmixed and unalloyed; drop the curtain of oblivion on the scenes that have past; banish the remembrance of political persecution; display the characteristic magnanimity of republicans, and prove the preeminence of republican virtue——call to mind that on this day, and perhaps, at this very hour the Citizens chosen by the suffrages of your electors to the two first stations of your government are inaugurated and sworn into office: reciprocate to them the obligations of fidelity and of duty, which they have this day entered into; respect the constituted authorities of your country, observe in all your conduct to citizens, a demeanor peaceful, orderly and temperate; render cheerful and prompt obedience to the Law: along with a vigilant attention to the security and preservation of republican liberty, and suffer not the magic of a name, or the imagined virtues of any man, ever to seduce you from that jealous regard of your rights, which constitutes the first in republican virtues, always remembering that the only safe depository of the public liberty is to be found in the virtue and integrity of the people.

Fellow-Citizens,

On this auspicious day, new hopes arise throughout the land, whilst joy exulting smiles in every face. The joy of millions in a nation's triumph! Happy then to retrospect the past or look forward to the future; see on the one hand, the voice of faction stilled, the strong arm of power fall nerveless before you, ambition discomfited, your oppressors, fled, and the banners of despotism prostrate before the standard of liberty. On the other hand, behold the guardian genius of America arise, with healing in her wings, leading by the hand her patriot son, the people's friend! Philosophy, science, wisdom and justice in high train; whilst seated in a triumphant car Liberty's fair Goddess, smiles benignant on the scene, and pointing to your charter of sacred rights and equal Laws, presents a spectacle of public happiness realized, in your country's peace, prosperity, and glory, conducted by philosophy, science and freedom supported by reason, truth and justice.

Glorious morn of freedom, lumens, beautifies and adorns our political horizon; may its meridian splendor be reflected as the sun beams of heaven to vivify and preserve the etherial flame and may the sons of America feel its animating influence to the latest period of time; and do thou "Almighty being" on whose eternal fiat depends the fate of nations, and the doctrine of the world you consecrate and perpetuate, the liberty, independence, and happiness of our lives and our beloved country.

JOHN BECKLEY, *AN ORATION DELIVERED. . . AT PHILADELPHIA, ON THE FOURTH OF MARCH, 1801.* [PHILADELPHIA, 1801]. MICROFORM, LIBRARY OF CONGRESS; AND PRINTED IN THE *AURORA* (PHILADELPHIA), MARCH 6, 1801.

1. Beckley delivered this oration in the German Reformed Church on Race Street in Philadelphia to a large crowd of Republican partisans eager to celebrate that day's inauguration of President Jefferson. In contrast to the quiet ceremony in Washington, Republicans held large and long celebrations in many urban areas including Philadelphia. Beckley's "Ciceronian" address was a highlight of a massive celebration in Philadelphia culminating in parades and toast-filled public and private celebratory dinners. Berkeley, *Beckley*, pp. 218–20; and *Aurora*, March 3, 6, and 12, 1801.
2. Belteshazzar, "king of the magicians." The biblical phrase which was written in Aramaic, was the handwriting on the wall interpreted by Daniel.

JOHN BECKLEY TO TENCH COXE

Dear Sir,   Philadelphia, 31st March 1801.

The Governor called on me to day, and gave me the reading of a long confidential letter from the president to him dated 26th instant, in which the president after referring to you and myself by name, and expressing in warm and feeling terms his <u>esteem</u> and <u>friendship</u> for us both, and the due estimate he has made of our <u>merits, Services & sufferings</u>, desires the Governor to inform <u>both those Gentlemen</u>, that as soon as the Administration get together, which he supposes will be about the last of April, and other more full and permanent arrangments are taken, <u>we</u> shall be immediately & particularly noticed. Thus much for the letter, which I informed the Governor I would advice you of, and he will do so himself.[1] What is particularly in contemplation for Either of us I know not, and in the same letter I perceive a hint that Genl. Muhlenburg will be supervisor—but this I must ask of you to keep to yourself as the Governor requested of me.

Excuse haste, the Court has this moment sent for me.

Yrs. Truly,   John Beckley

RC (COXE PAPERS, HISTORICAL SOCIETY OF PENNSYLVANIA).

1. Jefferson's March 26, 1801, letter to Pennsylvania Governor McKean is in the Jefferson Papers, Library of Congress. Despite their total commitment to seeking patronage posts and the political validity of their claims, both Beckley and Coxe were to remain frustrated office seekers for long periods. Beckley did not receive an appointment from Jefferson before his election as clerk of the House of Representatives on December 7, 1801, and Coxe was not rewarded for his political support until appointed supervisor of the revenue for Pennsylvania on July 28, 1802, and later purveyor of the United States on August 1, 1803.

For further information on Coxe's awkward and at times overweening demands for patronage, see Cooke, *Coxe*, pp. 392–416.

JOHN BECKLEY TO TENCH COXE

Dear Sir,   Philadelphia, 24th June 1801.

A severe attack of the gout, on my return from the Southward, has disabled me from writing you until now. Your friends Mr. Jefferson, Mr. Madison, & Mr. Gallatin particularly desired me to express to you their best respects and affectionate regard, and, at the same time to advise you, that an arrangement was making, and would <u>very soon</u> take place, by which you would receive appointments equal to 3500 $ per ann. within the State of Pennsylvania and most probably in this City. No precise explanation was given to me, but I conjectured that the Inspectorship of this Survey, with the addition of the collectorship, is meant.[1] I know your goodness will excuse my being thus laconic, as one of my Eyes is greatly affected and I write in much pain. Our best respects to Mrs. C. Your sincere friend,

John Beckley.

RC (COXE PAPERS, HISTORICAL SOCIETY OF PENNSYLVANIA).

1. Coxe rejected Jefferson's later offer of these positions. Cooke, *Coxe*, p. 396.

JOHN BECKLEY TO THOMAS JEFFERSON

Dear Sir,   Philadelphia 27th October 1801.

A short but severe fit of the gout has delayed my acknowledgment of your favour of the 22d. I sincerely regret the necessity that has occasioned Mr. Hansons reference to me, and in the just estimate of his character and merits, shall feel a twofold gratification in the possiblity that I may afford him a temporary relief from political persecution and intolerance. If, in the event of my contemplated Success,[1] the Station he asks will be acceptable, he cannot receive it with half the pleasure I shall feel in that acceptance. No circumstance of preengagement interferes with the performance of this promise, and I only lament that a previous contingent arrangement, precludes my offering him the more eligible station of principal Clerk.

I sought out and delivered your letter to Messrs. Fry and Chapman[2]—they are Germans, and not undestanding English, desired me to read it to one of their brethren to translate, which, being done, they requested that I would convey to you their high gratification and thankfulness, for so particular a Mark of your favor and attention.

In about ten days Mrs. Beckley and myself hope to be in Washington, when I shall have the pleasure to communicate to you, a singular overture to me, by letter, from a fœderal Senator,[3] to place me in the station of Secretary of the Senate. Mr. Duane desires me to express the deep sense he entertains of your favour, friendship and support—permit me to add a corresponding sentiment for myself, united with the most sincere esteem and attachment.

John Beckley

RC (JEFFERSON-COOLIDGE PAPERS, MASSACHUSETTS HISTORICAL SOCIETY).

1. The "contemplated Success" was Beckley's election as clerk of the House of Representatives. Jefferson had remarked in an October 22, 1801, letter to Beckley, asking Beckley to appoint Samuel Hanson as his engrossing clerk after he was elected clerk: "We all take for granted you will be restored to your former office in the House of representatives." Jefferson Papers, Library of Congress.

   Beckley was elected clerk of the House when Congress returned on December 7, defeating the incumbent clerk John Holt Oswald. *Debates and Proceedings, Seventh Congress*, p. 310.

2. Jefferson's letter to Michael Fry and Nathan Coleman of October 12, 1801, thanking them on behalf of the butchers of Philadelphia for the gift of a "Mammoth veal" is in the Jefferson Papers, Library of Congress.

3. The Federalist senator who offered to help Beckley secure the post of secretary of the Senate, then held by Samuel A. Otis, has not been identified. But on September 12, Otis had written to Jonathan Dayton, Federalist senator from New Jersey: "I have a hint from pretty good authority that endeavours are makeing to turn me out of office & to introduce Mr. Beckley. There hath never been an election of Secry of the S since the first. The Senate being a permanent body my office hath been considered permanent. Fairly in possession, I mean not to relinquish, as however small the provision, it is a chief dependence for the Support of my family; and it will be an odd measure to say the least of it, to elect a Secretary when one already holds the office, unless on a charge of malversation, which I defy." (Gratz Collection, Historical Society of Pennsylvania). Two other Federalist senators, John Q. Adams and William Plumer, reported that Otis retained his position because he agreed to give the Senate printing to Republican William Duane. Cunningham, *Jeffersonian Republicans in Power*, p. 270.

   In 1804 Beckley again considered making a serious effort to obtain the secretaryship of the Senate. See Beckley to John Brown, August 8, 1804.

JOHN BECKLEY TO TENCH COXE

Dear Sir,   Washington, 28th March 1802.

An obstinate and invincible gout, has adhered to me ever since my arrival here. My confinement & suffering, added to the state of my public concerns, and aggravated thereby, has nearly incapacitated me from any attention to my friends, or even the power of an epistolary correspondence. This will fully account for my past silence and seeming neglect. The great objects of the Session, are drawing to a close, and a few weeks will terminate this important Session. The reductions of the Army and Navy, and Civil list establishments; the repeal of the excressent judiciary; repeal of the Internal taxes; the permanent sinking fund appropriation of 7,300,000$ per ann. for the reduction of the public debt; the new act of naturalization; a revision and amendment of the old judiciary System; and a provision for the french Convention; and the one lately Effected with G. Britain, by which we pay 3 millions of dollars, in 3 yearly instalments, without interest—these, form the leading & characteristic features of the 1st Session of the 1st Congress of a republican administration, and will I trust, meet that decided approbation in the public mind, which measures so Eminently marked by pure regard to the public interest, ought to receive. In respect to one of these measures,[1] I know my friend, the personal inconvenience it may occasion to you, and in the anticipation of it I have, influenced solely by my own feelings, held full and free conversation with Mr. Madison and Mr. Jefferson on this Subject— they have both Explicitly declared their high regard and determination to embrace the first object that can be applied in your favour, and to do something adequate to your Merits & Services. What they may be, I cannot at present foresee, but from the unreserved manner of both, I doubt not they feel a particular interest in your situation. One thing I conjecture, if it may be in any way an object, and in that view I mention it.—the appointmt. of Commissrs. of Bankrupts will be vested in the president with power to appoint a limitted number in Each State, and I conclude a sole Commissr. will be named for your City, and if you should approve it, I have no doubt it will be yourself—I need not say, this all 'Entre nous'.

What may be the meditated changes, if any, in the Custom house department of your City, I know not, but am pretty sure, the president has, from the beginning, left it Entirely with Mr. Gallatin. No other object seems at present to occur.

I am, now, my friend, to ask the favour of your attention for me to a matter of private concern. It relates to an Effort I wish to be made to Sell my house & lot with the improvements in your City, at a price not less than 8,500 dollars—that being 1,500 dollars, less, than it cost for ready money. If that price can be got, one half in Cash, and the other in 6 months I will authorize you immediately to sell it, and now submit to your better judg-

John Beckley's memorandum book, page 1, Beckley Family Papers, Library of Congress.

246

Call on the printer for all Original papers.

States that have ratified 1st Article of Amendment to the
Constitution of United States. — 1. New Hampshire
     2. New York.
     3. Maryland.
     4. So. Carolina
     5. No. Carolina.
     6. Rhode island.
     7. New Jersey.
     8. Pennsylvania.
     9. Virginia. — (also all others.)
     10. Vermont. — (whole.)

Appendix to Journal matter for —
  1. Treasurers accounts.
  2d Ratifications of Amendments to Const. U.S.
  3. Statement in purchases of public debt.
  4. Census of Enumeration.
  5. reson of 30th Decr. — annual statement of Expenditures
  6. — proceedings on Secret Journal.

Book. for Standing rules & orders — Joint rules &c

Purchases of public debt —
          dollars   cents
    1,135,364 — 76 — purchases.
     699,163 — 38 — paid for it.
     432,201. 38 — profit to the U.S.

26. October — Standing Committee of Elections — Mr. Livermore, Mr. Boudinot,
Mr. Gerry, Mr. Giles, Mr. Bourne (R.I.) Mr. Hillhouse & Mr. Steele.

Schedule of Enumeration. — Have it executed by Mr. Lambert
and framed to be hung up.

22d November. Case of resignation William Pinkney, Member for Maryland via return of John
Francis Mercer in his room — see report of Committee of Elections thereon —

"   " Same day — In Comee of whole on a Bill to apportion representation acco. to first
Enumeration — see original Bill. — also amendt. agreed to in Comee.
                     (note arguments.)

10th Novemr. Report Secretary State on unappropriated Lands — 21 Millions
of Acres in N.W. territory, at disposal of U.States.

ment, the propriety of advertising it for 3 or 4 weeks, as to be entered upon the 1st day of June. The season of the Year is approaching, when it will appear to advantage and when merchants & others, think of removing from the Water side to more healthy & Eligible situations. My friend Mr. Smith, who now occupies the premises, will I am sure, so far cooperate with you that if a purchaser shall offer, he will, on two or 3 weeks previous notice, give possession, and I beg the favour of you to consult with him on the occasion—favour me with your opinion fully on this subject.

Does the prospect begin to open for Sales or disposition of Western lands? We are both deeply interested on this subject. It is generally believed here, that large investitures by Europeans will be made in American lands, this summer, but I know of no particular fact in reference thereto. Mr. Pichon,[2] supposes that a high degree of confidence is inspired in Europe, in favor of property in the U.S. and that the unsettled state of things there, will conduce to Encrease it.

Mrs. B. writes with me, in affectionate regards to Mrs. Coxe, and your family, and I remain, with great regard & esteem, dear Sir, Your sincere friend,

John Beckley

RC (COXE PAPERS, HISTORICAL SOCIETY OF PENNSYLVANIA).

1. The measure of particular concern to Coxe was the April 6, 1802, Congressional act abolishing internal taxes, because Coxe had just agreed to accept the post of supervisor of the revenue for Pennsylvania—a post which would be abolished under the Republican plan. Coxe was appointed to this position on July 28, 1802. Cooke, *Coxe*, p. 404
2. That is, Louis A. Pichon, the French chargé d'affaires, in whose house the Beckley's resided in the District of Columbia, before moving to a rented house on Delaware Avenue in late spring of 1802. Berkeley, *Beckley*, p. 235.

JOHN BECKLEY TO TENCH COXE

Dear Sir,   Washington, 11th April 1802.

Sunday, my only day of rest and respite, enables me to write you. Incessant labor all day, and my gouty foot which requires to be nursed & poulticed every night, to fit me for business the next day, and has constantly so required ever since Xmas, will not permit even a common attention to my own concerns; much less have I been able to break that Silence for which you so severely condemn me, or, to write to any person, about the presidents intentions as to the Customs, of which I am wholly ignorant—not having visited him but once these 3 months, and then Solely to mention my friend Mr. Smiths case, and deliver his Certificates.[1] What I ever mentioned, was in 2 lines to Mr. Smith, but it came from a Member of the Pennsylvania representation, and not from the president. Indeed, my friend, my best sympathies and feelings and along with them, every Exertion within my power, are pledged to serve you, and, would to God, they could be Effectual to do you that justice I know you are entitled to. But I am not a Cabinet minister, nor do I know any thing of interior movements or views, beyond what are expressed of the professions of regard and desire to serve you. The means of doing this, rests with those who possess the power. I cannot abandon the idea that you will be provided for, but in what I cannot say, altho' my mind leads me to presume it will be in the Customs. In respect to the Bankrupt Commissrs. it was merely a crude idea of my own, founded however on a suggestion of a Senator, that the Bill would be so modified as to authorize the president to appoint a Sole Commr. in the Commercial towns, in nature of a Judge, who at 8 dollars per day, should have a supervising and controuling power over each case of Special Commission—but the bill is differently constructed. I sincerely believe Mr. Madison & Mr. Gallatin, are equally with the president your friends, but I know not the reason of the delay to a restoration of you.

Our friend Mr. Duponceau is possessed of all my deeds and title papers for my house and lot—it is clear of ground rent, and I would take 8000 dollars, if the payments can be made certain in 4 or 6 months—provided the latter term is approved by Mr. Duponceau, who holds a mortgage on it to Mr. Hubert for 5700 dollars or thereabouts. If Mr. D and yourself deem it proper I will thank you to advertise it for me for about 4 weeks.

The first moment I am able to go about I will endeavor to ascertain what views or arrangements are meditated, particularly as it regards your situation, and advise you accordingly.

With sincere friendship, I am, dear Sir, truly your's

John Beckley

RC (COXE PAPERS, HISTORICAL SOCIETY OF PENNSYLVANIA).

1. Perhaps, John Smith, a former U.S. army officer, who had worked with Beckley in the previous presidential campaigns in Pennsylvania and had been appointed marshal of the Eastern District of Pennsylvania by Jefferson. Berkeley, *Beckley*, pp. 148, 207, and 222.

JOHN BECKLEY TO TENCH COXE

Dear Sir,   Washington, 21st May 1802.

A severe and painful illness has confined me to my bed and room from the hour that Congress adjourned,[1] and I now address you from a sick chamber, under a state of Convalescence which flatters me with a perfect restoration of health, and the use of my long afflicted foot. My situation since, and from some time before, the adjournment, prevented my seeing either the president or Mr. Gallatin, and I observe, with deep regret, that no nomination to the Senate took place which could possibly refer to you. Anxious as I was on the subject, I requested a particular friend to call on Mr. Gallatin, the day before he left home to escort his family to New York, and to ask him, in my name, if he knew or could say what was intended respecting your situation.—the answer I received, was, 'that you would not accept of any but a permanent situation, and that in a view to that it was the intention of the president to make a suitable arrangement as soon as possible'—nothing farther was said. Mr. G. will, about the time you receive this letter, be on his return thro' Philadelphia to this place, and as I am informed, will probably be engaged a day or two at the Bank. I know his friendship and good wishes to serve you, and wish you would take an opportunity to see and converse with him fully and freely.

Respecting the Sale of my house and lot, I have received a letter from Mr. Hubert, who holds my mortgage on it for 5000$ proposing to wait another Year from the 1st of July next, and to which I have acceded—this circumstance will enable me to embrace any favorable change which may occur, in the meantime, from a settled state of peace in the value of real property, without precipating a sale to immediate disadvantage. I was aware that your brothers late purchase, and similar ones under like circumstances, as well as the encrease of buildings, may serve to be adverse to my hope of obtaining 8500 dollars, but I cannot help flattering myself that a good look out may yet obtain it for me. On Brokers, nothing disinterested can be looked for, but on the joint friendship of Mr. Duponceau, Mr. John Smith, and yourself I will rely, that perchance the price I look for may be obtained, without a greater sacrifice than 1500$ which is the difference between 10,000$ it cost me, and 8500 which I now ask. If my three friends deem it advisable, they will advertise it for such time and in such manner as they deem proper. It is free of all Ground rent, and the title shall be given free of all incumbrances, the purchase money going to discharge what I owe upon it. Mr. Duponceau has all my deeds and title papers, and Mr. Smith will furnish a description of the property.

Will not the return of peace in Europe give a spring to the value and sale of landed property in the U.S.?

Be pleased to make my best respects to Mr. D. and Mr. S.—and make known the reason of my past silence. Excuse the incorrect scrawl I have labored to address you, and believe me, with unfeigned attachment. dear Sir, Yr. affecte. friend,

John Beckley

RC (COXE PAPERS, HISTORICAL SOCIETY OF PENNSYLVANIA).

1. Congress had adjourned on May 3, 1802.

JOHN BECKLEY TO TENCH COXE

Dear Sir,   Washington, 16th June 1802.

I am glad that the person you alluded to, is now out of the Question for the appointment referred to, altho' in consequence of your communication I took the effectual measure to have prevented it. My continued indisposition & confinement alone delays a visit to your City, when we may more fully and freely converse on many interesting topics. I trust however, and present appearances flatter me, that this cause will soon cease. I am at a loss in forwarding letters to Gales as my privilege[1] ceases during the recess. Excuse my being this brief, as I am very weak.

Your sincere friend,   John Beckley

RC (COXE PAPERS, HISTORICAL SOCIETY OF PENNSYLVANIA).

1. That is, his free postal mailing rights.

JOHN BECKLEY TO EPHRAIM KIRBY

Dear Sir,   Washington, 16th July 1802.

I take great pleasure in forwarding to you the enclosed official documents No. 1, 2, 3—authenticated by James Pleasants Junr. Keeper of the public rolls of the State of Virginia, and who is also Clerk of the General Assembly. I trust they will be in sufficient time to enable you to refute the shameful misrepresentations of Colo. Talmadge.[1] Be pleased to observe that the act for establishing religious freedom referred to in No. 1 is the same, Verbatim, with that in the Notes on Virginia, and was penned and presented to the Legislature of Virginia by Mr. Jefferson and passed by that assembly when I was their Clerk.

The new system and forlorn hope of the fœderalists to mislead the public mind by downright lying and falsehood, may serve to prop them for a moment and prolong the convulsive struggles of political death, but cannot fail ultimately to seal their eternal perdition.

Be so obliging as to favour me, occasionally, with any political communications from your quarter, and believe me, with great regard & esteem, dear Sir, truly your's.

John Beckley

RC (KIRBY PAPERS, DUKE UNIVERSITY).

1. Benjamin Tallmadge (1754–1835), a merchant-banker in Kirby's hometown of Litchfield, Connecticut, was a Federalist representative to Congress, where he served from 1801 to 1817. See Cunningham, *Jeffersonian Republicans in Power*, pp. 125–32.

JOHN BECKLEY TO CAESAR A. RODNEY

Dear Sir,[1]   Washington, 11th August 1802.

The gout in my stomach, has prevented, until now, my answering your late favour. I have given directions to package up in a small box, the documents you request; they will be addressed to you at Wilmington and the first safe opportunity, embraced, of sending them by the stage. My health compels me to retreat, immediately, to the Bath springs, and to abandon, for the present, the discussion of the merits of Mr. Adams's fiscal administration. In the interim, however, you will shortly see in the Aurora Nos. 1 and 2 of Cato's letters, exhibiting a fœderal listing of the duties on Salt, Brown Sugar, Bohea tea & Coffee, and a Justification, as well, of the repeal of the internal duties, as of the non repeal of those on Salt &c., with facts & reflections exposing the insidious conduct of the fœderalists on both grounds.[2]

On my return, the last of September, I shall be happy to hear from you, and am, with great regard and esteem, dear Sir, Your obedt. humble Servt.

John Beckley

[*P.S.*] My respects to Governor Hall.

RC (CHAMBERLAIN COLLECTION, BOSTON PUBLIC LIBRARY).

1. Caesar A. Rodney (1772–1824), Delaware lawyer and Republican politician, was engaged in a successful campaign to defeat Federalist James A. Bayard for a seat in the House of Representatives. He later served as a House manager in the impeachment trials of federal judges John Pickering and Samuel Chase, before being named U.S. Attorney General by Jefferson in 1807.
2. For Beckley's essays on federal duties, see the next two documents.

JOHN BECKLEY AS ANDREW MARVEL[1]

Wednesday, September 8, 1802

TO THE CITIZENS OF THE U. STATES

No. 1

That those who have said so much against the licentiousness of the press, and who by pretending to refrain from licentiousness, had nearly destroyed the liberty of speaking and writing, should so soon, forget their own principles, and become themselves the greatest calumniators, presents a strong feature of the character of the party. When the republicans under the late administration, reprobated its measures, on the ground of fact and argument, they were fined and imprisoned. They were pronounced guilty of sedition, declared the enemies of order, of government, and their country. Even when the proof of the truth might have exonerated the printer, the common law was resorted to in order to deprive him of the common rights of justice*² —and the truth itself has been punished as crime.

But the scene is now changed. What then was seditious in federal eyes, is now an evidence of attachment to order. What then was deemed repugnant to union, is now the offspring of a commendable jealousy. What then was enemy to our country is now the spirit of patriotism. Every newspaper of the opponents of administration, will witness these truths. Scarcely a page issues from their presses, but meets the sight befouled with the most shameless calumny. When no facts exist for misrepresentation, they are sure to fabricate falsehoods. When consistency of character gives no room for self approbation with an ingenuity peculiar to themselves, they attempt to extract merit from their inconsistencies. Every day affords proofs of this— but the history of the last session of Congress, from the importance of its transactions, gives the most striking and conclusive proofs of all. Till then the warmest friends of the minority never entertained a suspicion, that they wished to lessen public burdens, or to relieve the distresses of the poor. On former occasions every pretext to enlarge the revenues of the government was diligently sought after; and when one pretext was exhausted, another was created. But here, totally unlike themselves, with a charity for expressed poverty, which from their past professions and practice, was supposed to be foreign from their natures, they laboured to diminish the duties on *salt— Bohea tea—brown sugar* and *coffee*—With a modesty they never before possessed *popularity* was not their aim! *feelings like those of a virtuous man when he does an act of benefecence was their only expected reward.* Right worthy and noble Sirs! I would not detract from your merits, I would not rob you of the applause of one single act of your lives, which has the appearance of virtue. I am perfectly willing that your constituents should know the motives of your conduct. I am perfectly willing that they should *see*, that while you had the power to remove their grievances you preserved in *accumulating* tax upon tax, and when your power was *departed* you affected a veneration for the rights of the people, and an anxiety for the diminution of their burdens! To appreciate your services, they should be told, that rather than suffer the internal taxes to be repealed, you would be guilty of an inconsistency of character. . . . . The history of the duties on salt, bohea tea, brown sugar, and coffee, with a recurrence to the events which took place on the floor of congress during the last session, will be no small evidence of the duplicity and hypocrisy of your conduct. That history is intended to be now submitted to the understanding of the people of the union; — for they can have no interest in being deceived. When rightly informed their judgments will be correct. Neither a pretence to patriotism, nor a spurious sensibility for the drinkers of tea and coffee can protect the conduct of men from reproach and suspicion who have attempted to delude the common intelligence of the country.

A CONCISE HISTORY,

Of the Duties on Salt, brown Sugar, Bohea Tea, and Coffee, extracted from the Journals of Congress.

During the administration of general Washington—

The duty on Salt	was 12 cents per bushel
Bohea Tea	12 per pound
Brown Sugar	2 per pound
Coffee	5 per pound

On the 18th of July, 1797, in the first Congress of Mr. Adams's administration, an additional duty of 8 cents per bushel, was laid on salt, making the entire duty on that article 20 cents a bushel. The additional duty was limited in its continuance to two years; that is to the 8th of July 1799, and from thence until the end of the next session of Congress (1.) [(1.) See Laws of U.States, vol. 5, p. 35]³

But afterwards on the 7th of July 1800, a law was enacted, to continue this additional duty on salt for ten years, from the 3d of March 1800, to the 3d of March 1810. (2.) [(2.) Laws of U.States vol. 5, p. 144]

The duty on brown sugar was also encreased during the same administration, from two to two and a half cents per pound. By virtue of this act, and also of the acts of the 3d of March 1795, and of the 31st May, 1794, (3.)[(3.) Laws of the U.States, pages 295 and 333] passed during the administration of general Washington, all the *then* as well as the *further* proceeds of the duties on goods, wares, and merchandize, including of course all the duties before noticed, on *salt, brown sugar, bohea tea, and coffee*, were solemnly appropriated for the extinguishment of the public debt, until the whole of the said debt, foreign and domestic, should be paid and discharged.

When the additional duty of 8 cents a bushel on salt was first proposed in Congress, on the 9th of June, 1797, it was rejected in the house of representatives by the *strenuous exertions of the republican members.*(4.)[(4.) See the journals of the House of Representatives, pages 71, 72, and the debates published in the newspapers of Philadelphia of that month.] Soon after, on the 26th of June, 1797, a bill was presented by William Smith of Charleston, a federalist, to authorize a loan of 800,000 dollars, which was passed into a law; and on the 4th of July, 1797, being only *six days* before Congress adjourned, and when a number of members had left Congress and returned home, another motion was made by those then called the federal members, and carried, for imposing the additional duty of *eight cents a bushel* on salt.

On this motion the yeas and nays were taken, when the yeas were 47 and the nays 41—the names are subjoined in a note. (5).

[(5) The yeas and nays following are extracted from the Journal of the house of representatives pages 120, 121. YEAS: John Allen, George Baer, jun., James A. Bayard, John Chapman, C.B. Champlin, James Cochran, Joshua Coit, William Craik, S.W. Dana, J. Davenport, John Dennis, George Dent, Thomas Evans, Abiel Foster, Dwight Foster, Jonathan Freeman, Chauncey

Goodrich, Wm. Gordon, Roger Griswold, R.G. Harper, Thomas Hanley, William Hindman, Hezekiah L. Hosmer, J. H. Imlay, J.W. Kittera, Samuel Lyman, William Mathews, L.R. Morris, H.G. Otis, E.R. Porter, John Reed, Ja. Schurman, Samuel Sewall, William Shepard, Thomas Sinnickson, Samuel Sitgreaves, Jeremiah Smith, Nathaniel Smith, Wm. Smith (Charlest.) John Swanwick, George Thatcher, Richard Thomas, Mark Thompson, J.E. Van Allen, Peleg Wadsworth, John Williams.—47

NAYS: Abraham Baldwin, David Bard, Lemuel Benton, Richard Brent, Nathan Bryant, Demsey Burges, Samuel J. Cabell, Thomas Claiborne, Matthew Clay, John Clopton, T.T. Davis, J. Dawson, Lucas Elmendorf, John Fowler, Albert Gallatin, Js. Gillespie, W.B. Grove, J. A. Hanna, J.N. Havens, David Holmes, Walter Jones, Matthew Locke, Matthew Lyon, Js. Machir, Nathaniel Macon, Blair McClanachan, Joseph McDowell, J. Milledge, Anthony New, John Nicholas, T.J. Skinner, Wm. Smith (of Pinckney district), Richard Sprigg, Jun., Richard Stanford, Thomas Sumter, Abram. Trigg, John Trigg, P. Van Cortlandt, J. B. Varnum, Abraham Venable, Robert Williams—41]

Accordingly a bill was brought in, and *on the same day*[4] passed into law by those then called *federalists*, for laying the additional duty of *eight cents* a bushel on salt. The bill was without limitation of time, and of course designed to make the duty permanent and a perpetual tax. The *republicans* thereupon moved a *clause* to be added to the law, which would limit the continuance of this additional duty to two years. This *clause* was violently opposed by the federalists, but carried by the republicans on a vote 47 to 43.(6) [(6) See the journals pages 123 and 124—The yeas and nays fixed on this vote contrary to the former, the nays being the yeas only with the following alterations. John Chapman, George Dent, Thomas Evans, Thomas Harley, J.W. Kittera, and John Williams voted among the yeas, or for the limitation of the tax to two years, and Thomas Blount and David Morgan who were not present on the former vote, voted also for the limitation. Demsey Burgess, who had voted against the tax altogether, voted also against the limitation, and W. Grove was absent on the question.]

At a subsequent session of Congress[5] during Mr. Adams's administration, and after an act had been passed by the federalists to authorize another loan of five millions of dollars, at an interest of *eight per cent*, a motion was made by the federalists for a law "to continue in force the act passed on the 8th of July 1797, laying an additional duty on salt," this motion was carried by the federalists, 54 to 38.(7) [(7) See the Journals, p. 321–322—for the names as follows— Yeas: George Baer, Theodore Bailey, Bailey Bartlett, James A. Bayard, Jonathan Brace, John Brown, C.C. Champlin, William Cooper, S.W. Dana, John Davenport, Franklin Davenport, John Dennis, George Dent, William Edmond, Thomas Evans, Abiel Foster, Dwight Foster, Jonathan Freeman, Henry Glen, Chauncey Goodrich, Elizur Goodrich, William Gordon, Edwin Gray, William H. Grove, Robert Goodloe Harper, William H. Hill, S. Huger, J.H. Imlay, Aaron Kitchell, Silas Lee, Samuel

Lyman, James Linn, L.M. Morris, Abraham Nott, Robert Page, Josiah Parker, Thomas Pinckney, James Platt, Levin Powell, John Reed, John Rutledge, Samuel Sewall, James Sheafe, William Shepard, John Smith, R.D. Spaight, George Thatcher, J. C. Thomas, R. Thomas, P. Van Cortlandt, Peleg Wadsworth, Robert Waln, Samuel Williams. Yeas 54.

Nays: Willis Alston, Phanuel Bishop, Robert Brown, S.J. Cabell, Gabriel Christie, Mathew Clay, W. C. C. Claiborne, T.T. Davis, John Dawson, Joseph Dickson, Joseph Eagleston, Lucas Elmendorf, John Fowler, Albert Gallatin, Andrew Gregg, Thomas Hanley, Archibald Henderson, David Holmes, George Jackson, James Jones, Mathew Lyon, Nathaniel Macon, Peter Muhlenburg, Anthony New, John Nicholas, J.H. Nicholson, John Randolph, John Smilie, Richard Stanford, David Stone, Thomas Sumter, Benjamin Taliaferro, John Thomas, Abram Trigg, John Trigg, Jas. B. Varnum, Robert Williams, Henry Woods—Nays 38.]

The Bill was accordingly brought in and passed into law by the *Federalists*, directing the additional duty of *eight cents* per bushel on *salt*, to be continued in force, for and during the term of ten years from the 3d of March, 1800, to the 3d of March 1810. On the discussion of this bill, the republicans moved to strike out "ten years," so as to leave the law in force only until the 3d of March 1802, but the alteration was rejected by the Federalists, 44 to 50. (8) [(8) See Journals, pages 338, 339, for the yeas and nays, which were as follows: Yeas: William Allen, Phanuel Bishop, Robert Brown, Samuel J. Cabell, Matthew Clay, W.C. C. Claiborne, John Condit, John Dawson, Joseph Dickson, Joseph Eggleston, L. Elmendorf, John Fowler, Albert Gallatin, Edwin Gray, Andrew Gregg, J. A. Hanna, Thomas Hartley, Joseph Heister, A. Henderson, David Holmes, George Jackson, James Jones, Michael Leib, Mathew Lyon, James Linn, Nathaniel Mason, Peter Muhlenberg, Anthony New, John Nicholas, Abraham Nott, John Randolph, John Smith, John Smilie, Richard Stanford, David Stone, Thomas Sumpter, Benjamin Taliaferro, John Thornton, John Trigg, J. B. Varnum, Robert Williams, Henry Woods—44.

Nays: George Baer, Theodore Baily, Bailey Bartlett, James Bayard, J. Bird, Jonathan Brace, John Brown, Chris. G. Champlin, W. Cooper, S.W. Dana, J. Davenport, F. Davenport, John Dennis, Geo. Dent, Wm. Edmond, Thomas Evans, Abiel Foster, Dwight Foster, Henry Glen, Chauncy Goodrich, Elizur Goordrich, W. Gordon, Roger Griswold, Robert G. Harper, W.H. Hill, Benjamin Huger, J.H. Imlay, A. Kitchell, Henry Lee, Samuel Lyman, John Marshall, L.R. Morris, Robert Page, Josiah Parker, Thomas Pinckney, Jonas Pratt, Leven Powell, John Reed, John Rutledge, Samuel Sewall, William Shepard, Samuel Smith, George Thatcher, J.C. Thomas, Richard Thomas, P. Van Cortlandt, Peleg Wadsworth, Robert Waln, Lemuel Williams—50.]

From the foregoing facts, it will appear that the duties on salt, brown sugar, bohea tea, and coffee, were originally laid during the administration of George Washington.

That *additional* duties on *salt* and *brown sugar* were imposed by the Federalists, during the administration of Adams.

That the additional duty of *eight cents* per bushel on salt, was, when first proposed by the Federalists. . . . . rejected by the Republicans. . . .

That the same additional duty was afterwards, in the same session moved and carried by the *Federalists*.

That it was again strenuously objected to and opposed by the Republicans.

That this additional duty was first proposed to be made perpetual by the *Federalists*.

That this attempt was opposed and defeated by the Republicans.

That the first limitation of the said additional duty to *two years* was moved and carried by the *Republicans*.

That this limitation to *two years* was objected to and opposed by the Federalists.

That the law passsed May 7, 1800, to continue the additional duty of *eight cents* per bushel on *salt* for ten years, was first proposed by the Federalists.

That it was vigorously opposed by the Republicans.

That a second attempt to limit the said additional duty to *two years*, that is to the 3d March 1802, was made by the Republicans.

That this attempt was defeated, and the law as it now stands, to continue the said additional duty until the 3d March 1810, was carried by the *Federalists*.

That the increase and continuance of these duties were preceded by laws authorising loans of money to the public, and

That the proceeds of the duties on salt, bohea tea, brown sugar, and coffee were by law appropriated to the payment of the public debt until the whole of it should be discharged.

The reflections resulting from these facts, and from the repeal of the internal taxes, will in a future number be submitted to the calm and dispassionate judgement of a free and discerning people.

ANDREW MARVEL

TR (*AURORA* (PHILADELPHIA), SEPTEMBER 8, 1802).

1. Beckley was undoubtedly the author of these essays published over the pseudonym, Andrew Marvel. In an August 11, 1802, letter to Caesar A. Rodney (printed as the preceding document), Beckley spoke enthusiastically of the pending appearance of two essays in the *Aurora* "exhibiting a fœderal listing of the duties on Salt, Brown Sugar, Bohea tea & Coffee, and a Justification, as well, of the repeal of the internal duties." Even though Beckley refered to "Cato's letters," these essays by Andrew Marvel are almost certainly the two newspaper publications referred to by Beckley.

Andrew Marvell (1621–1678) was an English poet and political satirist known for his anti-royalist political satire and his fears of a military threat to representative government. See Alex B. Grossart, ed., *The Complete Works of Andrew Marvell*, 3 vols. (Privately printed, 1875).

John J. Beckley to James Madison, March 13, 1789, page 1, Madison Papers, Library of Congress.

2. The following statement marked by an asterisk was printed at the bottom of the page: "Mathew Lyon, a member of Congress, was fined and imprisoned, for a publication under the sedition law, which took place before the law had existence. Adams of Boston, printer of the Chronicle, was tried by a packed jury under the common law, and imprisoned. Frothingham printer at New York, was tried under the common law, and imprisoned. Both these cases and the following while the sedition law had existence. Luther Baldwin was tried and imprisoned by a sentence of Judge Washington, in Jersey under the common law. The crime a wish that the wadding of a gun had hit Mr. Adams's posterior, numerous cases might be added."

3. Footnotes provided by the author have been included in the text, enclosed in brackets. Additional citations to various actions of Congress can be found in the appropriate volumes of *The Debates and Proceedings in the Congress of the United States*.

4. That is, July 5, 1797.

5. That is, 1800.

JOHN BECKLEY AS ANDREW MARVEL

September 14, 1802

TO THE CITIZENS OF THE U. STATES.

No. II

The history of the duties on salt, brown sugar, bohea tea, and coffee, exhibits the opponents of the present administration, uniformly endeavoring to increase and perpetuate the taxes on what they have lately discovered to be the *necessaries of life*. Should we stop here, their conduct would appear consistent. But justice to their characters, and to the people of the United States, requires a consideration of their late proceedings on the floor of congress.

When the republicans, during the last session of that body, had ascertained that the expences of government, could, without injury to the union, be reduced more than the amount of revenue arising from the internal taxes, they proposed that the laws creating these taxes should be repealed.[1] This was considered as a measure of justice to their constituents. They knew there could be no justification of the retention of taxes, which were unnecessary for the support of government. They knew, that our government was formed for the protection of our persons and property, and not merely for the accumulation of public treasure. But the minority with a seeming anxiety for the preservation of national faith, for the diminution of taxes on the *necessaries of life*, and for the removal of grievances from the shoulders of the poor, *patriotically and humanely* wished to defeat the abolition of the internal taxes, by decreasing the impost on salt, brown sugar, bohea tea, and coffee. The attempt was insidious; but cannot long impose upon the mind of a people who respect their own interests. We were told that the public faith had pledged the proceeds of the excise duties for the payment of our national debt. But that same faith had no less pledged the duties on salt, brown sugar, bohea tea and coffee, for the same purpose. We were told that the repealing the internal taxes, one of the funds which the plighted faith of the nation had reserved for cancelling that debt, would be rescinded. But, to a common understanding, where two funds are created for the security of a public debt, there would appear no difference, between destroying one of those funds, and diminishing the other to an amount equal to the one which is proposed to be destroyed. The security in either case is equal; the infringement of national credit is equal. But it is difficult to tell on what ground these gentlemen could suppose, that our faith was plighted for the permanency of any particular species of revenue for the payment of our debts. For at the time debts were contracted, no particular fund existed, nor did we agree that any particular fund should exist, on the faith and security of which the money was advanced; a general confidence only in the integrity of the nation, and its future ability to reimburse the money borrowed, were the only foundations on which the loans were effected. It will not be thought that, had Great Britain subjugated us, an expectation would remain that these debts would ever be discharged. That the nation, when its independence was established would provide some means of payment, was undoubtedly expected, but they never pledged themselves, that any peculiar mode, or specific tax should be created for the reimbursement. Provided the instalments were satisfied according to contract, by whatever means it was effected, or from whatever resource, the national credit would remain unimpeachable. To annihilate therefore any particular portion of our revenue, or to divert any part of it to any other object, which heretofore had been appropriated to the payment of our public debt, can furnish no ground of imputation upon the faith of the nation, if a sufficiency remain for the discharge of the stipulated payments. The case is similar to a private transaction between two individuals. One loans the other a sum of money merely on the credit of his honesty. At the time the loan is made, the person receiving the money is involved in difficulties, his estate is unproductive, and there is no period in which the lender can look for repayment, but when his debtor is extricated from embarrassment; and no security which he can expect but the future improvement of the estate.

Should these events happen, the creditor may justly expect that his money will be repaid. But in whatever manner the payments may be made, must be totally immaterial to the creditor. He cannot claim his money out of any particular fund for none had been pledged. If he receives his interest one year out of one fund, and another year out of a different, as may best suit the private arrangements of his debtor, he can neither complain that the debtor has forfeited his credit, or broken the contract on which the loan was granted. The whole noise therefore which has been excited about public conscience, can be nothing more than the cant of a party to catch the breath of party applause, and to throw an appearance of patriotism on measures, to which they were not justly entitled.

The opponents of the repeal have told us that by retaining the internal revenue, and diminishing the impost on those *necessary articles*, the taxes, which are drawn from the opulent part of the community will be enhanced and those which fall most heavily on the industrious and indigent, will be lessened. But they must have forgotten, that the internal taxes operated like a sponge upon the purse of the people, drying up the very fountain of industry for the purpose of filling the public treasury. Every dollar, which was taken from circulation, decreased in proportion, the price of labor, rendered the poor and labourious less able to pay for salt, bohea tea, and coffee. These taxes could not be paid by the immediate produce of the land, nor by the manufactures of the mechanic. They gave the people no opportunity to commute the proceeds of their industry into cash. They opened directly upon the circulating medium, without supplying the means of our bringing back to the pockets of the citizens, the money which they had ferreted out. These evils would not result from continuing the duties on salt, brown sugar, bohea tea and coffee. The prices of these articles would be paid by the farmer and mechanic, without the hazard or the trouble of converting the produce of the earth or manufactures into money. But if cash were required, a sufficient length of credit would in general be given, to enable them to effect the exchange before payment would be demanded. The bad effects of the internal taxes were more immediately felt by the interior parts of the union, and operated upon them with peculiar injustice. For while the quantity of their circulating cash was small, their local situations were such, that the excise upon domestic distilled spirits with the aid of stamp duties, drained a great proportion of them of that money on which they depended, and which is necessary to facilitate the common intercourse of civil society. To remedy these inconveniences the pecuniary supplies which were brought by new settlers, must have been very inadequate, nor could much relief be expected from vending the profits of agriculture, after a circuitous voyage to the West Indies, or after a long and tedious transportaion by land to the place of sale. For the money, which is thus produced is usually left with the merchants of our sea ports, in payment for such articles of foreign growth and manufacture, as are required by the habit and necessities of those parts of the union. It is believed that they have paid more money yearly on account of the internal taxes, than would be sufficient for the payment of impost on that quantity of salt, bohea tea, coffee and brown sugar which is annually consumed in those parts of the country, especially when it is recollected, that the greatest proportion of the last article, is manufactured from their own native maple. But if the opposers of the repeal, were to receive credit for their newly acquired character of sensibility at the oppressions of the poor, let us recollect, that they were the oppressors, that, but a few sessions before, while the power was in their hands, instead of lessening the duty on salt, they increased it; instead of exonerating the public and the poor from taxes, they attempted to render them perpetual. To a person, however, not blinded by the enthusiasms of party spirit, to one, who is not determined to support the most absurd measures contrary to his own conviction, it would appear a duplicity of conduct unpardonable, an inconsistency of character irreconcilable, a shameless attempt to delude the understanding of the community, and to court that popularity which they affected to despise.

That the abolition or decrease of taxes, should be unpopular with any nation, seems a theory so paradoxical in its nature, that one would have thought an attempt to convince the citizens of the United-States of the justice and policy of the repeal of our internal taxes would be "like lighting a taper at noon day to assist the sun in illuminating the world." On ordinary occasions the absurdity of one, would be as great as that of the other. But so much has been said on the part of the opposition to government, so much artful misrepresentation has been used, that the minds of some may have been perverted. It is hoped however, that time will not long leave the advocates of delusion, even the most distant expectation of success, from schemes so hypocritical.

It is a maxim congenial with the nature of our government, that taxes should be imposed only when necessary. However necessary the internal taxes might be at the time of their creation, that necessity, when they were abolished, did not exist. The reduction of our army and of the navy, the repeal of the late midnight judiciary law, the dismission of useless officers, and various other retrenchments, curtailed the expences of government to the amount of a *million* of dollars. To retain therefore these taxes, would be an imposition on the community; would be extorting money from the pockets of the people for the purpose of lying useless in the public treasury, or of being appropriated to some unworthy object. For however wisely a *virtuous* administration might dispose of the surplus of national revenue, few have been so virtuous as to remit the temptation of a full treasury to run into extravagance. It has usually hurried them into wars, or into some scheme productive of public calamity. The nation can have no redress. For every thing is conducted under the sanction of law, or is covered with the cloak of pretended patriotism. The only means therefore for the people to keep the government upright, and faithful to the interests of the country, is to retain in their own hands whatever is not necessary to meet the exigencies of state. By pursuing this plan, they will, when actual danger approaches, be able to satisfy the just demands of administration. For the people are the best guardians of the wealth of the nation; and their pockets will better secure it from loss than all the bolts of a national treasury. The former is like the chest of economy, which nothing will open but the calls of prudence or necessity; the latter, like the desk of a spendthrift, which is unlocked at the impulse of every person. But it is not believed, that the excise and stamp duties were ever necessary. For at no period since their existence has it been necessary that the demands of the government should exceed those of the current year. It is true that fictitious necessities have been made, which served as a prelude and as a pretext to the augmentation of public burdens. A provisional army has been called to repel invasion when no enlightened and honest man in the union apprehended the least danger. A navy has been erected at an enormous and prodigal waste of public money. Useless, expensive and ridiculous embassies have been sent abroad to effect a reconcilliation with a foreign power, when one might have effected the purpose, or when misunderstandings might have been avoided. Many were deluded. The people seemed to be deceived into a momentary approbation of these measures. But fortunately, the folly and impatience of the projectors would not suffer them to act with prudence or foresight. They attempted the accomplishment of schemes in the short period of eight years, which the spirit and feelings of the country, would hardly support in the progress of fifty. The rapid accumulation of taxes, and the quick succession of expensive systems opened the eyes of the community, and blasted the full blown hopes of their authors. Their works have followed them. Systems of public extravagance have been succeeded by economy. The expenses of government have been reduced within the bounds of necessity. Though in this year an interest of $820,651 accrues.

On that part of one public debt which drew none under the former administration; though 888,888 are to be paid

In consequence of the late compromise with the British government, on account of her creditors; making in the whole 1,709,539 dollars in addition to our necessary annual expences—yet the resources of our country are adequate to every demand, without the aid of excise taxes and stamp duties.

Another principle of taxation, in a republican government is, that when taxes are *necessary*, those only should be levied which produce the most net revenue in proportion to the expence of collection, and in proportion to the number of officers employed. This principle would not justify the continuance of our internal taxes. For while that part of our revenue which arises from impost on foreign articles is collected, at about four and a half percent on its amount, the collection of that part, arising from the internal taxes, stamps duties excepted, costs nearly *nineteen and a half*. While by the former mode the treasury would be enriched 300,000 dollars, with a deduction of only 40,000 by the latter it would cost 175,000, making a difference to the people of the United States the sum of *one hundred and thirty-five thousand*. By repealing these taxes, an army of more than *four hundred and fifty officers* would be discharged, who were drones in society, living by the industry and the toil of their fellow-citizens—by retaining them and diminishing the duties on salt, brown sugar, bohea, and coffee, not an officer would be dismissed, not a *cent*, in collecting the revenue, would be saved to the union.

But necessity for the imposition, and economy in the collection, are not the only requisites for levying taxes in a government, whose basis is the rights of the people. It is necessary they be equal in their effects congenial with the spirit of freedom, and consistent with the welfare and happiness of the community. The nearer taxation and representation approximate to an equality, the more just will be the operation of government, and the higher its approach to the genius of republicanism. For where is the distinction between being taxed *without our consent*, and being taxed above that proportion, which the number of our representatives bears to the whole national representation! As much as we are taxed above that proportion, for so much we may truly be said to be taxed without our consent. An attempt by Great Britain to tax us without being represented in parliament, was considered a good justification for throwing off our allegiance to that country. And will not the same reason which would justify a *civil war*, justify also the *repeal* of a tax, which is founded on a similar principle of injustice. Yet, while *seven tenths* of the internal revenue were paid by the states north of the Potomac, which is far beyond their proportion of representation in Congress, we have been told that its abolition was dictated by southern interest, and calculated solely for southern benefit. Some might even be weak enough to believe it, but a large majority of the members from New England knowing the injustice their constituents would suffer by a continuance of these taxes voted against the repeal, and would have sacrificed the interests of that part of the union, to an affected and unfounded jealousy of Virginia. But the unequal effect of those taxes was not confined to states, nor to the interior quarters of the union only, it was also extended to individuals. For in certain instances, the excise on domestic distilled spirits was proportioned to the capacity of the still, and not to the quantity of liquor made. Many therefore were enabled by the extent of their capital, and by the aid of superior skill, to manufacture twice the quantity in the same time, as others who paid an equal tax, but were defective in skill, and destitute of resources. Consequences, still more unjust attended the operation of the license tax. Here one measure of taxation was applied to all, to him who in one year retailed forty gallons only, of wine or foreign distilled spirits, and to him, who in the same time, retailed five or fifty thousand. It will not be said then, that annuling the laws which created our internal revenue, is no relief but to the lazy and luxurious; nor that diminishing the duties on salt, brown sugar, bohea tea, and coffee was the only measure from which the industrious citizen would expect any exoneration from its burdens.

The operation of excise laws check the improvement of a country by taxing the industry and ingenuity of its citizens. The manufactures of the United States have obstacles enough to contend with, without being impeded in their progress by the hand of government. We are now sufficiently dependent on other countries for many of the necessaries and conveniences of civilized life, without being rendered more so, by the impolitic and injurious restraints of our own laws, upon the enterprising spirit, which would manufacture them among ourselves. Could every article of necessity, of convenience and of luxury, be produced by our labour within the limits of the union, it would encrease our wealth, and add to our national felicity. Losses by sea would not diminish our substance. A navy would not augment the expences of government; nor should we be involved in foreign politics, or lose our treasure and laws, by being entangled in the broils of other nations. But as this desirable situation will probably not soon be realised, an approximation to it, as far as lies with in the compass of our abilities, is devoutly to be wished. To impose a burden therefore upon our infant exertions to prevent these evils, and be a policy destitute of patriotism and contrary to the welfare of our country.

The oppression of excise laws opposes the principles of a republican government, and tranquility of civil society. The people to judge impartially of the measures and designs of administration, should be free from the influence of executive patronage. The fear of any army, and the impression of a body of officers, distributed through the country at the will and under the control of government, are alike unfriendly to the spirit of freedom. The former become eunuchs to guard the infallibility of administrations, and the other spies to watch every look to censure, and report every sentiment which sounds like reprobation of the proceedings of government. The power too which is usually placed in the hands of excise officers, is commonly odious in its execution.—neither the private habitations of families, nor the recesses of clossets, have been exempted from their search. The depositaries of wealth, and the chamber of retirement, have frequently been invaded by this band of parasites which administrates to the cupidity of government. This destroys the peace of social intercourse, and tears up by the roots that confidance on which society is founded. It endangers the existence of government, by exciting a spirit of hostility against the officers, which is usually transfered to those who appoint them. Though in this country such flagrant breeches of domestic security, such violations of the sanctity of private retreats, have not occurred; and we begin to tread on the threshold of that system, where almost every thing eaten must be measured, and almost every thing drank must be guaged, where every glass that admits the light of heaven for enjoyment, and very hearth that supports a fire for comfort, are objects of taxation. Under such circumstances no people will long remain quiet, nor, any government secure, without a military arm to awe the one into obedience, and to protect the other in its tyranny. For it is morally impossible, that an extensive excise system should be established, without a standing army to enforce its execution. The history of England and Ireland is proof sufficient of this fact. If we need further testimony, that taxation by excise is hostile to the sentiments of freedom, we have only to read our own. We there find one *principal* objection to the adoption of our present constitution was the power given to congress of raising a revenue by excise. We there find, that by encreasing this power, one insurrection has been excited, and did more injury to the harmony of the United States, than can be compensated by all the proceeds of the internal taxes, and by all the services which have been or will be performed, by the opposers to the repeal.

With so many reasons against the continuance of these taxes, opponents of administration could not with *appearance* of fidelity to their constituents, wish them longer to remain a burden on the community. To suppose it possible, we must attribute to them the grossest ignorance, or a temporary derangement of understanding. The former they will not assume to themselves, the latter the circumstances of the transactions will not allow us to grant, neither their ardor for preservation of public faith, nor the tears of charity which they shed over the distresses of the poor, can make us believe, that one was not pretence, and the other hypocricy, while one moment they pronounced that natural credit would become the victim of the repeal, in the next they proposed that a decrease of the duties on salt, bohea tea, brown sugar, and coffee, should be made a consideration for retaining the excise. When in the minority, they wept over the calamities of poverty, but forgot that their days of power were marked with austerity and oppressions. Their conduct through the whole wears an air of singularity, which a legislature seldom exhibits; their repeated attempts to prevent the passage of the repealing act, seem more like the petulant freats of a child, who, having been habituated to do what he pleases, is out of humor because he is opposed; than the dignified and manly conduct, which ought to characterise a legislative assembly of freemen. They sought rather to perplex, than convince their antagonists; to carry their point by preserverance, rather than by argument. To suppose they even *wished* a diminution of the duties on salt, brown sugar, bohea tea and coffee, would be an affront to their understandings. It could be nothing more than a finesse, an artful trick, to save that excise system to which they had been so long attached by principle. This system was a favorite point, from which the executive patronage could be extended to any limits, round it could be erected the energy of government. It was a child of their own loins, they could not brook the idea of its being strangled in infancy, and as soon as it had quitted the protected embrace of parental affection. By its death, the hope of enlarging official influence, and extending the sphere of taxation till the people should become unmindful of the measures of administration and force their oppressor in the weight of their own miseries, was extinguished. Should they regain their lost power, the terms on which they must hold it, would be changed. The people would look with a jealous eye on the restitution of the excise system. The popularity of their measures must rest on the long history of public utility. The artificial support of excise officers, of provisioned armies and sedition bills, would not probably be replaced with ease, or aid the enforcement of governmental exactions.

The fæd[eral] expectation of gradually asimilating the practices, under our constitution, to that of Great Britain, was decaying. The likeness to English *forms*, the etiquete and ceremonies of a British court, had been succeeded by republican simplicity. This they supported with reluctance. But to touch the substance similitude, was "death to their ambition."

ANDREW MARVEL

TR (*AURORA* (PHILADELPHIA), SEPTEMBER 14, 1802).

1. By an act of April 6, 1802, Congress had ended the collection of all internal taxes after June 30, 1802. *Debates and Proceedings, Seventh Congress.* pp. 1323–27.

JOHN BECKLEY TO JAMES MADISON

Dear Sir,   Philadelphia, 5th May 1803.

I have conditionally engaged a neat Hansome Chariot for you, with a pair of best plated harness at 500$. Particulars and a description of it, I will give in a day or two, having so far engaged, on the advice & opinion of Mr. Kerr without having, as yet, seen it, altho' under reservation to be finished as I may direct. If I conclude a purchase, I will arrange the payment to meet your accomodation within 60 or 90 days. The Carriages sold, <u>this day</u>, at Sheriffs Sale were tawdry and flimsey, no way sufficient in finish or fashion, being designed for South America.

War is confirmed between France & England, and happily so far as, since I have seen to day, a letter from an intelligent Emigrant, returned from this Country to Paris, in which under date 5th March he states a direct message to him from the first consul, advising him "not to interfere in political concerns & especially to avoid all reference to the Example of the Jacobin government of America, so dangerous to the repose & safety of European Systems."—the words of Bonaparte himself as quoted in the letter I saw.

NYork elections are decisively democratic thro' the State, for both branches, and leave no doubt that the mode for choosing Electors in that State for the presidential Election will be such as the democrats shall prescribe.

There are great jealousies & divisions here among the democrats on the question of removals from office, altho' a decided majority are in the affirmative of that question, and great feeling is Excited thereon pointed at Mr. Dallas here, and Mr. Gallatin at Washington, the alledged supporters of the system of moderation, as it respects Pennsylvania. It is difficult to restrain the turbulent spirits within any bounds of decency, and, as connected, with other intrigues of some designing men, but little suspected, I know not where it will end. I am laboring to effect an association & union of the principal characters now at variance, and wish I may be able to effect it.[1]

Mrs. B. writes in affectionate regards to Mrs. Madison & your family. I am, respectfully, dear Sir, Your's sincerely,

John Beckley

RC (MADISON PAPERS, NEW YORK PUBLIC LIBRARY).

1. Despite the efforts of moderates, such as Beckley and Gallatin, the dispute over the tempo of political removals from public office rose in intensity throughout Jefferson's first presidential term, badly splitting the Republican party in Pennsylvania. See Cunningham, *Jeffersonian Republicans in Power*, pp. 51–70.

JOHN BECKLEY TO WILLIAM EUSTIS

Dear Sir,[1] Washington City, 17th July 1804

A long absence from home on business at Richmond, must be my apology for past silence, whilst the same cause which calls me away a second time renders it the more necessary that I should now fulfill the obligation of friendship. Since we parted, the scene of politics foreign and domestic has become more critical and interesting than ever; and in the European world portends an immediate convulsion. France with gigantic strides treading back her revolutionary footsteps, and rapidly advancing to absolute Monarchy, whilst the military genius of Bonaparte is conducting him the race, and I trust to the fate of Cæsar. Great Britain attaining new worlds of Empire, and myriads of subjects in the East; whilst her own political being, stands as it were suspended and doubtful in the scale of Events. The great powers of Europe looking on, and anxiously marking the progress of this punic warfare, between the two rival nations hitherto the Arbiters and scourge of Europe. It does not bespeak the spirit of phrophecy, to foretell the issue. Every thing in France verges to the concentration and consummation of her Energies and resources, whilst every thing in Britain tends to weakness, disunion, distraction and despair—and, whilst the dynasty of France is changed under the auspices of Bonaparte, that of Great Britain will terminate with the life of George 3rd. In vain is the change of ministry and the return of Pitt to power; the pharoah of Great Britain has decreed his countrys ruin, he has dug the grave, and ominously called in the aid of Pitt to entomb his nations being. A single fact is worth a thousand speculations, by an official return to parliament, copy of which I have seen, the Exports of last year 1803, exhibited the alarming decrease of £8,400,00 Sterling value, and the letter announcing this fact dated London 13 May says, "Our manufactures are all at a stand, no business doing, no demand, no vent, no specie, no confidence, every body alarmed, a Spanish War and a treaty with Russia is talked of God only knows how our Salvation is to be wrought."

With such a picture before them I am led to admire the temerity of fœderalism in our own country, and can only account for it as the last convulsive struggles of an expiring faction, which like its prototype the monarchy of Britain, has dug its own grave, and is about to entomb the name and being of the party. At such a crisis the death of General Hamilton[2] will cause a deeper interest in his fate. His energy and talents placed him at the head of the party, and emphatically speaking they hear of a fathers exit, in the moment of their own dissolution. What were the causes and particulars of this duel we are not yet advised, but whatever they were I feel for his family, and drop a tear at his untimely fate—always his political enemy and knowing that he possessed great vices, I yet always admired his Energy and talents, and believe that he also possessed some commendable virtues. Nor will all his political sins, shade the remembrance of many useful public services.

It gave me great pleasure to see the spirit and union displayed at your celebration of 4th July—it augurs well of your future republican efforts, to ensure the Success of which, nothing but concert and exertion is wanting. Our countrys continued progress to national happiness and greatness, under the conduct of a faithful and intelligent administration, must eventually unite the people of every State in one accordant sentiment, and a few years more of peace, will seal the destiny of our republican Systems beyond the influence of foreign nations, empires, and principles.

I enclose you Donahoes rect. in full—he pertinaciously refused for some time to receive the money. My own health has been better this summer than for many years past. Our son Alfred is become a very fine boy—his mother and hers, are also in perfect health, and write with me in best regards to you. I shall not leave here until 5th August, and, in the interim shall be happy to receive a line from you, being with great regard and esteem, dear sir, Your faithful & obedt. Servt.

John Beckley

RC (FEINSTONE COLLECTION, MICROFILM, LIBRARY OF CONGRESS).

1. William Eustis (1753–1825), served as a Republican Representative from Massachusetts, 1801–5, until defeated by Federalist Josiah Quincy. He later was Jefferson's and Madison's secretary of war, 1807–12.
2. Only a few days earlier Alexander Hamilton had been shot and killed in a duel with Aaron Burr.

JOHN BECKLEY TO JOHN BROWN

My dear Sir,[1]   Washington City, 8 August 1804.

We are made happy by a letter from Margaretta to Maria received a few days ago, which advised us of the health and welfare of all your good family. Ours continue much as usual, nothing material having occurred in our domestic concerns. Alfred progresses rapidly, is very healthy and prattles every thing. In a few days I set off for Stanton to arrange my land concerns, and expect to be at home again in about a month. I was not surprised at the sensation excited in your State, by a Knowledge of the dirty intrigues for the Vice presidency. The man that could be the first and foremost to Exclude an old friend, from an office, to which he had been the first & foremost to invite him, and to render that circumstance subservient to his own contemptible views of influence and personal advancement, merits forever to be discarded from all public and private confidence. You well know the application of this remark, and how far the man in question merits it from me.[2]

Before this letter reaches you, the advice of Hamiltons duel with Burr, and his consequent death, will have been received. Burr is now at Clem Biddles, country seat near Philadelphia. A Jury of inquest on Hamiltons body, have brought in a verdict of Murder in the first degree vs. Burr, and the two seconds Van Ness & Pendleton as accessories. Federalism has monumented and sainted their leader up to the highest heavens, whilst the presses are made to groan under the weight of Orations, Eulogies, and mournings, and Burr is pursued with Vindictive and unrelenting fury. The Clergy too, are sedulously endeavouring to canonize, the double adulterer, as a moralist a

Christian, and a Saint. Our friend Mason, pronounced the Oration at New York. I have not seen it, and wish to forget the fact. It is generally believed that the indecent and intemperate efforts to render the event destructive to Burr, and subservient to other political views, will produce a strong counter current, and but one opinion prevails here of the sufficiency of provocation and correct conduct of Burr. Indeed it is only necessary to read the correspondence and Hamiltons confession to justify Colo. Burr's procedure, and to admit that nothing but the want of equal intelligence and equal nerve, would prevent any man from pursuing the same course.

The Electioneering campaign is very hot at Philadelphia—penrose vs Leib and Latimer vs Clay, are run by the fœderal and third party men, with great Earnestness and probable success.[3] In Massachusetts, federalism is gradually sinking, and it is believed a republican vote will obtain for their Electoral ticket. We have no news of the amendment of the Const. in Tennesse.[4]

Here is a perfect interregnum—the president and heads of department are all absent. French & English persecute our trade and blockade our harbors—strong remonstrances are made to both powers. Our fleet sailed for the Mediterranean the lst of July. Preeble has done wonders with his small force and by a late prompt and critical appearance before Tunis, prevented a War with that power.

Some appearances have Arisen of a renewed Continental War in Europe, whilst Bonnapartes Imperial diadem is not yet firmly fixed. The changes in the English Ministry, and dubious state of their Kings health, are as much indicative of peace as of War, and the crafty Corsican knows too well, how to pursue his game to Effect, without incurring the chances of a loss.

Have you heard from your brother James, since his departure? Genl. Wilkinson was here Several Weeks, and is gone to Balls town Springs. He dined and spent several Evenings with us, and said he had written you, as also to advise your brother against going to Orleans.[5]

Pray, if possible, be with us Early in the Session as the changes in Senate will induce me to press for the Secretaryship,[6] and as contingent consequence of my success will be the execution of my determined purpose to spend with Maria & her boy, our next Summer with our friends in Kentuckey. Maria has lately written very fully to Margaretta, and during my absence will write again. We all united in best wishes and most affectionate regards to your dear family, and I remain, dear Sir, Your sincere friend & Servt.

John Beckley

RC (BROWN PAPERS, YALE UNIVERSITY).

1. John Brown (1757–1837), a Virginia lawyer, moved to Kentucky, where he became a political leader in the post-war years. He had served in the U.S. Senate since 1792 and was later implicated in the Burr Conspiracy.
2. Beckley may have been referring to Kentucky's U.S. Senator John Breckinridge, who received 20 votes for the vice-presidency in the Republican congressional caucus. There

was a brief and unsuccessful effort in Kentucky to support Breckinridge for vice-president in opposition to the caucus nominee, George Clinton. Cunningham, *Jeffersonian Republicans in Power*, pp. 103–8.

3. Republicans Joseph Clay and Michael Leib were elected as U.S. representatives from Pennsylvania.

4. Beckley was referring to action on the proposed twelfth amendment to the constitution governing the choice of president and vice-president. On July 27, 1804, Tennessee had become the 13th state to ratify the amendment, which was declared in force on September 25, 1804, by a proclamation of the secretary of state. Herman V. Ames, *The Proposed Amendments to the Constitution of the United States During the First Century of its History* in *Annual Report of the American Historical Association for the year 1896.* 2 vols. (Washington: 1897), 1: 78–80, and 324–26.

5. James Brown (1766–1835) was named secretary of the Orleans Territory in October 1804 and soon thereafter became U.S. attorney for New Orleans. He later served in the U.S. Senate and as minister to France.

6. For Beckley's earlier consideration of seeking the secretaryship of the United States Senate, see Beckley to Jefferson, October 27, 1801.

JOHN BECKLEY TO JOHN BROWN

Dear Sir,   Washington City, 21st September 1804.

On my return home from Staunton, I heard with great concern of another affliction in your family by the loss of your little Alfred. Coming so recently after the severe shock you had before sustained, whilst it added to your distress, called for a full trial of all your fortitude & resignation to support the visitation and comfort the dear partner of your affection. It is perhaps more truly to those, who like us, have experienced similar affliction, that real sympathy belongs. We know what you feel, and have felt what you know. But thanks to him, "who giveth and who taketh away" and who endowed us with fortitude to support his dispensations, we have yet of comfort to make us happy. So also have you—two charming boys who have progressed beyond the dangers of infancy, with health and youth on the part of their parents that forbids not the prospect of more. I know the tender susceptibility of your Margaretta—but time, patience, absence & change of scene may and will restore her. Bring her to us, take the two boys along, come spend the winter, mingle in the bosom of friendship, the sympathies and affection of our past lives. Maria will be made happy herself, she will restore & make happy your Margaretta also. Consider too that the journey, change of air, and above all change of Scene, are the panacea of health to Margaretta, and we will return with you in the Spring.

I received a letter from James Brown, dated Washington Missisipi territory 25 Augst., he says he has totally recovered his health, strength & vigor, and should descend for N. Orleans in a few days. When at Monticello, a few days ago, the president told me he had offered him the station of Atto. for the U.S.[1]

Be so good as to ascertain amount of my taxes for 1802, 1803, and 1804, distinguishing the particular tracts charged to me, and which they <u>must</u> be paid. Mr. Fitzhugh wishes to draw on me for the amount, but if <u>it can</u> be delayed 2 or 3 months, it would be more convenient to me. Be good enough so to advise him.

I have brought suit <u>vs</u> all holders of my land under [?][2] and have discovered much valuable <u>property</u>. We have little or no news. The president returns 1st of October—at present all is vapid & dull at this place. Favour me with a line, and say when you will be with us. We shall prepare every thing for Margaretta & the boys. Accept our best wishes of health & happiness. Your ever affecte. friend.

John Beckley

RC (BROWN PAPERS, YALE UNIVERSITY).

1. See note 5 to the previous document.
2. One word illegible.

JOHN BECKLEY TO TENCH COXE

Dear Sir,   Washington. 10th January 1805.

Will you excuse my return of your letter of the 6th instant, with Mrs. Masons answer, interlined, to your several queries?[1] I have no copiest at hand, and am pressed for time. The political persecution and intollerance you mention is not matter of surprise to me. An unsuccessful effort has been made here, to effect a similar purpose, but its authors have been discomfited, and are equally despised and contemned by all.[2] Accept the united regards of all this family to Mrs. Coxe and yourself, in which Mr. Brown also desires to join, and believe me, always, dear Sir, Yrs. with true esteeem,

John Beckley

[*P.S.*] Is there any Sale for the Kanawha lands, say 170,00 acres? A most advantageous bargain may be had if any <u>European</u> wholesale purchaser would present.

RC (COXE PAPERS, HISTORICAL SOCIETY OF PENNSYLVANIA).

1. Beckley had written at the bottom of the letter: "Where ever any question has arisin in the Supreme Court which involves any of the questions that arose on his contract for the Fairfax estate the C.J. has uniformly refused to set." Coxe to Beckley, January 6, 1805, Coxe Papers, Historical Society of Pennsylvania.

2. Coxe was accused of trying to start a third party (the Quids) in Pennsylvania by splitting the Republicans. For a discussion of the Republican Party warfare in Pennsylvania, see Cunningham, *Jeffersonian Republicans in Power*, pp. 214–20 and Cooke, *Coxe*, pp. 432–48.

JOHN BECKLEY TO WILLIAM A. BURWELL

Dear Sir,[1]   Capitol hill 28th June 1805.

I enclose a copy, 'Second Edition published at Worcester,' of the pamphlet I wrote at Philadelphia, during our political struggles in 1800.[2] To you, it may be necessary to apologize for several inaccuracies as to dates in the Epitome of Mr. Jefferson's life contained in the latter pages. Written on the spur of the occasion, without communicating with any person, possessing scanty materials and relying too much on my own recollection, it was necessarily defective in some material points, and certainly erroneous in others immaterial. In pages 12, 13, 14 & 15, you will observe a full statement of my testimony in the cases of Arnold & Cornwallis's invasions, as I delivered it to Fenno for publication in the Year 1796, in part reply to William Smith's infamous publication under the signature of Phocion, and, in this statement, I am confident there is no error or inaccuracy, and shall be always ready to verify it.[3]

With great respect, I am, dear Sir, Your obedt. Servt.

John Beckley.

RC (JEFFERSON PAPERS, LIBRARY OF CONGRESS).

1. William A. Burwell (1780–1821) was serving as private secretary to President Jefferson and he used the material sent by Beckley in this "Vindication of Mr. Jefferson," which appeared in the *Richmond Enquirer*, August 23, 27, 30, September 6, 13, 17, and 27, 1805. Burwell later served in the House of Representatives, 1806–21.

2. William Beckley's *Address to the People of the United States with An Epitome and Vindication of the Public Life and Character of Thomas Jefferson* was first published in 1800 in Philadelphia by James Carey. It is published in this volume at the date of July 4, 1800.

3. Beckely's essay written over the pseudonym, A Subscriber, is published in this volume at the date, October 26, 1796.

JOHN BECKLEY TO JOHN BROWN

My dear Sir,   Washington City, 12th July 1806.

Your friendly favour of the 19th ulto. accompanied by another from Margaretta to Maria, made us very happy in the health and welfare of friends so dear. The deprivation you Suffer of the Society of two amiable brothers,[1] added to the retirement of your present mode of life, must not, however, much to be regretted, induce you to turn misanthrope, or to abandon those finer feelings of philanthropy, which cement friendships towards you, and yours, that never can be forgotten.

You have great and superior causes of thankfulness, and let me pray you in the name of friendship not to Encourage the wish to follow your brothers. They are nearly in the State of Single men, without families, and could remove without any great sacrafice or inconvenience; not so with you; a young and Encreasing family, a property not Easily convertible without great loss; domestic, rural, simple, plain republican habits, and Education of your fine promising boys, to be Exchanged for the gay, glitter, artificial and expensive modes and habits of a Country, where frivolity, vice and immorality mark the private, as licentiousness, duplicity and corruption the public character of the people. Besides, my dear Sir, with you more particularly the "amor patria", ought to be a governing principle of action. What signifies it, that you experience the temporary ingratitude of a giddy and thoughtless people? Emphatically, you are one of the fathers of Kentuckey, and in the innumerable instances of public usefulness and improvement you have introduced into your country, thro' a series of long and Eminent public service, there is erected for you an unperishable monument of honourable patriotism, of which you can never be deprived; and by no act of yours, ought your children to be deprived of this honorable inheritance. Posterity must and will render you complete justice.[2] The future historians of Kentuckey will record the name of Brown among those of its most distinguished & disinterested worthies. Myself, a living witness of the fidelity, zeal and patriotism of your well spent public life, I cannot believe in the ceaseless ingratitude of a whole people. Let us, nurture our children in the love of country.

I am very thankful for your attention to my business with Forbes and leave to your discretion the amount of a reasonable compensation for the Service required, but am anxious to obtain it, as soon as possible.

We greatly regret our inability to visit you this Summer, but Maria Expects both her brothers James & Isaac, to arrive next month from the West Indies; the former with his family; and I meditate a short trip to Bath until they arrive. Besides, I have made such a disposition for sale of my Montgomery land, in London, as promises great Success, and in another Six months we rely that from this and other causes, all my present pecuniary difficulties will Vanish, and permit us freely in the next recess after 3d March next, to pursue the object so near our hearts, of a visit to our dear friends in Kentuckey.

Our political horizon still remains clouded. In Europe, the deranged state of Continental Affairs, appears highly favourable to a Successful termination of our negociations both with England & Spain, altho' as yet no further advices are received. Skipwith reached France in 23 days, before, it is possible, that Randolphs mischief could have arrived.[3]

There is great apprehension here of a duel between the two Randolphs, John and Thomas Mann Randolph.[4] The former is universally reprobated for his inconsistent and incongruous course of conduct at the late Session. Without question, altho' fearful to avow it, he has imbibed an implacable resentment vs. the president, supposed to result from his mortification last year, of Armstrongs appointment,[5] after he had himself announced his intention of visiting Europe and had actually obtained from Madison his passport for the Voyage—hence too, his personal avowed hostility to Madison, and his paramount Vanity to become a president maker by the nomination of Monroe. You know the man and can easily see the operating motives of mortified pride and disappointed ambition. Sandfords[6] too honest, to be equal to these political tergiversations. My present opinion is, that Monroe will be prefered to Madison, if Mr. Jefferson shall not ultimately be prevailed upon to serve again. The fœds, and Madisons own trimming policy, will defeat his Election.[7]

Massachusetts, except as to Strong,[8] is completely republican. New York and Pennsylvania are both deeply divided and deranged as to their local politics.

As any thing worth communicating occurs, I will inform you. Maria, writes to Margaretta for herself, and will speak of all domestic concerns. Accept for yourself and yours, the most affectionate regards and sympathies of, my dear Sir, Your constant friend   John Beckley.

RC (BROWN PAPERS, YALE UNIVERSITY).

1. John Brown's brothers James (1766–1835) and Samuel (1769–1830) were living in the Louisiana Territory. James had been appointed secretary of the Orleans Territory in 1804 and in 1806 Samuel, a physician, had left Kentucky for New Orleans. Kline, ed., *Burr Papers*, 2:952 and 955.

2. For a discussion of the accusations that Brown was involved in the Burr-Wilkinson Conspiracy, see Beckley to Brown, September 8, 1806, and January 23, 1807.

3. Beckley is probably referring to John Randolph's denunciation of Spain and Jefferson's Spanish policy and his proposal that an army be raised to seize the disputed territories from Spain. Dumas Malone, *Jefferson the President: Second Term, 1805–1809* (Boston: Little, Brown and Co., 1974), pp. 71–74.

4. Thomas Mann Randolph, son-in-law of Jefferson, narrowly avoided a duel with his cousin and fellow representative, John Randolph, in the aftermath of a bitter verbal exchange in the House. See Malone, *Jefferson the President: Second Term*, pp. 127–32.

5. Randolph had been hinting that he wanted a diplomatic appointment in Europe, but John Armstrong (1758–1843), former U.S. senator, had been appointed minister to France (1804–10) and in 1806 had been appointed a special envoy to Spain. Malone, *Jefferson the President: Second Term*, pp. 88–92.

6. Thomas Sandford, two-term U.S. representative from Kentucky, was defeated in the 1806 election, because of his support for John Randolph. Cunningham, *Jeffersonian Republicans in Power*, p. 231.

7. For Randolph's support of Monroe's unsuccessful campaign for the 1808 presidential nomination, see the next document.

8. Caleb Strong (1745–1819), a former U.S. senator, served as governor of Massachusetts (1800–1807, 1812–16).

JOHN BECKLEY TO JAMES MONROE

My dear Sir,   Washington City, 13th July 1806.

Permit me to recommend the enclosed letter to your attention; I had the pleasure to write you by the gentleman to whom it is addressed, and to pray you, on my behalf, to render him any aid, which, consistently with your public functions, it might be in your power to do, for facilitating an agency committed to him by Andrew Moore Esq. and myself, for disposing (in Europe) of a joint property we hold in a body of 170,038 acres of land in Montgomery County, Virginia, universally admitted to be the most valuable, as to quantity and quality in all the Western Country. You will pardon the expression of that anxiety we feel upon the success of Mr. Hunts agency, therein, in the hope that so far only in the strictest sense of public duty, will admit, you will testify for the knowledge you possess of the public and private characters of Mr. Moore and myself, and as the nature of the business may permit and require.

I trust the confidential letter I wrote you during the Session via New York per packet has come safe to hand. It was not signed and was written in the 3rd person, so as to guard vs. accidental miscarriage. I unfolded the intrigues which caused us so much agitation during the Session; and the initials used I was confident you could not mistake. Since then the public mind has become fully tranquilised, and so far as respects the Executive measures and conduct there is but one unanimous sentiment of approbation to them, and reprobation of their opponents & calumniators. Not so however as respects the questions of who shall be next president? which was the spring and pivot of all the intrigues, and in which your name and character were made free use of by the leader of opposition (J. Randolph) as a declared candidate to succed Mr. J—,[1] but as it is generally believed, without your knowledge, privity or consent. Indeed the motive to this step was too obvious to admit a doubt that it was a masked friendship to you, to cover the resentment of disappointed ambition vs the president & Mr. Madison, for having overlooked him in the appointment of Armstrong to succeed Livingston, after he had last year announced his intention to go to France, and had actually obtained from Mr. Madison his passports for that purpose. Besides if to the reputation of making a president, could be added the object of creating a schism, between Jeff. Mad. and yourself, resentments would be more fully gratified. Nor is to be doubted that these were the operating views & feelings when I solemnly assure you that before the nomination of Pinckney to cooperate with you, it was made a "sine qua non" by Randolphs freinds, that they would relinquish their ground of opposition, if the republican members, would write with them in a declaratory vote of Neutral Rights and a recommendation to the president to send an Envoy to be the bearer of this strong expression of the opinion of the nation, and that Mr. R.[2] ought to be the man, A proposition which was instantly and in tota rejected by the republicans, and caused the warfare of opposition to be renewed. The termination of the Session, completed the defeat and mortification of the principal agitator, and the small minorities in which he was placed, have carried to the public mind full conviction of the folly and weakness of his conduct, which, if it does not materially affect and injure us in our foreign relations, will not be allayed by the ferment arising out of the presidential nomination. In respect to this, the public mind is taking a strong and decisive direction towards demanding Mr. Jeffersons continuance another term of 4 years, as the only means of preventing a Schism in the republican party, in which your friends are not disposed to yield your pretensions to those of any other candidate. Madison is deemed by many, too timid and indicisive as a statesman, and too liable to a conduct of forbearance to the foederal party which may endanger our harmony and political Safety. It is believed that in you, with equal knowledge of and talents to direct our foreign relations, the known energy and decisions of your character would Effectually put down all foederal views of disuniting us, and ruling themselves. Of this last opinion is the writer of these remarks, and whilst I live must ever hold that after Jefferson, it is on these that the Sheet anchor of republican hopes must rest. Adieu. present my respectful regards & those of Mrs. B. to Mrs. M. and believe me, most truly, my dear Sir, your affect. friend,   John Beckley.

RC (MONROE PAPERS, NEW YORK PUBLIC LIBRARY).

1. That is, Thomas Jefferson. Despite cautionary advice from political veterans, such as Beckley, Monroe openly challenged Madison for the presidential nomination after his return from France in December 1807. For further discussion of this split in the Republican ranks, see Harry Ammon, "James Monroe and the Election of 1808 in Virginia, *William and Mary Quarterly*, 3rd ser. 20 (January 1963): 33–56; and Irving Brant, *James Madison: Secretary of State, 1800–1809* (New York: Bobbs-Merrill, Company, Inc., 1953), pp. 419–68.
2. That is, John Randolph. For Randolph's unsuccessful quest for a diplomatic post, see the preceding document.

JOHN BECKLEY TO JOHN BROWN

My dear Sir,   Washington City. 8th September 1806.

I returned from Bath a few days ago, in a very impaired State of health, occasioned by a severe fever caught at that place, and I still continue in a low convalescent state.

I received at Bath your favour reporting the Kentuckey Conspiracy,[1] which truly occasions more ridicule and contempt for the authors than it excites any suspicion of the accused. Indeed it is not seriously deserving of notice as it respects any impression it was hoped to Effect out of Kentuckey. Wilkinson[2] is out with an able reply and full refutation of all the calumnies it contains, and I am glad to see that you are proceeding by libel to prosecute the malevolent defamers. I think you are bound to make a full development of the base intrigues of the Marshall family, of which I hold the Subtle & relentless Chief Justice the Main Spring.[3]

The president & heads of department are all absent—not a cyntilla of news foreign or domestic.

Let me now Entreat you my dear friend, to procure for me, as soon as possible, the particular description of my tract of land as requested in my former letters. I am really distressed for want of it, because if it comes near to my reasonable expectations from the information of others, I can immediately Sell it and relieve my dear family from distress. I wish an honest description of it, however I might desire it to be flattering, but as the quantity of the tract is large, there will doubtless be a proportion of good, of every acre of which I could wish a valuation to be put in the description. Other circumstances your better judgment will supply. Maria, her brother & Alfred are all well & desire their best love to Margaretta. Excuse this incoherent scrawl—I am very weak. Ever & affectionately, My dear friend, Yours truly,   John Beckley.

RC (BROWN PAPERS, YALE UNIVERSITY).

1. The "Kentuckey Conspiracy," which even Beckley soon began to refer to as the Burr Conspiracy, quickly developed into a more serious crisis of government than Beckley anticipated. The recipient of this letter, John Brown, and his brother, James, were implicated as a confederates of Burr in his plans to create his own empire in America's Louisiana Territory and adjacent Spanish territory, but they were never tried or convicted of any crime related to their participation. See Malone, *Jefferson the President, Second Term,* pp. 213–370; and Kline, ed., *Burr Papers,* 2:919–1046
2. James Wilkinson (1757–1825), governor of Louisiana, ranking general in the U.S. army, double agent for the Spanish government, and onetime conspirator with Burr, had publicly disavowed any connection with Burr's plots. Kline, ed., *Burr Papers,* 2:921–60 and Malone, *Jefferson the President, Second Term,* pp. 215–30.
3. In a July 25, 1806, letter to President Jefferson, Brown had accused John Marshall and his brothers-in-law, former U.S. Senator Humphrey Marshall, George Brooke, and Joseph H.

Daveiss, the U.S. attorney in Kentucky, of conspiring to ruin the Republican party in Kentucky by accusing all of its leaders of conspiracies to separate the western state from the United States. Chief Justice Marshall later presided at the treason trial of Burr. Brown to Jefferson, July 25, 1806, Jefferson Papers, Library of Congress; and Malone, *Jefferson the President, Second Term*, p. 238.

JOHN BECKLEY TO ISAAC PRINCE

My dear Sir,[1]   Washington City, 10th January 1807.

Last evening, I enclosed you a copy of the Bill reported yesterday, for continuing the Law suspending intercourse with St. Domingo, which is made the Order of the Day for Wednesday next. I am satisfied it will pass both houses without any difficulty, but you must not count upon its getting finally thro' so as to become a law, in less than 3 or 4 weeks. I will keep you advised of its progress.[2]

The letter I wrote you before you left Philadelphia on your last visit here, contained a full description of my house except noticing the Mahogany doors, & Marble hearths & Jams. In respect to terms of sale, if Mr. Duponceau can obtain Mr. Huberts consent to accept 2000 dollars (or 1500 I would prefer) and to let the remainder of the money due him rest for two or three years certain on the security of the Mortgage & judgment he now holds, paying him punctually the annual Interest, I would cheerfully consent to take 7000 dollars for the property, the purchaser to pay Hubert 1500 or 2000 (as the case may be) in Cash and 1000$ to myself, say 500 at 6 months & 500 at 12 months (negociable paper) and the residue of purchase to remain on interest for 2 or 3 years or as much longer as Hubert may agree on the security of the mortgage aforesaid. On this basis, my dear Sir, I will confide in your best exertions to serve me in this busines, and that you will as soon as you can ascertain & advice me of Mr. Duponceau & Huberts opinion or consent thereto if obtained. Could it be possible to associate a Sale or barter of the Kentucky tract of land I gave you the plot of, with a sale of the House for Goods or any thing else Convertible, so that 4000 dollars value could be secured for the land, it would be to me very desirable, altho' I much fear it will be difficult to effect it. You will ascertain of Smith, whether he has paid 100$ as I requested to Mr. Hubert, and as to arrears of interest due to Hubert you will observe that if a Sale is effected on the basis of this letter, he will receive all arrears in the proposed Cash payment which the purchaser is to make to him.

I know you will excuse my observing that in the proposed remittance to mother, we have rather calculated on it as a family aid, the better to enable me to apply the 600$ your friendship has loaned me, to my immediate pressing debts; but do not I beseech you suffer that or any other consideration to beget you inconvenience or difficulty. We all continue well and write in best regards. Tell Smith[3] his reappointment to office is fully secured.

Your ever affecte. friend   John Beckley

RC (BECKLEY FAMILY PAPERS, LIBRARY OF CONGRESS). ADDRESSED: "ISAAC PRINCE, ESQR., PHILADELPHIA. FREE J. BECKLEY."

1. Isaac Prince, youngest brother-in-law of Beckley, had been a merchant for many years on the West Indian island St. Bartholomew's and in 1803 had been appointed consul for that island—a position he held until March 21, 1809. Berkeley, *Beckley*, pp. 251–52.
2. The law suspending commercial intercourse between the United States and Santo Domingo for another year passed Congress on February 24, 1807. *American State Papers. Documents, Legislative and Executive, of the Congress of the United States: Commerce and Navigation. 1789–1815* (Washington, D.C.: Gales and Seaton, 1832), p. 717.
3. That is, John Smith, federal marshal of the Eastern District of Pennsylvania.

JOHN BECKLEY TO JOHN BROWN

Dear Sir,   Washington City 23d January 1807.

I hasten to enclose you the development of Burrs Conspiracy. The traitor has, I fear, abused your confidence and deceived you as to his real views.[1] I wish very much that if there Exists any communication from him to you, Either written or verbal, which may unvail his treachery both to yourself and others, or Either, you would possess me with it as a means to insure your character from that suspicion, which arises from your well meant, but as it eventuates, unfortunate civilities to the man during his late scenes in your State. It would be superfluous to add, what your discernment will perceive, the invidious surmises of your Enemies, that with such opportunites to know him as depravedly wicked & unprincipled, you have nevertheless at least outwardly adhered to him until the moment of the consummation of his treason. You know my unshaken friendship for you, and will duly appreciate the strong view I have given you of real impressions here—they must not be permitted to take root—it is only the esteem of the honest and good that can make life truly happy and enviable.

I have written you several letters since 1st Novr.—but fear that the mails are treacherous or intercepted. I hope this will arrive safe. We are all well. Maria wrote to Margaretta, two days ago. Excuse my adding more at present—the House is in Session. God bless you all.

Your ever affectionate friend   John Beckley.

[P.S.] Judge Innis is severely implicated. Swartout and Bollman are both arrived under guard and are now at the Marine Barracks.[2]

RC (BROWN PAPERS, YALE UNIVERSITY).

1. See Beckley to Brown, September 8, 1806, note 1.
2. The accuracy of Beckley's information on the Burr Conspiracy was at best spotty. Harry Innes, federal district judge of Kentucky, had denied a November 5, 1806, request for arrest warrants for Burr from U.S. District Attorney Joseph H. Daveiss. John Swartout of New York and Justus Erich Bollman of Pennsylvania had served as agents and messengers for Burr in his Western Conspiracy and had been arrested and sent under guard to Washington by General James Wilkinson. See notes 1, 2, and 3 at Beckley to Brown, September 8, 1806.

ISBN 0-16-048431-6